INCIDENTS CROWDED WITH LIFE

John Howard

FISHER KING PUBLISHING

INCIDENTS CROWDED WITH LIFE

Copyright © 2018 John Howard

Fisher King Publishing Ltd,
The Studio,
Arthington Lane,
Pool in Wharfedale,
LS21 1JZ,
England.

www.fisherkingpublishing.co.uk

A CIP catalogue record of this book is available from the British Library

Print ISBN 978-1-910406-72-4

Throughout this book names may have been changed at the discretion of the author.

Unless otherwise stated all lyrics are copyright of the author.

This book is dedicated to my mother, Brenda Longton Jones. I would also like to thank my husband, Neil France, for showing me the merits of succinctness.

John Howard
Murcia, Spain
2018

Chapter One

Don't It Just Hurt

On October 18th, 1976, at the age of 23 and three years after leaving home for London in search of fame and fortune, I lay in Fulham's St. Stephen's Hospital in a considerable amount of pain. I had broken my back and smashed both my feet, having launched myself from my Earl's Court bedroom window. At the time, I shared a flat with two Filipinos who for various reasons were on the run from Marcos. June, (Perfecto Terra Junior -'Son of The Perfect Earth', at least to his father) had written less than complimentary articles on the Philippines leader and only got out of the country by hiding in a delivery truck. My second flatmate Cid was a top art critic back home, but in London turned £30 a week as a clerical assistant.

And so it happened that on this fateful night my flatmates and Ricky, a friend of theirs, dragged back a bit of 'rough trade' - a rather large Russian sailor called Dimitri. I on the other hand hadn't dragged back any trade, rough or otherwise. I lay fast asleep in my little broom cupboard after a long day and night singing and playing the piano in AD8, April Ashley's Knightsbridge restaurant.

In the living room next door, things weren't going quite according to plan. Apparently after several unsuccessful attempts to screw each of them, (as Cid later told me – 'he was *such* a big boy, my dear'), he suddenly turned very nasty, and wielding a large kitchen knife, started to trash the room demanding money. Nothing new of course, many a queen has similar tales to tell. Not content with trashing the place he proceeded to throw the poor dears around the flat. With no ready cash to hand, June hit upon a brilliant idea.

Feeling rather groggy, I didn't really take in June's hurriedly hissed tale of mayhem and butchery being perpetrated in the next room and I rather generously told him to take the £20 I'd just earned that

1

night from my jeans at the bottom of the bed. Muttering his eternal gratitude, he departed clutching the note as though his life depended on it, which it did.

I lay back down in the hope of returning to my dream and hence the embrace of my perfect man - six foot four and built like a brick shithouse.

Unfortunately, this was not to be. A few minutes later and on the brink of being reunited with my hunk, the door flew open with a bang and Cid rushed across the room and dived into my bed.

"Oh John," he sobbed, shivering uncontrollably. "He won't go! What are we going to do?"

I could feel his racing heartbeat thumping in panic against my chest as his tiny frame lay shaking in my arms.

"He's got a knife John. He's going to kill us all!"

ALL! Suddenly I was wide awake. This was more serious than I thought. As we lay in the darkness I had to think quickly.

My room led directly into the front room where Dimitri was indulging in a bit of late night queer bashing and extortion. The only escape route to summon help was through my window. Before I could make a move however, there in the doorway loomed the Russian. Switching on the light he lunged towards us, grabbed Cid by the arm and dragged him to the floor. Not to be outdone, I immediately grabbed Cid's other arm and dragged him back onto the bed. For a few crazy moments we both tugged at the skinny creature as he shrieked hysterically, 'Please don't kill me! Please don't kill me!' (I think he was talking to the Russian).

Remaining surprisingly calm in the circumstances, I looked up at the towering angry giant and, trying to sound reasonable said:

"Look, let him stay here with me, you can see he's terrified. I mean it's not as if we can go anywhere is it?"

The logic of this penetrated his large skull, and with a grunt, he tossed Cid back onto the bed, as though flicking off a particularly sticky bogey. The petrified queen fell into my arms and whimpered pathetically.

Pointing very firmly, and I thought rather rudely at me, Dimitri growled:

"You stay here. You stay quiet. You behave."

"You bet we will," I replied ever so sweetly.

With another grunt and switching off the light decisively, he left the room closing the door surprisingly gently behind him.

I waited a few minutes and then crept out of bed. I pulled on my jeans, dived into a T-shirt and headed for the large sash window. It made the most dreadful racket as I struggled to lift it open. Then, making sure there was no movement from next door, and not even stopping to ask myself why it had gone so deathly quiet, I clambered out onto the small balcony, which overlooked Finborough Road.

As always, even at this late hour there was plenty of traffic about. I was sure someone would come to my aid.

Now, if this had been Twickenham or some leafy suburb in Wilmslow, within minutes someone would, I'm sure, have stopped to help.

But this was Earls Court, and in the 1970s it was an area packed with drug addicts, prostitutes, winos, opera loving leather queens and of course the ubiquitous Australians. (To think I used to find that exciting!).

Let's face it, the sight of an hysterical queen waving frantically from a first-floor balcony was hardly likely to cause a flicker of interest. People ambled by beneath me, one or two vaguely glancing up in my direction and then hurrying on. Most didn't even bother to look up. I couldn't shout for fear our Russian friend might hear. I sort of gasped for help, waving my arms about in dumb show. They must have thought I was on some sort of acid trip.

Meanwhile Cid was behind me cowering on the bed, wailing like a demented banshee:

"John, John! I think he's coming back! Ai'ee! No, it's all right he's not… Ai'ee! Yes, he's coming! Oh God John, he's coming. Oh God!"

Action was needed, fetching help a life-saving necessity. Looking down at the pavement twenty-five feet below, I decided it looked a lot more inviting and a lot more promising than it did up here. I took a deep breath and launched myself into the night.

The memory of my landing is still with me today. It hurt, badly, everywhere.

Cid stood hovering nervously on the balcony above me, unable to decide whether to follow. I waved at him croaking hoarsely, telling him to stay put.

Cars drove by - even a police car - as I lay on the ground. I waved at them pathetically. I tried standing, pulling myself up by hanging onto a lamp post. That hurt, and my feet made funny cracking noises. I slid back down to the ground and tried to think what I could do to get out of this mess. Cid had disappeared. Here I was, at 2 a.m. in the middle of October, lying on a pavement in jeans and T shirt, shoeless in Earl's Court. No wonder everyone ignored me.

Just then the front door opened. Down the steps and heading my way, calm as you like, came the Russian, the cause of all my misery and pain. He sauntered over, stood over me arms akimbo and said:

"Why you do that?"

"I don't know," I answered lamely. "I thought you were going to kill me."

"No. You stupid. If you kept quiet, I would not have killed you."

Where that left Cid and the others in his scheme of things I couldn't say and I didn't have the inclination to ask him at that precise moment.

Without another word, he turned on his heels and whistling tunelessly, disappeared into the night, never to be seen again, at least by me.

The next couple of minutes passed very slowly. I was beginning to despair that anyone would come along.

Suddenly, the sound of clicking stiletto heels broke the cold night air. A lady in black tights, leopard skin mini length coat and long peroxide hair came hurrying towards me. I smiled at her gratefully as she looked down at me. I breathed a sigh of relief. Help at last. I should, however, have realised that this was not going to be my night, for before I could say anything, she pulled her coat tightly round her, sniffed, stepped over me and walked on.

"Hey," I croaked at her retreating back, "where're you going?"

She slowed down and turned around. I could see what was going through her mind, 'Shall I help the poor bugger or what?' then she seemed to make a decision.

"I'm goin' 'ome love," she said, "I've 'ad enough problems for one night."

"Please help me, I think I've really hurt myself badly."

"I don't want to get involved, sorry."

As she turned to go again I managed to shout:

"Please! Just ring my doorbell. Please?"

A glimmer of doubt flickered across her face as she thought for a moment.

"Alright," she said. "But that's all. I don't want to get involved with the police."

I told her which of the numerous buzzers to press and just as she reached the door at the top of the steps, it flew open and three tiny oriental figures came sweeping past her down towards me like birds of prey. She decided to beat a hasty retreat as fast as her high heels would let her.

Hands to their mouths in horror, screeching 'Ai'ee!' in unison they gathered me up and carried me clumsily up the stairs to the flat, laying me out on the bed-settee in the front room. Around me lay a scene of total devastation. Cupboard doors hung open, their contents spewed all over the floor; drawers were smashed, wallpaper torn from the walls, and the hi-fi speakers were slashed to pieces. Tables lay upturned and vases, once full of beautifully arranged flowers, June's pride and joy, were now jagged bits of porcelain mixed with bent and broken blossoms, scattered around the room.

"We've called an ambulance," said June brightly, as though he was informing me my taxi was on its way.

"Oh my God, John," wailed Ricky, the prettiest of the three, and apparently the culprit who had picked up the Russian, "what have I done to you?"

"Ricky," shouted June officiously, "stop getting hysterical! John will be alright." Then he smiled at me persuasively as if to say, 'Won't you?'

Not really sure if June had grasped the seriousness of my injuries - my back and feet hurt murderously and I'd begun to shiver violently and uncontrollably - I nodded wearily at the distraught Ricky and assured him I'd be fine. Cid just stood over me shaking his head and murmuring, 'ai'ee' sadly to himself and stroking my feet as if they were sick children.

The ambulance arrived very quickly, and when they saw the extent of my injuries and the state of the flat, they insisted on calling the police.

"Oh, that won't be necessary surely," said June smiling so sweetly.

"I'm afraid it will sir," said the man in charge, not smiling so sweetly.

"Oh my God", screamed Ricky, throwing his hands up in the air dramatically. "We'll all be deported!"

As always in a crisis, June took control.

"You see sir", he said, taking a long dramatic drag from his cigarette and blowing the smoke out in true Lauren Bacall fashion, "John is not well."

"I can see that," snapped the ambulance man, indicating my smashed feet.

"No, what I mean is…" and here he dropped his voice to a

conspiratorial whisper, "he jumped out of the window *because* he's not well."

"Oh, I see, you mean he's...."

"Exactly."

They both nodded at each other, then looked at me as if to say, 'poor sod'.

By this time the room was beginning to spin. I had to get a hold of myself or at this rate I was going to end up committed.

"Look, I'm not mad!" I protested, realising at once how pathetic that sounded.

"Then why did you jump out of the window, sir? You must admit that's not normal behaviour."

I didn't like the way this was going.

"I jumped because..."

"Actually he fell." It was Cid who spoke this time.

Things were going from bad to worse.

"I did not fall, I'm not crazy, I jumped!" I was now starting to get angry. "I jumped for a very good reason, and my friends here know just what that very good reason is!"

I could tell from the look on the ambulance man's face I was beginning to get through. He turned to his companion and asked him to call the police. Then looking back at me he added:

"You can tell the police all about it in St. Stephen's, sir. For now, let's get you secured safely onto a stretcher and into the ambulance, OK?"

Ricky insisted on coming with me to keep me company and hold my hand. As it turned out it was me holding his hand, trying to console him as he kept wailing, "I'm so sorry, John. Oh, John!"

At the hospital, I was wheeled into the X-ray room, photographed, wheeled out, questioned by a rather dishy policeman and then accosted by one of those over-cheery nurses.

"You don't believe in doing things by halves, do you?" she cheered.

At last they found me a bed. I was told that I'd fractured my spine and my feet had been what they decoratively called 'powdered' by the impact.

So, I lay there on that winter night in 1976, not sure if I'd walk again, staring at the high white ward ceiling, hearing the sounds of people sleeping and dreaming around me. Whether it was the painkillers or the shock of what had happened to me taking effect, but slowly the last three years of my life seemed to appear on the blank 'screen' above me, my own private biopic. I watched in hazy wonder.

...Autumn 1973, I'd just arrived in London; signed by a manager and publisher; working on my first demos in Chappell Studios

...January 1974, I was commissioned to write and record the theme song for a Peter Fonda/William Holden movie and travelled to Rome to record it

...April 1974, I began recording my debut album at Abbey Road and Apple Studios

...Autumn 1974, my first single, 'Goodbye Suzie' was released, with all the hope and plans of everyone rolled into that four-minute opus; the single flopping, the resultant panic which ensued around CBS, 'what shall we do with him now?'

...Autumn 1975, my second album, *Technicolour Biography* shelved, recording another set of compositions with disco producer Biddu, *Can You Hear Me OK?* Waiting for CBS to announce a release date; none forthcoming

...As 1976 dawned, I was dropped by the label, no new album

released, no recording career, dreams shattered.

Like a spring uncoiling, a dam bursting, the whole of 1976 had turned into a hedonistic rush, lots of booze, casual sex and drugs, playing in bars and restaurants every day and every night, Blitz, April Ashley's, The Last Resort - how aptly named. Cruising gay clubs and bars every night, waking up with a different guy every morning, hash cakes easing the edges.

Just a couple of weeks earlier I'd started work on a song called 'They', a piece of paranoia and detachment which reflected how I felt about my life then. I'd gone into a bar drunk and high on hash, freaking out about the security guys on the door and running into the club shouting 'they've all got guns!'. Life had reached a point where something had to give.

And boy, that night, had it given.

As I lay watching all this unravel above me, and sleepily thinking all this through, wondering what the hell was going to happen to me, a large bulky Captain Birds Eye figure of man wandered down the ward, the male night nurse. He passed by the end of my bed and smiled at me, and for some reason I suddenly felt very safe, for the first time in a long time.

I was taken back to when, as a small child, I'd watch my parents passing my bedroom door on the dimly-lit landing. My dad would pop his head in and whisper.

"Goodnight, son," Captain Birds Eye whispered.

And, as he wandered off along the ward, from my warm secure bed I whispered back, "Goodnight, daddy."

Chapter Two

Miss Ashton's Disappointment

The curtain rises on a living-room in a semi-detached council house in Heywood, Lancashire. The sun is streaming through the large rear windows. The brightly-coloured three-piece suite and patterned carpet are circa 1957. A clothes horse - or 'maiden' as they are called in Lancashire at that time - stands in front of a coal fire, drying sheets and towels. The soft red glow of the coals showing through the damp steaming cotton.

In a corner of the room stands a large dark wood upright piano. A budgerigar called Joey hops from perch to perch in his cage on top. He stops, cocks his head on one side as the door slowly opens. A thin, pale looking boy, about four years old creeps in. Looking furtively around the room and seeing it empty, except for Joey, he smiles to himself and carefully closes the door behind him. He tiptoes over to the piano and with some difficulty clambers up onto the stool and leans precariously over the keys.

"This is for you, Joey," he says looking up at his budgie with affection. Joey bobs his head up and down and chirrups back, acknowledging the dedication.

The little boy moves the fingers of his left hand along the piano keys, searching for one in particular. It stands out from the rest by a brown nicotine stain on its tip - a lost memory of a wartime jazz session which his father had held for his musician friends every week in the room above his parents' Rochdale pub. With quiet satisfaction, he finds the key and gingerly presses it. Then he moves his right hand up to the treble section and presses another key. Slowly from this tentative start, a simple melody emerges. Joey chirps along as if in encouragement. With added confidence, the little boy attempts the tune again. Completely engrossed in his little masterpiece, he doesn't notice the door open and his parents creeping in. They sit down quietly and listen.

Father is slim, in his early thirties, of average height, with dark hair swept back with Brylcreem to conceal a small bald patch. His wife is a pretty woman, her thin delicate frame dressed in flowered cotton. They turn to each other and smile.

Their son finishes his recital and sits back, obviously pleased with himself. His parents' gentle applause makes him jump, then blush. He turns and smiles nervously at them both as his father nods his head slowly.

"He's a natural, Bren. He played with two hands without anyone showing him."

"That was very nice, love," Bren says to her son.

"I wrote that for Joey," he announces proudly.

"Well, it was lovely."

Father gets up and rubs his son's head affectionately, and lifting him off the stool says, "It's time for dinner now, cock. Go and get washed, there's a good boy."

The boy dashes off with a quick glance at his mother, who beams at him with pride.

"He's a natural pianist, you know. Maybe we should send him for lessons soon?"

"Let's see how Susan gets on first," Bren says. "There's plenty of time for

Ullswater Grove, Heywood, 1957, first May Day Walk

Howard."

My sister Susan. She'd been sent to elocution lessons, tap-dancing lessons, ballet lessons and she'd hated them all, coming home after just a few weeks saying, "I don't like them!"

My mum would put on her best coat, go around to the tutor in question and with humble apologies, explain that the lessons were interfering with her daughter's school work. A cancellation fee would be charged and a few weeks later another activity would be found to improve her daughter's education and social standing. My mother always failed to realise that Susan was quite happy with the way she was.

Now at the age of eight, it was piano lessons. Susan would come back from them sulking, plonk herself on the piano stool and bang away on the keys with about as much expression as a power drill. It was a great relief to her family, and probably the next-door neighbours, that after only a month, my father and sister came to a mutual understanding. She would never play the piano again!

That was the last attempt by my mother to get Susan to do anything she didn't want to. From then on, she was allowed to run her life more or less as was her wont - with one exception - me. Her tedious little brother needed looking after, and she had to take me everywhere she went. Susan would drag me from the house, grumbling under her breath that it wasn't fair and telling me to keep my mouth shut, especially in front of friends, and even more especially in front of male friends.

"Zip it," she'd growl as her smiling entourage approached us.

We'd usually go to the local 'rec' and I'd be told to play on the swings while Susan flicked her kiss-curls and giggled coyly at the boys surrounding her and her dolled-up mates.

"Don't go on the roundabout," she'd break off from the hilarity to warn me. "You were sick last time!"

And, she failed to add, she had been smacked and sent to bed as my fevered brow was cooled by my mother's loving hand and wet dishcloth.

I'd usually surreptitiously gravitate to the slide, land at the bottom on my arse, tumbling over and grazing my knees and burst into a fit of hysterical screams. Which meant Susan would have to drag me back home while her mates laughed their heads off. She'd be smacked and sent to bed and my stinging knees would be cooled by my mother's loving hand and a wet dishcloth.

No wonder my sister hated me so much.

You will have gathered by now that I was, to put it mildly, a bit of a wimp in Susan's eyes. "Yer cissy," she'd shout as I bawled my head off after some scrape or fall. "Me mum's going to kill me!"

To make matters worse, I had actually asked to have piano lessons, and if that wasn't bad enough, I was rather good. I was impatient, of course, wanting to 'play like daddy' straight away, but he told me I must do things in stages, practice my exercises, work hard and 'persevere.' So I did. And loved it. Susan would sit in the background as I practised my scales mumbling, "little goody-goody," just loud enough for me to hear. So I'd start crying and run from the room shouting, "I'm going to tell my mum over you," and she'd get smacked and sent to bed.

Matilda Emily Ashton. Miss, was a small squat lady of about sixty. She lived in a large dark red-brick Edwardian house on Ainsworth Road, Bury, with her older sister and younger brother. Many times I'd arrive for my weekly piano lesson and stand on the doorstep for sometimes ten minutes ringing the bell. Miss Ashton, the elder, was hard of hearing, Mr Ashton would be out in the backyard collecting coal, which he'd lug into the piano room, gasping for breath, stoically build up the fire, and trudge out again. Matilda would either be what she'd delicately call 'somewhere else in the house' or taking a lesson in the back parlour with the door shut. Eventually the front door would open, her pupil would bound out of the house like a prisoner released and Matilda would stare at me vexatiously saying, "Howard! You're late!"

My protests would simply be waved away and I'd be shown quickly into the piano room with a hurried gesture to 'sit!'. It was a stuffy room which was taken up almost entirely by a huge black grand piano surrounded and piled high with dusty old sheet music.

With more complaints about my tardiness, Miss Ashton would fall heavily onto the stool beside me and I'd begin to play for her what I'd been learning all week. Then it would start. The ritual taking out of a hair clip from her precariously mounted grey bun with which she would pick her ears, study what the clip had found, wipe the clip on a tissue she'd find inside her cardigan sleeve, and throw the soiled item onto the bottom end of the keyboard. Then the process would start again. I'd try to concentrate on the piece of music before me, but out of the corner of my eye I would be aware of this rather off-putting personal hygiene job going on. Occasionally, the dirty tissue would land near my fingers and I'd have to knock it out of the way as I went for one of the big deep bottom keys. This usually resulted in me playing a wrong note and being told off for not practising enough. By the end of my lesson, there would be a little pile of wax-laden tissues buffered up against the edge of the keyboard.

Then it would be time for Theory. And ritual number two. Plonking herself in front of the blazing fire (winter or summer, it was always a blazing fire), Miss Ashton would test me on my theory studies. I would stand before her as she'd begin to lift her skirt to alarming heights, displaying a lovely set of pink or blue bloomers beneath. Trying not to look, I'd answer each question, and with each correct answer the skirt would be lifted even higher. There was nothing salacious about it. She was simply warming her fanny, but I would always escape from that room at the end of the lesson with a bright red face, and it wasn't the fire which had caused it.

Occasionally, and usually when I'd played a piece particularly badly, she would sit and play it for me, her squat little fingers caressing the keys, her hunched shoulders rising and falling with each beautifully expressed musical phrase. I would look around the room at photographs taken across many years of her in evening dress, sitting at a grand piano in a large hall somewhere, or standing with groups of beautifully dressed people at musical recitals or functions, a vivacious little woman, smiling and laughing with her cultured companions. Then I'd look down at this dowdy little figure playing so exquisitely for me, and wondered what had happened that turned her exotic high life into one where she sat day after day, week after week, listening to the tuneless bangings of pupils who hadn't a chance of achieving anything like she obviously had.

In fairness, she did seem to enjoy taking piano lessons and derived a great deal of pleasure out of her pupils passing exams. They were always something of an event for Miss Ashton. She always insisted on accompanying her charges on the bus and 'for luck' would wear a bright canary yellow mackintosh, matching Wellington boots and bright yellow rain hat, whatever the weather outside. She would chatter away brightly throughout the journey into Bury Centre completely oblivious of the squirming child next to her, mortified at the stifled giggles from everyone else on the bus. Still, her bizarre attire seemed to do the trick as I always passed with flying colours.

My sister would mumble "Who's a clever boy, then?" as Mum proudly adjusted yet another framed 'Passed with Merit' certificate on the lounge wall.

During one examination, as I sat at the piano and prepared to begin my first piece, a road drill began pounding away outside the window. Even though the examiner closed the window the drill remained an unwelcome accompaniment to my piece. I doubt he heard much of what I played that morning, but I still got a High-Level Pass. Probably a sympathy mark for simply keeping going.

One day, I arrived for my lesson, stood the usual ten minutes ringing the bell, waited another five then decided to walk round to the garden window at the side of the house just to show my face and prove that I had arrived. I peered in and could just see the shape of Miss Ashton through the dirty glass. She was sitting in front of the fire, alone.

I tapped on the window gently.

"Who's that?" she jumped up and shouted.

"It's me!" I cried.

She came to the window, peered back through it, and opened it. I noticed she'd been crying.

"What are you doing here?" she asked, surprised.

"I've come for my lesson, Miss Ashton."

"But it's cancelled."

"Oh. Is it?"

"Yes. I told my sister to ring your mother. Didn't she?"

"No. No she didn't."

"Oh well. It's cancelled, I'm afraid." She leaned over and picked up one of her discarded tissues from off the piano and blew noisily into it. "I've cancelled all of today's lessons. I've had a bad shock. Charlie's dead."

Charlie was her English Bull Terrier. The treasured animal had sometimes been as much part of the weekly distractions as the waxed tissues and the moving skirt. His wicker basket lay atop the piano into which the huge brute would be lifted by Miss Ashton whenever he'd scampered into the room if her brother had opened the door to replenish the fire with more coal. He would be covered up with a smelly tartan blanket under which the dog would groan, grunt and gasp throughout the lesson.

She tearfully told me that she had been taking Charlie for his daily constitutional that morning and he had suddenly grunted, groaned and gasped for the last time, collapsing at her feet in a heap.

"Heart failure," she explained. She was dressed from head to foot in black, the matching dirty tissue grasped firmly in her hand.

At my next lesson, the large wicker basket still perched atop the piano, the tartan blanket waiting beside it for the master who would never return. Miss Ashton had a lacklustre quality about her that day, even forgetting to pick her ears or lift her skirt. Only her heavy sighs - as opposed to Charlie's grunts - accompanied my chirpy rendition of 'Blue Danube.'

"Very nice," she said at the end of my less than perfect recital.

I knew then how very heartbroken she must have been. I tactfully withdrew, leaving her with memories of the only thing I suspect she'd ever truly loved.

When I was eleven, I was given 'The Dream of Olwen' to learn for my next lesson. It was a difficult piece and I worked long and hard at it, trying to master it. Outside, my friends were happily playing in the street. Not getting very far playing it with two hands I stared at the infernal sheet music and instead tried picking out the melody with one hand to see if I could make sense of it that way. Then something happened. Lyrics came into my head to match the melody I was playing. I cautiously sung them with the tune and much to my surprise they sounded good. Another line of lyrics appeared as if by magic into my head and out of my mouth. So as not to forget the words I scribbled them down over the top line. In about ten minutes, I had a song. This was my first composition since 'Joey's Song.' Then I'd only had a melody, this time I had a set of lyrics. Their fluency to me was almost spiritual. I sang and played the song over again.

From behind me, through the window, the sound of applause rang out. My friends had stopped running up and down the street and had sat on the garden wall listening. My first public performance.

"We liked that," said Teresa from next door.

"Thanks," I said bashfully, flushing up.

"Play it again," said Teresa's older brother, Peter.

Happily, I performed my encore, more applause, the audience

swelled to three as Teresa's younger brother, Michael joined her on the wall.

I decided I would play it for Miss Ashton at my next lesson.

I shook like a leaf as I tentatively but rather proudly performed my new composition for Miss Ashton. By God, I thought, as I warbled my way through it, it does sound good.

When I'd finished, I waited for the inevitable applause. Instead, there was a very loud silence. Miss Ashton sat quite still, stony faced and merely nodded quickly as though an unpleasant task had been reluctantly performed.

As if to emphasise her displeasure, she got up, prodded the fire aggressively with the poker and yelled out, "Alfred! More coal!"

Alfred scuttled into the room, whipped the scuttle from the hearth and scuttled out.

"Should I do my scales now?" I asked feebly. Receiving merely a puckered grimace in reply, I began my C scales. I was just starting D when Alfred returned, puffing and panting with a full coal scuttle. As he struggled with it, Miss Ashton pushed him out of the way, grabbed the scuttle and threw the lot on the fire, stabbing it even more violently than before.

"Enough!" she yelled as Alfred made his escape, "Play The Dream of Olwen! Properly!"

It was a disaster. Mistake followed mistake, jarring wrong chord followed excruciating wrong chord, until, unable to stand it a moment longer, she pushed me off the stool and played it herself.

"Now go home and practice," she cried as she thrashed out the last perfect bar.

I picked up my things and rushed scarlet-faced out of the house.

On the long walk home I came to the conclusion that the life of a concert pianist was not for me. Cilla Black and P.J. Proby were my new musical heroes. I wanted to be like them. A Pop Star. If Miss bloody

Ashton couldn't recognise my talent, my friends certainly could. I made up my mind to tell Mum I wanted to give up piano lessons. However, as I reached home my steely determination evaporated. All that money my parents had spent on my lessons, all that hard work, all those exams passed. Maybe I'd give it another go. So piano lessons continued but my heart wasn't in it anymore. I entered more exams and passed them but the thrill had gone. I put words to all the pieces I was given to learn, which finally drove my mum to rush into the lounge where her pop star son was wailing ecstatically away and shout:

"If you don't play your music properly I'll tell your dad to stop your piano lessons!"

Perfect.

A couple of weeks later, Mum she wrote to Miss Ashton to explain why I was giving up my piano lessons. "Important school exams."

Years later, on a Memory Lane trip back to Bury I drove past Miss Ashton's old house. The plaque outside her front door which had read "M.E. Ashton - Teacher of Pianoforte (Qualified)" had gone leaving a lighter oblong of red brick. I got out of the car and took a photo of the house, arousing the suspicion of the new owner who came out and asked me what I was doing. When I explained, he told me Miss Ashton had died five years earlier, very old, in a nursing home, alone. He and his wife had bought the house at an auction.

As I got back in the car and had one final glance, I remembered the letter she had written in reply to my mother, words underlined in red pen to emphasise her disappointment:

"Of course, there are always those who do not, alas, come up to scratch, or who will not put that last extremely important bit of effort into their studies. They are the ones who fail, Mrs Jones. I am sorry to say that Howard is one of those. I expected so much more."

Miss Ashton had her dream. I had mine. And it wasn't Olwen's.

Chapter Three

Portrait Of A Mother

On July 10th, 1948, Brenda Marie Longton married Bert Jones in St. Joseph's Roman Catholic Church, Heywood. At 24 Brenda was almost eighteen months older than Bert. They did, however, have a lot in common. They were both only children; their fathers had died when they were young; they both worked for the same company - indeed that's where they met. And, of course, they were both in love.

Bert - or Herbert as his mother Ethel insisted on calling him in front of everyone - had been born into a middle-class home, 'one of the better public houses in Stockport', as Ethel would proudly tell fellow publicans at Licensed Victuallers do's. She was a proud woman. Proud of her father Joseph Sawyer who worked himself up at the local potteries in Burslem, Staffs, to become chief fire officer, proud of her mother Elizabeth who bore eleven children, all of whom survived infancy. However, by the time Bert was born in 1925, almost all of Ethel's brothers had been killed in the First World War and her sisters had died from illnesses brought on by the after-effects of a TNT explosion at a nearby factory. Ethel had been working at a munitions factory some miles away so missed it.

Her first son, Edward, had died at eighteen months of pneumonia, brought on, his mother always believed, by her maid dropping him when he was a young baby.

Gran Wood and Dad, about 1935

Her husband, Austin, weak from being gassed in the war and losing an eye at just seventeen, allowed himself to be dominated by 'Ma'. For a quiet life. Which became my father's mantra during his two marriages.

"We'd always go on separate holidays with your father, Austin and me," Gran told me during one of my many visits to her in my early teens. "We had to. There was the business to run. We could never be what you'd call a proper family, enjoying ourselves."

I have a letter Gran wrote to her husband during one of those holidays on her own with Bert. In it, she tells Austin that 'there are two lamb chops in the larder, and a nice piece of cod for your supper tomorrow evening in the cold cupboard.'

Encouraged by his ambitious mother's belief in his natural talent at the piano - Gran told me with no sense of shame that she had once made her young son play a piece so many times that his fingers bled - Bert became the local church organist before he'd reached his teens and was passing all his classical piano exams with ease. At fourteen, he discovered jazz, formed a band and, while his parents worked in the pub downstairs, he and his mates would bang away at the latest Benny Goodman hit, much to his mother's displeasure.

"Your father ruined his chances to become something when he wasted his talents on that darned jazz music. Bang! Bang! Bang! That's all it ever meant to me."

By his early forties, Austin's health was deteriorating, so Ethel decided they should move to a smaller pub in a quieter town. The brewery moved them to The Trafalgar in Rochdale. Just four years later, Austin contracted pneumonia and died at just forty-four. His sixteen-year-old son had been a working man for two years already, as a draughtsman at Heywood's Ames Crosta Mills, eleven or so miles from Rochdale, but a world away as far as Ethel was concerned:

"They all have bad legs in Heywood," she once told me as she strode along to the shops, "it must have been all that in-breeding."

In 1943, aged eighteen, Bert went against his mother's wishes and tried to sign up for the air force. His two loves were music and planes. His bedroom was full of model aircraft he and his cousin John had made together. It was merely a dream. Bert's eyesight even then was bad, certainly not good enough to shoot down enemy aircraft.

"Herbert used to wave goodbye to me each morning as he went off to school wearing his glasses. As soon as he got around the corner he took them off. No wonder he's virtually blind now."

Two years after the war ended, Ethel met and married fellow publican Harry Wood, "a nice little man." She moved into his pub The Grove where "the customers had no idea how to behave in public. I soon taught them."

The same year, Bert noticed a pretty young secretary at work and asked her out. He went home afterwards raving to his mother about this "lovely girl with the most beautiful skin I've ever seen." Within weeks they were dating regularly, and by the end of the year they were engaged.

Jane & Thomas Longton, my mum's parents, early 1920s

"Every Christmas, we'd get an orange. That was considered a real treat."

My maternal Great-Aunt Chrissie told me this once. It stuck in my mind from a young age, describing perfectly the difference between Gran Wood's upbringing and that of my mother's family.

Mum's mum was Jane Longton. She was born into the staunchly Roman Catholic family The Harts as the 20th Century dawned, within months of Queen Victoria dying and her son Edward becoming King. Jane's mother died shortly after giving birth to her, leaving her father Peter Hart to bring up five daughters and four sons single-handedly. The Harts had moved from Westmeath, Southern Ireland to Liverpool in the late 19th Century and then on to Wigan, following the coal mining and cotton mill trades. Peter and his sons became 'coal hewers', his daughters went into the cotton mills.

Jane and Chrissie moved to Heywood when they were in their teens. It was then a big cotton mill town, and this is where Jane met and married Thomas Longton, his family mainly cotton mill workers except Thomas himself who became a shop assistant at fifteen - less taxing on his weak heart. Their only child, Brenda, was born in 1924.

The Longton's married life was not easy. Jane discovered, shortly after giving birth to Brenda, that she had Parkinson's Disease, Thomas's heart condition was worsening and their daughter contracted polio when just a toddler. Thomas died at just thirty-eight

Mum & Dad early 1950s

in 1933. Jane's sister Peg, now living in one of 'the better areas' of the suburbs of Manchester with her accountant husband Jack, took them in. She forged a lifelong bond with Brenda, who recovered her health in her teens and, seeing how comfortably Aunty Peg lived with her successful husband, became determined to do better for herself. It was her drive and motivation from then on.

When she spotted the attractive young man coming out of his office at Ames Crosta's, she quickly found out that his name was Bert Jones, was an up and coming young draughtsman and that his parents ran a large pub in nearby Rochdale. Quite the catch. She made sure it wasn't long before Bert Jones noticed her.

Ethel Wood met Jane Longton, prospective in-laws, and they immediately disliked each other intensely. Jane found Ethel overbearing and snobbish - 'and a Protestant' - and Ethel saw that not only was Jane disabled but also Brenda had an under-developed leg, the result of her childhood polio.

"But Herbert, the girl's a cripple and so is her mother," she protested when Bert told her of his intention to marry Brenda.

"But Brenda, the boy's a Protestant and his mother's a publican," cried Jane when her daughter informed her of the couple's intentions.

"But mother, we're in love," they both replied.

As Brenda Jones stood smiling for the photographer on the steps of St. Joseph's Church that warm summer's day in 1948, her arm firmly linking that of her new husband, she knew she'd done well for herself. Bert smiled back at her and thought what a lovely creature he'd married. Ethel Wood and Jane Longton looked on, unconvinced.

One of the clearest early memories I have of my mum, from when I was about six years old, is of her sitting on the just-delivered new sofa, her just-delivered new summer frock flowing beautifully around perfectly positioned fully-fashioned nylons, new shoes lying in their tissue-paper-lined box on the deliciously new-smelling rug. She is discussing the colour schemes of the lounge with our next door neighbour Bernice. New carpets are rolled up in a corner of the room, about to be laid, and a glossy catalogue lies open on the coffee table at 'The Perfect Kitchen For Mrs 1960' page.

Mum wanted everything now. To ensure she didn't have to wait for anything 'until we could afford it' she purchased it all on HP. The Never-Never as it was known. We were therefore the first family in our street to get a fridge, a washing machine, a T.V., an electric cooker. Each 'newfangled gadget' was delivered to Number 2, Ullswater Grove before a crowd of onlookers who had straightened their twitched net curtains and rushed across the road to see 'what Brenda's having delivered today.' Mum would stand in the doorway, partially guiding the delivery men into the house, mostly allowing anyone who didn't know that it was Brenda Jones who was having yet another expensive piece of state-of-the art technology installed into her fast-developing modern home.

Gran Wood bitterly disapproved of this "downright irresponsibility", even more so her son's apparent lack of concern at how his wife was "spending every penny he earns on useless luxuries." But then Gran disapproved of everything Brenda did. Except one thing.

"When I saw her wash her tomatoes, I knew she was at least a clean woman."

In the summer of 1960, Mum dragged Dad to the Ideal Home Exhibition in Manchester. The council had told my parents they would have to be moved to a larger three-bedroomed house. My sister was approaching her teens and they didn't approve of a girl nearing puberty sharing a bedroom with her brother.

Mum and Dad had moved into their brand-new council house in 1954, when I was about eighteen months old, after Dad had insisted they leave Nan's house, where they'd lived since getting married. He was sick and tired of the back-biting Jane regularly threw at him because he wasn't "of The Faith."

"Either we leave, or I do!" Bert had finally told Brenda. He didn't insist on much during their married life, but this was one time he had to.

They'd been very happy in Ullswater Grove, it was a pleasant leafy estate with large front gardens and space for an allotment behind, which Dad would tend every weekend, growing all sorts of fruit and veg. Susan and I would help him pick and sort it and I can still remember clearly the beautiful smell of freshly podded peas.

But, now, after six good years they would have to move, and Mum decided she now wanted them to own their own home.

"It's what people do now," she told Dad over dinner one evening.

"People who can afford it," replied Dad.

"We will afford it. You'll have to do more banding."

'Banding' was 'gigging' with a jazz band at various clubs and pubs, which Dad enjoyed but it was tiring doing that as well as a full-time day job.

Walking round the Exhibition Hall, Mum was a woman on a mission. Checking out each 'house model', taking lots of leaflets off stands and handing them to Bert who scanned them with a sense of dread, she finally found the house she'd dreamed of. It was a three-bedroomed semi on a new estate on the outskirts of Bury. With a large garden and space for a garage it was "perfect!".

"But we haven't got a car!" Bert protested.

"Not yet." Brenda replied.

Eyes widening, Brenda pointed at the gorgeous architect's drawing:

"Look at the size of the master bedroom, Bert!"

"Look at the price!" Bert murmured.

After sweeping up to the receptionist and asking to see a rep, she was led around the show house with reluctant husband and two whining kids in tow, enthralled by everything "the smart young gentleman" showed them.

"We even get to choose the design of the kitchen units, Bert!"

"I heard the man," a defeated Bert replied.

A deposit was extricated from Bert's wallet, contracts signed and a happy Mrs. Jones floated home on Cloud Nine.

The new Greenhill estate quickly became known as Debtor's Alley, couple after couple unable to pay the mortgage and disappearing overnight, moonlight flitting back to mother's. Mum meanwhile hosted Tupperware Parties and Coffee Mornings, took driving lessons, passed her test and bought a new Vauxhall Viva. She'd pop round to neighbour's to talk about the new 'whistles and bells' central heating system she'd had installed, the rose garden Bert had planted out 'surrounded by miles of rustic fencing', and the posh new 'dinette' she'd had constructed out of bamboo and Formica. Brenda Longton Jones was in heaven.

Bert meanwhile spent sleepless nights trying to make the maths work, totting up what he earned with what Brenda spent, and never once ended up with a profit at the end of his calculations. More banding paid for more household gadgets. New carpets and top-of-the-range flock wallpaper were ordered 'on tick' from Kay's Catalogue. The bills came in, the money went out.

As the '60s waned along with The Jones' finances, Bert gently suggested they 'downsize'. He sold it to his wife as a new rural dream, a little cottage in the country.

"It's what everyone who's anyone is doing now," he told Bren, who'd read articles in Woman's Weekly which bore out Bert's claim.

In 1969, after two years of trying to sell their house and finally doing so with a small profit, Bert and Bren proudly stood outside their little stone terraced cottage in Ramsbottom and smiled. Dad turned to Mum and kissed her. Not only was his wife happy, but, finally, for the first time, The Jones' bank account was in the Black.

"I felt ten-foot-tall," Dad told me years later.

The war between mothers-in-law continued throughout Bert and Brenda's marriage. One of Ethel's abiding dislikes of Jane was how she "played on her handicap." She did not believe that Jane's illness was "as bad as she makes out."

Now widowed a second time and living alone in a tiny two-up-two-down cottage in Heywood - "to be near Herbert and the children" - Ethel once marched into Nan's nearby bungalow and proceeded to tell her that if she'd just hold her hands together they'd stop shaking.

"And they did!"

Unfortunately, this caused my mum to shake - with rage - when Nan told her about Gran's unsolicited advice. Brenda in turn marched down to Gran's, tore a strip off her and refused to speak to her until she apologised. The impasse lasted almost a year, my Gran picking my sister and I up for trips to the park or the cinema each Saturday morning from the top of our street rather than coming to the house. On our return, Gran would kiss us goodbye, watch us run home, see the door open as my mother let us in, then walk back home alone. Dad would visit his mum each week for lunch, she'd ask how Howard and Susan were going on at school, but the subject of Brenda would be avoided.

Finally, as Christmas approached, Mum told Dad:

"Ask Ma if she'd like to come over for Christmas Day. It's about time we let bygones be bygones."

When Gran came into the house that Christmas morning, Mum kissed her on the cheek and simply said,

"How've you been, Ma?"

"Fine, thank you, Brenda. I've been fine."

The two women never mentioned the episode again, at least to each other. But Ethel certainly steered well clear of giving health advice to Jane ever again.

Christmas Days were always something of an ordeal for Bert and Bren. There'd be Gran Wood in her latest home-made hat, discussing its net and sequin-embossed merits with anyone who happened to be sitting near her. Nan Longton would be at the other end of the room with her two sisters, where they would spend hours arguing about their respective ages.

"I'm sixty-two, Ribs! You're sixty-four!" Jane would yell at Chrissie.

"No, Jane," Chrissie would yell back, "I'm sixty-two, you're sixty and Peg's sixty-four."

"I am not!" Peg would protest. "I'm only sixty-three, which makes you sixty-one, Ribs, and Jane fifty-nine!"

"Yer what??"

"Peg said you were only fifty-nine, but you're older than that!"

"Well I am definitely not sixty-four yet!" Peg would yell.

"Yer what?"

And so it would go on. For hours.

Various great-uncles would be in the garden, puffing on pipes, away from the mayhem. But Dad, who was expected to act as host while Mum and Susan busied in the kitchen, would sit at the back of the room, his eyes directed at the floor, his arms resignedly folded as his mother repeatedly called out:

"Herbert! Play us something on the piano!"

Dad would slowly shake his head, either as silent comment on the whole horrific day unfolding before him, or in response to his mother's vain pleas to show everyone what a wonderfully talented son he had.

Mum would eventually save the day with her announcement that dinner was ready and we'd all troop out to The Dinette and tuck into turkey with all the trimmings. Paper hats would be donned, Christmas Crackers would be pulled, their inane jokes would be read out, and for a short while everyone enjoyed themselves as a family. Even Jane and Ethel allowed a thin smile at each other as they passed the gravy.

Once the Queen's Christmas Message had been watched and approved of, the mismatched brood would get ready to leave with much shouting and disagreement over whose was whose coat and which one brought the brolly. They would be bundled into taxis arguing about who should be dropped off first and we'd wave them off. I'd loved every minute, showing off all my new toys and annuals to everybody, made a fuss of and given sixpences and shillings for being 'a good boy'. Mum and Dad would collapse with a couple of sherries in front of the T.V., vowing never to do it again. Twelve months later, the whole sorry scene would be repeated, with maybe an occasional deceased aunt or uncle missing as the years went on.

Aunt Chrissie died in 1968, her mind gone back to the time her four young brothers would fight and she would scold them to stop. She kept asking my mum when she was going to get married and just looked constantly puzzled at me:

"Who this?" she'd ask my mum, nodding over at me.

"It's Howard."

"Howard? I haven't got a brother called Howard!"

"He's my son, aunty."

"Your son?! You're not married yet!"

Chrissie would turn away tutting and resume her staring at her brothers fighting in the corner.

"Tell them to stop," she'd order my mum.

"Tell who?"

"They're bad boys. When are you getting married?"

Nan gave up her sixty years of fighting Parkinson's ten years later, after whiling her final years away in an old people's home. The last time I saw her we had our usual high-volume conversation which gave no room for sensitivity or tact:

"Your breath smells," she yelled at me.

Nurses stopped in their tracks, bedpans in hand.

"Er - does it?"

"I said, yer breath smells!" she yelled even louder.

"I heard you the first time, Nan, and I…"

"You what?"

"I said, I heard you the first time."

"Cheese!"

"Sorry?"

"Cheese'll cure it. Always does. A lump of cheddar. Then your breath won't stink!"

"OK. I'll try that."

"I said that'll stop your breath smelling!"

I escaped from this final agonising hour, whispering quietly my destination to the bus conductor and afraid of anyone I knew coming to sit next to me.

Gran Wood suffered a fall a few months later. It turned her from the vibrant domineering character I'd grown up with to a frail shadow. Shortly before she died, I went to see her. She sat in her little warden-controlled flat, hands in her lap, staring across the room at something, an odd benign smile on her face. Then, quite unexpectedly she raised her head and looked at me:

"Are you still living with that man?" she asked, fiercely.

My sister sitting next to Gran shifted uncomfortably. Although I was by then an out gay man in London, my sexuality had never been discussed amongst the elder stateswomen of my family. Not in front of me anyway. I'd never even considered what they'd make of it. And frankly never cared.

"Which man?" I asked, as my sister wilted and Gran sat forward in her chair.

"You know which man. The one you've been living with. Are you still with him?" Her eyes pierced me for a reply.

"Yes. I am."

"Thought so."

With a loud sniff, she resumed her original pose, looking across the room, her benign smile returned, some pleasant memory playing itself out for her.

Silence returned, Susan and I smiling winsomely at each other, trying to think of something to say. A few minutes later, as though suddenly aware of nothing being said, Gran lifted her head towards me again, a kind of pity in her eyes. I wondered what was coming:

"God shouldn't make us live this long."

She stared at Susan as though a stranger had sat next to her, then glanced at me for a response:

"It isn't fair," she said.

"No," I agreed. "It isn't."

With a quick nod of her head she resumed her reverie across the room and Susan jumped up and brightly asked us if we wanted a cup of tea. But Gran was no longer interested.

I remembered the stout strong lady who had whisked me up into her arms as a child and rubbed her bristly chin against my face. 'Who's scrumptious?' she'd ask. 'You are,' she'd answer herself, laughing. Memories of home-made rice pudding and strong leaf tea served in tiny individual teapots, the sugar bowl and jug protected from flies by her hand-made crocheted little covers with the blue beads at each corner. A whole Sunday with Gran used to lie ahead as a delicious, story-filled afternoon of tasty baked treats and long conversations. Now the evening sun cast a long shadow across the room, the endless silence and my sister's embarrassment.

Aunty Peg lasted well into her nineties, tiny, busy, always baking, sprightly in her little pinny, proud of her tidy semi which always smelled of cakes fresh out of the oven, and with 'all her chairs at home' to the day she died. She'd had several miscarriages in early marriage so she and her husband Jack had adopted a little girl called Kathleen. As the teenage Kathleen regaled us of yet another trip to Rome to see 'The Holy Father', crossing herself and visibly excited at the remembered papal vision waving from his palatial balcony, Peg would mouth to my mum over homed-baked scones and tea, "she should have been a nun."

Peg not only outlived her sisters but also her favourite niece.

Mum was found in a coma in the October of 1972. She'd taken to bed after the doctor had told her she had a bad case of constipation. Close. It began with C. After a major operation which, the doctors told my father, would only give her a short respite, she returned home refusing to give up. Her health and strength seemed to return and along with it a determination to give something back for the care she'd had in hospital. She started doing voluntary work for the local Cancer Research Society, becoming secretary within a few weeks. But another more personal plan began to hatch in her mind.

The need to get back to Heywood became her final intention and it got increasingly stronger. In early 1974, she suggested she and Bert sell up and buy a little shop there, "to give me something to do while you're out at work." It was the same shop my friends and I had gone into on the way to Queen's Park in the 1960s. It had ice lollies, a 'Penny Tray', and fabulous sarsaparilla sweets which were made using a secret recipe handed down from owner to owner.

Dad reluctantly agreed, and as he feared, Mum's health deteriorated just before they were due to move. She was carried into the shop and three months later, her body was carried out. She was never strong enough to serve behind the counter. Even so, the last time I saw her she told me how happy she was to be back in her hometown, and we reminisced about our Sunday afternoons at the park armed with our lollies and sweets, listening to the brass band and watching the little boats on the lake. Though she was in constant pain, numbed by morphine, I do believe she was at peace with herself in her last days. Dad had held her hand as she lay dying in the front room and they'd talked about Susan and her young family, about my teenage ambitions appearing to be bearing fruit as I'd begun my London adventure, and her plans to visit me soon.

When I saw the look of determination on her face in the Chapel of Rest, I knew that even at the end she had tried not to give in, tried to fight, tried to win through. As I sat in the front room with the little polythene bag of her possessions I realised just how insignificant we all really are. Fifty years of a life struggling against ill health and supporting a sick mother, raising two kids, creating a lovely home, sure in herself she would make her life better than her own mother's had been. And here it all was, gathered together in a polythene bag. The sum total of one existence.

Or was it? Mum left behind a lot of great memories for me and for everyone who knew her. She'd enjoyed her life after marrying Bert and had lots of friends who stayed loyal to her till she died. She was very popular with everyone who knew her. She'd attained most of the things she'd wanted, she'd usually got what she'd gone after, even if she didn't own most of it.

The first time I played 'Goodbye Suzie' to her was on the piano in the Ramsbottom sitting-room in the summer of 1973. I'd just written it and wanted her to hear it. I turned around when I'd finished and she was in tears.

"Oh, Howard," she said as she wiped her eyes, "you've got to go to London. You could make it big down there, son. You're too good to stay here."

Mum died on 19th September 1974. Five weeks later, 'Goodbye Suzie' became my first single.

Chapter Four

Sacred Heart

It was on a cold damp foggy evening, a pea-souper as we used to call them, when I was ten years old, that my mother escorted me and my sister to church. It was time for our regular 'Confession', the ritual bearing of souls to the embodiment of God on Earth - the priest. As always, we were hoping for forgiveness and expecting some kind of penance in return. The Father and The Confessor anonymously opposite one another in divinely blessed rabbit hutches. Anonymous? My mother always ended up discussing my father's agnosticism about which the local priesthood showed immense concern.

Being a dreadful goody-goody, I usually had very little to tell in the way of sins. So I did what anyone would do in my position. I made them up. I always ensured I had a nice long list for the priest to savour, tut about, and absolve me of - thereby adding a real sin in the process - lying.

I entered the tiny wood-panelled, polish-smelling inner sanctum of The Confessional with a suitable sinner's expression on my face. Kneeling on the hard, thin piece of wood which was never wide enough to be comfy, I joined my hands in supplication and began:

"Bless me, Father, I have sinned. It is one month since my last Confession..."

Pausing for encouragement but receiving instead a gruff heavy cough and the whiff of peppermint, I ploughed on. As carefully and solemnly as I could, I trotted out my usual list of misdemeanours, which I would have loved to have actually committed. They had been learnt by rote, pulled out of my Sin Hat each month like a naughty rabbit:

"I've felt jealousy, four times; I've been cheeky to my mother, er... three times; I've been disobedient to my father at least five times."

Silence from the room next door. I tried a new one:

"I've been greedy... well, only with midget gems, and then just the red ones."

Another whiff of peppermint floated through the metal gauze on a stifled yawn.

I took a deep breath. It was now or never. This time, I had The Big Finish:

"And... I have had Immoral Thoughts!"

Up until a couple of days earlier I hadn't even heard of Immoral Thoughts, let alone had them. I'd sort of stumbled on them during our Religious Instruction class with Miss Maplin, a severe God-fearing spinster with a well discussed crush on The Headmaster, William 'Puffing Billy' Banks. Her hair was scraped back into a tight bun, so tight I used to wonder what would happen if it fell down, would her face collapse with it?

On this particular occasion she'd asked the class what special quality God possessed which none of us enjoyed whilst on Earth.

An annoyingly enthusiastic classmate shot his hand eagerly into the air:

"Miss! Miss!" he cried. "Me Miss! Me!"

With a sigh, Miss Maplin dropped her glasses to the end of her nose and stared over them:

"Yes, Stephen?"

"Well, Miss," said the thrilled Stephen. "God is Immoral!"

Miss Maplin's thin smile fixed onto her face:

"Er... I think you mean *Immortal*, Stephen, actually."

Stephen went a lovely shade of puce while Miss Maplin screwed up her nose as if detecting a particularly evil smell.

"To be *immoral* is quite a different thing," she went on sternly. "It's a nasty, dirty, disgusting sin. To even have immoral thoughts is considered evil in Heaven."

She raised her eyes to the ceiling and blessed herself, relishing her revelation of the Devil's work to her flock. Pulling her knitted cardigan more tightly around her, she visibly began to enjoy herself:

"Many of the older boys in this school probably indulge in immoral deeds every night, alone, in their beds. Oh yes! You can be just as immoral alone as with another dirty person."

She glowered at the unfortunate Stephen whose arm was no longer raised above his head, it hung rather limply behind it as though hiding from the wrath of Miss Maplin. But there was no hiding place.

"I am quite positive, Stephen, that your extremely wicked elder brother is probably doing something immoral right now, killing thousands of innocent babies in the process."

This was an astonishing discovery, not only that Stephen Mason's brother was a suspected mass murderer, but that, deliciously, you could commit a really big sin without actually doing anything. I liked the sound of these Immoral Thoughts. I had found my piéce de resistance for Saturday night's Confession.

And so, there I knelt, awaiting the priest's reaction with bated breath. There was a long pause. A deep sorrowful sigh. I saw his large shadowy shape slowly gather itself up. With a grunt, he moved his face closer to the gauze. I leaned forward too. This was going to be good.

"You are forgiven, my child. But for your penance you must say three Hail Marys, two Our Fathers and one complete Rosary."

How disappointing! Was that it? I waited, but I saw him sit back. It was over. My cue to leave. Silence reigned once more.

"Thank you, Father," I said dejectedly.

I got up to go, almost mumbled "s'not fair' as I trudged out. Then…

"Before you go…"

I stopped and spun round. My heart raced.

"Yes, Father?"

"I'd better have words with you about these… immoral thoughts."

I threw myself back down onto the kneeler, pressed my clammy hands together and waited. This could change my life, I thought. I'll no longer be the bullied skinny goody-goody dumped into a bin at playtime. I'll be the naughtiest boy in the class with a really Big Sin to my name!

The priest heaved himself forward and pressed his face against the gauze as if to prevent even God hearing what he had to say:

"You see, my child, you must try to stop having them."

"Yes, Father. Of course I must."

"Because just one immoral thought could do irreparable harm."

That made me feel slightly uneasy. Recollections of the older boys saying 'it' could make you go blind sprang to mind.

"Because you see, when you grow up and get married... your husband will not like it."

I swallowed hard, staring at the gauze in stunned silence. I opened my mouth to explain but he was suddenly in full flow, his voice beginning to tremble as he went on. "For to be a good wife and a good mother, you must have a clean mind as well as a clean body."

"B-b-b-but, Father, I..."

"No buts, my child! This is the Word of God! Heed it!" I saw his finger rise towards Heaven. "You will soon be a young woman. What decent Catholic man wants a wife with a dirty mind?"

He thundered on. I felt dizzy. I needed air.

"And remember! God is *forever* watching you! Now, go in peace, my child. Blessed are they who are pure of mind and heart. Be a good girl. God will know if you are not!"

I emerged from The Confessional my face on fire. My sister gawped at me and yelled,

"What's up wi' you? Yer all red! Look mum, he's all red!"

Her shrill laughter echoed round the vast church, heads turned, faces stared at the little boy with the red face.

"You alright, love?" Mum asked me.

"Yes, I'm fine."

"You don't look it," Susan bellowed.

"The Confessional was too stuffy, that's all."

Susan prodded my cheek and sang,

"Who's embarrassed, you's embarrassed, that's who's!"

"Oh get lost!" I hissed back.

"Mu-um, he shouted at me!"

"I'll shout at both of you if you don't be quiet. Now, Howard, do your penance. Susan, get into that Confessional before I take you both home and put you to bed without any supper."

As I mumbled my penance, the rosary beads slipping oddly comfortingly through my fingers, I thought things over. But the more I mulled, the more confused I felt. The priest was supposed to be all-knowing. That had been one of the attractions when I'd decided I wanted to join the priesthood. That and 'all those flowing robes,' as my mum had observed when trying, successfully, to talk me out of it. Now my whole Faith was in turmoil. Why didn't he know he was talking to a boy? Why didn't he?! Then it hit me. The revelation. He wasn't Jesus incarnate after all. He was just a silly old man. A silly stupid old man. I was shattered.

That night, for the first time in years, I didn't bother to kneel by my bed, look up to my Sacred Heart statue and pray thanks to God for my day. Instead I lay in the dark, feeling quite alone. The seeds of atheism had been sown.

Many years later, I was having a few friends round for dinner. We'd got onto religion and jokes about cardinals with burning handbags and I recounted this story. When the laughter had subsided, a particularly dry old queen observed, "Well, my dear," she drawled, taking a long drag from her cigarette. "It just goes to show that the little boy was right after all. The priest was all-knowing. Hallelujah".

Chapter Five

Finally Adored

When we moved from Heywood to Bury in December 1960 something very unsettling happened to my school life. I'd been a contented kid at St. Joseph's Junior School, a modern building constructed for, and ingrained with, a purveying sense that we were there to learn something new and exciting. However, once at Guardian Angel's School in Bury, a derelict decrepit place with plaster literally falling off the ceiling and a central heating system that hardly ever worked, my happy days were over. It was as though all the rough kids of the county had been sent there, with cissy old me thrust into their den.

They perceived my Heywood accent as 'posh' and my voice as 'soft' and very soon I was The Bullied Child. Skinny of frame and unworldly by nature, I couldn't understand the taunts of 'Posh boy!' and 'Listen to 'is Nancy Boy voice!' as I walked home. At playtime, I would be grabbed and thrown into the janitor's rubbish bin, rolled around the playground and dragged out again, their cries of 'Not so posh now, Jonesey!' ringing in my ears.

I was happiest when, in morning assembly, the deputy headmaster stood at his upright piano and conducted the school sing-along. 'Jerusalem' and 'The Happy Wanderer' were my favourites and I'd trill the melodies with full gusto. The other kids would mock my high-pitched singing and imitate me with operatic whoops but I didn't care. For half an hour each day I was in my perfect little world of music, inwardly mocking their tuneless meanderings and ugly cackling. It set me up for the dreadful day ahead.

One of the horrors of the day was when I needed to go to the loo. Not because of what would happen in there but what one was expected to do beforehand. We had to go and speak to the teacher-with-the-key, in full view of the class he was taking, and ask for some toilet roll. After one had hissed as quietly as one could, "I want to go to the toilet, sir", which he would never quite hear and so insisted on it being repeated another couple of times, he would get up, go to a cupboard on the wall, open it and slowly move his finger along a row of keys until he came to the one marked 'Lavatory' in big red letters. He would then take that to another cupboard, unlock it and delve into the back of it, finally extricating the roll of toilet paper. He'd carefully tear off two pieces of loo roll which he would place on his desk, put the toilet roll back in its cupboard and return the 'Lavatory' key back onto its hook, close that cupboard door and then sit at his desk. In one's outstretched hand he'd dismissively place the two pieces as though they'd already been used.

With a hurried 'Thank you, sir' one would run off to the outside loos clutching those two shiny pieces of Izal like they were five-pound notes rather than horrid disinfectant-smelling and utterly useless bum rubber. It smeared, never soaked, it scratched, never soothed. It was another example of the torture which that God-forsaken school devised for what they viewed as their disgusting brood of nit-infested unwashed hoodlums.

The outside 'lavvy' itself was a cold, draughty wee-smelling sanctuary at the farthest end of the playground and the fact it was connected to the church behind made it even more of an ordeal. There was always the sense that God was even watching us on the loo.

Much to everyone's surprise, I failed my 11-plus. This meant that, rather than go on to a good grammar school I would have to start afresh as the new boy at St. Gabriel's Secondary Modern, a newer building than Guardian Angel's but even rougher. Here the head case older lads roamed the playground each day looking for victims of their wrath.

One of their favourite pastimes was the New Kids' Initiation

Ceremony. This involved some poor new boy being held by the scruff of his neck over a dustbin full of broken glass and, as the unfortunate child squealed for mercy, he would be dropped feet first into the bin. Oh, the laughter emanating from the bubble-gum-chewing Big Boys. They'd clap each other on the back, pop their gum and wander off for a sneaky fag behind the bike shed while the younger kids would rescue their pal and dust him down. Amazingly there were never any serious injuries, and, small blessing, it only happened to you once.

The police, however, were regularly called to sort out other more serious larks such as a stabbing in the girl's playground, or to find and punish the culprits of a blazing case of arson on the railway embankment behind the school. Other times an ambulance would be called to someone passed out from swallowing too many 'black bombers', the regular lunchtime drug-snack for some of the older pupils. Their Highs were the school's Lows, as the reputation of St. Gabriel's worsened, while the intake numbers ironically increased, to the point that the A - D streaming had to be extended to an E stream.

The streaming was based initially on 11-plus results then on end-of-term exam results. If you rose into the Top 5 of the B stream you were moved to the A stream the next term, and vice versa. Like a Hit Parade of brain power. The A-streamers automatically took their GCEs in the fifth form, the B and C-streamers sat CSEs. D & E were expected to aspire and work towards going up to at least the C stream by the fourth year, otherwise they simply left school at fifteen with no qualifications.

As we lined up in the playground each morning, watched by the line-duty teacher and his patrol of beefy Prefects, it was usually a first year E-streamer who would be grabbed by the ear and dragged to the front of the line. The teacher would shout at him for a few minutes then cane him in front of us all. I was always amazed when, a couple of hours later during playtime, the punished boy would be showing his reddened swollen hand to his admiring classmates, laughing and joking about how much it hurt, their wounded hero for a day.

I remember some of the E-stream boys wandering round with shaven purple heads, the treatment for lice in those days. Again, who the hell devised that? They were little beacons of shame and filth to the higher-streamed boys, fair game for a bit of bashing up after school.

The social hierarchy game, without any prompting, had already begun.

Sadist teachers also roamed the corridors, looking for anyone likely to need a damned good thrashing. One teacher had wrapped shiny copper wire around his cane so it had that extra bite and weight when it landed on a kid's outstretched hand. The female staff were mainly elderly single ladies living with 'mum'. I used to wonder if they'd ever been in love, perhaps left alone by the war or ditched at the altar. Whatever their story, their love for Jesus only increased their contempt for the pupils.

The only exception to this band of ancient crazy monsters was the P.E. Teacher, Mr Richmond. He was a tall lean man in his thirties who talked rather loudly, walked very quickly and ran around the football pitch with his 'lads', blowing his whistle enthusiastically and shouting 'Shot!', whenever a goal was scored. His eagerness to exhaust left me completely uninspired and as often as I could I would 'forget' my kit or come down with some dreaded lurgy which prevented me from moving any further than the changing rooms. As the mumbled 'cissy Jonesey's ill again!' taunts faded into the winter air I would sit blissfully happy, snug against the heater on the shiny pale green wall for whole games periods.

Then, one awful unexpected day as I was settling onto my cosy bench, Mr Richmond decided he'd had enough of this and, insisting I take part in the match, thrust a pair of ludicrously oversized shorts at me, a filthy shirt which looked more like one of Mum's well-used dusters, and a beaten-up pair of old football boots.

"Put them on," he ordered.

My school tie kept the shorts up and my feet barely held the boots on. Stinking of someone else's B.O., I trudged outside to the delighted gasps and guffaws of my 'chums' and stood on the edge of the frozen field, pulling the over-long sleeves down over my blue hands and hopping from foot to foot to try and get warm.

Just as I was daydreaming that Mr Richmond would take pity on this pathetic freezing kid, blow his horrible little whistle and tell me to go back to the changing room, he took charge of the ball, dribbled it round and kicked it towards me. In slow motion, I saw the terrifying object hurtling through the air in my direction and foolishly lifted my foot to kick it back. What felt like a lump of concrete slammed into my foot, a numbing sharp pain shot up my leg and, in true football hero fashion I fell to the ground and writhed in agony.

I looked up to a circle of faces staring down at me, puzzled and even concerned faces, so I screamed very loudly. They parted like a wave and began shouting:

"It looks pretty bad, sir!"

"I think he's broken his leg, sir!"

And more alarmingly, "Shall I call an ambulance, sir?"

Mr Richmond's authoritative voice broke through the mêlée. "Come on, lads! Let me through!" In the guise of St Christopher, he bent down towards me, swept me up in his strong arms and carried me, Scarlett-like off the pitch. "Don't worry, son, you'll be alright," he told me.

I felt suddenly rather fine. I could have lain there all day.

In the changing rooms, he laid me gently onto the bench and inspected my leg for any damage. Finally, with a quick decisive nod, he said,

"Better just rest up here, Jones. We'll see how you are at the end of the match."

He efficiently ushered his mumbling brood back out onto the pitch and I was left, once more blissfully alone in the stale-feet smell of the clothes-strewn room, the silence periodically punctuated by the distant enthusiastic cry of 'Shot!' and a long piercing whistle breaking through the freezing December air.

I got even lankier as I entered my teens, my limbs and neck stretching almost alarmingly, a large Adam's Apple appearing like an unwelcome guest in my throat. Developing acute short-sightedness as puberty beckoned was the sour icing on a bitter-tasting cake. I was now the skinny lanky wimp with glasses.

My elastically thin legs meant I wasn't bad at Long Jump but I had "no discipline!" according to Mr Richmond. When you're scratching around in the sand for your glasses after landing rather awkwardly on your arse, a whole classroom of kids baying, "Useless! Useless!", 'discipline' is the last word which comes to mind.

When I was fourteen, I auditioned for the annual school play. Drama rehearsals always crossed over Games Periods, so it was an absolute no-brainer for me. The new drama teacher, Miss Shaw, who also taught art and was a stylish ray of light on a grey landscape of dull tweeds and flat shoes, had chosen 'Nicolo & Nicolette'. It was a fantasy piece which called for someone to play The High Cockalorum. He was a dandy character with fine plumage and a crow which was 'feared for miles around, from country field to town.' After reading a bit of it for Miss Shaw, I got the part.

In the first rehearsal a few days later I got to the crowing bit, where everyone else on stage cover their ears and wait for the thunder. I was just about to crow ever so loudly when Miss Shaw stopped me and said she wanted a slightly different take on The Crow. To demonstrate what she had in mind, she minced on, limp wrist dangling by her side, the other jammed onto her waist and shimmied to centre stage.

Standing to attention she lifted her head proudly and, in a very refined, very slow, rather precious high-camp voice, she cooed,

"A-cock, A-doodle, A-doo."

It was utterly brilliant and made everyone laugh. She instructed the other performers to slowly take their hands from their ears and look mildly puzzled rather than awe-struck.

"Try it, Jones," she told me.

I did, and it worked, people were in fits of giggles.

"It's only a small part," Miss Shaw told me, "but you will be remembered for the rest of the play, Jones!".

Home time came, and as we were leaving the assembly hall, rehearsals finished, she asked me,

"You live Bolton Road way, don't you?"

I told her yes, I did, and a few minutes later was sitting next to her in her open-topped green MG sports car as she sped, film-star-like out of the school gates. Boys stood gawping at me as I rather grandly waved at them, Miss Shaw chuckling to herself and pushing the car into full throttle.

Miss Shaw was a real beauty, the stuff schoolboys' wet dreams are made of. High cheek bones, shoulder-length dark hair, slim figure hugged into tight mini-skirted outfits, knee-length high-heeled boots which literally shook the corridor every time she stomped stylishly along. She had this bird-like way of looking round her as she walked, head going from side to side in quick sharp movements, taking in everything as though it was the first time she'd seen it. Her wide dark mascara'd eyes seemed to dare anyone who stared - and they usually did - to look away. Boys would sigh as she passed. Their youthful lust was palpable. Think of the lady on the front cover of Bob Dylan's *Bringing It All Back Home*, and you have a virtual twin of Miss Shaw.

And here was I, the effeminate loser wimp of the school, side-by-side with the untouchable siren of every boy's fantasy. The lads could not believe their eyes as we va-va-voomed past them.

Over the noise of the engine, in her gorgeous deep husky voice, she talked about herself, how long she'd lived in the area, where she'd lived and taught before. It was all rather lovely and I felt very special in her company.

Then, we came to my road and she stopped to let me out. I thanked her and was just about to open the door when she pushed her sunglasses onto the top of her head and said to me:

"Howard?"

"Yes, Miss?"

"You're ok doing this part in the play, aren't you?"

"Yes, Miss."

"You don't mind the, well, the campness of how I want it played?"

"No, Miss."

She paused, continued looking at me, then said, "I know what a difficult time you probably have... with other boys in the school. You are quite different from anyone else. You know that, don't you?"

"I do, yes, Miss."

"And you do have a hard time sometimes, don't you?"

"Sometimes, yes, Miss."

"Well, listen to me." She stopped the engine and held me with her eyes. "You *are* different. You have a style about you. I watch you walk about the school and you have an aura which is very self-contained and rather wonderful. You are not like the other lads and that's why they make fun of you. I see them doing it. But be proud of what you are, Jones. *Be* different. No matter what anyone tells you, or calls you, or however much they make fun of you or laugh at you. Life will occasionally be very difficult for you, my boy. People and their prejudices will make it so. But face it, head-on, don't be afraid. Hold your head up high and stare them down. It works. I know it does."

She beamed a huge smile at me, squeezed my arm and briskly said,

"Now, off you go for your tea. Have a nice evening. See you tomorrow."

Feeling rather odd, a little shaky even and resisting the urge to give Miss Shaw a big hug, I quickly thanked her, got out of the car and waved as she sped off. Her black shiny hair blowing wildly, she waved back as though casually drying her bright red nail-varnish.

The following evening was the play's first night and my High Cockalorum brought the house down. My parents and Gran Wood were sitting in the second row and my abiding memory is of Gran clutching Dad's arm and laughing her head off, her hooting laughter ringing out above everyone else's.

The next day, lads were coming up to me in the playground and patting me on the back. One-by-one they stood round me, full of smiles, suddenly my friends:

"Well done, Jonesey!"

"You were fantastic!"

"My mum thought you were the best thing in it!"

Then someone tapped me on the shoulder. It was Mr Richmond. He held out his hand and said,

"Put it there, Jones. I thought you were utterly amazing last night. You might be rubbish at football, but, boy, you are something else on stage!"

On the last night of the play, we were given an after-show party in the Assembly Room, orange juice and sandwiches and a fair sprinkling of mutual congratulation. As we all stood round chatting excitedly about our performances, feeling very pleased with ourselves and extremely relieved it was over, someone mentioned that I played the piano.

"A piano player too!" Miss Shaw shouted. "On you go, Jones!"

"And he can sing," one of the girls added.

"Oh! Even better!"

With just a little cajoling and encouragement, I sat down at the piano and did 'Homeward Bound'. Very quickly I realised that the hilarity and hubbub which had buzzed around me had melted away and in its place was total silence. When I got to the last chorus everyone joined in. It was a truly beautiful sound. At the end, the room erupted into applause.

"Excuse the language, boys and girls, but Bloody Hell!" cried a delighted Miss Shaw. "Another, please, Howard!"

I wished I could have played all night but, with my encore of 'Blowing in the Wind' wildly applauded, I had used up my entire catalogue of songs I knew off by heart. I stood, soaked in the cheers and looked across the room. Miss Shaw was beaming at me. She raised her glass and did a little bow.

"Well done," she mouthed.

The playground the next day was abuzz about my High Cockalorum's special mention in the Bury Times' review. And it got better. The kids who had been at the last night party told everyone about my impromptu performance. I was suddenly aware of a crowd of admiring faces, staring and smiling at me.

I was never bullied or picked on again.

Chapter Six

Small Town, Big Adventures

The first record I fell in love with was 'On the Street Where You Live'. My parents had the Cast Recording E.P. of *My Fair Lady* and I discovered this lyrical gem one afternoon going through the pile of discs by the record player. I would have been about four or five and instantly was taken by the internal rhymes in lines like '*I have often walked down the street before/But the pavement always stayed beneath my feet before.*' I played the track repeatedly until I knew it off by heart. The singer had a gorgeously rich deep baritone and I wanted to be the one he waited each day for under those lilac trees.

The first record I bought was Elvis Presley's 'It's Now or Never'. It would have been late 1960, and I found it at the Bury Market record stall while out shopping with my mum. I'd never heard it before but wanted to buy a single. At least, I wanted my mum to buy me a single! I liked his name, it sounded very odd and oddly appealing. I'd never heard of anyone called 'Elvis' before. When I played it back at home I adored his voice, it was so majestic and in control. His earlier stuff had gone by me unnoticed. In fact, Rock 'n' Roll had no impact on me whatsoever. For one thing, I didn't hear much of it. Pop radio in Britain hadn't got going, and though we got our first TV in 1957 there was little pop music on there, and any there had been, such as Jack Good's *Oh Boy!* would have aired long after I was tucked up in bed. Even if I had heard anything remotely rock 'n' roll, I was too young to identify with it or understand the social and musical revolution it had caused in the 1950s. To this day, the genre leaves me stone cold. Rather like the Blues does.

I didn't know who Buddy Holly was until I saw his name in the writer's credit brackets for 'Words of Love' on the sleeve of *Beatles For Sale*, which my sister got for Christmas '64. *(Holly)*, it read. I had no idea if this was a girl's Christian name or a boy's surname.

"Buddy Holly died five years ago," Susan told me with great authority. I assumed he must have been very old.

Our house in the late '50s and early '60s had been full of Cliff Richard singles. 'Gee Whiz It's You', 'The Young Ones', 'Living Doll', 'High Class Baby', 'Theme for A Dream', 'Dynamite'. Sue and her friends, in multi-coloured headbands and Sweetheart Swing dresses, would pick each record up and dance across the room singing the opening lines to each other. Susan would stack the records on her pink and grey Dansette turntable, her beehive and kiss curls bobbing up and down as she and her pals hand-jived round the sitting-room. Each 45 wowed more than the last as they slipped around on top of each other, but the girls were oblivious. They bopped happily around to the wowing sounds of their Brylcreemed hero, kissing his smiling laminated face and giggling naughtily.

One of their games as the singles played was standing in a circle and seeing who could keep their hoola-hoop going the longest. I did try having a go once but quickly got a stitch, much to everyone's amusement. The Cliff Club, as the girls called themselves, was their secret society for which membership to me was never offered. I was an under-age onlooker to their Go-Go-Daddy-O fun.

I did have one personal Cliff favourite, 'The Shrine on The Second Floor', from his 'Expresso Bongo' E.P., which I'd play on my own when Sue was out. It sounded so exotic, the words telling of this 'grey-haired Madonna' who lived there, 'the face of this lady of grace on the shrine on the second floor.' It was surreal and otherworldly. I'd lie on the floor and try to imagine this 'shrine'. In my mind, it was carpeted with soft purple wall-to-wall and had shiny lifts on every floor out of which beautifully dressed couples would wander, smile at each other and disappear down the softly-lit corridor which smelt of polish and spring flowers. I'd discuss it with my imaginary friend, Barbara, and she would agree with me that, one day, we would visit it and say hello to the grey-haired Madonna.

Sue stayed loyal to Cliff right up to early '63. But once The Beatles shot to the top of the charts with 'Please Please Me' he was ditched. All we then heard in the house were the exciting raw strains of 'From Me to You' and 'She Loves You'. She was enthralled with The Fab Four, especially Paul, who'd she'd scream at in the front room whenever the group were on TV, which in 1963 seemed like every night. Her love affair with everything Beatles extended to a Beatles wig, Beatles boots, Beatles stickers on her school satchel, even Beatles wallpaper (which I now wish we'd peeled off carefully and saved rather than getting my parents to steam it off when Sue got married in 1965 and left home, bequeathing her larger bedroom to me).

The British pop explosion that year meant the scene was blown wide open for a lot of new names to suddenly start selling a lot of singles, and because many of them came from the North-West of England it had an even greater impact for me and my friends. It felt very local and as though they belonged to us, in a way that American pop stars never could. Even at ten years old, I knew something was happening. I have a clear memory of seeing a school friend combing his crew cut down with water, trying to get a fringe and singing 'I'll send it along with love from me to you,' bobbing his head around like Paul and George did on Thank Your Lucky Stars.

In January 1964, Top Of The Pops started. It helped burgeoning pop fans like me to tune in every week to the latest hits by The Hollies, The Searchers, The Rolling Stones, Cilla Black, Sandie Shaw and Dusty Springfield. I was fascinated each week to see where a single had risen or fallen to. My love of lists, which I've had all my life, was satiated beautifully with great music into the bargain. I liked especially the wondrous drama-pop platters like 'Anyone Who Had A Heart', 'Always Something There To Remind Me' and 'I Just Don't Know What To Do With Myself', while on the solo male front I was actually keener on the few American acts still dominating the charts.

P. J. Proby was a particular favourite. He was my first pop star crush. While Sue shrieked at The Beatles I secretly lusted after P.J. Well, lust is probably too strong a word at that age. It was more a feeling that I wanted this man to literally 'Hold Me'. I would imagine myself in his arms as I watched him leap around in front of the cameras in his blue velvet shirt, tight velvet pants and cute little pony tail.

"He looks daft," my sister would yell as I got closer to the TV to watch his every move.

"He does not!" I said.

('He looks gorgeous!' I thought).

Gene Pitney and Roy Orbison were the Kings of Drama Pop in 1964, and anything they released had me spending my pocket money down the record shop in Bury Centre. Their big doom-laden echoey ballads with tortured tales of love lost and broken hearts would boom out in my listening booth at Javelin Records, door shut, staring faces ignored, as I mimed happily away to each purchase. Heaven.

On holiday in Torquay in the summer of '65, my friend Anthony and I would listen to Radio Luxembourg every night in our room on my little transistor radio. Even with the signal fading in and out, the station played some of the best pop music around. We fell in love with a new one which had just come out, 'I Got You Babe.' Fab 208 played it at least three times a night. We learnt the words by heart so that we could enter the local holiday talent contest as Sonny & Cher. On the Friday evening before the contest, we sat in the guest house's darkened TV room and waited excitedly for the duo to appear on Ready Steady Go. Cathy McGowan joyfully announced them and voilà, there they were. And horror of horrors, they were husband and wife! We'd thought they were two blokes, with Cher's deep voice and Sonny's slightly higher one. Anthony turned to me and said,

"Well, I'm not being Cher!"

"Neither am I!" I protested, rather vacuously.

"That's that then!"

So, the next day, I entered the contest on my own, telling the compère, one Billy Bright, that I would perform Cilla Black's 'It's For You'. He turned to the piano accompanist who shrugged his shoulders and shook his head:

"Our pianist doesn't know that one, Howard," the blue blazered Billy smilingly announced to the audience. Out of the corner of my eye I could see Anthony hiding behind someone in the crowd, grinning to himself.

"It was a Top Ten hit last year," I informed Billy. "Got to No.7!"

"Did it now?" Billy mugged at his fans and turned to the pianist again, who shrugged his shoulders even higher and looked bored.

"OK, I'll sing it on my own then."

"Acapella," the compère laughed, getting an 'Ooooh!' from the crowd.

'Whatever,' I thought, and launched into, "I'd say, someday, I'm gonna give my heart away, when I do, it's for you."

My knees shook, my hands shook, my head shook, my voice quivered. Anthony sidled up to the front of the stage and smirked up at me the whole way through. I stared at the out-of-focus microphone and wished I was dead. The audience gave me a mild sympathy clap and I ran off the stage.

"You looked so funny!" Anthony crowed.

Our friendship never really recovered.

My love of Sonny & Cher, however, continued to grow. I got their debut album *Look At Us* for Christmas that year and fell in love with tracks like 'Just You' and 'The Letter'. Sonny was a great songwriter and producer, while Cher had the most incredible voice, deep, resonant and very emotional. They stood side by side on the cover of the L.P. which I studied and stared at each time I took the orange-labelled gem out of its white paper inner sleeve. They were, I guess, the first

Hippies, at least the first I'd ever seen, and they always looked so in love. I adored the open-handed rather child-like clapping Cher did on Top Of The Pops as she belted out *'And when I get scared, you're always arou-ou-ou-nd."* It was my idea of pop paradise every time they appeared on TV. Sonny didn't have the greatest voice, but when he harmonised a third above Cher the sound they made together was glorious. I bought every single they released for the next two years, 'Little Man', which almost gave them their second UK No.1, a particular favourite. And I will always scratch my head that the utterly brilliant, multi-layered gem that was 'Living For You' never reached any higher than No.44.

Even though I wasn't an avid fan during their mop-top days, I liked a lot of what The Beatles brought out. *Beatles For Sale* was a favourite of mine, and I rather liked the Derek Taylor track notes inside the gate-fold sleeve where John looked very dishy with his loosened tie. The fact the group weren't grinning from ear-to-ear on the front cover also struck me as extremely cool. I even bought 'I Feel Fine', beating Sue to the record shop with my three-and-eleven. John and Paul's shimmering double-tracked harmonies thrilled me, Ringo's smashing cymbals thrashing away throughout, that fab distorted bass note at the start then into George's superb complex riff which John then doubled when it all got going, it all made a really tremendous noise. The group's biggest-sounding single up that point seemed so polished and complete and utterly joyful.

'We Can Work It Out/Day Tripper' was my Christmas '65 present for myself, paid for with the postal orders Nan and Gran had given me. I loved the way Paul giggled at John's gurning antics at the harmonium during the 'Work It Out' promo film, and they all looked the business in their black roll-neck sweaters. But my main singles purchases that year were records by The Kinks, The Pretty Things, The Fortunes, Marianne Faithfull, Sonny & Cher and Dylan's 'Like A

Rolling Stone'. Bob's earlier folk-protest stuff had bypassed me, rather like Elvis's rock 'n' roll stuff had. A girl at school had sung 'The Times They Are-A Changing' to me, but when I heard Bob's version on the radio I assumed he was an old man so dismissed it. Then one day, while making myself a cup of tea, 'Like A Rolling Stone' blasted into the kitchen out of the transistor. I'd never heard anything like it. It sounded so angry, but in a truly erudite way. The energy of the thing pulsed into the room and the words Bob was singing were like a new language. He spewed them out, each line tumbling into the next. God, it was wonderful. And that organ! Beautiful riffs and ghostly motifs curling round and under Dylan's gorgeous rant. I knew I had to have it. Just a few weeks later came 'Positively Fourth Street.' It was even more wonderful. Four exhilarating minutes of astonishingly phrased and perfectly sung venom. I pitied whoever Bob was singing about, but kind of wished it were me just to be the inspiration for such a stunning song. Out of nowhere, or so it seemed to me, came this searing star, and when I saw his latest photos in Melody Maker I wanted that polka dot shirt and those shades like nothing else.

In '66 I grooved along to The Mamas & Papas, Ike & Tina Turner, The Mindbenders and Harper's Bizarre. Although The Beach Boys' goofy striped-shirted surfer-boy image prevented me turning onto them wholesale, 'God Only Knows' took my breath away, and I still consider it the ultimate piece of pop perfection.

Once Susan had left home at the end of 1965, the regular influx of Beatles singles and LPs ceased, and while I thought 'Paperback Writer' was great, I found a comment a friend made at the local Bury Palais disco, on hearing the single played there, more interesting:

"This is the best record The Beatles have made. They were finished before this one came out."

In retrospect that seems a ridiculous thing to say. 'We Can Work It Out' had been No.1 for five weeks over Christmas '65 and Rubber Soul had sold millions round the world. But there was a definite sense among general pop fans by the early summer of 1966 that The Fabs had had their day. There hadn't been a single released for six months, their live performances and their public profile had lessened, certainly in the UK, and other bands like The Small Faces, The Walker Brothers, The Yardbirds and The Troggs were riding high in the charts which The Beatles once dominated and now seemed to have lost interest in. Even The Rolling Stones, always runners-up in the public's mind next to The Fabs, had achieved two huge hits during the year and had become rather dangerously hip with tremendously off-the-wall singles like '19th Nervous Breakdown' and 'Paint It Black'.

When The Beatles' Double 'A' side 'Eleanor Rigby/Yellow Submarine' came out in August that year, the group didn't even bother to make a promo video for it. For a thirteen-year-old pop fan like me who could only afford to buy singles most of the year and followed the charts avidly each week, the apparent lack of Beatles to be seen anywhere meant that other acts were taking a hold in their absence. The Beach Boys, for example, who had always been the American underdogs when compared with The Beatles, were suddenly going from strength to strength, bringing out amazing 45s like 'Sloop John B', 'God Only Knows' and the astonishing chart-topper 'Good Vibrations.'

I couldn't afford Revolver, my sister was busy rearing her new daughter so didn't buy records any longer, and it was singles, TV shows and the charts which made up my pop landscape. From my vantage point, the once-mighty and omnipresent Beatles were notable by their absence.

By the end of the year, with no Beatles Christmas single release for the first time since 1962, along with all the kafuffle on the news about John Lennon's so-called 'anti-Jesus' remarks prompting Beatles record burning parties in America, and rumours abounding that the group were on the verge of splitting with just occasional rare glimpses of one of them alone in India or another filming solo in Spain, one had the definite impression that the times were definitely a-changing for The Fab Four.

In February 1967 I was watching the weekly Saturday TV show Juke Box Jury when the new Beatles single came on, their first 45 release for six months. Host David Jacobs played both sides, 'Penny Lane' and 'Strawberry Fields Forever.' Only about a minute of each but that was enough to completely change my world - and my opinion. When the opening mellotron strains of 'Strawberry Fields' and John Lennon's mournful slightly odd vocal began I fell hook, line and sinker in love. I remember Simon Dee, one of the J.B.J. panellists that evening, covering his face with his hands, shaking his head and murmuring, "they are AMAZING!". I simply sat and stared at the TV nodding in silent agreement. I bought the single a few days later and played it until it virtually wore out.

The group's two psychedelic promo videos for the tracks, featuring the no longer Mop Top foursome, also signalled that something was happening here and we didn't know what it was. They were now moustachioed, exotically attired, rather mysterious and beautiful people, displaying the kind of confidence only Gods achieve. There was no attempt to be cheery or funny, the chirpy boys-next-door look and leaping about antics had gone and been replaced by something, for me at the age of fourteen, altogether more artistic and much more fascinating.

From that moment on there was no other pop act for me. With one single, they had left every other pop star behind, the sound of pop music changed forever with just two incredible recordings. When news broke that their new L.P. *Sgt Pepper's Lonely Hearts Club Band* was to be released in June, I saved up weeks of pocket money. Just the title alone was enough to intrigue me. My determination to buy it was fuelled even more when our history teacher, on the day of its release, instead of giving us our usual history lesson, played it to us in its entirety. "This is history in the making", was Mr Reilly's prophetic excuse for straying off the beaten curriculum track.

While we'd all been decrying the fall of The Fabs, they had been working away in the studios on a masterpiece. 'Pepper' became the L.P. that all record buyers had to own. Walking around Bury Centre with it under your arm became a kind of badge of honour. You were suddenly cool and other kids smiled knowingly at you as you wandered nonchalantly by singing 'Good Morning, Good Morning' to yourself: 'I got nothing to say, but it's ok'.

In the UCP Tripe Shop, I'd prop the L.P. up on the empty chair next to me, feeling very hip as I tucked into tripe and chips with a hot steaming Vimto, assured that adults would stare disapprovingly while their kids looked on in wonder.

"I liked them," the girl at the till said to me one day, nodding towards my proudly displayed Pepper sleeve as I paid her my one and a penny, "until they went weird."

Truly nothing could have made me love The Beatles more at that point.

Listening to the intricacies of 'Strawberry Fields' and much of 'Pepper' repeatedly in my bedroom, a new ambition overtook me. I had already begun writing songs, albeit not great songs. But now I wanted to be a recording artist. To try and create something close to what The Beatles were doing became an obsession. I dreamed of being in a recording studio like my heroes were in the Beatles Monthly photos, working on my own masterpiece.

I begged my parents to buy me a new Grundig multi-tracking tape recorder which I'd seen in a music shop on the way home from school. It was an expensive thing to desire and pay for but, God bless them, they bought it for my birthday. For months afterwards, I would record the piano in the living room while my parents were out, then take the tape recorder upstairs to my room and spend delicious evenings alone overdubbing salt cellars, banged knees and oohs and ahhs, before adding the final double-tracked lead vocal with an occasional third-above harmony. Oh my word was I happy. The songs still weren't up to much but the fun I had was top notch.

On Christmas Day 1967, I played my latest creations to our visiting guests. My sister and her husband, Dave, along with Gran Wood and Nan Longton sat and watched me carefully thread my reel-to-reel tape through the heads on the machine, choosing which channel configuration I needed and turning the enormous plastic knob to 'Play'. They were more interested in the complexities of what I was doing rather than what was to come.

My parents had left me more or less alone the previous few months to indulge myself in the weird banging's and oohings and aahhings they heard coming out of my bedroom while they watched Coronation Street. Now they perched themselves at the back of the room, my mum with one ear cocked for the oven timer, Dad with that amused frown he always had when I was trying out something new.

As the strains of the first track floated round the living-room, I sensed bemusement turn to fascination.

"Is that you singing?" Susan asked, staring at me.

I nodded.

"Bloody hell!"

"Language!" my mum said to the back of her head.

"No, bloody hell is right!" Gran Wood broke in. "This is great!"

"Who did all those voices?" Susan asked.

"Howard did," my dad replied. "We can hear him doing them in his bedroom every night."

"And the harmonies!" Gran Wood exclaimed. "All you??"

I nodded again, blushing up.

Dad winked at me, Mum beamed, Sue looked increasingly astonished. She turned to Dave and said,

"My little brother can sing!"

"Aye, he can that," Dave answered. "Good on yer, son!"

It was the best Christmas Day I'd ever had.

A few months later, I sent off a tape of thirty songs I'd recorded at home to Apple Records, which had advertised in Disc & Music Echo that they were looking for new talent. I never heard a word back from them, of course. I read years later that all the tapes they'd received through the post got thrown in the bin. But it didn't put me off. More songs, more multi-tracked opuses flowed out of me onto that overworked tape recorder, which finally gave up the ghost after a year or so. With a puff of smoke and a loud bang it refused to ever multi-track anything for me again.

But the seed was planted and the recording continued, although done more simply, live in the sitting-room, mike propped up on the piano as I banged out my developing catalogue of compositions. My future was decided. Any thought of becoming something other than a successful pop singer no longer occurred to me. It was just, as far as I was concerned, a matter of time.

Chapter Seven

A Wardrobe Dreams

This new-found self-belief that I was 'a talent' seemed to alter my personality. Having discovered myself in my music I developed a new assertiveness. It transformed me from an unsure gangly young lad, aware he was different but not of what that would mean in the future, into someone very certain of his place in the world. In my head, I had become A Star. Basically, ambition took over. Not only ambition but a belief that my dreams would come true. Which meant that anyone who did not view me as different in a positive way was, in my youthfully arrogant opinion, 'wrong'.

I think timing was important too. Just as The Beatles lost their family-friendly Mop Top image and became more anti-Establishment in both their dress and their collective attitude, I fell in love with them. I read every interview I could find with any member of the group and took what they said as Gospel. Their rather off-the-cuff and often badly-thought-out views on drugs, religion, authority, society, you name it, what The Fabs thought and said became the template for my life at the age of fifteen.

I began to reject all forms of conformity. The previously studious, bespectacled, obedient lad turned into a self-opinionated burgeoning hippie. By 1969 I had grown my hair to my shoulders and replaced my square tortoiseshell plastic-rimmed glasses with John Lennon metal round jobbies. I began spouting extremely naive views, to anyone who was unwise enough to stop and ask me how I was doing, on reincarnation and The Meaning Of Life, absorbed mainly from what George Harrison had said in Disc & Music Echo.

At school, I pinned slogans to the Events notice-board such as 'Peace Not War!', 'Grow Your Hair For Peace!' and 'Talking 'Bout A Revolution!', most of them pinched from the constantly sloganeering

John and Yoko. As each of my garish home-made posters was ripped down by a tutting teacher, I pinned up another. Badly designed and poorly executed pieces of simplistic propaganda, they were daubs of reds and greens and lots of exclamation marks. Nevertheless, they got me noticed, which was my intention. I became the self-anointed School Rebel which acquired for me a certain amount of kudos with some of the other pupils, while peeing off many more who believed it would, in the end, reflect badly on them.

For me it was a natural progression towards stardom and fame. For the school, it meant that the previously admired 'talented lad' was now a 'pain in the arse' who needed taking down a peg or two. This newly acquired overbearing confidence also coincided with studying for my 'O' levels, which caused great concern amongst those teachers who thought I had a real chance of good results in the forthcoming June exams. I had no such great hopes. My positions in the Top 20 class rankings had plummeted from a regular fourth or fifth in my first three years at the school, to a lowly nineteenth by the end of my fourth year. Something, the teachers decided, had to be done.

At first it was a few man-to-man chats with the Headmaster. He'd sit me down in his pipe-smelling book-lined office and with great respect try to cajole me into "behaving" and "getting your head down to some proper work." I would try and explain why I was acting up so much and what my long-term intentions were, but he'd just shake his head and ask me what my parents thought. The fact was, I hadn't given that any consideration at all.

In my final pep-talk with him, he had another go at making me see sense:

"Howard," he began, sitting next to me and adopting an affectionate uncle's tone of voice. "All this malarkey and really unacceptable behaviour is not only shaming your parents but is creating a lot of unrest amongst the pupils. It has to stop."

"But sir," I explained as though to a child, "young people have to make a stand and change the world. That is why we are here. To right the wrongs our elders have created."

With a sigh and a definite smirk, the Head stood, walked round and looked down at me patiently, laying a fatherly hand on my shoulder:

"Howard. We all want to make the world a better place. We all think at your age that we can do better. I was a bit of a rebel myself in my time." He allowed himself a nostalgic tip of the head. "The truth is, you are a good student, you are well-liked here, but you are not doing yourself any favours with this disruptive behaviour. What I want to know is, where did it come from? You were such a good boy."

Sighing impatiently and crossing my legs as if preparing for a TV interview with Robin Day, I began a diatribe about peace and love and the after-life. I was in good form today, I thought, and prattled on like a male Germaine Greer preaching to a roomful of perceived dimwits. I crossed the other leg and had just launched into my theories of the uselessness of the Roman Catholic Church when his patience snapped. With a threat that "any further nonsense like this will result in me having to speak to your parents" I was sent packing.

A final barked order as I left of "and get your hair cut!" ensured that, as I strode off down the corridor past a Physics Lab full of craning necks and staring eyes, I became even more determined that I would do things my way. The road ahead was clear. The one behind me littered with the mistakes of predecessors. It felt good to be so right about everything. 'Change It!' became my new mantra which I thereafter pinned up daily on the noticeboard.

One of the things I decided to change was my school attire. Dark blue blazer, white shirt, yellow and dark blue striped tie, black Terylene trousers and black shoes were "So boring, man!", as I'd moan to school pals on the walk home. At weekends, I'd taken to visiting The Toggery clothes shop in Bury Centre. With its array of flowered shirts and ties, striped hipsters and garish tie-dye scarves I'd try several combinations out, wafting in front of the mirror knowing I could only afford one. With its links to The Hollies, who apparently had a share in the shop, one regularly brushed shoulders with other dedicated followers of fashion. A school friend told me she'd seen Graham Nash coming out of there one Saturday afternoon, so I'd browse the merchandise for hours in the hope of bumping into him. By early '69, with Nash relocated to L.A. and his place in the group taken by Terry Sylvester, I had to hope that the less cool Allan Clarke or Tony Hicks may walk in. It never happened.

One Monday morning, I swanned out of the house in my latest outfit of purple dotted roll-neck shirt - with the Velcro seal at the back which sounded like your head was ripping off when you undid it - and golden-brown trousers which shimmered like a sunset as I walked. A bright yellow Paisley floor-length scarf brushed mauve shoes which were neatly set off by canary yellow socks.

My mum took one look at me as I reached the front door:

"You're not going to school like that, are you?" she said.

I told her that, yes, I was.

"Well, I expect you back home by lunchtime."

"I'm not coming home for lunch."

"Oh, I think you probably are!"

I walked through the school gates and was met by wolf whistles which were meant to embarrass me. Instead, I preened from within.

"Jonesey!" one boy hollered. "You going to a fancy dress party?"

I waved rather royally and went straight to the fifth form common room, usually a welcoming sanctuary where we listened to Radio 1 and chatted about what we were going to do with our lives after 'O' Levels.

I did a little twirl as friends stood and admired. Less impressed lads just sniggered:

"You know who's coming this morning, don't you?" one of them said, nudging his pals.

My friends nodded at me and looked worried.

"The Bishop!" the boy bellowed.

"You're going to be for it!" another lad said as he pushed past me.

My friends nodded at me again and looked even more worried.

As the fading strains of "Jonesey's in the shithouse!" echoed round the corridor walls I inwardly, reluctantly, agreed with them. My friends' thin smiles and poorly disguised fear seemed to confirm it.

In Assembly, I stood near the back and tried to look as inconspicuous as I could. My brave purple and gold fashion statement was turning into a 'wish I hadn't done this' moment. I was thinking through how I could perhaps sneak out with an excuse that I felt sick, when the doors at the back of the hall swung open and in walked the beaming, slightly flushed Headmaster. Obviously excited about the thrill and pride of this magic career moment, he was puffed up like a randy cockatoo and seemed not to have noticed dandy old me hiding behind a rather large boy I'd strategically placed myself next to.

My relief quickly evaporated when in sailed the Bishop, radiant in - Oh No!! - purple and gold! A canary yellow sash hung on for dear life round his ample waist, the whole shimmering ensemble topped off with a purple and gold satin creation which bobbed from side to side on his huge wobbling head. Stately as a galleon, he glanced benignly at his youthful flock who all stood to attention and stared respectfully. Sadly for me, some of the pupils were not only staring at the Bishop, their eyes kept moving off rather too purposefully to where I was hiding. As his eyes followed theirs, I hunched my shoulders, lost about two inches in height and prayed for mercy. It was no use. His eyes fell on me and his cheeks sucked in air. His golden sash strained at the waist while his enormous hat bobbed about even more dangerously. I tried a smile as if to say, "Oh look! We twinned our outfits," but he looked ready to explode. As I squirmed under his gaze he took a deep breath, regained his composure and floated off like someone on wheels to the front of the Hall. I saw him lean towards the Headmaster and whisper something. The two men looked in my direction and the Head nodded. A boy in front of me murmured "Jonesey's for it now," but any sniggers that followed were drowned out by a booming "Let us pray!" The Bishop roared out the Lord's Prayer ending with the sonorous "And deliver us from Evil!", accompanied by a resolute glare at me.

Prayers over, Bishop gone, I slipped out at the back of the Hall surrounded by a protective mêlée of pupils from which I soon broke off and found an empty classroom. I settled down into the welcome silence and immersed myself in revising French Essays. Apart from the occasional wanderer who stared in and wandered off again I was blissfully alone.

Suddenly, the door flew open and a palpable energy of contained anger flooded into the room. The Deputy Head stood stock still and just stared, taking in the offending outfit which had seemed such a good idea earlier in the day. I felt, rather than bedecked in glorious multi-colour splendour, like someone had stripped me naked.

The Deputy Head was a man we seldom saw except when taking Woodwork classes. As I hadn't had the pleasure of those sawdust-smelling hours of tedium for some time, I'd forgotten how he'd always made me laugh by pronouncing foyer 'fwayay', cup 'curp', come 'carm' and pursing his lips rather seductively as he spoke in his bizarre 'posh-Northern'.

"Carm with me!" he ordered. But this time, I wasn't laughing.

He silently and solemnly marched me down the corridor, knocked on the Head's door and led me in. The Headmaster stood with his back to me, staring out of his window at the playing fields in the distance. The delicious smell of freshly cut grass wafted in which momentarily cheered me. But only for a moment.

There began a five-minute rant, and though I saw his mouth

moving and watched his reddening face perspire, I inwardly heard 'Give Peace A Chance.' With very little response from me except a shrugged shoulder and a bored look up to his tobacco-stained ceiling, the Head stepped towards me and grabbed hold of my Prefect's badge.

"You won't be needing that anymore!" he yelled and ripped it off my chest.

I was just about to protest at the hole he'd created in my gorgeous new sweater when the Deputy Head handed me a letter addressed to my parents.

"Goow haoume nowww!" he ordered in his mangled excuse for English, "give that to your marther and calm back within one aarrr dressed in your schoooool youniform!"

As I left, he added, "and leeeave by the fwayay!"

I began to shake as I ran to the bus stop, and it wasn't from laughing.

"Thought so," my mum said as I trudged through the front door.

"This is for you," I replied, handing her the letter and going upstairs to change.

Mum was waiting for me when I came back down:

"Well, you've done it now, son," she said, waving the letter at me. "They want to see your dad and me tomorrow morning to -" she glanced down at the letter and read it out, "- 'to discuss the future of your son at this school.' Well done, Howard. I hope you're pleased with yourself!"

"You're a very lucky boy," Dad said to me as he and Mum left the Headmaster's office.

"I'm not being expelled?" I asked, rather incredulous.

"Oh yes, you're being expelled." He held up a hand to stop me responding. "You *are* being expelled, but not until after you've taken your 'O' levels."

"I don't know how you do it, son," Mum said. "In spite of everything you've done the Headmaster seems to really like you. He was genuinely upset at what's happened, but feels he has no choice."

"Should I go and thank him?" I asked, moving off to the Head's door.

"No!" Dad grabbed hold of my arm. "I wouldn't do that."

"You are to come back with us," Mum explained. "You'll revise at home from now on, and only come back into the school to take your exams. Unofficially, you are no longer a pupil at this school, it will only become official once you've sat your 'O' Levels."

The drive home seemed very long and very silent. Once there, Mum put the kettle on while Dad stood quite still in the middle of the kitchen. As I went upstairs I saw the two of them hug each other. In my room, I took off my satchel, set out my study books on the bed and burst into tears.

That summer, we went to Belgium for two weeks, visiting Ghent and Bruges. It was my first holiday abroad and my first time on an aeroplane. For the trip out I wore my new John Sebastian sunglasses, a polka dot cravat, rainbow-coloured cheesecloth shirt and my shimmery golden trousers finished off with maroon leather sandals. As we stood at the check-in desk I tried out my latest pose which I'd practiced in the mirror for about a week. It was the Lennon look, breathing in through the nose and showing one's two front teeth. I looked around nonchalantly, expecting someone to ask for my autograph. No-one did.

Once landed and settled into our hotel I wandered down to the cosy little bar and asked the barman, "Quelle heure est'il?" and was thrilled when he replied, "Deux heures, mon ami." I'd just had my 'O' level results and achieved Grade Two in French. Along with Art History it was my only really good grade but I was happy. I'd just been accepted into Accrington College of Further Education to study

Fine Art and 'A' Level French. As I sat with my cafe au lait and listened to Mireille Mathieu on the radio, life seemed very good.

Later that evening I walked with my parents through the little cobbled streets of Bruges. Mum looked great in turquoise cut-off slacks and white blouson, her emerald green cardigan thrown across her shoulders. Dad held her hand and seemed at peace with the world, having no idea that, in just five years' time, he would lose his 'Bren'. He did seem to treasure that time with her and I would imagine it stayed with him for a long time after she'd passed away.

A clear memory of that holiday is the delicious smell from the Waffle kiosks which floated on the air. The vendor would top them off with a thin spread of mustard and they were utterly delicious. I also loved the bitter-sweet taste of strong espressos in wood-panelled coffee bars full of the noise of excited chatter and the smell of Gauloises cigarettes. Everyone looked so chic. It all seemed very exotic. Cafe Culture, which had not yet hit the North of England, was in full swing there and everything seemed to me like a movie scene. Most of what I'd encountered on holiday before were packed seafront chip shops in Blackpool, everyone crowded in to escape the rain which streamed down steamed-up windows. We'd eat cod, chips and peas washed down with stewed tea and the pungent smell of B.O. escaping from wet pac-a-macs.

One afternoon, while my parents slept off a particularly large lunch, I popped into a cafe near the hotel and, as I sipped my espresso, I noticed a young girl sitting in the window across the room. She stared out at the passers-by with a kind of half-smile on her face, reminding me of Audrey Hepburn in Breakfast At Tiffany's. A song came into my head and I quickly wrote down the lyrics which were pouring out of the ether onto my paper napkin. I sang the melody to myself over and over as I rushed back to the hotel, spread out my notes on the bed and spent the afternoon developing what became 'Blue Lady'.

It was my first observational song, and the earliest of my

compositions which I still perform today. I'd never written about anyone else before, my previous song writing attempts all being plaintive love songs about how I felt, what I'd gone through, the angst of youth, etc. This one was different. Once I got home a few days later I sat at the piano and finished it, recording a rough demo on my clapped-out Grundig. In 2006, I found that demo in a dusty pile of reel-to-reels I'd carried around from house to house for almost forty years. A few months later, I performed it at The Briton's Protection in Manchester. The show was recorded and became my live album *In The Room Upstairs*.

'Blue Lady' always takes me back to that little cafe in Bruges and the Audrey Hepburn look-alike who inspired it:

Blue Lady
Lost in your loss
Your mirror reflects
What a broken heart cost
Tomorrow's the longest day away

Blue lady
Lost in the night
Your angels of mercy
Have all taken flight
And left you with nothing left to say

Time after time
You spent day after day
Simply loving the way that you lived
Letting love slip away

Blue Lady
Nothing to prove
The stars are your witness
Your alibi moon

Is sailing from dawn before the day

Blue Lady
Known coast to coast
You wait in the sunset
For those you liked most
But sometimes the best of time's delayed

Something for nothing's worth nothing at all
All the moments you treasured are torn letters
Piled in the hall

Blue Lady
Look in his eyes
Where past is receding
Your future arrives
There'll always be someone's brighter day

Make every moment
A memory that you want to last
Make every movement
*A message whose bottle you've cast**

*Featured on the 2007 album 'In The Room Upstairs - Live at The Briton's Protection'

Chapter Eight

The Flame

I can't remember when I first realised I was gay. There was no big revelation. Nobody changed my life. No-one forced anything on me or forced me to do anything I didn't want to. It crept up on me, really, the unsensational truth nibbling away at my ear as I grew up. What was true is how natural it felt, it had always felt right. I was entirely happy to be who I was. Only others seemed to want to direct me another way.

I've known guys who have come Out later in life, creating turmoil within a previously, on the surface, happy family life, a home broken along with a wife's heart and kids' expectations. I've known young guys who never came to terms with being gay, fought it, hated it, wished it were not so, craved for a 'normal' life. Wrecked by grief and dismay at their situation before they've had time to find anyone to love them for who they are. On the other hand, I've known guys who seemed to go out of their way to outrage, to shock, to prove to everyone they walk past that they are different, who enjoy being stared at just so they can pout back and blow a kiss.

I never was any of those. I was just me.

Even at school, where I was tagged 'Queen Hilary' by many of the boys, their name-calling never intimidated me. In fact, I would often use it to my benefit as I did one cold and rainy morning. I usually walked to school but, on this day, as the weather was awful, I boarded the old double-decker Routemaster for the ten-minute ride. I would normally sit on the lower deck with the girls, much more fun and not as rowdy as upstairs where all the lads were, as usual making a racket and running all over the place. But that day the lower deck was packed so I had to join the boys. As I climbed the stairs I heard one of them say, "Hilary's here!" and, when I reached the top, much to my thrill they all stood to attention. A boy at the front of the bus stood in the aisle and shouted, "Hail Queen Hilary!", which everyone repeated. It was rather a marvellous noise. I smiled at them all, waved grandly and made my way to the front, flopping down in the seat vacated by the ringleader.

"Thank you!" I said to him, beaming gratefully. And to the rest of the bus, "you can sit down now!"

They did, leaving this one lad without a seat and looking most disconsolate that his prank had backfired. Everybody laughed, one of them shouted, "good for you, Jonesey!" and the 'Hailing' one, instead of objecting or - as I thought he might - dragging me out of my seat, walked to the back amidst a bus full of jeering and went downstairs, where he had to stand on the open rear platform, getting blown to buggery by the wind and rain. As I got off the bus outside the school gates he mumbled at me,

"I'll get you for that."

"No you won't," said another boy.

Feeling really quite protected and special, I emerged from the bus with pride and body intact. Intact and smiling, in fact.

When I was five, first year at Infants' School, I was allowed a sneak peek at Jane Malding's underskirt in the playground. She was a year above me and locally famous for winning a Butlins talent contest singing 'Last Train To San Fernando.' She'd sing it for anyone who asked, throwing her head back as though catching the spotlight and concentrating very hard on getting all the words right. Curtsying at the end to the inevitable applause and admiration of boys from her class, she seemed set for stardom. I always found her voice a bit thin and screechy but never said so.

Fate made the right decision. She married the local mayor's son, an ambitious lad who whisked Jane off to America where they set up a successful carpeting company called 'Completely Floored'.

They had four Harvard-educated kids and an apparently beautiful home in fashionable Westchester. I imagined Jane marching onto the stage at one of her Marquee-tented charity do's, taking the mike and thrilling all her rich society friends with 'Last Train To San Fernando'. I wondered if her voice had remained thin and screechy. I'm sure her friends didn't really care.

Anyway, I digress. Little Miss Malding, as she'd been billed at Butlins, had been threatening to show me her underskirt for weeks and finally, one afternoon, she took my hand, led me behind the headmistress's Morris Minor and told me to, "stand there." She hitched up her frock and looked very pleased with herself. I thought she looked a bit daft but the underskirt did fascinate me. It was a voluminous multi-layered net rainbow-coloured thing. Like something from 'Come Dancing' without the sequins. I recall being more interested in the material than the naughtiness of what we were doing.

"Doesn't it scratch?" I asked her.

"Have a feel and see," she replied coquettishly.

I did, but more like a customer in a dress shop would rub a fabric to check it out for quality.

To Jane it felt naughty and she giggled when I rubbed the net. To me it just felt a bit scratchy. Bored, I wandered off to get a Jammy Dodger biscuit from the teacher who handed out Jammy Dodgers and Wagon Wheels at playtime. She was chatting to the janitor, laughing at his jokes. He was a handsome man whose smile thrilled me so much more than Jane Malding's net underskirt.

When I was twelve, a school mate, Ronnie, held my hand as we watched TV in his house. He sort of ran his hand over mine and then held it, stroking it gently. As the TV mumbled away in the background and my eyes got increasingly blurred, he squeezed my hand and I squeezed his back, not sure what this meant but enjoying myself.

Ronnie was the school Romeo, good-looking and funny, girls of all ages fancied him, some of them regularly spending a happy half hour with him in one of the unfinished new-builds down the road. I'd sometimes see them coming out of the doorless doorway, tucking in their shirts and blouses, hair ruffled, lips a bit red. They'd giggle at each other and swap secret smiles as I waved at them from across the unmade road, trying to look as though I didn't know what they'd been up to.

Back on the sofa, my heart was thumping in my chest and made a noise in my ears, bang! bang! bang! I was sure Ronnie could hear it, especially as he edged closer. Out of the corner of my eye I saw him turn towards me. I could feel his warm breath on my neck and noticed how lovely he smelt. I was just about to turn my head to him when the sound of a key in the front door, much bustling in the hallway and a cry of "I'm home!" put paid to that.

Ronnie quickly thrust my hand away and jumped up.

"Hi mam! You're back!" he shouted, running into the kitchen.

"Yes. Who else were you expecting?"

I followed him out and smiled at his mum busying away with her shopping.

"Hallo Howard!" she said. "What've you two been up to?"

"Nothing!" Ronnie said. "Just watching TV!"

"Has he been looking after you?" Ronnie's mum asked, tapping her son on the shoulder playfully.

"Of course I have!" Ronnie said, laughing.

She looked at her son and shook her head,

"Little monkey. Always up to something you shouldn't."

Five more minutes, I thought, and who knows what he'd have been up to?

Sadly, I never found out. Ronnie didn't hold my hand again. In fact, I was never invited to watch TV with him again. The moment had gone.

As long as I can remember, I enjoyed being with men, but never feeling I was like them. I just wanted to be near them. I loved the way they sat. I loved the way they talked. They'd rub my head and call me 'cock'. I'd blush and want them to do it again. My dreams from a young age were always about men kissing me. Not passionately, more like Prince Charming kissed Cinderella in the Disney cartoon.

Even by my teens, my fantasies weren't particularly sexual. It wasn't sex I craved. It was a man sitting next to me, smiling at me and telling me I was his world. Sex was a mystery really. It was something other lads did with the girls in the park on a Friday night. On a Monday morning, before class started, I'd listen to their detail-laden stories of what they'd got up to in the bushes, trying to picture it and failing. I was more confused than turned on when one of the girls, Barbara, told me she'd sucked Colin's lollypop.

"Would you like to come and polish *my* tits this Friday night, Howard?" she purred, seductively undoing her top blouse button.

One of the lads licked his lips and winked at me. It wasn't an invitation but it stayed with me for the rest of the day, long after the thought of Barbara's available boobs had gone completely out of my mind.

I'd snogged a couple of girls at friends' parties, mainly because that's what everyone else was doing. I think they'd enjoyed themselves but I never did. One snogee, Julie, a blonde-haired lovely all the other boys fancied, who'd chatted me up over an orange one afternoon, decided after a startlingly little amount of time that I was her boyfriend. This entailed visits at weekends, flowers in hand for my mother, long walks down country lanes and stolen kisses under blossom-filled trees. While this Mills & Boon idyll kept her happy for a few weeks, I watched, like a fascinated observer, as it all unravelled, a disaster waiting to happen.

"Maybe they were right," she said, when the inevitable 'are you finishing with me?' moment took place in a bus stop in Rawtenstall on a wet Saturday night. "Maybe you are a pooftah."

The first man who fell in love with me was George. He lived in Ramsbottom and resembled an Edwardian porn model, short and stocky, broad shoulders, droopy moustache and thick sideburns. He was a couple of years older than me and always brightened a room with his killer smile. I didn't know he felt this way about me until one evening, when my parents were away for the weekend, I asked some friends from the village to come back to my house to listen to some music. We'd often get together at each other's houses, a sort of house-crawl, ending up at whoever's parents were out for the night. We'd put the world to rights, listen to great records and sing in front of the fire together. It was that time in one's life when it felt like every tomorrow was made for you, only the future mattered, and we were going to be a part of making things different. George was usually there and always ready to sit and chat to me, which was a pleasure. Eye candy wasn't in it.

He'd asked me once, when everyone else was chatting amongst themselves, if I was gay and I'd replied I was but that I hadn't done much about it. I remember him smiling even more broadly at me, nodding and drinking his beer thoughtfully.

On this particular evening as we all walked back to my house, George suddenly began picking all the daffodils which grew in the turfed areas along the pavement. He ran along the road and wherever daffodils grew he picked them until his arms were full of yellow. As we reached my house he ran in front of me and declared,

"These are for you, Howard!"

Knowing he was a bit pissed, I smiled and thanked him while his mates whooped and hollered.

"Georgie!" one of them shouted, "you getting amorous with Howard?"

"If that's what he wants, then yes, I am!" he replied.

I took some of the daffs off him while he carried the rest into the kitchen, looking in cupboards for vases and arranging them on the work surface.

"Do you like them, Howard?" George asked me, looking extremely pleased with himself.

"They're lovely," I replied.

"They're all for you, because you know, Howard, I love you!"

Believing this was one of those bromance moments when straight blokes get pissed and become extremely affectionate with each other - 'I love you, I do, you know that?' - I just smiled at George and patted his face. He kissed my hand and stood looking at me with swimming eyes, smiling from ear to ear.

Forever after wishing I hadn't, I moved away and said,

"I'll just put some music on, then I'll be back."

"You'd better be," he replied and watched me go.

Leaving him in the kitchen putting more flowers in more vases, I went through to the sitting-room and looked through my LPs, picking T.Rex's *Electric Warrior*.

"I love Marc Bolan!" one of the girls shouted as I held up the sleeve for their approval.

"He's gay!" one of the blokes said.

"He's married!" the girl replied.

"So what?" another bloke shouted and laughed.

As 'Mambo Sun' blasted out and people danced and sang along I went back into the kitchen. Five beautifully arranged vases of daffodils sat on the work surface but no sign of George, then I heard the soft sound of snoring from upstairs. I went up to my room, took off his shoes, covered him up and left him there, a moustachioed angel.

Nobody noticed he was missing as they sat around chatting or bopped to 'Cosmic Dancer.' When 'Jeepster' blasted out we all did Bolan impressions in a circle, joining in as one when Marc sang 'And I'm gonna suck ya!' Girls screeched, blokes winked back at them. Finally, when they'd all left I tiptoed upstairs, glanced in at the sleeping beauty, decided common sense should overcome temptation and crept into my parents' bedroom. When I awoke the next morning George had gone, only five vases of daffodils remained of his declaration of love.

A few nights later, I was walking home with a couple of friends and saw George across the road. He'd obviously been drinking as he scampered over, shook my hand and put his arm round my shoulder.

"Howard?" he said, staring at me very intensely, arm still round my shoulder. "Can you give me some advice?"

"Sure."

He looked around conspiratorially and then said, very quietly:

"The thing is, Howard, I love two people right now, and I don't which one to pick. Should I follow my heart or my head?"

Stepping back as though waiting for words of wisdom, he folded his arms and quickly looked me up and down.

Trying not to blush and to keep my voice steady I replied,

"Do what you think is best for you, George. Whichever would work out best for you."

George thought about it, nodded, shook my hand again, squeezing it very tightly and said,

"I knew you'd know what to do for the best. Thanks, Howard. Goodnight."

As he wandered off one of my companions said,

"Was that Daffodil George?"

I laughed, "Yes, it was."

"Was he speaking in code for our benefit?"

I shrugged and made a face as if to say "Dunno."

"Don't you want to find out?" my other companion said.

"What do you mean?"

"Go and ask him."

I shrugged again.

"Go on! Go and talk to him properly about it. You'll regret it if you don't."

I saw George disappear around a corner.

"Nah," I said, "he knows where I am."

Over the next few weeks I'd see him walking through the town with a pretty red-headed girl, kissing and canoodling her as they went along. One time, I caught his eye and he smiled and nodded across the street, then said something to the girl who smiled and nodded at me as well. I smiled back at them both. George gave me a thumbs-up sign, as though saying, 'Right decision.' I felt pleased and sad at the same time.

They were married a few months later and left the village to start up home together nearer her job in Manchester. I'll never forget those daffodils. I never saw him again.

The first man I slept with was Big Nigel, a bass player in a friend's band who I met one evening at a party in Edenfield, a couple of miles from my parents' house in Ramsbottom. Chris, the host, told us his mum and dad were away so he'd decided to have a few mates round for beers and good music. Looking like Robert Plant's twin brother, he was a popular guy and the house was packed.

As Thunderclap Newman's 'Something In The Air' blasted out of the hi-fi I took myself upstairs to the loo. On the way back I noticed a tall hairy Adonis quietly crying to himself on the landing. I've always melted at the sight of a big man weeping and asked him what the matter was.

"Me girlfriend's finished with me," he said through tears falling down his bearded cheeks.

Dying to wipe them away I asked, "what's her name?"

"Maureen," he replied and began to sob again.

"Well, it's Maureen's loss," I said, which elicited a gorgeous smile and an adorable blush.

"What's your name?" he asked.

"Howard," I replied, suddenly aware that he was stroking my arm. Voice shaking, heart beating, legs trembling, I said, "yours?"

"Nigel," he replied and smiled again.

He continued to look at me and smile and stroke my arm. Then the film jumped and I was suddenly in his arms with his tongue down my throat. As if in a dreamlike gay ballet, he lifted me up into his huge arms, carried me across the landing, pushed open a bedroom door and lay me very gently on the bed. He was about twice my weight and at least six foot four. 'Bloody hell,' I thought, 'you're beautiful.'

Getting naked seemed to take seconds and very quickly hands and mouths were everywhere. We rolled around the bed, or more accurately he rolled me around the bed. It was the most exciting thing that had ever happened to me and while not quite the Disney cartoon I'd imagined, it was near enough for now. After more groping and rolling, he lay me on my back and knelt up in front of me, putting my legs over his lovely wide shoulders.

"Yeah?" he asked, grinning at me.

I looked at him in what I hoped was a Lauren Bacall kind of way, but inside I screamed, 'Oh yes!'

And then the door opened.

Pat, a rather odd girl I'd been talking to earlier, wandered into the room. She was apparently famous for labelling all her food in the kitchen cupboard 'Property of Pat', and making sure everything in there read out perfectly face on to whoever was looking in. She closed the door, stared at us, put her tiny little hands to her tiny little face and said in a tiny little girl's voice,

"What are you doing, Howard?"

Thinking 'Isn't that bloody obvious, dear?' I instead replied, "What are you doing in here, Pat?"

Nigel promptly leaned over the bed and with an enormous groan threw up all over the rather attractive and probably brand-new beige rug.

Seeming to freeze on the spot, Pat opened her mouth more widely than I thought was humanly possible, clasped her hands to her ears and, looking like the model for the Edvard Munch painting, she screamed. And screamed. And screamed. Her huge shock of wiry black hair appeared to rise ever higher as her scream got ever louder. It added an extra touch of horror to the already ghastly scene.

The door opened again and this time several people ran in, witnessing a naked Adonis retching over the floor, a skinny naked me pleading with Pat to stop screaming, and Pat screaming so loudly one of the girls said, "Shall I call the police?"

Someone outside the door said, "They're going to call the police!"

"No-one's calling the police!" We all looked to the girl who said this. It was Chris's girlfriend, Andrea. She was a tall Amazonian creature and stepped forward, hands on hips, waiting for silence. Even Pat shut up, her scream turning into a kind of muffled sob.

"Now, let's all just calm down!" Andrea continued. She looked at me with a kind of disdain.

"You, get dressed!" she ordered.

Looking down at the vomit-covered rug she pointed at Nigel:

"You, clear that up!"

Then, putting her arm round Pat's shoulder and stroking her hair with the other hand she led her out. Everyone else followed her and, finally, a sort of peace returned. As I found my knickers and socks and sat on the edge of the bed, Nigel looked over at me and wiped his mouth:

"I'm sorry about this," he said. "What a mess, eh?"

Not sure if he meant the pile of vomit on the rug or the situation, I smiled wanly back at him.

"Don't worry," he said, pointing at the vomit, "I will clear it up."

"You'd better," I replied, "or Andrea'll have your guts for garters."

Nigel pointed at the vomit, "D'you think?"

I treaded carefully round it and found my trousers and sweater, thankfully out of range of the spray. Sitting next to him, I patted his arm.

"Saved by the belle, eh?" he joked.

'Even after throwing up he looks gorgeous,' I thought, and was about to kiss him on the cheek when the retching restarted. I pulled on the rest of my clothes, and, knowing this wasn't the time for fond goodbyes, walked out onto the landing.

A crowd of onlookers queuing up the stairs gawped at me, all trying to peer through the closing door at what was going on in the bedroom, as though a murder had taken place.

"Can I just squeeze through?" I asked, edging my way down the stairs. They parted like a Biblical sea and I made for the front door, slipped on the shoes I was carrying and stepped out into the warm evening air. As I breathed it in I heard Chris let out a wail upstairs:

"Oh No! Nigel! That was me mum's favourite rug!"

I closed the door and walked home.

"You have a nice evening?" Mum asked as I let myself in.

"Interesting," I said and, without elaborating, went up to my room. Dylan's *Highway 61 Revisited* seemed a good choice to blow away the confusion in my head, until 'Ballad Of A Thin Man' came on. It could have been written for me.

I saw Nigel a couple of weeks later at a local disco standing alone at the bar. I was just weighing up whether I should go over and speak to him when a group of his mates joined him, accompanied by a skinny dark-haired girl. She smiled at Nigel, stepped up to him and said something into his ear. He grabbed hold of her, gave her one of those tongue-down-the-throat kisses I remembered so fondly and his mates burst into applause. By the beam on Nigel's face I knew this was Maureen who he'd been crying over at the top of the stairs. Luckily, some of my own friends came over and pulled me onto the dance floor. 'The Ballad of John & Yoko' was playing and we sang along at the top of our voices:

"Christ! You know it ain't easy, you know how hard it can be, the way things are going, they're gonna crucify me!"

I think I sang the loudest.

My first platonic girlfriend was Pauline. She was my best friend at school and the first girl with whom I never felt any pressure to 'make a pass' at or appear at all interested in sexually. We shared a love of music and the easy ability to make each other laugh, all the time.

We'd spend evenings joyfully miming to *The White Album*, Pauline playing Paul, and me, with my new round-rimmed glasses, John. Our favourite was 'Helter Skelter'. Pauline had the mono L.P. and so one night I took along my stereo version. She nearly jumped out of her skin when Ringo cried at the end of the track, *"I've got blisters on my fingers!!"*. It wasn't on the mono version and she'd insist on me bringing my copy along after that.

It was through Pauline that I discovered Simon & Garfunkel were more than just one song. She had all their albums and would play, especially for me, 'For Emily, Whenever I May Find Her', my own S & G favourite. We'd both lift our heads and holler to the ceiling the last line of the song, *'Oh how I love you!'*.

She also introduced me to Joni Mitchell's *Song To A Seagull* album, then a recent release. Pauline imagined 'Michael From Mountains' was about a boy she was having an on-off relationship with at the time. She'd dissect the lyric and say, "That is SO Michael!"

My love for The Beatles was matched only by her adoration of Dylan. She would proudly show me the front cover of *Freewheelin'* and point out how much she resembled Suze Rotolo, the girl on Bobby's arm on a freezing Winter New York street. While The Fab Four stayed top of my list, I did marvel at the delicious ghostliness of *Blonde On Blonde*, with its dreamlike druggy lyrics and Bobby's wonderfully exhausted '66 voice. I was especially impressed by 'Sad Eyed Lady of The Lowlands' which took up a whole Side Four of the album.

Our friendship went on into 1970, then, for reasons I can no longer remember - but am certain they were my all of my doing - we had a big falling out, rows on the phone, things said I certainly now regret. I was too proud to apologise and she was too angry to accept an apology, even if it had been offered. No longer seeing each other at school every day and living far enough apart to not bump into each other in the street, we lost touch.

Once, in the early '70s, I saw her sitting in a folk club in Manchester where her now permanent boyfriend Michael was performing. Pauline looked over at me and smiled so, after his set, I joined them at their table. I'd not met him before and, not getting a particularly warm reaction as we were introduced, I said, rather gauchely,

"So, you're Michael From Mountains."

It went down like a lead balloon and conversation became so stilted I excused myself and took my leave.

The very last time I saw Pauline was in Bury Town Centre. It was a few days before I was due to move to London, Summer 1973. I was waiting for my bus back to Ramsbottom from which, when it arrived, Pauline jumped off.

"Hi!" she said brightly.

"Hi!" I replied brightly back.

We did the usual "How are you?" and "How's life?" thing, until I finally told her of my plans to move down South.

With very little reaction except a 'thought you would' expression, she just said,

"Well, enjoy your new life in London. I hope it goes well for you. Take care. 'Bye!"

This episode is covered partly in my 1974 song 'The Flame,' though its lyric also covers the wider theme of lost opportunities, friendships gone, chances missed, regretting what-ifs. Pauline is also the subject of a song I wrote just after our row in 1970, titled, unsurprisingly, 'Pauline's Song.' I recorded a rough demo at home and performed it a few times in various folk clubs during the years before I moved to London. But, once down South, and with a pianoful of new songs under my arm, it was forgotten about. In 2009, I discovered the reel-to-reel demo in my trunk, liked what I heard and after a few lyric re-writes finally recorded it properly for my E.P. *Songs For A Lifetime.* The E.P. is in many ways dedicated to Pauline, featuring a cover of Dylan's 'Sad Eyed Lady Of The Lowlands' and my interpretation of Joni's 'Michael From Mountains.'

Pauline's Song

When are you coming back to me?
When are you coming back to me?

You know, when I'm sitting here
In silence, save for the sound of rain
I know there's nothing I could say
To undo the hurt and see you smile again

But as I lie around
And watch the dog lie unconcerned with life
I wish that I could worry less about you
(You're on my mind all the time)

Shadows play upon the wall
They dance and writhe like fire
But still my nights are colder now
I never thought that I could feel this down

And as I watch the buses full of people
Going by my window
I wish that one would stop

And leave you standing there
Freewheelin' with me again

When I wore your coat and you wore mine
Our spotlight shone as we both mimed
To records we'd just bought
The candlelight always caught our best sides
The room was small
Our dreams were vast
A trace of dust that floated past
"It fell down from the moon" you said
And like our dreams
I believed you
And now I wish that I could worry less about you

You know that there are songs
We listened to that kept us singing
I still play them on my own sometimes
And I can hear you harmonising

But as I lie around and watch the door
Opening and closing
I wish that I could see you
Walking down the path
Bringing it all back home again

When I wore your coat and you wore mine
Our spotlight shone as we both mimed
To records we'd just bought
The candlelight always caught our best sides
The room was small
Our dreams were vast
A trace of dust that floated past
"It fell down from the moon" you said
And like our dreams

I believed you
And now I wish that I could worry less about you
Now a candle only lights a corner

I know I said some things
I'll never forgive myself for
You know those words can't be unsaid
And we'll never be like we were before
But time passes by
Passes by
Passes by
And we still have time
Still have time
Still have time
Don't we?

I just can't bear for it to end this way
And hey! this is no way to say goodbye

And I wish that I could worry less about you
Yes I wish that I could worry less about you
Oh I wish that I could worry less about you
Now a candle only lights a corner
When are you coming back to me?

Chapter Nine

(I'm The) Talk Of The Town

Accrington College of Further Education, where I began studying 'A' Levels in the Autumn of 1969, was housed in a detached old red-brick Victorian building. It was fronted by an overgrown lawned garden, weed-infested flowerbeds and rusting sycamores. Surrounded by chipped metal railings atop a crumbling high stone wall, it reflected, but no longer boasted, a better time in its long life. These days, I'd want to tidy it up and plant out herbaceous borders filled with radiant hollyhocks, delphiniums and foxgloves. Back then, its neglected Bohemian mess seemed deliciously run down and conveniently hid us from the main High Road which ran past the college into the centre of town.

Climbing the well-worn steps, entering the musty echo of corridors full of the bustle of students going to class, I felt lighter and ready to take things on. This was not like school with its strict dress codes and an expectation that you might be 'in trouble' at any moment. This was finally becoming An Adult. Making your own way. I was mixing with people who chose to bring their cornucopia of styles, personalities and ideas to a forum of discussion. While we were all blissfully unaware - or ignoring the fact - that real life was waiting as we lived the student myth of holding off our futures for a while, responsibility had arrived. It was, however, disguised as irresponsibility. It was extremely liberating.

Rather like record labels such as Island and Immediate, and their label bosses Chris Blackwell and Andrew Loog Oldham, sent their top pop groups to sprawling old farmhouses for the summer, a place to allow their creative bankables to compose their next million-selling opuses in peace and quiet, so we had been allowed, by the education system, to shut ourselves away and hone our particular talents, increase our knowledge, develop our personalities.

Whether the college housed any future creative bankables is debatable, but I soon discovered, on the top floor, the haven I had sought. There, at the top of the stairs, was the Fine Art Department.

I would pass second-year art students and the occasional home-knitted-pullovered tutor in the corridor and smile as they greeted me with a gentle "Hey man". I would meander round the huge high-ceilinged white wood-panelled room like a visitor to a gallery, studying the many canvases which leaned against the walls. Some were finished, a sea of abstract floating brown and white oblongs here, or a landscape of lavishly executed Bosch-like figures there. Others were still works in progress which sat on easels, usually accompanied by their affectionate creator who would nod at you then turn their attention back to the matter in hand.

There was always the heady mix of linseed and patchouli oils filling the air alongside the music, which gently floated out of an old record player in one corner of the room. It was a different kind of music to anything I'd heard before. This wasn't pop music, it seemed to go beyond that and come from a place I had never been. I'd study the L.P. covers thrown casually around the place and wonder who The Incredible String Band were, Roy Harper, The Third Ear Band, The Mothers of Invention, King Crimson. They were all totally new to me. My previously perceived coolness for carrying my copy of *Sgt Pepper* around Bury Town Centre felt suddenly out of time, out of place and embarrassingly gauche. I soon discovered that 'image' was unimportant here, what mattered more was possessing an inherent talent for painting and an ability to appear interesting whilst remaining benignly aloof from even trying to achieve such a lofty ideal.

At school, once I'd reached fifteen, I had done my best to be noticed and to be considered different. Indeed, it was my raison d'etre. Now, such self-possession - nay, obsession - felt extremely uncool and far too noisy. The first thing you noticed on walking into the Art Department was how quiet it was, save for the soft strains of Mike Heron's 'A Very Cellular Song' or Roy Harper's 'McGoohan's Blues' wafting through the room. The sound of raucous laughter never dented this idyll of tranquil confidence. If anyone did laugh it was silently, shoulders moving up and down as though holding in a sneeze, as if afraid that outbursts of any kind would blow away the ethereal mist of familial harmony. You would never hear anyone shouting across the room, 'Hey, Tim! You got a spare pencil I could borrow?' Such needs were much more confidentially handled. A mumbled request to your nearest neighbour was answered with a silent passing of the required pencil or paintbrush, all the while neither requestor nor provider taking their eyes off their works in hand. If you cocked an ear you could just about hear a 'Thanks, man,' murmuring under the sonic radar.

During my first couple of weeks there, whenever I entered the Inner Sanctum, I felt like a loud car horn in a deserted street. I'd been so used to bursting into rooms ready to make people laugh or tell them about the latest Beatles track I'd heard. My days 'Before Accrington' had been full of people shouting, 'Look what Howard's wearing today!' and the sense, however misplaced, that I shone like a welcome glow in a roomful of grey observers. This new silently unobtrusive world both fascinated and confused me. I didn't understand, or belong, but desperately wanted to.

Opinions were whispered and agreed with by a gentle nod of the head. Disagreement would be conveyed by the slightest wince, as though responding to a mild storm outside the window. I very quickly learnt that, instead of hailing everyone with a cheery "Hi guys," in the morning, one merely nodded and said, ever so quietly, "Hey" and then wandered over to one's work area, head down, shoulders stooped.

Work areas were smallish screened-off bits of the room which felt surprisingly private. I quickly made mine feel homely, pinning up sketches and ideas I'd done on 'college field trips', when we visited local bits of wasteland and scribbled away at our interpretations of a piece of wood in a muddy puddle or a particularly interesting chunk of rock. I'd use my sketches as the basis for a larger oil painting and this was where, almost by accident, I discovered a new and acceptable way to 'shout' a little louder. I loved the Fauves and the Impressionists, who I'd found out about in my History of Art classes, and wanted to achieve their intoxicating freedom of colour and vibrancy in my work. No longer for me subtle skin tones or gentle blue skies behind fluffy white clouds. Everything now had to dazzle and surprise. Bright purple and red hills under vermilion skies became my landscapes. They were my route to a shineworthy status amongst respected colleagues I wished to impress. And, as the weeks went by, it seemed to bear fruit, some of the students occasionally creeping on tiptoes into my work area and watching me paint. Never commenting, of course, that would have been far too presumptuous. But the fact they were interested in my splashings and daubs made up for what I quickly came to realise, that I was unlikely to find, create, or adopt the new, more laid-back persona I thought I needed to match my surroundings. If I was to survive this world I wanted to be part of, it would have to be done through my work.

The Head Tutor, Mr Bownass (or 'Bone-Arse' as he was known) paid me an unexpected visit one day as I was tossing another primary colour onto my vibrant canvas. One saw art tutors very occasionally, they were like shy nocturnal animals who only came out when the coast was clear, so this was quite a thing. He stood behind me, smoking his pipe, puffing away as I worked. After a few minutes of silent observation, he sort of shuffled to the side of me and said,

"You have an extremely unbridled sense of colour, Howard."

I, perhaps mistakenly, took it as a compliment, smiled over my shoulder as one might to an awed fan, and sallied forth on my quest for resplendent perfection. He crept out and never commented on my work again.

As my confidence in my art increased, so too did the size of my canvases. They got increasingly larger, with life-class paintings especially often measuring five-foot square. I'd sometimes have to stand on a chair to reach the top of the canvas, which could be deemed precocious, and probably was by some, but as usual in my case, as confidence grew, so too did a lack of regard for how others may disapprove. I began my own weekly regime, which I tagged 'A Developing Project In Abstract', where each new canvas was a more abstract variation on the previous painting. So, a life class model became, over several developments, a series of shapes and colours in a room once housing tables and chairs which had morphed into indeterminable cubes and triangles.

Of course, Picasso and Braque had already done this decades before with Cubism, but I was blithely unconcerned about that. Eventually, tens of canvases of my work leant against the wall. I was convinced that one day very soon I would have the opportunity to exhibit my Project to an admiring world of art lovers. It never happened. In fact, I imagine that every single radiant 'Howard' was painted over white and reused once I'd left college.

We were allowed to take one of our canvases home on our last day. I chose a huge self-portrait glaring out from its world of primary colours with wide-eyed fury. My mother cooed when she saw it and hung it on the landing.

"It makes the top of the stairs look so much brighter!" she announced.

Dad wasn't convinced, complaining that it gave him the heebie-jeebies.

"It's looking at me every time I come out of the toilet," he complained.

When I finally took it down and rolled it up, deciding it would fill a bedsit wall perfectly on my imminent move to London in the summer of '73, Dad quickly suggested a Boots Still Life would fill the vacant space very nicely. I carried that canvas from flat to flat during my first few years in London, finally leaving it under my bed in the Earl's Court room from which I'd leapt in 1976. I wouldn't think it's still there.

One afternoon, as I was busying away on my multi-coloured interpretation of a kettle, Bob, a wide-eyed peace child from Freecloud Blake, crept into my work area and asked me if I fancied going to see The Incredible String Band at The Free Trade Hall. I had been intrigued by what I'd heard in the art room and without hesitation said yes, I'd love to.

Two things happened to me that night. One, I fell in love with The Incredible String Band, and two, I decided that I wanted to perform on large stages just like these magical troubadours.

They looked like hippie gods, lit in mauves, blues and pinks which danced upon their white blousons, dressing them in shirts of many colours for each song. With leather breeches tucked into thigh-length boots they strode the stage like medieval minstrels. There was something masculinely feminine about Robin and Mike, beautiful yet rugged at the same time. They played a mind-boggling variety of instruments and percussion, rushing round the stage during a single number. At what seemed unrehearsed moments but were obviously perfectly planned, they'd drop a guitar and take up a sitar, dash off the piano stool and perch with a lute, seamlessly continuing to play the song at hand with no break in rhythm or performance. Grinning to each other like thrilled little boys at the best ever party, their delight radiated out to adoring fans who clapped and laughed throughout an evening of song and communal involvement. We supped at their banquet of sound, our hearts dancing to the rhythm of optimistic joy.

The two girls in the band, Rose and Liquorice, looked like woodland nymphs. Their headbands of knitted daisies sat atop pre-Raphaelite flowing locks, which fell around their Laura Ashley flowered frocks. Bob was convinced Rose was smiling at him, but in fact most of the males in the audience were under that illusion. While chinking finger cymbals, tapping tambourines and patting bongos, they possessed a visual presence both evocative and unforgettable. It was as though they'd arrived on a cloud of love, staring dreamily out at men who wished they were theirs and women who wished they were them.

I hadn't been to any concerts up to that point, my love of popular music being limited to buying records and watching my heroes on TV. I had been invited that Autumn to go with some of the other students to the Isle of Wight Festival to see Bob Dylan. It was a big event as he hadn't performed outside America for three years. While tempted, I decided that a weekend of sitting and sleeping in a field of mud along with several hundred others wasn't for me. Just the thought of queuing up for overflowing filthy loos every morning was enough to put me off. While I enjoyed the conviviality of hippie company at college, I only partially embraced the life it offered. Living in a commune would not have suited me at all. I liked to go back home every evening to a warm bath and the privacy of a spotless loo. I guess I was what they used to call a Weekend Weirdo.

After the Incredibles' show, as I was leaving the theatre, I spotted a flyer for an upcoming concert by Roy Harper. No-one else at college seemed interested in seeing him so, a few weeks later, I made my way on my own on the bus, bought my ticket and settled down for what would be one of the best concerts I have ever seen.

Roy walked on with no announcement, how cool was that, and, lit by a single spotlight alone on the stage, began strumming his guitar.

'The kettle's on, the sun has gone, another day,' he sang. I was instantly hooked. For two hours, he sang his glorious songs to an enraptured audience. What fascinated me was the way he would stop halfway through a number to tell us a story of what he'd got up to the previous evening. The stories were always long, always funny, outrageously so sometimes, and one felt he was sitting with each one of us in a cosy front room, regaling us with his adventures. Even more brilliant was how, once the story had been told and the audience were in fits of laughter, he would simply continue with the song he'd interrupted at the exact point he'd broken off. His songs were funny, sad, personal and observational, his guitar playing was astonishing. A fairly small man in stature, he was a giant on stage, owning his space and holding us all enthralled by his warmth and genius.

The next day, I took myself off to Javelin Records and bought Harper's new album, *Flat Baroque And Berserk*. I played it for hours on end, especially the utterly gorgeous 'Another Day'. I vowed that one day I would record that song, and in 2009, finally, I did.

In March 1970, the Students Union arranged an evening of music, dance and sketches for parents and governors. It was to take place in the college's second, newer building down the road, a rather featureless, late '60s state of the art place with language labs and an enormous performance hall. Knowing I was a pianist they asked me if I would 'do a couple of tunes'. I readily accepted and put together a short set of four songs I'd recently written. With a few of the other students showing some interest in being involved, a combo was formed for the evening. We had a couple of rehearsals but soon it became obvious that it was just me and the drummer, Tim Whittaker, who took it seriously. So, on the night, Tim and I, who had named ourselves Rubber Nun (Tim's suggestion) performed our fifteen-minute spot. As the final number ended, the place literally went mad (even the four nuns sitting in the front row stood and applauded!). I got goose bumps hearing the cheers, and this for songs I'd written!

Tim soon got bored (he actually went on to join the Liverpool band Deaf School) but I continued to give monthly lunchtime solo concerts in the Maths Room, which had an old upright piano. I designed my own little posters which I'd stick up around the college, 'Howard In

Concert at 12.30 today' and each month, to my surprise and delight, the room would be full of attentive listeners. I rarely performed the same song twice, I was writing at such a rate by then. I don't recall ever feeling nervous or unsure, I knew that I could do it, I had no doubts. What really stayed with me was how some of the audience would wait behind as I was putting lyrics away in my bag, and tell me how much a certain song had resonated with them. I realised that not only could I perform, but my songs also affected people in ways I had never dreamed they could. For all my love of painting and my recent ambition to take it up more seriously, I knew now for certain that my future was with my music.

During one of the concerts, I noticed Mr Bownass sitting at the back. He leaned on his knees listening intently to every number. Afterwards, he told me that a friend of his was a gig promoter and, if I was interested, he'd mention me to him. A couple of weeks later I got a phone call from a chap called Steve who, as well as referring to everything as 'cool!', told me he would like to see me play and had lined up a gig at a folk club in Manchester for me if I wanted it.

I was only booked to perform three songs and they seemed to go down well. Once again, I noticed how people would stop talking and listen to me intently. After my set, a very skinny bearded guy approached me:

"Hi man, I'm Steve," he said cheerily. "That was cool!" He took out a packet of Kool cigarettes and lit one up. I'm not sure he saw the irony. He said he'd like to have a go at getting me some 'proper gigs', the first being at the Octagon Theatre in Bolton which showcased local artists each month in Saturday afternoon concerts they called Bluesologies.

I told Steve that I wanted to be billed as 'Jon Howard'. It was a name I'd come up with while mulling over what I should call myself if I ever turned professional. I liked the way names such as Rod Stewart,

John Lennon, Bob Dylan, ran off the tongue and wanted something similar. 'Howard Jones' just didn't sound Pop Star-ish enough to my ears and it was also the name of a singer in the Joe Loss Band - in fact, that was who my mum had named me after. I took the 'es' off 'Jones', put it in front of my Christian name, and voilà, there it was.

"Cool!" said Steve, though whether he actually thought so was always hard to tell.

The following Saturday, I arrived at the theatre and noticed, outside the building, a little poster on the wall announcing the four acts performing that afternoon. There I was, 'Jon Howard', second on the bill.

'Yeah,' I thought, 'That's cool!'

I'd been to The Octagon with the college a few months earlier to see Chekhov's The Cherry Orchard, and couldn't imagine how a theatre in the round would work as a music venue. How wrong I was. They had cleverly left the set of the play they were doing that week intact and so we performed 'inside' a sitting-room in front of the French windows which led out onto 'the garden'. My upright piano looked very at home surrounded by 1920s-style tables and chairs and a telephone stand by 'the door'.

I had a whole half-an-hour to myself. As soon as I began, the lights dimmed and a beautiful purple glow filled the stage. Shivers ran down my back.

'So this is what it feels like,' I thought.

For each number, the lighting man gave me a different hue, which in turn affected the way I performed the song. My Incredible String Band dream had actually come true. I loved the atmosphere of a 'proper' legitimate theatre, the wonders of a superb sound system which rang out around me as I sang. The full house of people hadn't a clue who I was but when I got a 'More!' at the end of my final song I felt ten feet tall.

The headlining act that day was Spirogyra, a Canterbury-based band whose sound was enormous and songs were rousing anthemic folk-rock wonders. Their lead singer, guitarist and main songwriter, Bolton-born Martin Cockerham, had a pop star charisma. He was supported in the band brilliantly by a Nick Drake-ish violinist (Julian Cusack), along with bass player, Steve Borrill. Their female singer, Barbara Gaskin, stood closely beside Cockerham throughout, her light breathy harmonies adding a gossamer touch to their sound. They looked fantastic on stage and I was certain they would achieve big things.

As I was getting ready to leave, a small bespectacled chap tapped me on the shoulder.

"Hello," he said, "my name's Max Hole. I manage the band. I just wanted to say how much we enjoyed your performance."

He stood smiling at me, nodding his head enthusiastically, and reminded me of a tiny college professor.

"We're doing another gig in December this year here," he continued, "and wondered if you'd like to be our support for the evening?"

When I told Steve on the way to the bus stop, he nodded into his stooped shoulders, took a drag from his Kool cigarette and said, "Cool!"

The gig was a joy, the group having now hired their own sound man who sat a few feet from me as I performed, tweaking the mikes and adding more reverb when needed. The theatre's set that evening was a magical forest of giant plants and butterflies, obviously for a children's play they were putting on for Christmas. The gently bobbing nets of greens and blues, which wafted over me as I sang amidst this fantasy woodland, made me feel like a character from Alice's Adventures In Wonderland. Max took a photo of me during my performance that night which I still have. I look utterly knocked out to be there. I was.

I was booked again by Max a year or so later to support Spirogyra at The Octagon, but, while it was another lovely evening, it marked the band's swansong there. Splitting up shortly afterwards, with just the duo of Martin and Barbara remaining, a lot of the momentum and the growing fan base they had achieved as a four-piece dissipated. I'd bought their debut album, St. Radigunds, as soon as it was released in 1971, and it's still a joy to hear. It takes me back to that Autumn afternoon when I first witnessed what I believed would be acoustic-rock's Next Big Thing.

On a four-day visit to London in the Spring of 1973, I visited Max at his flat in Thurloe Square. By then, he was a founding partner in Gemini Artists, an agency and management company. I was kind of hoping he would offer to manage me and show me the way to record deals and touring. But instead he made me a lovely cup of Jasmine tea and we spent a pleasant hour or so chatting about what we were up to. Finally, when it became obvious that my visit had run its course, full of 'But - er' pauses and starings out of the window, I took my leave.

Max went on to work in A & R at various record companies, rising to Global Head Honcho at Universal by 2010. He was referred to in Billboard as 'a serious contender for title of most powerful label executive outside America'. In 1983, while working at Warners, he ironically signed up singer-songwriter Howard Jones who, in an even odder twist of fate, was actually christened John Howard Jones! Isn't life strange?

Barbara Gaskin had her own solo UK No.1 hit in 1981 with a version of Lesley Gore's 'It's My Party' while Martin Cockerham drifted off into a reclusive nomadic life during the '80s. He is now back performing with various musician friends, and I'm happy to say we are back in touch via Social Media. He told me recently that Max's health is not good and he has taken temporary leave of his position at Universal while he recuperates. Even though his initial obvious interest in me didn't lead to anything more permanent, I'll always be grateful to Max for giving me the opportunity to develop and show off my performing talent back in those halcyon days at The Octagon.

At one of my early gigs, in April or May 1970, at a folk club in Prestwich, a guy came up to me after I'd played my set and told me I reminded him 'of a guy called Elton John'.

Not knowing who that was, I searched out and bought Elton's recently-released eponymous album. Back at home, while I enjoyed the L.P., I couldn't really hear any similarity to my style. John was much more bluesy Gospel-sounding with a boogie-style on the piano and a marked American accent. I also noticed that, while he wrote the music, his lyrics were written by a guy called Bernie Taupin. I am, to this day, compared to Elton John on many websites which sell or promote my work, and, to this day, I can still not hear the likeness others do. We both sing, we both play the piano. That's it as far as I'm concerned.

I've admired some of Elton's music. I consider *Goodbye Yellow Brick Road* his finest achievement as a cohesive piece of work but somehow his songs never really touch me. I don't know why. I do recall, after playing *Elton John* all the way through, I put it away, found Roy Harper's *Flat Baroque* album and let it steal my heart once more. Who knows why this happens? Why one artist leaves us relatively cold or unmoved, while another tugs at our heartstrings and takes us to another place, is one of the unanswerable questions.

By early 1971, with Roy Harper as my inspiration, I'd begun to tailor my act for audiences who seemed to enjoy listening to my stories as well as my songs. I was getting my own headlining nights at some of the folk clubs and, even more thrilling, I was packing them out. One club manager told me he'd never seen his place so full.

"They've been queuing down the stairs into the street," he told me.

"That's never happened before."

One afternoon in April '72, after closing a Bluesology session at The Octagon, I was sitting in my dressing-room when I heard a gentle knock on the door.

"Come in!" I called out.

Two guys poked their heads in and smiled at me.

"Hi!" one of them said. "Do you mind if we disturb you?"

"Not at all," I said and offered them a seat.

"We really loved your set today," the other chap said.

"You're in Iron Maiden, aren't you?" I asked, remembering their set from earlier on in the day.

"Yes, we are, but our lead singer is leaving soon and..."

"...and we were wondering if you'd be interested in joining the band as his replacement?"

Iron Maiden, I hasten to add here, was not a Heavy Metal outfit back in 1972. This earlier incarnation was much more about market squares and fair maidens than bringing anyone's daughter to the slaughter. Their tales of minstrels running in sun-dappled meadows were all delivered in a gentle Fairport Convention-esque style.

I didn't want to be rude to these guys, they were sweet gents and I was very flattered:

"Hey, thanks," I said, "but I really want to investigate for a bit longer a solo career. It might not work out, but I'd like to give it a go before making any changes."

Bless them, they kind of bowed and walked backwards out of the room saying,

"No problem, man."

"We understand, man."

"Thanks for your great music!"

And they were gone. Just as I was wondering if I'd made the right decision turning them down, I heard an audience member, leaving the theatre, shout, "We want Jon Howard!"

It was the unsolicited and well-timed consensus I needed.

I can't remember why, but during 1970 I developed a new and eager love of everything Bob Dylan. I'd bought a couple of his 1965 singles when they were first released and, of course, Pauline used to play me his albums whenever I was round at her house in the late '60s. But, probably because I was hearing his LPs every day on the art room record player, I became a belated ardent fan and bought every one of his albums released up to that point. I even scoured the specialist record shops for the under-the-counter bootleg albums such as Seems Like A Freeze Out, Talking New York City Blues and Stealin'. The studio outtakes from Dylan's '65/'66 sessions, featured on clear yellow vinyl bootlegs, were the most intriguing. Tracks like 'I Wanna Be Your Lover' and 'She's Your Lover Now', which never made it onto the released albums, were fascinating. They often broke down at the end or contained vocal fluffs, but were still entirely brilliant. (Columbia finally woke up to these outtakes many years later and began an official issue programme of all Dylan's bootleg material).

Around that time I wrote and demo'd a song called 'A Kind Of Aching', full of *Blonde On Blonde*-esque imagery and internal rhymes. I performed it for a few months then, like so many others, I discarded it. Going through my old reel-to-reels one day in 2004, I rediscovered the 1970 home demo. Listening to it over thirty years after it was first written, I was fascinated to hear - and had totally forgotten that - I had re-used a part of its lyric for my 1973 song 'Kid In A Big World'. The line *'the press they'll flash their cameras, they'll test you and guess your words aren't like theirs'* pops up in both songs. Self-plagiarism, the useful tool of any songwriter.

Although it needed some work to lessen the blatant Dylan styling, I felt that 'A Kind Of Aching' could be a contender for *As I Was Saying*, my 2005 'comeback' album. Both Phil King and Andre Barreau, my bassist and guitarist on the album, agreed, and happily it became one of the most downloaded tracks from that release.

Another discarded song from 1970, 'I'm Dead Again', always got a great reaction at my college lunchtime concerts, but for some reason I never demo'd it. I found a scribbled lyric for it, one summer's afternoon in 2007, while flicking through a box of unused lyrics and poems I've carried round for years. Sometimes, something in there interests me enough to attempt a remodel and, for some reason, the first line of 'I'm Dead Again' - *you changing right before my eyes* - struck a chord that day. It took me immediately back to performing the song at college, its tune jumping into my head like a forgotten friend. Surprisingly quickly, I reworked it to a standard I thought deserved preserving at last and recorded a simple piano/voice demo. In 2010, that became the starting point for yet another rewrite. Re-titled 'I Am Dead Again', I included the final version on my album *Exhibiting Tendencies*. Maybe one day I'll release the 2007 demo of that early '70s composition?

Chapter Ten

The Other Side Of Town

One Monday morning, in the late Spring of 1971, I was sitting in my work area, eating a cheese sandwich my mum had packed for me. The strains of the amazing new Roy Harper album, *Stormcock*, which I'd bought that weekend and brought in to play to everyone, sailed gloriously around the room. Over Roy's and Jimmy Page's astonishing guitar playing, I heard the heavy tread of Doc Martin boots thudding past. Not used to such definite footfall here, I peered out around my screen and saw a stocky short-haired chap in a billowing white cotton shirt, walking purposefully to the far end of the art room. His red braces held up white baggy trousers over the black boots.

Sitting down with his back to us, he began setting out his paints, brushes and pencils with great consideration. 'What a lovely back that man has,' I thought as he began sketching away at what looked like a Hockney-esque line drawing.

"That's Anthony," Anita in the next work area said, emphasising the 'th' in his name.

"Anthony?" I asked, trying to feign nonchalance.

She wandered into my area with a coffee, a knowing look, and sat down.

"Never Antony, and whatever you do, do not call him Tony."

"So who is he, this Anthony?"

Looking behind her to make sure he wasn't listening, she said, "He was here a couple of years ago."

"Why is he here now?"

Anita took out a banana from her bag and munched away happily on it.

"He didn't like it at Liverpool," she said, lowering her voice even more. "So they let him come back and study for his diploma here."

I peered again and watched his creation developing, as he drew another sweeping line across the paper.

"What's he like?" I asked, wondering how she always knew everything about everybody before anyone else.

She stopped munching and grimaced, "Weird." She drained her coffee cup and got up. "He's weird."

I had another look and smiled at Anita, who widened her eyes and mouthed 'Really weird' like a warning. She wandered back to continue what had been a three-day exercise in drawing an orchid. Anita specialised in orchids. Careful, unexciting pastel drawings of orchids.

"Ah, another drawing of another orchid," Mr Bownass would say wandering by her work area.

Later that morning Bownass walked in, glanced at Anita's orchid with sagging shoulders then, seeing Anthony, bucked up and went to greet him warmly. Bizarrely clapping his hands as though calling for silence at the beginning of a meeting, he introduced his new arrival to us all. Nodding at each one of us meaningfully he said,

"I think Anthony may act as an inspiration for you."

The more he went on, the more embarrassed his hero became, flushing up and waving weakly to a room full of curious onlookers. Finally, cutting Bownass off in mid-gush, Anthony excused himself and rushed out, mumbling angrily to himself.

"Well, that was fun!" Anita said to a downcast Bownass as he left the room.

Taking advantage of the moment, I ran down to Anthony's easel for a quick peek.

"What are you doing?" Anita squeaked.

The line drawing was now a pencil and gouache study of what looked like naked blokes lying around the place, bleeding from various orifices. A tiny window was roughly sketched above them, the only light source on a grim setting. It wasn't erotic, it wasn't even particularly disturbing, but it was intriguing. The returning clump of boots announced that Anthony was back. I put on my best smile and turned around.

With a quizzical look and, pointing his bottle of lemonade rather threateningly in my direction, he said,

"'ello?"

"Hi!" I said. Then pointing at his drawing, "I kind of like this."

He sat down and narrowed his eyes:

"'Kind of'?"

"Yes. Kind of."

"Gee, thanks!"

He took a swig of his lemonade, picked up his pencil and continued to draw. He might just as well have said, 'Dismissed.'

For the next couple of weeks, Anthony would wander in at different times, sit at his easel and begin another homo-semi-erotic study. He wouldn't speak to anyone and always sat with his back to us. The only time I saw him come to life was when a former student from the previous year, Paul, turned up. There was an immediate empathy between them. At one point, Paul said something which sent them both into fits of giggles then, just as unexpectedly, their laughter stopped. Paul bid him a quick goodbye, and nodding to the room, left. Anthony went back to drawing in silence.

The detached aura surrounding him fascinated me. It wasn't the benignly pervading containedness which I'd experienced from the older students in my first year. This was a man who clearly wished to be left alone and, for some reason I still don't fully understand, I was determined to break into his isolation. I guess I found him rather sexy. He wasn't a handsome man, far from it, but he had a physical presence which I found alluring. I was the only one there who did. All the other students completely avoided making any contact with our unwelcoming visitor.

I'd try to strike up conversations with him, all my attempts being met with a gruff "Mmm." I'd put on various LPs lying round the room and see if there was a reaction. There never was. Then, one evening, when everyone had gone home or to the pub across the road, I was dipping an etching in the acid, situated conveniently near Anthony's work area, when he put down his pencil, turned around and watched me. He didn't speak, he just watched me. I smiled and he continued to look at me.

"Alright?" I asked in a friendly casual way.

He just nodded and carried on looking.

"Nearly finished," I said, pointing to the acid tray. "Are you going across to the pub?"

"Maybe," he said. "Are you?"

"Probably."

"Then, yes. I am."

"OK," I said nonchalantly as my heart thudded in my chest. "See you later!"

Dylan's 'Lay Lady Lay' was playing on the juke box when Anthony walked in, pushed past everyone and wedged himself into the seat next to me.

"Don't mind us!" one of the girls said.

"I do, actually," Anthony replied. Then to me, "OK?"

"Yes. Fine." I smiled at everyone as though apologising for my companion's bad manners.

Anita mouthed "So-o-o-o weird!" at me but I was enjoying myself. Anthony's warm leg squeezed next to mine felt very good.

He didn't engage with anyone, even as I chatted to people on our table there was no attempt to join in. He'd occasionally go to the bar for another pint, buying me one each time but no-one else, then settled back down next to me and supped his beer, staring straight ahead. As last orders were called and everyone drank up and left, Anthony walked me out onto the street. I'd come to college that sunny morning with a flimsy jacket and the night air felt cold. I shivered and, without any preamble, he put his arms round me and hugged me tightly.

"Better?" he said.

"Mmm. Much."

"Come and stay for the weekend at my house."

Bloody hell, I thought.

"Thank you, yes, that would be nice."

"Nice?"

"Well, yes, it would."

"Nothing worthwhile is 'nice'."

I smiled at him and said, "Whatever, I'll look forward to it."

"Good."

On the Friday evening, my heart fluttering like a captive bird, we sat together on the bus to Oswaldtwistle. He didn't speak for the whole journey but that was fine. I rather enjoyed our silences together. Getting off at the Terminus, we walked up a road of newly built semis, past perfectly clipped hedges and tidy flowerbeds. As we reached a small exclusive-looking cul-de-sac, he pointed to a large detached house at the end, surrounded by a sizeable lawned garden which spread down to the pavement, like the houses I'd seen in American TV series.

"That's where I live," he said in a strangely dismissive way.

"My God, it's huge."

"Mum's dream house which Dad built for her. Now a fucking nightmare."

After taking off our shoes in the boot-room, we entered through a side door into an impressive kitchen, all fitted units in light blue and cream, with a state-of-the-art oven and a huge American style fridge. I noticed a distinctly sickly-sweet aroma.

"You can smell it?" he said as I lifted my head and breathed in.

"It's pretty strong."

He opened one of the cupboards. It was full to bursting with jars of sarsaparilla sweets. Another cupboard was equally packed with them. His face broke into a huge smile:

"My mum's addicted to them. She has them delivered."

"What does your dad think?"

"He's too busy wanking off over gay magazines in his bedroom."

I let that one hang in the air and followed him into the enormous sitting-room. Floor-length heavily braided cream curtains swept down to wall-to-wall chocolate brown shag pile. Crimson and cream Regency design wallpaper, over which hung large gilt-framed mirrors, acted as the backcloth for repro antique furniture. Two candelabras stood atop a long highly polished sideboard, which Anthony opened to reveal the largest TV I'd ever seen housed inside a piece of furniture. The plush heavy sofas and chairs were arranged in a semi-circle, around a red-brick and brass-surround farmhouse style fireplace. Above it hung numerous reproduction masters in fussy ornate frames, a Matisse, a Van Gogh, a Durer, a Monet.

"Woolworth's," Anthony said, watching me take them in. "Mum's always had an eye for shit. That's why she married my dad. Do you want a cup of tea?"

We sipped our Darjeeling as Leonard Cohen's 'Avalanche' droned around the room. I was a big Cohen fan and liked this new raw sound he had come up with for Songs Of Love And Hate, his third Top 20 album. The poet turned successful recording artist had become the singing bedsit Lothario. His songs spoke to thousands of doomily romantic teenage souls. They offered wide-scape tales of exotic women he had bedded or lusted after, or of nights in the desert fighting long-gone wars, with only a good woman's company as his medicine. They appealed to our generation's wounded sense of battling against a system, with only love and erudition for weapons.

"I wouldn't have seen you as a Cohen fan," I said.

"I'm not."

"So - why-?"

"I like to play stuff I hate. It makes me angry, which makes me paint."

"And the stuff we play in the art room?"

"All crap."

"So, what *do* you like?"

He got up and put on a Jacques Brel album, handing me the sleeve. I hadn't heard him before but recognised the song:

"Scott Walker did this, 'Jackie'," I said as Anthony sat down.

"Unfortunately, yes, he did."

"I bought that single."

He nodded and smiled to himself.

"It's brilliant," I protested.

"No. *This* is brilliant."

I liked what I heard. It had much more light and shade than Walker's version. I had loved the frenetic sweeping strings and crashing cymbals of Scott's hit, but Brel's French language original had many more subtle layers of sound and instrumentation. The arrangement was one minute blasting out in oompah-pah Sunday bandstand fashion, the next an intimate accordion-backed thought piece wove its way into your soul. It never let you rest or relax, you were constantly challenged as to where the song might go next. It scurried by and fondled you, rushed away and then returned in a different form. I found it fascinating.

Walker had used the Mort Shuman English translation, 'authentic queers and phoney virgins' being the line I loved the most. But sung by Brel, as he spat words out like a curse, then just as unexpectedly murmured them into your ear like an attentive lover, the song drew me in even more. It was as though he was letting me into a secret, only me. Looking at the sleeve photo of his gaunt figure sitting at a table in a bar, cigarette in hand, I could imagine him wringing out every line to a gripped group of enthralled fans.

"I loved that," I said as it ended, waiting for the next track. But instead, Anthony jumped up and put on The Velvet Underground's 'Waiting For The Man'. He threw the Warhol Banana sleeve at me and laughed. I was about to say something gauche like "That's a big one!" when I heard movement in the kitchen behind us. Anthony's face fell.

"Fuck!" he said as the sitting room door behind us opened.

I turned and saw a very small skinny lady walk in, her cigarette holder dangling from scrawny ringed fingers. Swaying slightly, she shut the door very slowly and gently behind her, as if thinking very hard about what she was doing. She put her hand on her hip Bette Davis style and smiled at us. A huge fur coat slipped off her tiny shoulders and fell to the floor. With heels too high for her, she tottered towards us, a drunken leer on her face the whole time. Anthony rushed to the radiogram and yanked the stylus off the record with a loud scratch.

Flinching just slightly, she continued to slowly approach us, never taking her eyes off me:

"Hello," she said. "I'm Vivienne. Not Vivien. Never Viv! Vi-vi-enne!" She pronounced the last 'n' with a grand twitch of her head.

Anthony's face had reddened and his lips were tight.

"What do you want, mum?" he said, shaking his head.

"I want to meet your friend," she purred.

She leant over the back of the sofa and, sounding like a Lancashire Eartha Kitt but smelling like a sarsaparilla brewery, said,

"What's his name, Anthony?"

"Howard."

"Ooooh! Hello, Howard! Aren't you lovely?"

I was just about to say hello back when she fell into a heap behind the sofa. I heard a kind of gurgle and a hissed 'Shit!' and waited for Anthony to go and help her up. But he just stood, arms folded, breathing heavily. From the back of the settee, a clawed hand appeared. Like a spider suspended, it floated over my head then landed, thin bony fingers scraping their way through my hair, huge diamond rings scratching my scalp.

"Oooh!" a muffled voice cooed. "He has such lovely hair, Anthony! Have you felt it yet?"

"No."

"Can I have him?"

"No. Now fuck off!"

With a sigh, Vivienne heaved herself up and teetered back towards the door. She slid round it like an aging pole dancer and, eyes swimming, slurred:

"The clean bedding is in the airing cupboard. Goodnight!"

She blew a kiss into the room and shut the door.

Anthony put the record back on even louder and sat next to me.

"Sorry about that," he said. "Do you want to play cards?"

"Hey white boy," Lou Reed snarled, *"what you doin' uptown?"*

By one-thirty we were on our umpteenth game of Snap – the only card game I've ever been able to play - a Francoise Hardy album shimmying out of the radiogram. After several brandies I was ready for bed, though beginning to think that, after all, I would be kipping on the sofa on my own. I was just about to suggest that we retire for the night when there was a loud crash from the kitchen, cutlery fell to the floor and a bloke swore very loudly.

"Dad's home," Anthony said with a sigh, turning off the record again.

We listened in silence as more mumbled effing and blinding went on next door. A clump of feet began ascending the stairs, accompanied by grunts and curses. I was reminded of those table-top Papier Mache landscape constructions, the ones Michael Bentine had used on his weekly TV shows. I'd loved his small unseen creatures, bumbling and squeaking their way around their tiny world. This, though, was less endearing. As the clumping stopped, there was a loud banging on a door and a man hollered,

"Are you in there, bitch?"

"Yes I am! So fucking what?" a woman's voice yelled back, Eartha Kitt having now turned into Elsie Tanner.

"I wanna fuck ya!"

"You?! Fuck me?! Don't make me laugh, you fucking bum stuffer!"

"Yeah? Well, I'm gonna stuff your arse tonight, you old slag!!"

"Go and toss yourself off over your dirty magazines!! Fucking pervert!!"

More banging on the bedroom door followed. Something was thrown and smashed against the wall. I wasn't sure if it came from inside or outside the room.

"Fucking bitch!"

"Fucking bastard!"

Then there was a scream.

"You fucking idiot. That was my mother's vase!!"

"Yeah, well, I wish I'd thrown it at her fucking head!! She was more of a bitch than you!"

The row continued to rage for another five minutes, until, finally, with a last 'bitch' and 'bastard' hurled across the landing, doors slammed shut and silence returned.

"Dream house, eh?" Anthony said, and cleared away our glasses. "Time for bed."

I followed him up the stairs and he stopped on the lower landing, pointing to one of several doors:

"That's the spare room," he murmured quietly. "You can sleep in there."

He pointed to another door on the next level:

"Or you can sleep in there with me."

When I awoke in Anthony's arms the next morning, I was very pleased I'd chosen the second option.

On the bus home, I felt very surreal, as though I'd crossed a threshold. I'd finally Done It. Watching the Rossendale countryside floating by, I noticed an old bloke opposite staring at me. I looked back at him and thought, 'Have I got the word 'Fucked' on my forehead, or something?'. But it was the usual 1970s old Northern bloke thing, 'Is that a boy or a girl?'. I nodded at him and he immediately turned away, feigning fascination with some sheep in a field.

I didn't care. I had much pleasanter things on my mind. I remembered how, during a brief rest from rolling me around his surprisingly spacious single bed, Anthony had lain on his back and studied me.

"What?" I'd asked him.

"You're dead 'ot, you."

'Yes, I am rather,' I'd thought, seeing myself in the mirror astride my big man. Shaking my mane of long hair, I'd smiled at my reflection.

The following Friday night we went to a pub in Blackburn, The Merchants. It was the first gay pub I'd ever been into. Old and rather run-down, it boasted signed photos of long-dead 'celebrities' on the nicotine-stained walls, recalling its former days as a Variety artists' after-theatre haunt. Now, instead of raucous laughter ringing out from visiting showbiz turns, the juke box blasted out The Supremes' 'Stoned Love' to little groups of elderly men. They shyly eyed up the younger talent draped along the bar, arses squeezed into torn jeans on full display for their admiring elders.

'God,' I thought as one of the prettiest boys winked at me, 'if I looked like that, I wouldn't be standing in a dump like this.'

Anthony made his way to the bar and asked for two pints of bitter. The barman was dressed in a kind of half-drag, garishly made-up like a seaside landlady on a night out, long dangly earrings clacking as he pulled our pints. Nipple clips hung across his bare tattooed chest and handcuffs dangled at his waist. He clicked his fingers in time to the record as he took Anthony's money, not looking at him but checking his own reflection in the glass-tiled wall opposite. He caught me looking at him and licked his lips salaciously. As he went off to serve another customer, someone at the other end of the bar dropped a glass on the floor. Everyone cheered and somebody shouted out, "Another earring gone, Shirley!".

I followed Anthony into a huge room next door, completely empty except for two old ladies sitting closely together near the stage. I wasn't sure if they expected cabaret but certainly nobody else did. We sat at a table long in need of a good wipe with a clean cloth and drank our pints in silence. 'Stoned Love' had been followed by Lynn Anderson's 'Rose Garden' and I could hear the queens in the bar happily singing along. Anthony looked at me and we both smiled just as the two old dears came and sat with us.

"Hello, me loves!" one of them, wearing a rather large knitted pink hat, said brightly, "Do you mind if we join you?"

Neither of us responded.

"It's a bit lonely over there!" the other lady said, her fox fur having seen better days. "We thought it would be busier than this, didn't we, Norma?"

Norma nodded, her hat wobbling away atop a tight perm.

"Yes, Lizzie and I thought, well, Friday night, bound to be busy."

"It is next door," Anthony said.

"Yes, but we wouldn't fit in there would we?"

"It is rather full," I said, which made them smile, and then realising what they meant I smiled too.

"This your girlfriend?" Norma asked, settling down and nodding at me as she sipped her Double Diamond.

Anthony burst out giggling. The two old ladies stared at him then back at me. Lizzie nudged Norma and pulled a face at her.

"Oh! Sorry love!" Norma said, blushing up, "I thought you were a girl."

Anthony was now in fits of laughter.

"He's very happy!" Lizzie said.

"That's 'cos he's gay!" Norma cried, and then hooted with laughter.

Anthony shut up immediately and glared at them both.

Taking our empty glasses, I escaped to the bar and asked for two more pints. This time the barman took off one of his nipple clips and waved it at me invitingly. Leaning over the bar, he sang along to Lynn, flicking his tongue like a lizard on all the 'L's, 'Smile to yourself and let's be jolly, love shouldn't be so melancholy'. One of the young queens next to me nudged his friend and they waited to see what I would do. Just then I felt a heavy prod in my ribs and heard Anthony saying, "we're going."

I turned around to see him rushing through the crowd for the door.

'Sorry' I mouthed to the barman. He pouted, and flinched as he put his clip back on a very red nipple.

As I ran towards the door, one of the old blokes, surprisingly nimbly, jumped in front of me and said, "Hello, love. I'm Barry. I love your hair!"

"So does his mum," I replied, pointing to my retreating friend.

Just then a harridanesque screech came from behind us:

"Hey! That bloke tried to strangle my friend!"

I turned and it was Lizzie from the large empty room, jumping up and down and pointing. Anthony had gone, so I made a similar speedy exit.

Out on the street he was running for our bus which had thankfully just arrived. I ran after him and just managed to jump on the platform as the bus was pulling away. I saw the old dear running out of the pub as we whisked by. She shouted something like "Loony!" as we ran upstairs.

Settling down on the empty top deck and sorting out my change for the fare, I asked him,

"Did you really try to strangle that woman?"

"No. I just made her think I was trying to strangle her," he replied.

"Because she called you gay?"

The bus conductor had arrived and Anthony gave me a look which said, 'drop it'.

Walking towards his house and, breaking a ten-minute silence, I asked him why he'd not liked Liverpool Art College:

"They thought I was a poof because I sound all my S's and T's."

I looked at him quizzically:

"I say 'Yes' instead of 'Yeah'," he explained.

"But -" then I got that look again and decided I didn't want to be his next fake strangler victim.

Anthony was much more aggressive in bed that night, wanting to get it over and done with, and fell asleep very quickly afterwards. I lay in the dark, wondering what his problem was, when, right on cue, the marital ritual of banging and cursing started on the landing. For ten minutes, various objects were thrown against walls, threats were screamed at each other, until, with their sign-off 'bitch!', "bastard!' flung across the landing, doors were finally slammed shut and the storm subsided once more. Their son slept fitfully through it all, just once turning over and saying in his sleep 'Oh fuck off', and then going back into a deep slumber.

I was woken by the sound of the dustmen outside at around 6 a.m., quietly got up, dressed and left for the early bus home.

At college on the Monday morning, Anthony walked past my work area and went straight to his easel and began to draw. I'd noticed in his bedroom that he was building up a large portfolio of sketches and gouache studies and I took the opportunity of collaring Bownass as he wandered in:

"What are Anthony's plans?" I asked him quietly.

Bownass looked a little askance at my question but said, "He's applying to Sheffield Art College, to carry on his diploma there."

"He's not happy here?"

"Anthony's not happy anywhere, Howard. That's what makes him a potentially great artist."

I was about to disagree with his 'Genius is Pain' rot when there was a commotion at the far end of the room. Anita screamed and we ran out to find Anthony with his hands round her throat, laughing manically as she gasped for breath. Bownass pulled Anthony off her as Anita fell to the floor.

"Your fucking boyfriend tried to kill me!" she rasped at me but pointing at Anthony, who was dusting himself off and bright red in the face. Bownass held him off from attacking her again as other students rushed in to see what all the fuss was about.

"Anthony!" Bownass shouted, "Go and get some air, go on. Now!"

Anthony dropped his head and, without looking at anyone, trudged out. I wasn't sure whether to follow him or stay and comfort the weeping Anita. I chose the latter and she fell into my arms sobbing.

"What happened?" I asked.

Through sobs and little throttled gasps she said, "I just asked him if he'd had a nice weekend with you, and how you two were getting on together."

"Just that?" I asked, unconvinced.

"Well, I did say how pleased I was he'd finally found a nice boyfriend."

"And?"

"And I told him that he didn't need to hide the fact that he was gay. I was trying to be nice!"

I remembered his words to me before our first weekend together, 'Nothing worthwhile is nice' and patted Anita's head as she rested it on my shoulder and wept.

"He's fucking crazy and shouldn't be here!" she wailed.

"He won't be much longer," Bownass said and left.

We didn't see Anthony at college for the rest of the week and he didn't call me to arrange a weekend together. I didn't have his phone number, he'd never offered it. Then, about ten days later, I noticed him sitting at the back of the Maths Room during one of my lunchtime concerts. I hadn't seen him arrive so he'd obviously slipped in when I was sorting my lyrics out or chatting to those arriving. I watched his reaction at the end of the songs and he clapped and even smiled at some of my stories but, as he'd arrived, he left when I wasn't looking. He wasn't in the art room later and no-one knew where he'd gone.

"He's not back, is he?" Anita asked, panic in her eyes.

"No," I replied, "he's not."

Maybe this was his odd way of saying goodbye?

That Friday evening, I was lying on my bed listening to Joni Mitchell's Ladies of The Canyon when the phone rang downstairs. With that odd feeling that you know who's calling, I let my mum answer it:

"Ramsbottom 2502...Yes, he's here. Who's calling? Ok, wait a minute... Howard, it's Antony for you."

"OK," I said as nonchalantly as I could muster, and went down to get it.

Taking the phone off mum I covered up the receiver and said, "It's Anthony, not Antony."

"Oh, excuse me!" Mum said and disappeared.

"Hello?" I sat on the stairs which, being in an old terraced cottage with its original boxed-in staircase, hid me from the rest of the house.

"It's me," he said quietly.

"I know," I said. "How are you?"

"Missing you."

My heart did a little leap but I kept my cool:

"That's nice," I said purposely. No rebuke came.

"Can I see you this weekend?"

"What, tomorrow?"

"No, tonight, soon as you can get here."

"Sure. I'll get there soon as I can," I replied, but as I replaced the receiver said 'Idiot' to myself.

When he opened the door Anthony looked odd, odder than usual that is. He had shaved his head rather badly, leaving longer tufts of hair sticking up. He resembled a rescued puppy and I brushed his head with my hand.

"That's different," I said. He looked embarrassed, mumbled something, and opened the door to let me in.

The familiar sarsaparilla smell wasn't as strong as usual and, as though reading my mind, he said,

"Mum and Dad are away for the weekend." He led me into the sitting room. "Majorca."

I had visions of their fellow sun-seekers' horrified faces as they lay in bed each evening, listening to effings, blindings and smashed hotel vases in the room across the hall. Maybe one of the other holidaymakers had told Anthony's dad to keep the noise down, and there'd been a fight. Maybe they'd been thrown out of the hotel. Lordy, I thought, they may be on their way back already! So, with this scenario playing out in my mind, the fact they were away didn't really have the calming effect it should have done. I realised how uneasy I felt in the house, and he seemed to sense it:

"I'm sorry about all the mess up the other week. It's all a mess really."

"I hear you've applied to Sheffield?"

"Oh! Yes. Did Bone Arse tell you?"

I nodded.

"I asked him not to tell anyone."

"When's your interview?"

"Next week."

"You'll have no problem getting in."

"Paul said that as well."

I remembered that Paul was at Sheffield and smiled.

"Are you coming to bed?" Anthony asked.

He was very tender and caring that night and, as I fell asleep in his arms, I thought that maybe I'd done the right thing coming back after all. But, waking out of a recurring dream about large derelict rooms leading up rickety stairs, I became aware of Anthony's voice saying, "Wake up." I looked at the bedside clock, it was 3.15.

"Get up," Anthony said. "We're going for a walk."

"What do you mean? A walk? It's the middle of the night."

"Come on." He was already dressed and, picking up his camera, marched out of the room.

Like a fool but oddly intrigued, I quickly put on my clothes and followed him out. It was late Spring but still quite chilly. I shivered but got no hug this time. He walked so quickly he was almost running and it was hard to keep up, especially as I had no idea where we were going. Finally, after trekking for ten minutes he turned into a graveyard and stood by one of the stones. It was rather a large thing, with the statue of an angel looking down sadly and praying.

Turning on the camera flash Anthony took a picture of it.

"Lie down," he said.

"What?"

"Lie down."

Thinking this was probably for one of his gouache studies, I did as he said. But instead of taking a photo he lay next to me. The camera round his neck clattered on the stone beneath us as he kissed me and fumbled with my clothes, trying to pull my trousers off.

"What the fuck?" I said, jumping up.

Anthony looked bewildered as I did my trousers up and stared down at him. He moved his head and I saw the name on the gravestone.

"Yes, it's my grandma's grave," he said. "Always hated her. I thought we'd fuck on top of her, that'd teach the old bag."

He giggled and snapped a picture of me as I fastened my belt and marched off.

I arrived back at the house before Anthony did, but, once he'd let us in I made for the airing cupboard, got some bedding out and settled myself on the sofa.

"Oh, by the way," I said as he came into the sitting room, "I didn't ask you what you thought of my songs the other day?"

"Oh, yes, they were shit."

"I don't think anyone else there thought that."

"Yes, well, they're stupid, with no taste."

He shrugged, turned off the light and went upstairs. The early morning bus home was cold and gloomy, matching my mood. I was determined never to go there again.

I slotted back into 'normal' college life easily, chatting with the other students about everything but the elephant no longer in the room. Weeks went by, I sailed through my Mock Art 'A' Levels, thrilling Bownass with a life class painting of our very ancient model, Nina.

"If you paint like that in the actual exam, Howard," he said, "you'll get a Grade 1."

I did consider asking him what had happened to Anthony but decided against it. Not mentioning him sort of made the unsettling previous few weeks disappear. Only his empty easel and chair waited for him to return.

The summer came, exams taken, the long break at home ahead until I started next term at Rochdale Pre-Dip college. The fact was, I could have applied to go straight to a Dip AD course at one of the larger colleges further from home, but I wasn't sure I wanted to commit to that yet. My music was now taking up so much of my life, filling my thoughts and ambitions, that I wanted to hold off making any decisions. I was still convinced that someone was going to see me performing and offer me a deal, or at least an exciting proposition. Waiting while painting seemed a good option.

One sunny July afternoon, I was enjoying a John Newcombe/ Roger Taylor tennis match on the telly, when the phone rang. Mum and Dad were out so I went to answer it.

The familiar dulcet-toned ''ello' made my heart sink.

"Oh, hello," I said, as coolly as I could.

"Will you come over this evening?"

I hesitated and was about to say 'I don't think so', when Anthony said, "Please!"

I hesitated again, and said, "Oh, Anthony…".

It was the opening he needed.

"Please come over. I'm leaving for Sheffield next week, and would like to see you before I go."

I sighed and, wondering what the hell I was thinking, said, "OK, see you later."

Anthony wasted no time in getting me upstairs and in bed. Love-making was much more adventurous than before, and a couple of times I thought, 'Who taught him this one?'. During one of the breathers, as he lay on his back smiling at the ceiling, he said,

"I actually quite liked one of the songs you sang. 'I'm Dead Again'."

I realised he meant the college lunchtime show he'd come to weeks earlier, and tapped him on the chest playfully:

"Oh! So you did like something then?"

"Of course."

As I was floating off to sleep, I heard Anthony mumble "I'm hungry", the sound of padding feet and a door closing. I wasn't prepared at all for what followed..

…The sound of someone eating and banging a spoon against a bowl woke me up. Sitting on the edge of the bed, Anthony was tucking into what I thought at first was a huge helping of cereal in a cake mixing bowl. But closer inspection revealed a disgusting mixture of what looked like melted strawberry ice cream, currants, cornflakes and lumps of meat. It all swam in a congealed brown gravy and he was slurping it down as though he hadn't eaten for days.

"That looks foul," I said, as he swallowed down the last piece of ice cream-covered meat.

"It was," he said, obviously delighted nonetheless.

Too tired to ask any questions, I lay back down and left him to it. I was just nodding off again when I heard a loud retching noise above me. I looked up just as the whole of his revolting snack cascaded out of his mouth, all over my head and face. As I was spitting and coughing it out frantically, I could hear him laughing like a maniac. I wiped the goo out of my eyes and saw him lying on his back, kicking his legs in the air with delight.

"You bastard!" I yelled and, rather ridiculously, hit him extremely hard on the legs, like mothers used to scold children in the street. It was the only part of him I could get to as he rolled around cackling. "That's it! No more!" I shouted, as more bits of vomit trickled into my mouth. I spat it out in his direction and ran out onto the landing.

As I was making for the shower room, Anthony's mum came out to see what the noise was. She was naked except for a pair of scanty panties and curlers bobbing around on top of her tiny head.

"Yeugh!" she said, covering her mouth, as bits of meat and corn flakes dripped off my head onto the floor.

I flew into the bathroom and slammed the door shut.

Anthony's father called out from his bedroom next door, "Keep the fucking noise down!"

"Oh go fuck yourself !" I screamed, locking the door just in case.

I stood in the hot shower and scrubbed away at my face and hair, poured oodles of pine-scented shampoo on my head, rinsing and re-washing it, washing and re-rinsing it. I let the clean fresh warm water run down my face for what seemed ages, a sense of calm returning as the pink and brown juice around my feet finally cleared. I found a very large bath towel in the airing cupboard and wrapped myself in its comforting hugeness. Inspecting myself in the full-length wall mirror, to make sure all remnants of vomit had gone, I crept out. The house had fallen eerily quiet as I tiptoed downstairs and settled myself on the sofa.

I dreamt of crossing wide highways with a large group of friends, all hanging onto my every word of wisdom as we made our way to the other side. Everyone was laughing and having a great time. Suddenly, we were all in a packed bar sitting cross-legged on the floor, the flickering light from wall candles reflecting off my friends' faces. There was a bloke I couldn't make out by the door and he was mumbling something at us. I was just about to ask him what he was saying when I started to wake up. As I came to, I heard Anthony reading what sounded like poetry to someone.

I gingerly lifted myself up and there, at the corner telephone table, he sat, as ever with his back to the room. He was stark bollock naked, and I wondered what his mother would make of his sweaty arse on her prized mock Chippendale. Clutching what looked like handwritten verses, he was reading them down the phone in a monotone murmur. I had to strain to hear what he was saying but caught the occasional line.

"I want to feel your dick in my mouth and suck your life south, into mine," he droned. It was hardly Keats.

He did an odd little chuckle, like a child does when it's pleased with itself.

"These were written especially for you, my darling Paul," he cooed.

I had an image of the round-shouldered recipient of this foul stuff, gurgling with pleasure in his Sheffield bedsit. When Anthony asked lasciviously,

"You are naked aren't you, Paul? I want you to be naked when I read these to you, Paul, my love," that image suddenly got much worse.

I must have shifted slightly because he stopped reading, sat stock still, put down his 'poem' and turned round. He stared at me, so I stared right back at him.

"I won't be a moment, my darling," he sighed into the phone.

Putting it down remarkably gently, as though it were Paul himself he'd been holding, he stood up and glared at me. His full erection bobbing up and down was almost as red as his face.

"Stop looking at me!" he growled.

I widened my eyes and stared even more intensely.

"OK," he said to himself and rushed into the kitchen. I heard him frantically searching in the cutlery drawer. Seconds later, like a warrior in battle, he ran back in brandishing a huge carving knife, hurling it and himself at me. Whether he wasn't as strong as he looked, or I had more strength than I could have imagined, I managed to hold him off. His cock was now disturbingly engorged as he pushed himself onto me, the knife inches from my chest. I had the bizarre thought that he was going to come all over me. Somehow, the idea wasn't turning me on right then. I screamed at the top of my voice,

"Help Me!!"

There was a noise upstairs, then the sound of running on the landing.

Anthony stood up and looked furiously at me, as if to say, 'What have you done?'

There was a crash, several heavy thuds down the stairs, and a final bang against the wall as someone fell in a heap at the bottom of the staircase.

I heard Anthony's father moan "Fucking hell."

"What the fuck's going on?" Vivienne yelled as she ran downstairs, then screamed, "William! Don't move!"

"I can't," he groaned back at her.

"Fuck!" Anthony shouted as his mother rushed into the room.

"Anthony!" she screamed, ran towards him and slapped him hard on the arse. He yelped, leapt backwards and fell against the wall, looking terrified of this tiny over-tanned lady in curlers.

"Put that away!" she yelled at him. I wasn't sure if she meant the knife or the erection, but, in both cases, it worked. The knife dangled from his hand, the subsiding erection hung beside it. He crumpled down the wall and put up his hands as if protecting himself. Vivienne took the knife from him and shook it at him angrily.

"What are you doing with this, you stupid boy?"

He uncovered his face and pointed at her accusingly.

"Oh go fuck yourself!" he screamed.

Jumping up and sprinting to the door, he turned round and yelled, "ALL of you!!" and ran out of the room. Cursing his father – "Get up, you cunt!" – as he flew upstairs, he slammed his door shut.

Vivienne took a deep breath and wrapped her dressing gown around her tightly. As she sucked on a sarsaparilla sweet her curlers twitched up and down, like little rag-roll creatures on her head. Seeing the phone off the hook, she went and picked it up, listened for a moment and said,

"I think they've gone."

Placing it back on the receiver, she turned to me and beamed:

"Are you alright, Howard?"

I nodded.

"Would you like a nice cup of tea?"

I shook my head.

"Okay then."

Flicking off the light, she whispered "Sweet dreams," and closed the door.

"You'll be alright, my love," I heard her murmur gently to her groaning husband in the hallway. "Let's get you back into bed, shall we? My poor, poor William baby boy."

Manly sobbing progressed up the stairs, a door shut above me - but only one – and silence, like a forgotten friend, reigned once more.

Mum was dusting when I got home.

"Did you have a nice time?" she asked, picking up and polishing one of her many Toby Jugs which sat on the piano.

Wanting to cry my eyes out and tell her everything, I just said,

"Er – Anthony and I have had a falling out."

"Oh, I'm sorry to hear that. You were such good pals."

"Yes, well, if he rings, could you tell him I'm not in?"

"What if he keeps ringing?"

"He won't."

And he didn't, in fact I never heard from him again... except...

...One evening, in the late Spring of 1975, I was standing at the bar of The Bolton's Pub. Situated on the corner of Earl's Court Road and Old Brompton Road in West London, it was then one of the most popular gay pubs in the area. There was a bustling large bar, where one could 'vada' the assembled talent, and an adjacent quieter 'Snug' where you could take your pick-up for a more intimate chat. Victorian Bohemia in style, stained-glass windowed screens lined the back of the bar, and ornately sculpted steel light fittings hung from high yellowing ceilings. I rather enjoyed its decaying grandeur, and my flat was just a two-minute walk away. Extremely handy.

I had just come back from a recording session at Nova Sound Studios in Marble Arch, completing a track for my second CBS album, *Can You Hear Me OK?*. The song was 'You Keep Me Steady' and the session had gone well. Pip Williams had scored a gorgeous string arrangement and Biddu, the producer, was knocked out with the track. Life felt good as I sipped my vodka and lime. The new Peter Fonda film I'd written the theme song for, *Open Season*, had just been released into cinemas. On the way from Leicester Square tube station that evening, I'd noticed my name on a poster for the movie – 'Casting Shadows performed by CBS Artiste John Howard' it read along the bottom. If I'd had a mobile phone back in those days it would now be in my photo collection.

I was considering whether I should have a meal at the Stockpot eaterie round the corner or go home and do myself a salad, when I noticed two blokes looking at me from their table in the Snug. With sinking heart, I realised it was Anthony and Paul. They whispered something to each other and, thrusting his hands into his pockets, Paul got up and came over.

"Hi!" he said, smiling amiably amidst shoulders that looked even more rounded than I remembered.

"Hello, Paul," I said, as non-committal as I could.

"You look great!" he said brightly.

Unable to honestly return the compliment, I just thanked him and sipped my drink.

"Er, would you mind if Anthony came and spoke to you? He has something he wants to say."

I clapped my hand to my face in mock horror,

"Oh God! He doesn't want to read me a poem, does he?"

A reluctantly withheld giggle made Paul's shoulders bob up and down, like a broken down jack-in-the-box.

"No, he's stopped writing those, thank God."

"Well, as long as he doesn't vomit on me, try to stab or strangle me, I don't see why not."

He looked over and waved at Anthony, mouthing 'Come on!'.

As I watched the man, who'd meant so much to me four years earlier, shuffle towards me like a beaten dog, I thought, 'My word, life has not been kind to you, my dear.'

"Hi," he said. "You look really great."

Ditto Paul's compliment, I just said, "Thanks."

He looked strangely smaller than I remembered and, with an irony only I was aware of, he said,

"You look taller."

"Are you here for the weekend?" I asked him.

"No," he took a swig of his drink. "We live here."

I tried to hide the expression on my face, but as though he'd read it, he said,

"We live in the East End, Shoreditch. We don't usually come this side of London."

"Right," I said. 'Thank God for that,' I thought.

"Do you live near here?" Paul asked.

I wasn't about to tell them that my flat was just three doors down the road.

"Quite near," I said.

"So, what are you up to now?"

I took great pleasure in going into a lot of detail. I'd got to the point in my story where I'd just been told that I was going to be performing my new single, on a BBC TV show starring Johnny Mathis and Lynsey de Paul, when Paul checked his watch:

"That's really good to hear, Howard," he said with a frozen smile, "but we have to get back." Anthony looked at him meaningfully. "But I'll leave you two to chat for a few minutes."

Anthony waited for us to be alone then moved closer in. I automatically stepped back.

'Just you dare,' I thought.

"I just want to say…" Anthony began nervously. "That I am really sorry for the way I treated you."

So you should be, I thought, but said, "Thank you."

"You're a really good person and I was very bad to you. I was a very fucked up person back then."

"Indeed you were, on both counts."

"Yes, well, I'm sorry."

"Did Paul tell you to say this?"

He flushed up, and I momentarily thought he was going to have one of his strops and throw his beer over my head. Instead, he smiled rather sadly and said, "No. I've been wanting to apologise ever since that night. You know, when I – ".

"There he is!" a familiar voice shouted behind me. I turned round to see my boyfriend, Bry, coming in. The difference between the two men could not have been greater. Blonde, rugged and tanned from the Jo'burg sun he lived under, Bry made Anthony look oddly parochial and even smaller.

"Hi gorgeous," he said, hugging me. Then, looking at Anthony, "who's your friend?"

"Bry, this is Anthony. We were at art college together."

Bry extended his hand and said, "Nice to meet you, Antony!" – I didn't correct him – "You must be very proud of this guy. Not only gorgeous but talented as well!"

Bry's pride was Anthony's discomfort. He sort of sidled on the spot and giggled out a weak,

"Yes. He is. OK then…" he waved over at Paul who was getting up to leave, "it was nice seeing you, Howard. 'Bye!"

He scurried back to his table and picked up a couple of carrier bags. He and Paul nodded at us and left.

"Weird bloke!" Bry said laughing. "What did you see in *him*?"

"How did you know?"

"The way he looked at you. That 'why did I let this one go?' look."

"It's a long story," I replied.

"I'm all ears…over dinner."

As we left the pub, Anthony and Paul were standing at a bus stop. Bry hailed a cab and, as we got in, I smiled over at them. Anthony watched as we sped by.

"Missing him already?" Bry asked.

"Hardly."

Chapter Eleven

The Exquisites

'The future belongs to the dandy. It is The Exquisites who are going to rule.'

Oscar Wilde

Glam Rock, like Merseybeat nine years earlier, arrived just when British Pop needed it most. It also, like its Liverpudlian predecessor, harboured impostors. In 1963, after ditching the Brylcreem, many previously unsuccessful acts adopted a Mop Top fringe, put on a suit and tie, pulled on Beatle Boots and aped the Mersey sound. It was the route to success in the charts which had eluded them. In 1972, artists and bands, similarly desperate for a hit record after years of releasing flops, or at best so-so singles, raided their sisters' wardrobes and jewellery boxes and took the glitter plunge. They pinned on big garish earrings, squeezed themselves into glittery over-tight outfits and caked their faces with badly-applied make-up. After practicing walking in five-inch platform heel boots in front of their bedroom mirrors, banging their heads a few times on the lampshade, they clumped excitedly out onto streets now suddenly paved with golden glitz.

Like transformed Cinderellas at the Glam Rock Ball, their new image and sound offered them the Prince Charming of record deals, singles in the charts and glittery appearances on Top of The Pops.

Glam Rock appeared like a multi-coloured rocket in the sky. Everyone went 'Wooo!' as it billowed out twinkly gorgeous stars for a short while. Then, when people had moved their gaze onto something different and more interesting, it fizzled out and fell to the ground. Its burnt-out stars floated gently down, their beautiful but temporary lights fading. As they lay forgotten and ignored by the screaming crowds in the next field, a kid in torn jeans and safety-pinned T-shirt stomped on them and yelled "Anarchy!" .

Glam's main protagonists and leaders in the parade, Marc Bolan and David Bowie, were, again like those who'd fronted the Mersey Boom of 1963, artists who had been around for years. Through the mid-to-late-'60s, they'd both gigged and released several records under various monikers, trying out several images, and playing with different bands. In the end, as with the Merseybeat stars, fame and fortune only came knocking when they created something new, entirely their own and, because the time was right, wildly exciting to millions.

But it was Bolan who had actually lit the flame. In November 1970, Marc took a match to the very blue-grey touch paper of the British Hit Parade, and set off one of the most eagerly-awaited firework displays in pop music.

I became initially a 'distant shore' fan of Marc Bolan when, in 1969, my school friend Pauline first played me *Unicorn*. Tyrannosaurus Rex stared beautifully out at us from the L.P. sleeve, which I remember was a glossy gorgeous thing. Marc and his fellow Rex-er, percussionist Steve Peregrin-Took, made a great noise together, a surprisingly big noise for two such elfinesque pretty chaps. Occasionally given an even more panoramic sound by their producer Tony Visconti on piano, the duo impressed me greatly.

I particularly liked 'The Seal of Seasons', with its lovely falsetto backing vocals and catchy chorus, *'Just like a prancer, a gypsy dancer'*, and 'Cat Black', with lines like *'Spun in lore from Dagamore'*. Marc's lyrics wove fantastical tales, poems set to music, with their Lord of The Rings construction and fairytale woodland-warlock imagery. Indeed, Took, born Stephen Ross-Porter, had renamed himself after a Tolkien Hobbit character.

The songs were all presented with Marc's heavily strummed acoustic guitar, accompanied by Took's wild bongo slapping and occasional bangs on bits of a drum kit. Together they created a sound you couldn't find anywhere or from anyone else. It was cute without being cloying. Hippie-esque without being over-long. With short catchy melodies and hooks, it was pop-py without being Pop.

And then there was Bolan's voice. His warbly mangling of the English language, strangulated vowels and bizarrely hiccuped words, tripped and skipped along over the acoustic ocean Marc and Took skilfully helmed. I found it fascinating and, again, unlike anything else around at the time. Of course, odd vocal styles in popular music were nothing new. Buddy Holly had hiccuped and cackled his Texan way to No.1 more than ten years earlier, followed by his British imitator Adam Faith; at the same time, Elvis had burbled and gurgled his way into teenage hearts and the global charts.

The Beatles had promoted a much less mannered way of singing, but they still kept a decidedly American accent in their delivery. Bolan brought something entirely different. Hippie fey, beautifully tousled, this warbly, wobbly-voiced girlishly pretty man sang in a very posh, very English, enunciated voice. Every consonant was pronounced with a kind of camp sibilance, every vowel stretched surreally out of shape.

Consequently, his lyrics were often hard to understand or grasp. They became more a sound, a light drone, a fairyland wobbly chant. He actually sounded as though he lived and made music in a forest. Even more delightful, Bolan made words up, e.g. 'doopy-doopy doi doi', to provide his own vocalised bass and rhythm lines. His music made one smile. Always.

There was actually an odd commerciality to what Tyrannosaurus Rex were coming up with, which separated them from the currently big-selling singer-songwriter, albums-only brigade. The Incredible String Band were doing something similar in terms of woodland, whimsical, pastoral folk music. But their songs, unlike Bolan's, were never written with an ear to what could possibly – just possibly – be a hit single.

On the other hand, it was all too strange and otherworldly, in fact a million miles away from what mainstream pop radio was playing in the late '60s, to ensure anything like singles chart superiority.

Most people in the know believed (and their big fan, John Peel, hoped), that Tyrannosaurus Rex would forever remain a niche act. They were selling enough albums to the Uni and Hippie crowd to mildly, briefly, dent the UK Top 30. The duo even had a couple of singles, 'Debora' and 'One Inch Rock', played by their gushing fan Peel enough times to see them briefly trouble the lower echelons of the UK Hit Parade. 'Yes,' many pundits decided, they were 'fun to have around, and brightened the place up a bit.' But pop idol? Marc Bolan...? 'Never!'

In the Spring of 1970, I heard a record on the radio which pricked up my ears and intrigued me. It was the new one by Tyrannosaurus Rex, called 'By The Light of A Magical Moon'. It had a great melody, some lovely guitar licks – was that an electric guitar I heard??! - and featured that familiar, strangulated sibilant warble out front. *'I'll barefoot dance – da-dance, with my baby – a-baby, by the la-light of a ma-magical moon – alright!', Marc trilled*, like a pixie inviting us to a lovely party in the woods. This new one, though, was much poppier than anything on *Unicorn* and I thought, 'Ooh, that sounds like a hit!'. It wasn't, in fact it didn't even touch the Top 40, but I liked it enough to go to my local record shop and buy the brand new album it came off, *Beard Of Stars*.

Another great quality L.P. sleeve showed a black and white slightly fuzzed photo of Bolan on the front, his curly hair now cascading down his back. On the back sleeve there was...no, not Peregrin-Took, but another chap, who Pauline told me was one Mickey Finn. I loved the album, it was full of what I could see as potential hit singles (what did I know?). The urgently compelling 'Fist Heart, Mighty Dawn Dart' –

which today, over forty-five years later, sits amidst my iPod 'Gorgeous' playlist – frenetically bounced along with a great chorus, *'Funny how the day comes, funny how the day comes slow-oh-woh!'*. 'Woodland Bop', a very cute dancey number, was short on lyrics but made up for that with their beauty, *'In the hallowed morning see her in the moon-white, streaking across the skies.'* 'Great Horse' was another lovely piece, with adept, evocative lyrics, *'Tall bowman from the burnt pastures, saw Champer and he bowed, ground kissing to his lord, Strange beastie from the legend lair, Sire, I can master with the aide of this skull-powdered cord.'* The majestic 'Dove', which soared within a stunning melody, wound around a simply, but eruditely, told love song, *'All my days are leafy blue, because I'm not with you, All my words are ragged steel when I'm not with you, See how the sun shines like an arc where you walk.'*

The album was full of gloriously melodic folk-pop, the songs creating their own special scenarios, like temples built in landscapes from another world. It also boasted a much fuller sound than before. Marc was, yes, occasionally playing electric as well as acoustic guitar, there were more backing vocals and percussion, and an altogether more dynamic, tighter pop sound. The Lord of The Rings-style lyrics were still there, but somehow simplified and more accessible. And of course, there was the astonishing album closer, 'Elemental Child'. It was Eddie Cochrane Rock'n'Roll meets 1970 Hippie Folk. A message was being sent to his fans, though, at that point, they weren't really hearing it.

The truth was, Marc was challenging himself and his listeners, progressing, albeit gently, to another level. I had a definite feeling that Bolan was now onto something, and in time would hit paydirt. He just needed *that* record to do it.

One evening in mid-November, I was mildly enjoying watching Christie perform their latest Top Ten hit, 'San Bernadino', quite fancying a hairy-chested bloke called Neil Diamond growling out 'Cracklin' Rosie', and yawning during White Plains' 'Julie Do Ya Love Me'. It was the usual 1970 Top Of The Pops fare, not bad but not great MOR pop. Tony Blackburn chuckled on set, bobbed his head around and almost had me heading for the kettle, when his next announcement kept me in my seat:

"Okay everyone! Now we have a new name to many of you, with their first Top 30 hit record, in at No.30 this week, it's T.Rex!"

The camera panned quickly right, and there stood Marc Bolan. Electric guitar to the fore a la Chuck Berry, his wild corkscrew hair blowing in the wind of beckoning stardom, he was a cameraman's dream. As he warbled out the utterly wonderful 'Ride A White Swan' – 'Wear a tall hat like the people of the Beltane, wear your hair long, girl, you can't go wrong' - he pouted and preened, clicked his head and neck like a catwalk model, and shimmied his pink-jacketed shoulders at the gawping girls out front. Charmingly, constantly, he always found the camera, wherever it was, and then watched himself on the monitor. With a "Look mum, it's me on the telly!" smile, you could almost read his mind – 'This is what I was born to do! I look fabulous!!'. You could also read the minds of millions of teenage TOTP viewers. As one, they went 'Wow!'. I remember thinking, 'At last! A new bona fide pop star! He has finally arrived!'.

Bolan had, with one glorious single, exploded across the pop galaxy, and bopped sensationally into kids' hearts. He'd thrown down the mantle, claiming the deserted crown which The Beatles had thrown aside months earlier. It suited him well. And, for a while, it looked like it would sit on his head for some time to come…

One morning before Christmas, a college friend of mine, Dave told me that T.Rex were playing a gig in Blackburn that weekend.

"Do you want to go?"

Not knowing what to expect, I said yes.

It was an unforgettable evening…Marc wandered on unannounced to a full-house and smiled at the audience, who wafted patchouli oil round the room as they applauded him. He sat on a pink satin cushion, placed centre stage on the floor by a stage-hand a few minutes earlier, as a shy Mickey Finn followed him on and took up his place stage left on a tall set of bongos.

"Hi, thanks for coming, it's cool to see you all!" Marc said in his lovely lisping London brogue, "I hope you like our music tonight."

The duo launched into 'Salamanda Palaganda', a song I didn't know. As though reading my mind, Dave leaned over and whispered, "It's from *Prophets, Seers and Sages*," and I made a note to self to buy that one very soon. For forty five minutes, Marc thrilled the hippie crowd with acoustic gems from his first four albums - Dave kindly enlightening me to songs I didn't know, prompting another note to self, 'Must buy *My People Were Fair*' as well.'

Bolan was utterly delightful, looked gorgeous in his little pink satin top, green slacks and powder blue pixie slippers. His curls bobbed about as he beamed over at Mickey, grooving to the rhythms they were creating together. During the final number, I think it was 'One Inch Rock', I heard a stifled squeak of 'Marc!' from the back of the theatre, followed by a couple of other similar girlish squeals. The rest of the audience didn't seem to notice. They were too busy gently swaying their long manes in time to the music, feeling as one, wholly part of Marc and Mickey's enchanted gathering. Head-banded girls sitting with their boyfriends were smiling, but much too cool to squeal their hero's name.

"Okay," Marc said at the end of the song, standing up and wandering over to a mike next to Mickey, "we'll be back in about fifteen minutes…hold on for some fun!"

As Dave and his girlfriend Christine and I stood in the bar during the interval, I noticed a distinctly young crowd of girls hovering by the doors which led into the theatre. Many of them were wearing Marc

Bolan T-Shirts, holding copies of 'Ride A White Swan' and giggling every time one of them kissed Marc's photo on the sleeve. Nearby, a bunch of long-haired guys, resolutely ignoring the cooing teenagers, were downing their pints and discussing the finer points of 'Stacey Grove'.

"Yeah, he's a nice guy, man!" one of them said, laughing at his own in-joke.

"Cool gig," said another. "I thought he'd gone 'pop'."

"Yeah. So did I. But he's still the same. The commercial stuff pays the rent, but he knows what his real fans want."

Just then, a statuesque bald-headed woman wandered by and headed for the Ladies.

"My God," the first chap said, open-mouthed. "That was June Child!"

"Marc's wife," Dave quietly prompted me.

"What's she done to her *hair*?" the second guy said, horrified.

"Oh my *God!*" they both moaned.

After the interval we took our seats as the room filled back up. I noticed the pink satin cushion had gone, while, resting against a speaker, there stood a white sparkly electric guitar. It emitted a low static buzz which matched the mumbling hum of concerned hippies, spreading round the theatre. As a white light hit it like a star-bolt, Marc strode on in a gold satin jacket, silver satin pants, silver-sprayed boots, and a sequinned T-Shirt. He put his hands on his hips, revealing 'NYC Rocks!' emblazoned across his chest, shook his curls provocatively, and gave the audience the thumbs-up sign. Nodding at an expectantly nervous Finn, he strapped on the guitar and walked to the mike, now centre stage where the cushion had been.

"Hi everyone! You're still here!" he giggled and I was struck at how charming he was. "Okay, we're gonna do something new now, and it goes like this…"

He slammed his hand into his screeching guitar strings like a stroppy electrified pixie, screamed out a lung-throttling "Oooowwww!" and 'Rip Off' hit us like a bomb blast.

Two things then happened…several shell-shocked hippies began standing up, pointing at the stage angrily and chanting 'Traitor! Traitor!', while a whole group of the girls I'd seen during the interval aptly let rip and ran to the front of the stage, screaming their heads off. At that, huge swathes of the sheepskin-and-jeans brigade angrily got up and walked out, shouting 'Sell-Out!' as they left. Bolan, obliviously, was having a marvellous time. He strutted across the stage, phallically jutting his guitar out at the growing groups of fans who had crowded at the front. They waved and screeched, singing along with every number, arms held aloft their yelling heads. The place was bedlam. It was wonderful.

During a searingly brilliant guitar solo, Marc looked up and beamed at them all. It resulted in even louder screaming. He then launched into 'Raw Ramp'. 'Oooh woman, I love your chest, ooh baby I'm crazy 'bout your breasts' he sang, shaking drenched curls at his adoring hysterical fans. I was wondering if the song would prompt some mass ripping off of blouses, but thankfully it didn't.

I looked at Dave, who shrugged his shoulders, glanced at Christine, and the three of us stood up and boogied for the rest of the evening. I was exhilarated. I had witnessed the birth of the UK's new pop superstar. Even the mass walk-out of his hippie fans thrilled me.

"It's like Dylan goes electric all over again!" I yelled at Dave through the ear-splitting rock, which two tiny little guys were making on stage.

Marc finished the astonishing evening with, of course, 'Ride A White Swan', and there wasn't a person in there who wasn't jumping up and down, singing along – 'Catch a bright star and place it on your forehead, say a few spells and baby there you go', we trilled ecstatically. I was in love.

The week that 'Ride A White Swan' peaked at No.2, at the end of January, Dave came into college one morning with *T.Rex*, Marc's brand new album. He put it on the record player and by track 2, 'Jewel', I was literally dancing round the room. Marc had lessened the warble and concentrated on writing even catchier fantastic melodies and hooks, through fifteen terrific pop nuggets. They included the instantly adorable 'The Time of Love Is Now' and 'The Visit', while beautiful string arrangements adorned the likes of 'Diamond Meadows' and 'The Children of Rarn'. He boogied with ease through 'Is It Love' and the sensational Motownesque 'Beltane Walk' – *'Gimme love, gimme little love, gimme little love from your heart, and then we'll-a-walk'*, he chirruped to thousands of new adoring fans. The song also hinted at a bisexuality we hadn't heard from pop stars before. It would come to define the Glam Rock movement: *'Walking down by the west wind, I met a boy he was my friend, I said Boy, we could sing it too, and we do – ooh!'*. On so many levels, the album set a new bar in the creation of fun, commercial pop music for a new decade.

While *T.Rex* was still riding high in the Top Ten, Marc released his new single, 'Hot Love'. It got blanket airplay on pop radio and hit the Top 20 first week of release.

"Have you heard the new T.Rex single?" my friend Anita exclaimed, eyes wide with amused shock. "I mean, really – *'well she ain't no witch and I love the way she twitch, ah-ha-ha'*. Who does he think he is? The new Elvis fucking Presley?!"

'Yes,' I thought, 'That is exactly who he thinks he is. And he's absolutely right.'

Glam Rock, of which Bolan is rightfully credited with being the creator, actually began rather by accident in March 1971, when T.Rex appeared on Top of The Pops to perform 'Hot Love'. Marc now fronted a bona fide band, a four-piece consisting of him and Finn now broadened out with drummer Bill Legend and bassist Steve Currie. Before going in front of the cameras, Marc had two spots of glitter placed under his eyes. The studio lights caught them beautifully as Bolan preened and pouted his way through what would be his biggest-selling single yet. A simple rolling rock rhythm trotted along as he intoned gleefully, 'She's my woman of gold and she's not very old, ah-ha-ha'. Toss of curls. 'I'm her two-penny prince and I'll give her Hot Love, ah-ha-ha!'.

The ending alone ensured it would hit No.1. With the repetitive intoxicating chant of La-la-la's, interspersed with Marc's little spoken bits of sexy hokum as he stomped gorgeously in front of his new band, a nation sang along and took it to No.1, where it remained for six weeks. The single became the UK's Spring pop anthem overnight.

His shows were now entirely peopled by screaming girls, the hippies had left the theatre for good, even John Peel derided Marc publicly for 'selling out'. T.Rexstasy had been born, and Bolan's starry glittery face was splashed across every music magazine, Sunday supplement and pop music TV show. T.Rex became the biggest selling British pop band since The Beatles. The T.Rex album stayed in the UK charts for over six months, while alongside it his record company cheekily issued an extremely premature 'Best of T.Rex' compilation to cash in on their most successful act ever. It too hit the Top 30 with ease. But the best was yet to come.

That summer, T.Rex once again appeared on Top of The Pops to perform their new No.1 single, the stunning Chuck Berry-riff-happy, 'Get It On'. Marc even quoted a line from Berry's 'Little Queenie' as the track faded – 'and meanwhile, I'm still thinkin''. Elton John, then a burgeoning pop star with just one UK Top Ten hit and a Top Three album to his name, sat in on piano for some of the TOTP sessions (though he was actually miming to Rick Wakeman's playing on the record). The track was augmented with terrific sax riffs, courtesy of King Crimson's Iain McDonald, and the falsetto backing vocals of the former lead singers from one of America's big pop groups of the '60s, The Turtles.

Mark Volman and Howard Kaylan had hit it big during The Summer Of Love with the ecstatically multi-harmonied 'Happy Together', the even better 'She'd Rather Be With Me', and their brilliant '68 pop song send up, 'Elenore' – 'You're my pride and joy, etcetera'. Now with flowing locks and renamed 'Flo & Eddie', they became as much 'the sound of T.Rex' over the next couple of years as Marc himself. In fact Volman was once quoted as saying that when Marc stopped using them, his records stopped selling. Whatever the truth of this, they certainly added a new gloss to T.Rex's productions, usually singing a full octave above Bolan, whose vocal range was in fact quite limited.

In October, T.Rex's new album, *Electric Warrior* got rave reviews, huge sales figures and topped the UK charts for weeks. It was Marc's last bona fide release on the indie Fly Records. He'd begun negotiations with EMI to start up his own label, T.Rex Hot Wax, so Fly cutely released a track from 'Warrior' as a single to ensure they had at least one more Bolan smash for Christmas. It worked. Even without the band promoting it at all on TV, 'Jeepster' smashed into the Top 10 within a week. Because T.Rex were by then so huge, just the sight of another slice of Bolan on vinyl was leapt on and snapped up by his ever-hungry fans. They were already screaming their heads off whenever Marc performed the song on stage, as he got down on his knees and sang, *'Girl I'm just a vampire for your love, and I'm gonna suck ya!'* to a sea of waving arms.

The single stayed in the Top Three for seven weeks, and even though its release pissed Marc off, it actually set up his next venture rather brilliantly. It ensured that his profile stayed high, as 1971 came to an end and 1972 dawned. When he released his first Hot Wax single in January, 'Telegram Sam' – *'Me I funk, but I don't care, I'm no square with my corkscrew hair, Telegram Sam, you're my Main Man!'* – 'Jeepster' was still hovering around the lower echelons of the Top 40.

'Sam' entered the charts at No.3 and climbed effortlessly to No.1

the following week. T.Rex were officially named the biggest selling singles group of 1971, with *Electric Warrior* one of the Top Five best selling albums of the year. It was a tremendous feat of self-belief and sheer hard work which, in just two years, had lifted Marc Bolan from cult hippie elfin troubadour to the biggest thing in pop Britain had seen for eight years.

In April 1972, while 'Telegram Sam', was still in the charts, and their reissued *Prophets, Seers & Sages* album was at No.1, I was offered a job selling posters at one of their Manchester gigs. It was an outdoor show and the deal was I did the hawking for nothing but got in free to see the band play. I was struck straight away by not only the size of the audience, but their average age. All of them, bar me and a mate who'd also sold Marc posters before the show, were pre-pubescent teenagers – teeny boppers. They all sported glitter and stars on their cheeks and screeched Marc's name before he'd even taken the stage. Once he appeared my ears began to hurt, as thousands of girls bellowed and yelled, screeched and screamed 'Marc! Marc!' for two hours. At the age of only nineteen, I felt rather old.

What also stayed with me afterwards was how aggressively the kids screamed at Bolan to 'Stand up!' when he'd sat on his little pink cushion to perform 'Debora', which had recently been reissued by Marc's former label, Fly, and was rapidly climbing into the Top 10. T.Rex's audiences were now so huge, with everybody standing screeching their heads off every time Bolan so much as scratched his nose, they actually couldn't see him sitting on the floor any longer. Met with a barrage of screams and yells as he stood up to do 'Get It On', Marc was the kids' property now. They had invested many pounds buying his releases and they wanted their money's worth.

The following month, T.Rex released their biggest selling single, 'Metal Guru'. It was a glorious Spector-ish Visconti production, utterly huge sounding from the get-go, and enormously successful. Flo & Eddie wailed gorgeously along as Marc sang what was in fact a very simple song with a chugging infectious riff, repeating several times the same chant-like lines, 'Metal Guru, is it you, all alone without a telephone, Metal Guru, could it be, you're gonna bring my baby to me?, Metal Guru, is it you, she'll be wild, you know a rock 'n' roll child'. It was all rather nonsensical but totally fabulous. It stayed at No.1 for four weeks and one began to think that this guy could do no wrong. But there was trouble ahead...

T.Rex's summer '72 album, The Slider, coincided with the band's concentrated attempt to break America. They spent weeks over there gigging and trying to repeat the modest Top Ten success they'd had in The States a year earlier with 'Get It On' ('Bang A Gong' as it was renamed there). It meant that, while the cats were away, the new kittens on the block came out to play. A new band of Glam Rock pretenders to the throne, who'd been waiting in the wings, were ready to pounce and steal Marc's glittery crown.

Former skinhead combo Slade had reinvented themselves in 1971 as everybody's mates, with brilliant, sing-along football chant chart-toppers like 'Coz I Luv U', 'Mama Weer All Crazee Now' and 'Take Me Bak 'Ome', the misspelled titles a direct attempt at appealing to school-kids (or 'skoolkidz'). But whereas they had initially struck gold with a mainly male audience, as opposed to the T.Rex teen-girl fans, their image gradually changed. In evermore radiant appearances on Top of The Pops, they began donning sequinned hats, ever higher glittery platform boots, promoting an altogether more Glam Rock image. As the group's guitarist, Dave Hill, paraded up and down TV sets like some glammed-up Boadicea, they became the assumed successors to the T.Rexstasy dynasty. It was reminiscent of when The Rolling Stones had vied for The Beatles' top pop position in the '60s – though The Stones never quite pulled the coup off.

Other Glam contenders were also hitting the chart highs. Gary Glitter, formerly failed '60s pop singer Paul Raven née Gadd, shot into the UK Top Three with his Mike Leander-created 'Rock 'n' Roll Parts One & Two', setting up what became a two-year career as the Baco-Foil Prince of Glam. Art-rock band Roxy Music, fronted by glamorously sleazy lounge lizard Bryan Ferry, and the futuristically adorned Eno on electronic keyboards, hit No.4 with their divine debut single, 'Virginia Plain'. With its exotic Hollywood-esque lyrics, *'Baby Jane's in Acapulco, we are flying down to Rio!'* warbled out in true Bolanesque style, it ensured glitter fans, starved of seeing Marc on TOTP for the summer, bought it in the hundreds of thousands.

While I loved Roxy, I always found them slightly detached. They looked beautiful and otherworldly, but they could never be yours. Look, admire, but don't touch. As he sneered stylishly on TV, Ferry's fans were, in effect, being given an audience by their louche Lord of Leopardskin Pop. Keeping the Vogue-ish glamour, they featured top models on their album sleeves. Kari-Ann Muller lay draped on a rug on the band's eponymous debut L.P., while the stilettoed fully-fashioned legs of Amanda Lear paraded a jaguar on a shiny lead on their second – and finest album, *For Your Pleasure*. That L.P. included the Roxy single that should have been, the utterly fabulous 'Do The Strand': *'Tired of the Tango, fed up with Fandango, dance on moonbeams, slide on rainbows, in furs or blue jeans, you know what I mean, Do The Strand'.*

But there was another, much more significant threat to Bolan's still-accepted place as The King of Glam Rock. One David Bowie, the late-starter in the Glam Rock race. He'd hit the UK Top 5 in September 1969, with his single 'Space Oddity', promoting a rather fey, gentle persona as he smiled nervously at the camera and strummed his jangly guitar. His odd, rather doomy little song about 'Major Tom', a spaceman lost amongst the stars, struck a chord with a public still mesmerised by the recent first manned moon landing. But, as quickly as he had apparently appeared in the firmament, Bowie had fallen down pop's hungry black hole. Unlike Apollo 11, he failed to return to Earth, unable to follow-up his novelty hit single. There he stayed, *'floating round my tin can, far above the moon,'* until in 1972, Major Tom metamorphosed into a certain Ziggy Stardust...

In the Spring of that year, Melody Maker had featured Bowie on its front cover, looking foppishly coiffured and heavily made-up, with the headline 'I suppose I'm bi-sexual'. The piece, along with some small but significant gigs around Britain with his new band The Spiders From Mars, encouraged music buyers of both sexes and all persuasions to try out his recently-released offering, the album *Hunky Dory*.

It featured on the sleeve a long-haired David, heavily made-up and cleverly tinted to give him the appearance of a movie starlet. It was actually a look he'd already ditched, having also used it on his previous, unsuccessful album, *The Man Who Sold The World*. The image chameleon Bowie was, as became the case throughout the rest of his career, ahead of the fans.

Within that divinely decadent wrapping there inhabited some great songs. The utterly camp 'Queen Bitch' harkened back to Velvet Underground – *'Well, I'm up on the eleventh floor and I'm watching the cruisers below'*, and the sumptuous chorus, delightedly self-mocking his previous image, *'She's so swishy in her satin and tat, in her frock coat and bippety boppety hat, oh God, I could do better than that!'*. 'Life On Mars?' was a pop symphony extraordinaire, featuring probably David's greatest ever melody and a breathtaking lyric, *'Sailors fighting in the dance hall, oh man, look at those cavemen go, it's the freakiest show, Take a look at the lawman beating up the wrong guy, oh man, wonder if he'll ever know, he's in the best-selling show, Is there life on Mars?'*.

And then there was the stunning album closer, 'The Bewlay Brothers'. It knocked me sideways when I first heard it. 'Good God,' I thought, 'Something incredible just entered my life.' It talked of *'mind-warp pavilions'*, *'the crutch-hungry dark'*, and how *'Their heads of brawn were nicer shorn, and how they bought their positions with saccharin and trust'*. *'It was stalking time for the Moonboys,'* Bowie yelled gloriously, *'The Bewlay Brothers'*. Setting out surreal, slightly disturbing panoramas, like a screenplay writer in a moonlit park at midnight, Bowie intoned each line perfectly. He described each scene within each sculpted phrase, poetically, beautifully, set within a new intriguing scenario. He sang of times gone, like a lost Atlantis, while sounding utterly 'Now'. None of the scenes he described seemed wholly real, yet you could imagine them so easily. Like Bolan had before him, Bowie was turning the English language on its head and making it work differently. Moulding words into sentences which made no sense, and yet made perfect sense.

But, whereas Bolan had used a mix of folkish woodland whimsy and raunchy teen love as the base for his great pop songs, Bowie was using literature, surrealism and erudition to create catchy enthralling pieces. While his songs had the potential to net the teeny pop fans from Bolan's arena, they had already captured the hearts and minds of the older teenage intelligentsia. This was perfectly executed in the irrepressible 'Changes': *'I watch the ripples change their size, but never leave the stream of warm impermanence, and so the days float through my eyes, but still the days seem the same, and these children that you spit on as they try to change their worlds, are immune to your consultations, they're quite aware of what they're going through, Ch-ch-ch-ch-changes, don't tell them to grow up and out of it'*. We had a new spokesman for all teenage youth, our generation's Dylan, in fact.

When Bowie sang *'Oooh, look out you rock 'n' rollers, pretty soon now you're gonna get older'*, it was like a direct challenge to Bolan, who had constantly alluded to his fans wanting him to 'rock' and absolutely refusing to change tack.

Indeed, Marc's producer, Tony Visconti, has been quoted as saying that he was constantly nagging Marc, during the height of T.Rexstasy, to finish his Children of Rarn Suite to give the fans something new and more challenging, to which Bolan would reply each time, "Nah, the kids want another rocker."

One Thursday evening in July '72, the nation and I were watching Top Of The Pops. There were highs in that week's programme – Roberta Flack's beautiful 'First Time Ever I Saw Your Face', Dr. Hook's plaintive country-rock odyssey, 'Sylvia's Mother', Love Unlimited's soul-pop 'Walking In The Rain With One I Love' (created, written and produced by the then-unknown Barry White), and the breathlessly breathtaking harmony-fest, 'Betcha By Golly Wow', by future soul sensation The Stylistics. But in between these gems, one made cups of tea or went to the loo while The Sweet performed their inconsequential fourth bubblegum hit, 'Little Willie', Gilbert O'Sullivan astonished me as he trilled out the truly awful 'Oh-Wakka-Doo-Wakka-Day', and The Partridge Family's 'Breaking Up is Hard To Do' indicated a new addition to the teeny-bop stable was about to emerge onto the race track. As I waited for Slade to finish the show, doing their latest chart-topping scream-a-song, 'Take Me Bak 'Ome', a new star appeared, like a newly-emerged butterfly, in front of the cameras.

In at No.29 that week with 'Starman', David Bowie shimmied up to his mike, an exotically white-faced androgynous alien with spiky red hair, and caused my mother to gasp, "My God! What is that?" While a nation's parents were simultaneously outraged, the nation's youth inwardly shouted, 'Yes!' In a tight padded jump suit, and with a confidently impudent glare at an astonished TV-viewing public, he began his gorgeous tale about a man in the sky who was coming down to meet us all, a Starman who would be a saviour for kids everywhere. 'He told me, Let the children lose it, let the children use it, let all the children boogie' went the fabulous chorus which, for good measure, pinched part of its notation from Judy Garland's *Wizard of Oz* hit 'Over The Rainbow'. How could this not fail?

And then David clinched it. He grabbed hold of his heavily mascara'd guitarist, Mick Ronson, put his arm salaciously over his shoulder and made lyrical bruv-love with his band-mate in front of millions of viewers. It became a clarion call to any young person who was unsure about his or her sexuality. It said, "Come on, be like us, be yourself, it's ok. We're here now."

A couple of weeks later, I was at a college disco when the DJ put on a track which stopped me dead as I was going to the bar: *'A soldier with a broken arm fixed his stare to the wheel of a Cadillac, a cop knelt and kissed the feet of a priest and a queer threw up at the sight of that,'* it gave me goosebumps. I sat down and listened as the singer, whose voice I recognised as Bowie's, wailed, *'We got five years, stuck on my eyes, five years, what a surprise!'*. But there was more, the next track – *'Soul love, the priest that tastes the word and told of love, and how my God on high is all love, though reaching up my loneliness evolves by the blindness that surrounds him.'* 'Moonage Daydream' then slammed out across the hall, *'Keep your mouth shut, you're squawking like a pink money bird, and I'm muzzing up my brain for the words'*. It sent me into an ecstasy as the chorus told us all to, *'Keep your 'lectric eye on me, babe, hold your ray gun to my head, press your space face close to mine, love, Freak out to a Moonage Daydream, oh-yeah'*.

As Ronson's supersonic guitar screamed gloriously around the hall in the track's fade-out, I walked over to the DJ.

"What is this album?" I asked him, just as 'Starman' ooh-hoo-hoo'd out of the speakers.

He proudly gave me the sleeve. *Ziggy Stardust & the Spiders From Mars*, with its orange-haired space troubadour grinning out at the world, became my Must-Have Summer '72 album.

Up in my bedroom during those hot days and nights, I soaked

in every nuance, every camp yelp and sexual innuendo. I stood in front of the mirror, miming that pointing limp hand gesture Bowie had wiggled at the camera during his 'Starman' TV performance – '*I had to phone someone so I picked on you-hoo-hoo*' - and fell in love with David Ziggy Bowie. There is no doubt that my own song-writing style changed forever with that album. Its influence on me was as big as Roy Harper's had been two years earlier, as huge as my late discovery of Dylan had been a year earlier. In effect, it set the template for *Kid In A Big World*. Shortly after buying *Ziggy Stardust* I wrote 'Small Town, Big Adventures' and 'Third Man'.

Ziggy was a brilliant creation, born of a clever Magpie's imagination and nous. It was as though Bowie had been wondering just what he could do to achieve the pop domination his mate Marc was enjoying. One can imagine him, sitting on the balcony of Haddon Hall, his decaying grandeur mansion in Beckenham, sometime in 1971, and thinking, 'Now, what was successful for me before? – a song about space travel. And what's selling now? – great pop songs by a beautifully androgynous man wearing make-up. Hm.'

"Angie!" he'd (possibly) called to his wife, "what do you think about this idea?"

However he arrived at it, David had struck gold. By September, both *Ziggy Stardust* and the previously critically welcomed, but low-selling, *Hunky Dory* were in the albums Top Five.

That month, Bolan re-emerged from his failed American tour with 'Children of The Revolution', a track lifted off August's under-performing *The Slider*, which had surprised everyone – not least I would imagine Marc Bolan - by failing to dent the UK Top Three. The track was slower than usual for a T.Rex single, with quite a good chunky rhythm and an excellent cello arrangement. As had become his norm by then, it was full of both self-reverential references, aligned with car images to create a glossy dynamism – '*I drive a Rolls Royce 'cause it's good for my voice*' - along with a rather self-conscious 'nod to the kids' chorus, *'But you won't fool the children of the revolution, no-no-no'.*

It was roundly beaten to the punch by the latest offering from new teeny-bopper screamathon, American TV actor turned pop star, Partridge Family front-man, David Cassidy. 'How Can I Be Sure?' leapfrogged the T.Rex '45' to No.1, after Marc had been been kept off the top spot the previous week by Slade's 'Mama Weer All Crazee Now'. Somehow, the writing was being quickly scribbled on the wall.

Bowie increased the pressure by hitting the Top 20 in October with the out-and-out bisexual love song, 'John, I'm Only Dancing' - *'She turns me on, but I'm only dancing, don't get me wrong, I'm only dancing, oh John!'* - and in November his first two albums, which had failed to make a mark when first released, now repackaged with Ziggy photos replacing the originals, also entered the Top 30.

In December, T.Rex issued, with almost indecent haste, the riff-laden, frantically breathless 'Solid Gold Easy Action', once again full of the usual self-aggrandising nonsense lyrics, *'All my hair will keep her smiling, with my wondrous walk and my telephone dialling'.* It reached No.2, but was knocked off that perch after just one week by Bowie's grindingly gorgeous 'Jean Genie', his pop peon to the openly gay author, Jean Genet. *'The Jean Genie lives on his back, the Jean Genie loves chimney stacks, he's outrageous, he screams and he bawls, Jean Genie, let yourself go!'.*

And it wasn't just Bowie who was proving that you could still make it big in your mid-twenties, still achieve pop superstardom, if the time - and the music - is right. The newly-glammed-up-camped-up Elton John was in the Top Five through Christmas '72 with his '50s pastiche, 'Crocodile Rock'. Bedecked in glittery, impossibly high-heeled platform boots, star-studded jump-suits and an array of outrageously huge Designer spectacles, he was not only making waves in Britain, he had also become America's new pop darling.

Ziggy was also starting to make strides across the Atlantic too, preparing the ground for Bowie's larger-scale invasion of America's pop scene a year or so later. Meanwhile, T.Rex were never to have a hit record there again.

Although they were the best-selling UK singles group in 1972, and third in the best-selling albums category, just twelve months later T.Rex had fallen to sixth in the year's singles best sellers list, and didn't even figure in the albums listing. Cruelly, David Bowie topped both best selling listings that year.

As T.Rex's fortunes continued to fade during 1973, ironically, the Glam Rock bandwagon was firing on all cylinders. Former bubblegum group Sweet enjoyed their first No.1. 'Blockbuster', written and produced by Mickey Chinn & Mike Chapman, took every Bowie/ Bolan element known to record buyers, mixed it all together in a pseudo-hard rock coating, and crashed to the top of the charts within three weeks of entering at No.16. The band had now ditched stripy tops and summer slacks for full-on glitter-suits, caked-on make-up and girly eyelashes. Guitarist Steve Priest fluttered them prettily at the ever-ready camera as he mock-wailed, "I haven't got a clue what to do!" like a frantic housewife whose washing machine had broken down. The fact he was straight as a die meant not a jot to anyone. This wasn't Gay Pop, it was Glam Rock, and as we all know, many straight men absolutely love wearing a dress and high heels for 'fun' occasionally. Have a Vicars & Tarts party and you can be sure most of the Tarts will be the husbands.

Slade followed Sweet at the top with their fourth chart-topper, 'Cum On Feel The Noize', now equalling Bolan's four-time No.1 chart feat of the previous year. Gary Glitter hit the Top Three with 'Do You Wanna Touch Me?', equally self-obsessed as Bolan's recent fare, but with more of a twinkle in the eye. Where Marc seemed to believe in his lyrical proclamations of greatness and sexual prowess, Glitter completely sent himself up. Alice Cooper, previously a Goth-rock act from America who'd specialised in demonic on-stage displays of Draculaistic proportions, had turned campy Glam the previous summer, with the beautifully timed 'School's Out' hitting the top just as kids went on their annual six-week break. Lead singer, Vincent Furnier's devilish make-up and leather jump suit was no longer frightening the kids, it was Vaudevillian excess, which they lapped up as he camped it up like a rather creepy children's entertainer each week on TOTP, with three further Top Ten hits through '72 and '73.

Mud, another bubblegum act from the 'Chinnichapp' house of hits, began clumping about various TV studios in the prerequisite platform boots, long dangly earrings, lipstick and rouge, pouting out hit after hit, their lead guitarist becoming just a tad away from a full-on drag act. Roxy Music hit the Top Ten again with another slice of vampy art-rock, 'Pyjamarama', which burbled along prettily as Ferry leered from highlighted slitted eyelids, without ever acknowledging the fans who danced beneath him. '60s pop star Roy Wood, who had been responsible for some of the catchiest hits of that decade with his band The Move, painted his face, put on a scary wig, created a new band Wizzard and delighted hundreds of thousands with rock'n'roll gems turned Glittery stompers like 'See My Baby Jive', my own personal juke box fave during the Summer of '73.

Even former Velvet Underground man, Lou Reed, turned up in pan stick and mascara, droning out the brilliant Bowie-produced 'Walk On The Wild Side' to great effect and Top Ten honours. *'Sugar Plum Fairy never once gave it away, everybody had to pay and pay, a hustle here and a hustle there, New York City's the place where they say Hey babe! Take a walk on the wild side!'*. His lyrics told of pimps, prostitutes, drug dealers and life in the back streets, as they had always done since the '60s in songs like 'Waiting For The Man' – *'I'm waiting for my man, twenty-six dollars in my hand, up to Lexington 1-2-5, feeling sick and dirty, more dead than alive, I'm waiting for my man'* - but he now performed them with a Ziggy limp wrist and more than a handful of stardust.

Another refugee from niche world rock, Mott The Hoople, also benefited from the magic touch of Bowie the producer, as well as top-notch songwriter. He wrote the magnificent 'All The Young Dudes' for them (after they'd turned down 'Suffragette City'!), sang backing vocals on the session, and gave them their first, and biggest, hit single. He even cheekily name-checked his Glam buddy Bolan in the lyric, *'Television man is crazy, says we're juvenile delinquent wrecks, oh man, I need T.V. when I got T.Rex!'* while cleverly decrying what had gone before Glam hit the scene, *'My brother's back at home with his Beatles and his Stones, we never got it off on that Revolution stuff, too many snags, what a drag!'*. Utterly wonderful and absolutely right for its time, the single took just three weeks to crash into the Top Five. Mott were never really a Glam-Rock band but they certainly looked the part while it gave them three Top Ten smashes and a Top Ten album.

Even label owners jumped onto the Glamwagon. Peter Shelley, who co-owned Magnet Records with Michael Levy, wrote and recorded a glitter hit called 'My Coo-Ca-Choo' under the pseudonym 'Alvin Stardust'. Ripping off Norman Greenbaum's 'Spirit In The Sky' riff (as Bowie had done for 'Jean Genie' and The Sweet had done for 'Blockbuster') it entered the charts at No.50 and two weeks later had cracked the Top 30. With Pop TV producers keen to book 'Alvin' to perform his hit record, Shelley, who had no interest at that time in becoming a pop star, hired one Bernard Jewry to adopt his pseudonym and mime to the record.

It was probably a surprise to both Shelley and Jewry when 'Coo-Ca-Choo' shot to No.2 and 'Stardust' became the talk of the nation. With his leather-clad, diamond-ringed, moody guy image he took the UK by storm. Even Russell Harty had him on his chat show, featuring a hilarious non-interview when Alvin famously refused to speak to him.

Jewry was no stranger to either the pop charts, nor to the phenomenon of performing in another man's shoes. In 1960 he had been a roadie with the band Shane Fenton & The Fentones. The band's lead singer, Johnny Theakstone, died suddenly of rheumatic fever so Jewry stepped in, adopting the singer's pseudonym. The band had four Top 40 hits before going the way of most rock'n'roll acts in late '62 with the onset of Beatlemania, which swept almost all before it onto the wasteland of yesterday's heroes.

With another single demanded by his fans, Stardust/Jewry released the even more successful follow-up, 'Jealous Mind', which topped the charts in early '74, showcasing an uncannily perfect imitation of Shelley's voice. The leather-clad moody guy image, however, soon began to pall. But very adeptly, Stardust adopted a new, softer, nice-guy-next-door look, and went on to have several hits through the '80s.

Just one girl got in on the all-male Glam act. Mickie Most prodigy Suzi Quatro bopped her own leather-clad frame to No.1 with Chinnichapp infectious pop froth. 'Can The Can' and '48 Crash' were lyrically utter nonsense, but they sounded great and did the trick in cashing in on a wave of Teen-Glam fervour.

And what of Mr Bowie? Well, he did what he did throughout his career, just when we thought we had him sussed, he changed tack. Publicly killing off Ziggy Stardust to a gasping spiky-haired London audience in the summer of 1973, he replaced one alien persona with another. *Aladdin Sane* became his first No.1 album. It featured two hit singles and a swathe of dark, cascading pianoed, Orwell-esque visions of a scary post-Apocalypse future. Written while on tour in America, and reflecting the increasing paranoia he was experiencing, as success, gigging and various chemicals took over his life, the album rejected the lighter Glam-Camp which had made him a star in 1972. He continued the theme with 'Diamond Dogs' in the Summer of '74, which was filled with even doomier scenes of canine/human mutants walking city alleyways in a bleak, unforgiving landscape of the future. The hit single from the album, 'Rebel Rebel, harked back to his Ziggy sound, but now, without Ronson alongside him, it was harder and less decorative. It chilled, rather than embraced. Featuring an effective Jagger impression, David yelped his way through the UK Top Five hit which signalled the end of his particular Glam road: *'You've got your mother in a whirl, she's not sure if you're a boy or a girl... Rebel Rebel you've torn your dress, Rebel Rebel, your face is a mess, Rebel Rebel, how could they know, hot tramp, I love you so!'*. The Exquisites were in disarray, the make-up was running, the glitter had fallen, the streets were awash with the decadent remnants. The album's title track bade a final farewell, and opened the door to their destruction: *'In the year of the scavenger, the season of the bitch, sashay on the board-walk, scurry to the ditch, just another future song, lonely little kitsch, there's gonna be sorrow, try and wake up tomorrow, will they come?'*. It set the scene for his next planned chameleon-like character change. The Thin White Duke waited in the wings while Aladdin stood weeping over the body of Ziggy Stardust, torn to pieces by the Diamond Dogs. *'The Diamond Dogs are poachers and they hide behind trees, hunt you to the ground they will, mannequins with kill appeal.'*

During his Ziggy heyday, David had become the supreme creator of Theatre-Pop. Incorporating mime, costume changes, and songs which gave his fans hope that they could be whoever, whatever they chose. During 1973, his shows, and his full houses of hypnotised Ziggy lookalikes, proved that he was the new Supreme Pop Being. Even old tracks like 1971's 'Life On Mars', issued as a single with a Ziggy-upped new video, hit the Top Three.

Everyone wondered what 1974 would bring for Bowie. We needn't have worried. His White Soul tour of America was a triumph, he became the darling of U.S. chat shows and New York scenesters, and began work on what was one of his finest albums, released in the Spring of 1975, the funk-sassy *Young Americans* with its incredible title track: *'They pulled in just behind the bridge, he lays her down, he frowns, Gee my life's a funny thing, am I still too young? He kissed her then and there, she took his ring, took his babies, it took him minutes, took her nowhere, heaven knows she'd've taken anything but all night, she wants the Young American'* .

Of course, as we all know, this was just the beginning of the global domination Bowie achieved. He constantly, seamlessly, changed creative course over the next four decades, adopting, just as his fans thought they had him sussed, a dizzy array of new looks and musical styles. Brand Bowie became a self-created phenomenon, which is still in top gear years after his death in January 2016.

Through 1973, Bolan strutted about the TOTP studios ever more desperately. Clad in feather boas and increasingly heavier make-up, he began to look like one of the drag queens Lou Reed sang about. His previous, intuitively light touch had become a clumsily leaden attempt to keep up with the panto-Glam excesses of his competitors. In March, he entered the charts at a respectable No.3 with '20th Century Boy' - which is now considered one of T.Rex's classic singles. At the time, without benefit of retrospective rewriting of history, it sounded suspiciously similar to his No.1 hit of a year earlier, 'Telegram Sam'. But where that song had boasted fun lines like *'Bobby's alright, he's a natural born poet he's just outtasight!'*, and *'Purple Pie Pete, your lips are like lightning, girls melt in the heat'*, this new take on the same chord structure and melody, bombastically boasted, *'I move like a cat, charge like a ram, sting like a bee, babe I wanna be your man!'*. He growled it out and searched for the monitor, flailing his arms around his thrust-out cock-guitar. What had been fun-camp two years earlier now looked simply ridiculous. And oddly, he looked much older. As his feather boa looked ready to throttle him, he had become a pastiche of the younger, more nimble Bolan. Admittedly, the single had a very big sound, touching on an almost rock vibe, but it got no higher than its first week position. It remained there for three weeks then fell out of the Top 20 just three weeks later.

He'd guested on Cilla Black's weekly TV show earlier in the year, duetting with her on 'Life's A Gas', and performing 'Mad Donna' from the just-released *Tanx* album with the band. Looking fresh and prettily made-up, his performance with Cilla, complete with feather boa, was actually charming. The bombast was in check as he sat next to her and turned on the Bolan charm for the '60s chanteuse-turned-Family-Favourite. Ms Black obviously found him extremely alluring too, quoted as saying, "It was like being jealous of your best girlfriend. He had everything – the hair, the eyes, the makeup, the glam. The worrying thing was you did kind of fancy him, being this feminine-looking guy. But then you had the music as well, both things together, and the combination was unbelievable."

The *Tanx* sleeve pictured him sitting astride a toy tank, pumped-up pecs on view, the now mandatory feather boa slung around his neck. If it was meant to look sexy, it failed. He just looked a bit daft. It did ok chart-wise, matching *The Slider's* peak of No.4, but it hung around the charts for much less time and spawned no hit singles.

Rolling Stone's reviewer, Paul Gambacinni wrote, "This one album might have made a good EP, since there are four worthwhile tracks, but the remaining nine are flights of Bolan's fantasies, that might be interesting to his numerous devotees, but less so to more casual listeners. It's a sad indication that Bolan really hasn't progressed, and I can't see many people being truly pleased with it."

The album did, however, feature the title song from the T.Rex movie, 'Born To Boogie'. Filmed by Ringo Starr at the band's 1972 sold-out Wembley Empire Pool show, and featuring edited-in vignettes featuring Bolan, Starr and Elton John, filmed partly on the estate of John Lennon's Tittenhurst Park mansion, it was something of a curate's egg. The live concert scenes captured T.Rexstacy really well, while the odd pseudo-surreal performances filmed later seemed out of place and badly inserted.

I went to see the movie in early '73 and was struck by how poorly attended it was. The hysterical scenes at Wembley seemed sadly out of time, bizarrely vapid in such a cavernously empty cinema. It brought it home even more clearly that T.Rex as Pop Phenomenon were no more.

Bolan's next offering that summer was his worst single release to date. 'The Groover' began with a 'butch' male-chorus chant, spelling out his band's name like some cheap advert for a cleaning product. Maybe he felt we needed to be reminded who and what T.Rex was. A chugging rhythm then supported boorish, joyless lines such as, *'When I'm on the floor the kids they yell for more, more, more!'*. Fact was, they weren't yelling any longer. They had, as one, begun to yawn. The picture sleeve showed Marc on all fours, wearing oversized shades and a strange shapeless little white cape. He resembled an aging disco diva. 'The Groover' entered at No.6, climbed to No.4, dropped to No.5 and had left the charts two weeks later. His singles were reaching increasingly lower positions in the chart, and selling less each time.

What had, in fact, happened was that Marc's hard-core fan-base were, while dwindling in numbers, still rushing out to buy his singles in the first week of release. But the records were no longer sustained in the charts by the wider general public also falling in love with them, and keeping them in the Top Three for several weeks more. This was what had made gems like 'Hot Love', 'Get It On' and 'Metal Guru' such enormous sellers.

His year-end offering, the woefully slight 'Truck On Tyke', did not even bother the Top Ten, stalling at a peak of No.12 after four weeks in the charts. Visconti called it quits, realising that Marc would never complete his Children of Rarn Suite, leaving T.Rex to fend for itself in their increasingly bleak new world of diminishing returns.

On the other hand, Marc's once possible heirs to his throne were not only biting at his heels, they were gobbling him up whole. During 1973, Slade hit No.1 again with 'Skweeze Me, Pleeze Me', Dave

Hill's outfits becoming increasingly more bizarre with every TOTP appearance; Gary Glitter, after several No.2 smashes, finally hit the top with '(I'm The) Leader of The Gang'; Wizzard hit the Toppermost for a second time with 'Angel Fingers' and Sweet crashed into the Top Three with their blistering GlamSlam goldie, 'Ballroom Blitz'.

Elton John also was going from strength to strength, enjoying his biggest-selling album yet with *Goodbye Yellow Brick Road*. It spawned numerous State-side million-sellers for an adoring public who cheered every extravagant costume he modelled on stage, a feather-encrusted Janet Baker lookalike one minute, a strutting Glitter Michelin Man the next. Excess to Success seemed the order of the day. And we loved them all for it. This was Pop Music! This was fun! This was what pop was all about.

The Glam Circus truly came to town in 1973, but T.Rex, as we'd known and loved them for three years, had finally fallen from the tightrope. In January 1974, Marc released what was, in effect, a solo single, 'Whatever Happened To The Teenage Dream?' and declared in the music press that "Glam Rock Is Dead." A music journo wrote that, where once a T.Rex spot on Top Of The Pops ensured they would be No.1 the following week, it had now reached a point where the opposite happened. Marc appeared on TOTP with 'Teenage Dream' at No.13 after two weeks on the chart, the following week it dropped to No.18 and was gone seven days later. It kind of answered the song's question.

Ironically, it was actually a really excellent record, the first of his I'd bought for twelve months, and his first one recorded without Visconti. Sweeping pianos and chunky acoustic guitar were the backdrop for a superb heartfelt ballad which housed some terrific lyrics, some of his finest, in fact: '*Silver Surfer and The Ragged Kid, all are sad and rusted, boy, they don't have a gig, believe me Pope Paul my toes are clean, Whatever happened to the teenage dream?*'.

In March '74, Bolan had one last moment in the albums Top 20 when *Zinc Alloy and The Hidden Riders of Tomorrow*, an apparently belated attempt to do a *Ziggy Stardust and The Spiders From Mars*, briefly climbed to twelve, stayed three weeks in the charts and was gone. His next single, 'Light Of Love' crept to No.22 and got no further.

So why did this happen? Why did the public en masse desert the Elfin Glam Lord? I think there were several reasons, some of Marc's own doing, and other circumstances beyond his control. Mainly, it was a matter of timing. This had worked in Bolan's favour in 1970, when he'd come along just when pop music needed a kick up the arse. He'd done that beautifully and garnered the suitable rewards. But by 1973, he was literally in the wrong place doing the wrong thing. He was out of time, as Chris Farlowe had sung so magnificently in 1966: *'You don't know what's going on, you've been away for far too long, you can't come back and be the first in line…you're out of touch my baby, my poor discarded baby, I said baby, baby, baby, you're out of time.'*

In effect, Bolan got stuck in the netherworld between the art-rock of Bowie and Roxy Music and the teeny stuff churned out by Glitter, Wizzard, Sweet et al. The former was, I think, beyond Bolan, he didn't have the theatrical nous to offer that; the latter was what he'd done so well as T.Rex first took off, but was now too wrapped up in himself, and his own self-image, to give the kids the unharnessed fun-pop the new Glam stars sold by the bucket-loads. The joy had gone, replaced by a desperate need to tell everybody how fantastic, how sexy, how 'The Best' he was. That wasn't his job, or indeed necessary, his fans had been telling him he was great for the previous three years, by buying his records. That should have been enough. But as he lost the plot and slipped further down the rankings, his need to still claim greatness sounded ever emptier and more desperate, like a man shouting from the bottom of a well.

Then there were the new younger record buyers, those kids whose older sisters had screamed at Marc in his heyday but who had now grown up and moved on, most likely to Bowie and Ferry. The new teeny-boppers were spending their pocket money on Donny Osmond, Michael Jackson and David Cassidy. And, it's fair to say, being so aligned to Glam Rock as Bolan and T.Rex were, literally the fathers of the genre, it was hard to find another scene to move onto. There were no more left to him. And, truth be known, he was no longer capable of developing his style or his sound, beyond what he'd succeeded at between 1970 and 1972.

Marc had deserted his Hippie followers in 1970 for heights of pop stardom he could only have dreamed of a year earlier. But to change again and attempt, say, a concept album approach, which Bowie had done so successfully, or woo the cool art college crowd, who Roxy Music appealed to, was not possible for him as an artist. I think he was tired and disenchanted, puzzled and unsure what he could do to get back the fans he'd lost. They had moved on. He had not. Bolan had reached that dreaded pop desert of 'Has-Been World', and from that there is rarely any true recovery or comeback.

Bolan became, in effect, pop music's Norma Desmond –

"You used to be big, Marc Bolan"

"I AM big! It's the records that got small!"

Bowie stole Glam Rock when Marc wasn't looking, made it his own, then, when it had done its work for him, threw it away, walking into a new sunrise of global domination; but what of the others who briefly feasted on Bolan's hors d'ouevres? What became of them all once the genre was overdone, the kids had grown up and out of it, and their former heroes' careers were on overkill…

…1974 was the last year that Wizzard had any hits, each one a less interesting retread of their '73 chart-toppers; Sweet 'went heavy' in '74 and managed a couple more Top Three hits until 1975, when their sales rapidly fell off; Suzi Quatro had also abandoned the Glam route by '75 and found the hits were few and far between on that particular new highway; Gary Glitter's pantomime dame act had palled by 1975, with no more Top Five hits coming his way; Roxy Music split up in 1976 and reformed three years later with a new, sophisticated dance-soul sound which proved even more successful than their fling with Glam; Slade had their final No.1 album in early '74, and by '75 found the charts a harder slope to climb; Mud were the only Glam-band who actually became more successful once the earrings had been left at home, hitting No.1 three times between January 1974 and April 1975, and scoring their last Top Ten hit at the end of 1976.

And that was the year, of course, when a wholly different kind of pop genre took off. Punk was unleashed, spitting and snarling, onto a quivering stage-full of former Glam stars and rock legends. The Sex Pistols sneered at anyone who just wanted a nice time, at anyone who had been there before them. They were the self-professed new voice of angry kids who 'needed an outlet for their venom'. At the time, it felt threatening, but in fact was just another publicity stunt by a clever marketing man. The Pistols' manager, Malcolm McLaren, portrayed himself as some kind of Svengali of the Disenfranchised Youth of Britain, as his band tore up the charts and ripped shreds out of any pop magazine which didn't feature them. I found it hilarious that music papers like NME and Melody Maker, who had ignored Punk at first, suddenly realised they were missing the boat and began only featuring any act which claimed to be 'Punk, man!'. It was all too tuneless and angry for me, based on some stupid premise that you didn't have to be good to be great. It was all an empty marketing ploy, a vapid prat-pose on a barren stage. It worked, to a lesser or greater extent, for various punk bands, but, like anyone who shouts for too long, people eventually stopped listening to them. And of course, McLaren fell out very publicly with his former charges, whose movie 'The Great Rock 'n' Roll Swindle' said it all.

Punk's only saving grace was that it led to New Wave, The Stranglers, Elvis Costello, Blondie, The Clash, The Jam, The Boomtown Rats, who all knew how to write a great melody housed around fantastic lyrics. They had grown initially out of Punk, had tried the snarly pissed-off thing, but quickly discovered that making truly creative and ground-breaking records was the only way to find lasting success. The Pistols lasted for a couple of years at the top, finally imploding in the mire of their own saliva and manufactured ire.

Bolan accurately announced Glam-Rock's demise in January 1974 and T.Rex never again reached the heights they'd achieved three years earlier. The band's final Top 20 hit was 'I Love To Boogie' in the Summer of '76, his biggest hit at the time for almost three years. What was interesting about it was that many of the people who bought it were not T.Rex fans. I had friends who, while it was climbing the charts, told me, "I've never really liked T.Rex, but that 'I Love To Boogie' is great!". They simply loved the record, and their enthusiasm kept it in the charts for over two months. It was his best single – and best lyric - since the glory days of 1972. It basically said it all about the Elfin King who'd bopped into the history books at the end of 1970:

> 'The passions of the Earth blasted its mind
> Now it's neat sweet ready for the moon based grind
> We love to boogie
> We love to boogie on a Saturday night
> High school boogie, jitterbug boogie
> We love to boogie on a Saturday night'

Marc was killed while being driven home by his partner Gloria Jones on 16th September 1977. He'd just enjoyed something of a career resurgence, hosting his own six-week TV series, 'Marc', aimed squarely at 'the kids'. It was an interesting format, being not only a showcase for Marc and his new-look T.Rex, but also featuring guest performances from other acts. It was an eclectic mix of artists, The Jam and Showaddywaddy on Show 1, 10cc, Mud and The Bay City Rollers on Show 2, The Boomtown Rats and Hawkwind on Show 3, Steve Gibbons Band and Queen's Roger Taylor on Show 4, Thin Lizzy and Radio Stars on Show 5, Generation X, Eddie & The Hot Rods and David Bowie on the final Show, which was recorded on the 7th September. Marc looked well, slimmer and healthier than he had for years, and obviously newly energised.

He briefly duetted on the final show with Bowie, but the number was cut short when Marc tripped over a cable during their number, and fell off the stage. Bowie was left looking down at his old pal, highly, and rather affectionately, amused. The moment was left in, unedited.

The two old Glam Dames actually wrote a song together after the recording, 'Madmen', which was covered by New Wave band, The Cuddly Toys, who took it in the Indie charts after Bolan's death.

Marc died just nine days later. The show was transmitted shortly after Bolan's funeral on the 20th September. The series had been a big hit, and a second series had been commissioned. Marc seemed to have finally left the demons behind, back on TV, looking great and having a ball. Perhaps even on course for a chart comeback too. We'll never know.

Years after his death, Bolan was re-evaluated by media and music fans who weren't around when he'd hit the Melody Maker and NME headlines each week. He was posthumously given the accolade of Father of Glam, Grandfather of Punk, although I never quite saw the latter as in any way true or accurate. His recordings were used in TV commercials and films, prompting, in 1991, the return to the Top 20 for his 1973 Top Three hit, '20th Century Boy' and a Top Five placing for *T.Rex - The Ultimate Collection.*

At his peak, Marc had shone like a multi-coloured beacon amidst the monochrome pop world of the early '70s. Without Marc, there would have been no Glam Rock, none of the fantastic singles which lifted our charts and hearts for those three glittery years. It's even debatable that, without Marc's success, there would have been a Ziggy Stardust – i.e. a Bowie comeback. Glam Rock certainly gave Ziggy The Starman the lift-off he needed. The public's minds had been opened to the possibility, and the delight, of androgynous pop stars, via the pouting, preening prettiest star. It opened a new door for the cleverly opportunistic Bowie, who saw the way, and seized the day.

Marc kissed us with his gorgeous songs, blowing them to us like wishes in our ears. Flashing his starry eyes, he'd waved his electric guitar wand and made a wish:

"Let my songs do you good and make you happy!"

I believe that's all he ever wanted – that his music make us smile and want to dance. And it did. And still does.

The scene in *Billy Elliott,* where Billy jumped delightedly on his mattress as T.Rex's 'Cosmic Dancer' rang out around the cinema, was one of those movie goose-bump moments for me. You could almost see that gorgeous smile once more, beaming around the place, as we sang along to his simply beautiful lyrics: *'I was dancing when I was eight, is it strange to dance so late, I danced myself into the tomb, is it strange to dance so soon?'.*

Chapter Twelve

3 Years (I'm Gonna Make It)

On the hottest day of the year in August 1973, I sat on a thankfully almost empty train headed out of Manchester Piccadilly station bound for London Euston. I'd finally decided to make a go of it and leave home in the hope of finding a record company who believed, as much as I did, that I had something to offer as a singer-songwriter. The previous three years had proved to me that I could perform successfully and build up a following. The response I'd been getting, wherever I played, suggested that, with promotion and a record label's vision, my music could work outside of the relatively small world of Manchester area folk clubs.

I had no illusions, however, that getting a record deal would be easy. I knew I had talent, but was also aware it wouldn't be a doddle persuading a record label to take me on. I just needed a break…and a couple of months earlier it looked like I'd had one, which had led to me taking this train journey to a new life, and what turned out to be the beginning of a new career.

One evening in May, I was performing at a folk club on the outskirts of Manchester. The packed room had listened to the songs I banged out on a delightfully out of tune upright piano. As I'd stepped off the stage to enthusiastic applause and went to the bar for my free drink, a smiling bearded chap in glasses and, I noticed, a very good suit, walked up to me and, shaking my hand, said,

"Hello. My name's Peter. I'd just like to say how much I enjoyed your music tonight."

Behind him stood a lady who reminded me a little of a dark-haired Joni Mitchell. Peter put his hand round her waist, beaming at her and gently brought her forward.

"This is my wife Ann," he said, obviously completely in love with her, and as she told me in a beautifully husky southern counties voice,

"We utterly loved your music," I fully understood why.

Peter continued to radiate adoration in her direction, then he turned to me and said,

"I work for Polydor Records."

I actually felt my eyes light up as I thanked them both for their compliments. He must have seen that as he quickly added, "I'm nothing to do with A & R! I work in international marketing." He handed me a business card. "But I am sure someone at the label will love what you do, if they could hear it."

I was half-expecting him to offer to arrange an audition for me at the label's offices but instead he said,

"Ann and I are going back to London tomorrow, but what if I came back in a couple of weekends' time, brought my tape recorder and recorded some of your songs to play to them?"

I enthusiastically agreed that would be great, and, with the plan for me to call Peter when I had somewhere arranged to do the recording, they left.

On the bus home, the glow of potential discovery faded as the black cloud of 'where the hell am I going to find somewhere for Peter to record my songs?' descended.

It was a friend who lived in the same village as me who came to the rescue:

"Ramsbottom Town Hall has a civic room with a grand piano," he told me. "My dad works there. I'll ask him. You may be able to rent it for an afternoon."

Sure enough, a couple of weeks later I sat at the newly-tuned Steinway grand piano and sang my songs into Peter's mike as he taped each one of my performances, smiling delightedly and giving me the silent thumbs-up and an encouraging nod of the head. We recorded about ten songs, then Peter packed the machine away, put the reel-to-reel, which he patted like a favourite pet, into his bag and, with a promise that he'd be in touch, he said farewell.

"You write fucking fantastic songs," he said, as he went smiling off to his four-wheel-drive in the car park. I walked home feeling like I'd just passed an audition.

I was further encouraged when he called me a couple of days later to say he'd listened to the tape, was extremely pleased with how it sounded, and signed off by saying that whenever I wanted to, I was welcome to go and stay with him and Ann at their house in Epping, as he was sure I would need to be in London very soon.

Lying in bed a few mornings later, listening to my mum chatting over the backyard fence to our next-door neighbour, Iris, about how "Howard's been discovered by a record chap in London", I was mulling over travelling down there. More to the point, how I was going to pay for it and the weeks I would need to feed myself before being signed to Polydor. Peter had offered me a place to stay but I couldn't expect him to keep me while I was there, and surely I'd have to eventually find a flat to rent. I needed to build up some savings. Certainly the earnings I got, cash in hand, from folk gigs paid for a couple of beers and the train or bus home, but there was nothing left to add to a London Expenses piggy bank.

"Go and sign on," my mum suggested an hour later, as I explained my dilemma, munching on toast and jam and sipping a nice strong cup of tea she'd made me. "If it's only for a few weeks that should help you save up for London."

Her initially good idea collapsed in my mind into a frightening possibility:

"What if they find me a job?" I asked, wide-eyed with horror.

Mum looked me up and down, at my split-ended hair floating around my skinny shoulders and down my back, at my paint-covered jeans and second-hand ill-fitting cheesecloth shirt, at plimsolls which had given up the thought of ever being washed, indeed contemplating falling to pieces as we spoke. She smiled at me as one would at an abandoned puppy, and said,

"They won't, son. Don't worry your head about that."

The lady behind the counter at the local DHSS office also eyed me up and down, but lacking the same maternal affection, as she adjusted her Mary Whitehouse glasses to get a better look. She actually tutted as she stared at me. On her ample bosom, a plastic badge displayed her embossed name, the wholly inaccurately playful 'Babs'.

"Fill this in," she barked, sliding a multi-layered green/pink/white form across her counter, retrieving her hand quickly as though terrified I might touch her. "Then bring it back to me and I'll assess you."

Trying, and failing, to avoid her disgusted glare I went over to a shelf which ran around one side of the room and realised I hadn't brought a pen. There was the glued-on plastic base and rather dirty frayed string for one, but no pen. I went back to the counter and was met by Babs' proffered hand holding out a Biro for me.

"You might as well fill it in here," she said, then as though bestowing a huge favour, "I'm not busy."

I wanted to feel grateful, but just didn't. She watched me fill in the first box, making sure I could actually spell my name, then every time I came to the next question, she peered over her glasses and made an odd humming noise. I inwardly gloated at her obvious disappointment as I returned the completed form, sliding it across her counter like a challenge.

As she read it through very slowly she exercised her long red-varnished nails, like talons prepared for the kill. Occasionally she looked up at me, pulled a face, sniffed, and then read on. Finally, at the box which had asked 'Qualities Possessed For Possible Work Available' she read my answer twice, guffawed to herself and looked up at me, her over-red lips staining her teeth as she snarled:

"Singer-Songwriter?? What use will that be?" She patted her

hairdo a la Mrs Slocombe, and snorted rather unattractively.

"It's what I do," I replied.

"So why are you signing on?"

"So I can save some money to go to London. I already have a record company interested in me," I said, stretching the truth just a little.

She took off her glasses and leaned on the counter, exercising her jaw:

"So! You have no intention of working?"

"Oh yes, if you found something, but nothing permanent. I'll be going to London within a few weeks. As soon as possible."

She contemptuously drew her head into her shoulders, stamped the form with three loud bangs, and handed me back my pink copy. She told me to come back at 9 o'clock the following day, to sign on and collect my £12 weekly benefit pay.

"Nine prompt!" she ordered as I thanked her and left.

For two weeks, I duly signed on, collected my £12 in a little brown envelope from 'Jack' the cashier, a kindly old soul with an always grease-stained tie and an off-white shirt with sweat marks under the arms. They seemed to be the only ones he possessed. I'd go home and put my 'earnings' in a cardboard box on my dresser marked 'London Money', which with a few quid I had left over from folk club fees, already stood at £31. My train fare to the Big City, in fact. Great. The plan was coming together.

Then, on the third week, as I stood at the cash desk waiting for my money from 'Jack', 'Babs' saw me, marched forward and whispered something to him. He mumbled a "Righty-ho then" and respectfully moved aside for her.

"You have an interview for a job," she told me triumphantly.

"Doing what?" I asked, as witheringly as I could muster above shaking knees.

"It's at a paper-packing factory, across the road from where you live as it happens, so you won't have a problem getting there on time."

She passed me a handwritten note with the disdain of a nouveau riche tipping a doorman. In her unsurprisingly childlike handwriting, it had the company name and address.

"They're waiting to see you now. Ask for Mr Redman." She turned and nodded at 'Jack', who almost tugged his forelock at her, rushed forward and handed me my envelope. With a sympathetic glance he mouthed 'Good luck.'

Mr Redman sat opposite me, showing off good strong arms, rather inviting thighs and a lovely sideways smile. He looked at me in a 'what the hell have they sent me this time?' kind of way, raising his eyebrows as I told him, with absolute honesty, that anything I took, whatever it was, would only be temporary. He read the form again, as if to find a reason, any reason, why he should employ me.

"It says here you're a songwriter, Howard."

"Yes. I am."

He smiled that gorgeous lopsided smile.

"Are you any good?"

"Yes. I am," I smiled back, and nodded at him confidently.

"Excellent. Glad to hear it, son. Because there is no way in hell you can work here."

I wasn't sure whether to feel pleased or disappointed. I was rather enjoying his company.

"You are an obviously intelligent chap," he continued, winning me over even further. "And quite frankly, most of the blokes here have got just about one brain that works between them. You wouldn't survive a day here, son, you'd go mad."

He stood up to signal the interview was over and extended an enormous hand, which enveloped mine as I shook it.

"Let me know when you're on Top of The Pops," he said, offering me, for the last time, that smile.

The next morning, when I told 'Babs' how my interview had gone she looked horrified, her badge bouncing up and down like a labelled baby on her bosom as she did an odd little dance of frustration:

"Why did you tell him you won't be staying?"

"Because it's the truth. I always tell the truth."

Drawing herself up and shimmying her shoulders like Norman Evans, she said:

"Good luck with that for the rest of your life!"

With a 'never mind' shrug I was about to turn and leave, when she held up her hand to stop me:

"No, no. Don't go." Propping her glasses firmly on the end of her nose and licking her finger, she drew out a piece of paper from a pile of stuff she'd been going through when I'd arrived. "I have another job for you! *And* it's a temporary position."

"As what?"

She thrust the piece of paper into my hand:

"A postman! It's all there. Ask for Mr Hodge. Tell him Babs says hello."

I sat opposite the rumpled Mr Hodge as he rolled up a rather thin lumpy fag and explained what being a postman entailed. It didn't take long. When he asked me why I wanted to become a postman, with that long up and down study I was used to by now, I told him my now rote story, that I was going to London to get a record deal in a few weeks and needed to save some money for the trip. He lit up and puffed on his roll-up, blowing out a cigarette-reeking breath.

"You a singer then?" he spat out a bit of tobacco.

"And a pianist."

"Are you now? What do you sing?"

"My own songs. I'm a songwriter."

He chuckled and began cackling out, 'ave you got a loight boy?' and then, rather unnecessarily, with another spit, said, "The Singing Postman!"

I was trying my best to look mirthful when he looked round me and shouted, "Ralph! Come 'ere!"

A rather overweight chap, a couple of years older than me, appeared, sweating and puffing as he approached us.

"Yes boss?"

"Take our Singing Postman to his work station and show him the ropes. He won't be here long, so don't go into too much detail."

"Right boss!" Ralph replied cheerily and flicked his thumb ahead of him. I took it as a 'Follow me' and duly did so, realising that in his wake wafted the most ghastly dirty-knickers smell. He stopped in front of various pigeon-holes full of mail. "You'll be stationed here," he said, pointing at them. "Next to me." I tried to look pleased.

For the next ten minutes, he showed me how mail was sorted, all the while throwing, with great but smelly aplomb, various letters into their numerical narrow pigeon-holes. As he did so, breathing an odd shit-smelling odour in my direction, he said, "You like tennis?"

Trying to imagine this stinking heap of gasping flab in a changing room, and quickly eradicating the image from my mind, I told him I watched it on TV, but, as emphatically as I could, that I didn't play.

"No, neither do I. But that Chrissie Evert, eh? Wouldn't mind knocking my balls her way!" Another terrible vision was created as he nudged and leered at me. I think I actually winced. "Ah," he winked. "I suppose you prefer John Newcombe?" He smiled a rather surprisingly lovely smile and I felt myself blushing up. "Thought so. Each to his own. Ok! We start dead on 5.30 in the morning. Be here on time, the boss hates late-comers."

My alarm went off at 5 a.m. and, wondering where my head was, I wandered to the bathroom and prepared for my first day of work. I sprayed myself from head to toe with cologne as a safety shield against Ralph's B.O. and traipsed off wearily for the first job I'd had in my life. The dawn chorus sounded much more excited about the beginning of the day than I felt.

Ralph looked mightily impressed as I walked in dead on 5.30. He shouted across the room,

"That's a fiver you owe me, Brian!"

A five pound note rolled up with an elastic band shot over my head and was unexpectedly nimbly caught by the still reeking Ralph. Bath night had obviously not been last night.

He watched me as unobtrusively as he could as I began sorting the mail and, in fact, when one got used to the smell, he was quite a nice chap. Very helpful when I had a query, and always showing me, with great attention to detail, how to bundle up letters at just the right point so the elastic wouldn't snap, and then how to shove them, in the correct order, into a rather large sack behind me.

Just before six o'clock, with the sack full to bursting, reminding me of childhood Christmases, when my sister and I used to wake up to pillow cases stuffed with toys, I stood and waited. Ralph looked at me, then at the sack, then back at me.

"What you waiting for, mate?" he asked.

"You."

"Why?"

"You're coming with me, aren't you? It's my first day."

Ralph stared at me with twinkling eyes and whistled to the ceiling:

"No, mate, I'm not! You're on your own."

The horror of my morning ahead was still hitting me as he lifted the bag with a heaving grunt, tossed it manfully above his head, and dumped its lead weight onto my shoulder. I thought my legs were going to buckle under me. Somehow, and without screaming in agony, I managed to stay upright.

"Grab hold!" he cried, pulling the strap into my hand. "All yours!" Giving me the thumbs-up as I clung for dear life to the strap, he said, "First bus goes at 6.15 from Rammy to Longsight, which..." he glanced at his watch, "...is in about ten minutes. Should take you about an hour and a half to walk the round and get back here to sort your second post. See you back here at eight!"

As I trudged out wondering if I'd make it to the bus stop, I saw the boss wink over at Ralph then nod at me.

"Don't get lost," he murmured with a chuckle, the strains of "'ave you got a loight, boy?" following me out.

After a ten minute bus ride to Holcombe Hill and a near disaster as I was getting off, the bag almost falling off my shoulder and pulling me off the platform into the gutter, my first stop-off with the mail was a recently-built parade of shops. I'd got out my first bundle of mail on the bus so felt rather pleased with my foresight as I searched for a letter box at the first shop, 'Cornucopia – A World of Household Dreams'. The door was one of those new all-glass things, and try as I might I couldn't see where the letterbox was. I peered through into the unlit shop to see if anyone had arrived early, but apart from extremely stylish long-backed metal chairs, lots of glass and chrome shelving units and tall twisted multi-coloured vases from which gold spray-painted ferns were attempting to escape, there was no sign of life.

'Maybe I'll do this later at the end of my round' I was thinking when I finally – and wished I hadn't - spotted the letterbox. It was right at the bottom of the door, fitted into the only apparent piece of wood in the whole thing, and camouflaged beautifully by someone having painted it the same colour as the wood. I got down on my haunches to post the wodge of mail through and, just as I was retrieving my hand, I felt the weight of the mailbag start to pull me backwards. In panic I tried to grab a parking sign pole near me but just scraped my hand on it as, in horrifying slow motion, I continued to fall. My legs slipped from under me as the bag landed finally and firmly on the pavement, with me above it, helplessly kicking my legs in the air like a marooned tortoise. Try as I might, flailing this way and that, I could not get up. I tried to heave the strap from off my shoulder but it was trapped under the bag. Finally, I lay there with not a soul around and visions of still being there when the shop owners arrived to start their day. I had another go at more flailing, cursing and kicking my legs about, until I gave up, inwardly dying, dreading the next two hours, when..

"You need some help, mate?"

A figure stood above me, silhouetted against a golden street light, his hand reaching down. It felt almost biblical.

I gratefully grabbed hold of his hand and he pulled me onto my side, got hold of the strap and heaved the bag off my shoulder onto the ground. As I struggled back up and dusted myself down, I saw that my Good Samaritan was a boy of about thirteen.

"I'm just starting my paper round," he laughed. "Good job, eh?"

Embarrassed but extremely grateful, I thanked him profusely then, even more embarrassing, realised I knew him. He used to live a few doors from us in Bury. He was a small kid then but, apart from being about four foot taller, looked more or less the same. I was hoping he hadn't recognised me and, so as to hide my face with my hair, bent down to heave the bag back onto my shoulder, planning a quick exit once upright.

"Howard?" he said, as I rose back up, "You're Howard Jones, aren't you?"

"Yep. That's me," I reluctantly admitted.

"Your sister used to babysit me and my sisters." The years piled on me as his youthful smile beamed at the rising sun.

"Marcus, isn't it?" I asked, trying to sound as though I'd just realised who he was. "Do you live round here now?"

"Yes. I live across the road from here." He pointed to a large red-brick detached house, a shiny green Land Rover parked in the driveway. "We moved here about five years ago."

"Well, I'm very glad you did!"

He looked at me in a way that reminded me of his mother. It was that quiet confidence which is immediately apparent in people with 'good breeding' and private education. It's always both fascinated and eluded me.

Marcus's parents, Sadie and Simon, were the 'groovy couple' on our brand new housing estate in Bury, moving in with their young family when we did at the end of 1960. She was quite small and very skinny, with an olive complexion and always beautifully dressed. Her long dark hair either fell around her shoulders or was tied up loosely with a silk scarf, in that casual but artistic way only film stars and models knew how to do properly. She had one of those laughing voices, and threw her head back with a smile like Audrey Hepburn when she greeted you. Her accent was posh Northern, not put-on posh a la Thora Hird, it actually signalled her background, entirely, very coolly, natural.

Her languidly lanky husband always drove the latest Land Rover, upgrading it annually. He wore a waxed green jacket over crisp white cotton shirts, perfectly fitted Levi jeans, and Burberry scarf cravats, which he tied with a cheeky little nautical knot. He drove to work each morning waving at the neighbours like a Squire acknowledging his serfs.

Sadie and Simon were the first people I'd known who wore sunglasses on cloudy days. They were officially the hippest people I'd ever met. Many of our neighbours disagreed, but never to their faces:

"Ideas above her station, that one," I heard grumpy Mr Sykes next door saying to his wife, just minutes after they'd cried out a cheery, "Good morning Sadie! Lovely day!" across the back garden.

She'd waved back like Jackie Kennedy from the steps of the White House. Even hanging the washing out looked glamorous when Sadie did it.

Other than babysitting their three porcelain doll children, my sister and her best friend Pam sometimes used to visit Sadie at weekends, while Simon was at the office. I would envy their jolly '60s get-togethers listening to The Rolling Stones, looking at back copies of

Vogue and talking about film stars. Sadie would occasionally give Sue a silk blouse or a trendy haute couture sweater as an extra thank you gift for the babysitting. My sister would come home on a Sunday evening, catwalk the gift for us, and in a dreamy mist of teenage-girl-crush, tell us all how 'Fab' and 'With-it' Sadie was.

"She has a dishwasher!" Sue once told my mum, who looked at Dad meaningfully, who looked back at Mum with a 'No, we're not' look on his face.

They'd moved from the Greenhill Estate in the late '60s, about the same time we did. My sister by then was married with her own kids and had lost touch with Sadie, so I had no idea where they'd gone until this chance 'meeting' with Marcus. I asked him to give his parents my best, thanked him again for coming along when he did, and waved goodbye. The next time I posted any mail for Cornucopia, I took the bag off my shoulder first!

One afternoon, I got a call from The Bury Times. I wasn't sure how they found out about me or got my phone number, but the chap from the paper, Terry, told me he'd like to do a piece on me. He sounded highly amused that I was known locally as The Singing Postman, a fact I hadn't given him in our short conversation. It was then I realised who had called him.

"How would today be for you," Terry enquired, "if I came to your place with a photographer, and did the interview?"

I hadn't acquiesced to being interviewed but thought 'Why not?'.

Terry was very pleasant, a small, stocky man with piercing blue eyes and an odd habit of giggling nervously whenever he asked me a question. I wondered naively if he was star-struck, but it was just his way. He asked some innocuous questions about how long I'd been a songwriter and my recording ambitions and, oddly, whether doing my post round helped inspire me:

"You know, meeting so many people each day on your rounds,

does it give you ideas for songs?"

The fact was, most people were in bed on my first round and at work by the time I delivered their second post. But he was thrilled by my anecdote about a lovely old lady, who would regularly invite me in when I was delivering her mail and give me a cup of tea. As she'd poured from her lovely Clarice Cliff teapot into matching cups, her sitting room full of the delicate scents of lavender water and face powder, she'd chat away about her late husband and her daughter who lived in Australia.

"I hope to go and visit her one day," she'd say mistily, staring at the photo of her only child, who she hadn't seen for ten years.

She was thrilled when I mentioned her beautiful roses, which looked particularly colourful one morning as she led me into the house.

"Ronald loved his roses," she'd replied beaming at me, reminiscing about their life together as she boiled the kettle and set out the tray.

She would always finish our conversations with enquiries about when I was leaving for London. My reply was always virtually the same, but, with each visit, as the remaining time before I left got less, she would become increasingly excited for me, clapping her tiny hands and saying, "Good boy".

On my final visit to her, as we said our last goodbyes, she pulled my head down and kissed me on the cheek. "I wish I was coming with you," she'd whispered. "I wish you were too," I'd replied. For a moment, as her eyes sparkled up at me, her age fell away and she was a bright young thing with her whole life ahead of her. "Be wonderful," she'd said, holding her hands together as if in prayer. "For me. You darling boy."

His interview, and my story, over, Terry snapped his notebook shut and asked me to pose at the piano, "with your back to the photographer, turn round over your shoulder and smile." Two photos were taken, then Terry asked for one more.

"Ready?" he asked.

"Mmm," I replied, as the camera flashed.

The following weekend, my pursed lips, raised eyebrows and inane expression as I'd 'Mmmmed,' to Terry, looking like someone had goosed me, sat embarrassingly on the paper's front page, beside the headline: 'Don't Look So Surprised, Jon! - Our Singing Postman Has Success In The Bag!'

It's one of the few press clippings I didn't keep.

"I never thought you'd stick at this," Mum told me one day, as I blissed out on my aching feet soaking in the warm salt water she'd put in a bowl for me. "You've gone up in my estimation, son. A great deal."

I was just thinking how funny it was that sticking at a postman's job for a few weeks was more impressive than three years packing out folk clubs with my music, when the phone rang. I heard Mum say to the caller,

"He's just drying his feet. He won't be a moment." She popped her head into the lounge and mouthed, 'It's Peter!'

"Been treading grapes?" Peter joked as I took the phone.

"Long story!" I replied.

"I'd love to hear it! And on that subject, Ann and I were wondering when you were planning to make the move to London?"

Imagining that was a hint that he had good news, I suggested the first week of August, in two week's time.

"Perfect!" Peter said.

"Oh!" my mum said when I told her.

"You suggested it's what I should do, mum."

"Yes. It is. It is. Yes."

"This is it!" I said, hugging her.

"Yes. It is. Yes," she murmured into my shoulder.

To my surprise, on my last day at the post office, I was given a farewell card by Mr Hodge and a copy of T.Rex album, *Tanx*.

"Something to remember us by," Ralph said, as everyone smiled at me and wished me the best of luck.

"We'll miss you," the boss said, "it's been good having someone a bit different around. Brightened the place up!"

"Hear! Hear!" said Ralph, sounding just a little emotional. He even smelled rather nice for a change.

Enjoying the round of applause, I thanked them all, feeling rather touched they'd remembered me saying how much I loved Marc Bolan. As I reached our house, Enid, an elderly neighbour who lived a few doors down from us called out to me:

"I hear you're going to London!"

"Yes!" I replied brightly.

"Pah! London! Full of robbers and scoundrels!"

I laughed. She didn't.

"You be careful down there. They'll have the shirt off your back!"

I almost replied, "I hope someone does," but thought better of it.

A few days later, I was waving at my mum and dad as they stood on the steps of our little cottage watching the bus taking me off on my new adventure. I had no idea what lay ahead, but I was determined to do my best to make my dreams come true. Dreams that had started three years earlier after my first gig at Accrington College in March 1970.

Finally, this was it. No going back now.

Chapter Thirteen

Guess Who's Coming To Dinner

As I stepped from the train at Euston Station, on a warm late afternoon, August 4th 1973, the unsolicited thought 'I'm home' sprang into my head. Hundreds of people milled around as I made my way to the Underground, and headed for the recently opened Victoria Line. I immediately loved the bustle of it all, and something else, the anonymity. I had been so used for years, living in small Northern towns, to being noticed by those I seemed to outrage, shock or simply amuse. With my hair down a back covered by my mum's blouses and jacket cast-offs, I'd been the local effeminate skinny queen, mentally batting away cries of "Get yer 'air cut, Dorothy!" as I'd walked from my house to the pub. I'd ignored grins and smirks as I'd settled on the bus home from college or a friend's house, or overheard a kid ask his mum "Was that a boy or a girl??". I'd learnt to look beyond those people, knowing that one day I would no longer be living near them, putting up with them, pretending they didn't exist. I would be gone and they would be left behind. I'd longed for the day when I found a larger, more exciting world which accepted me.

As I strode through the tube system, hopping from train to train with my little suitcase and record player, settling finally on the Eastbound Central Line, it was even better than I'd imagined. Not only did no-one look mockingly at me, in fact no-one looked at anyone. It was A to B priorities that swept everyone along, how people around them looked was of no importance to these city dwellers. What also struck me was how great everyone looked, so different, individual, all dressed in ways which would have made the idiots who'd name-called me for years back home stop dead in their tracks. They would have stared unbelievingly and probably shouted something derogatory, feeling ever so clever as they'd yobbed it across the road. Now, here in this amazing hub of society to which, after less than an hour, I already belonged, no-one shouted anything, we were all as one, assured in our own worlds of isolated, anonymous uniqueness.

As I arrived at Peter and Ann's lovely red-brick Edwardian semi in Epping and rang the bell, I sensed not only a new beginning but that a road ahead was already being cleared for me. I looked forward to chatting with Peter that evening, over dinner and a glass of wine, about the career path he had planned for me, arranging discussions and a deal with the head honchos at Polydor. However, after five minutes and three more rings of the bell, when no-one came to the door, those plans I'd been hatching were going up in smoke. I thought at first I may have the wrong day. I searched my memory for my last conversation with Peter, when we'd agreed I would arrive today at around this time. Trying not to worry, I settled on a wooden bench in the front garden, enjoying the late sunshine and the scent from the honeysuckle weaving its way round the trellis behind me.

As I read an old NME I'd brought with me for the journey, a car flew past with its radio blasting out Gary Glitter's 'I'm The Leader of The Gang' which had gone to No.1 that week. I was once again filled with the excitement of the possibility that soon I would be making my own mark on the pop charts. An hour later, as I re-read an interview with David Bowie about his recent 'retirement' from live shows, I heard a car pull up outside the house. The doors opened and four children piled noisily out, shouting their heads off and rowing with each other as they flew through the gate. When they saw me, the noise stopped and as one they screeched to a halt. Eight little eyes stared from four huddled little figures, and as I stood up to greet them their eyes widened even more, slowly following me up from my worn plimsolls to my billowing hair.

Standing at the front of the group was a girl of about twelve, behind her a slightly younger boy and hiding behind him were two much younger boys, about four or five years old, who peered suspiciously from behind their older brother. The girl seemed to make a decision and stepped forward, stretching out her hand:

"Hello," she said, "you must be Jon."

As I was shaking her hand, and about to ask her name, a heavily pregnant Ann struggled through the huddle of little boys, carrying several bags of shopping. I rushed forward to help her and took what she indicated was the heaviest bag and a couple of others which looked ready to fall on the floor.

"Hello!" she said, as brightly as she could while obviously exhausted. "I hope you haven't been waiting long. I had to pick up the kids *and* go shopping, Peter called to say he'd be late at work."

With his mum's obvious acceptance of this stranger called Jon in his garden, one of the younger boys pushed through, and, hand extended, declared, "I'm Matty!"

I bent down to shake his hand which prompted the other boys to join in. Their sister just tutted:

"Leave Jon alone! He must be exhausted!"

"Yes, you must," Ann said to me, "come in and sit down."

As she opened the door and I followed her through to the large kitchen which smelled of fresh baking, her children careered past us, throwing down satchels and bags, kicking off shoes. Matty jumped in front of me:

"I'm four, Carl's five, Jake's eleven and Sophie's twelve and a half."

"Twelve and three-quarters, actually," Sophie said.

Undeterred, Matty continued: "How old are you, Jon?".

"I'm twenty," I replied, to which there was a quick huddle and whisper amongst the boys.

"Younger than daddy then?" Jake said.

"Everyone's younger than daddy!" Sophie said and everyone, including me and Ann laughed.

As her mother busied away emptying her bags into various

cupboards, Sophie asked me if I would like some tea. I had never known a twelve year old like her, asking if I preferred Earl Grey, Jasmine or "common-or-garden PG Tips?". I'd only heard such well-spoken tones from children in 1950s British films. "Jasmine tea, please," I replied, to which Sophie danced round the table and chimed,

"He wants Jasmine tea! How delightful, mummy! *He* can stay!"

Ann gave me a look as if to say, 'Well, *you've* scored highly!' and began preparations for dinner.

"You play the piano, don't you?" Jake said, purposefully opening the lid of an upright in the corner of the dining room which led directly from the kitchen.

"Oh please play for us!" Sophie cried, doing a perfect ballet pirouette in front of me.

"Yes!" all the kids shouted as one, "Jon's going to play for us!"

Ann smiled over at me with an expression that said, "Only if you want to."

I went and sat down and did a recently-written song, 'Guess Who's Coming To Dinner', which got a "*You* are, Jon!" from Carl when I announced its title.

"Do another one!" Matty shouted as I came to the end, and he came and sat next to me on the piano stool, humming 'Flash just flew by my window' to himself.

I gave them 'Family Man', which made them all laugh when I sang the 'she's got a double belly and she's got a double chin/she watches lotsa telly and she drinks a lotta gin' line. For days afterwards one of them would be singing it to themselves around the house.

Peter arrived later that evening looking tired but happily surrounded by his four children, who excitedly gave him a detailed account of what we'd had for dinner and offering interrupted overlapping tales of my short impromptu performance.

"He's very good!" Sophie told him.

"I know," Peter replied, smiling over at me.

Ann stroked Peter's face very affectionately and said,

"Have you had any luck with John's tape, darling?"

It felt more like a prompt to let me know what was happening, rather than an enquiry based on ignorance.

"I want to discuss that with Jon tomorrow evening," Peter replied, giving his wife a knowing glance. Then looking at me, "I'm playing a gig tomorrow night. Would you like to join me for an evening of medieval song?"

"As long as I'm not expected to join in!"

"Oh do!" the kids all shouted.

I just shook my head at Peter, who winked back.

As I lay in bed that night, I decided I couldn't stay in this house for very long. Lovely though Peter and Ann and their children were, I actually had no idea they had any kids when I'd agreed to come down and stay with them. No mention had been made of their large – and soon to be extended again - family when I'd spoken to Peter on the phone. I naively had imagined the couple as just the two of them living a Bohemian London life together, travelling from gig to gig watching Polydor artists perform, a kind of 'music biz' version of Joni Mitchell and Graham Nash.

The piano, being in the dining room-cum-playroom, would be the centre of the hustle and bustle of family life. Ann obviously loved cooking, baking, and pottering in her gorgeous huge kitchen which was open to where the piano stood, so the idea of any privacy as I worked on songs was out of the question. I've always needed total isolation to write songs, where I can sit on my own for hours, trying ideas out over and over again, getting things wrong, re-doing sections of songs, playing a new composition ad nauseum until it's wedged firmly in my head. It was likely either I would drive Ann mad or I would go slowly crazy trying to compete with the noise and chaos of a truly happy household rushing around me. There was also another baby on the way within a couple of months, which would make the situation, as far as I was concerned, completely untenable. I adored this intelligent and classy family, certainly the nicest I'd ever met, and if I had been merely a guest staying for a short vacation, it would have been delightful to get to know them much better. But I simply could not live with them if I was to stay focused and forge ahead with my plans to write enough songs for an album and get a record deal. The next evening made up my mind once and for all that I had to find myself a flat of my own.

The medieval banquet was in full swing as, feeling just a little uncomfortable, I watched rowdy couples at long wooden tables heckling Peter and his minstrel troupe, as, dressed in tunics, feathers and pantaloons, they sang and played their Elizabethan hearts out. Their audience of executives and their expensively bejewelled wives ate lots of meat, drank huge tankards of beer, and laughed heartily as wolf-whistled bosomy barmaids coped admirably with tweaked bums and tickled chins. Wondering why I'd agreed to come, I longed to be on the drive back to Peter's house.

He hadn't brought up my tape at all as we'd made our way there, sticking to light conversation about his family, his forthcoming baby and the gig ahead of him. I'd been too fearful of what he might say to broach the subject, so sat simmering away to myself as overfed, overindulged businessmen fantasised openly and noisily about bedding one of the 'beer maidens'.

Finally, as we were getting back in the car to head home, and I complimented Peter on how he'd cheerily sailed above the raucous behaviour of his god-awful audience, he laughed and said,

"But now, to your music."

As he drove on my heart began to sink. He told me, in a very stalled and stuttered way, how he still loved what I did, and believed someone out there would recognise my talent, and make it happen for me, but,

"Sadly, that won't be me."

Relieved that the car was relatively dark, save for occasional street lights which bathed us momentarily in a dim yellow glow, I listened in silence as he explained that none of the A & R people at Polydor had liked the tape,

"In fact one of them said he couldn't understand what I saw in you."

His voice became a blur as he went on to say that the pop scene had changed a lot in recent months, with less singer-songwriters hitting it big, and more out-and-out bubblegum and MOR artists selling records.

"Look at the charts now, Barry Blue, Peters & Lee, Donny Osmond, The Carpenters, First Choice. Even Al Martino and Perry Como are making a comeback! Record labels want hot pants and hooks it seems to me. Talent and individuality are out, for the time being anyway. I don't want to say this, but you may have missed the boat, unless you change your writing style, or unless you are extremely patient."

I reminded him what he'd said to me just three months earlier, 'You write fucking fantastic songs', which prompted a deep sigh from behind the steering wheel:

"I still think that, but last week, I went off-piste and played your tape to a couple of friends of mine from other majors, and they had exactly the same reaction as my Polydor colleagues – 'what the hell are you bothering with this bloke for?'. It's very depressing, but I had to tell you, you have to know what you'll be up against."

His final comment suggested something else. That I was on my own now. As we reached his house and he parked the car in the drive he confirmed that:

"The truth is, Jon, I can't help you. I love what you do, but I can't convince the people I know of your huge talent. As far as

I'm concerned, you are now free to go and find someone else who believes as much as I do, someone who can get you that deal. I'm so sorry. For you, and for me."

Feeling like a bus had hit me, but feeling more sorry for Peter, who had steeled himself to tell me this, I tried an unconvincing smile and shook his hand:

"Thanks for trying anyway," I mumbled, and got out of the car, my legs just a little shaky beneath me as we crept into the silent house of happy sleeping children. Peter offered me a coffee but I declined, unsure what I could find to say at this point, and went up to bed. I awoke a little while later and heard a mumbled conversation in the bedroom along the landing, imagining Peter telling Ann what he'd told me. It sounded very sombre and matched my rather doomy mood as I fell back to sleep.

As I rose for breakfast the next morning, Peter long gone off to work, Ann out shopping with the toddlers, the older kids at school, I browsed the ads section of their Evening Standard, found 'Flats To Let', and rang a few.

I spent days traipsing round London looking at flats, my heart sinking at each one as I saw a queue of other interested potential rentees. They were lined up and down streets, winding up staircases, crowded round packed lifts, and snaking for what seemed miles round blocks of apartments. I would get back to Epping every disheartening evening with no flat, aching feet and a dull sense that this was going to be a hopeless search. I couldn't believe so many people were looking for accommodation, and wondered how most of them ever found somewhere to live.

Then, one morning, in another scouring of Flats To Rent ads, I noticed one which said 'Only gay men need apply', which could have sounded a little dodgy but I was intrigued enough to ring the number. A jolly-voiced chap answered, introduced himself as Roger, immediately checked I was gay and then explained that he didn't want any "straights bringing back palone trade, dear, bras and knickers on the floor every morning, jubes bouncing by me ricicles as I read me paper, ugh!! Only omi-palones in my lattie, darling!". With more Camp Polari than a Julian and Sandy sketch, some of which lost me completely, he agreed I could go to view the house in East Twickenham about eight that evening.

"Come and have a bijou buvare with me, it'll be bona!", Roger signed off, with a delighted giggle.

I walked from Richmond station, past rather elegant restaurants and High Fashion clothes shops, over the bridge which straddled the river and enjoyed the fabulous view of the exquisite houses along it.

"One day…" I thought.

Feeling quite enchanted by the place, I found Roger's little Victorian terrace tucked down a side street near the tree-lined tow-path, and thought how charming it looked. I was initially surprised to see that there was no-one else there to view it but guessed Roger's catchment of potential lodgers, especially after talking to them on the phone, was quite limited. After the first ring of the doorbell, I heard much moving around inside, little shrieks and huffs and puffs, giggles and whoops, and clattering of what sounded like furniture being pushed into place. I could see a small figure through the stained glass rushing to the door and with a grand opening and a beaming smile:

"Hello! I'm Roger! You must be Jon!"

He was a tiny little man of about forty with wet shoulder-length hair which dripped onto an odd one-piece corduroy outfit, topped and tailed with a little green scarf draped over one shoulder and burgundy satin slippers.

"Come in. Vada the lattie, darling. Excuse the riah. I've just washed it. And, by the way, it's *not* a switch, it's all mine."

He flitted and fluttered about the hallway as I followed him into a long corridor, where walls were lined with photos and framed posters of him in younger years, many of them showing him performing and posing in drag with his double-act partner. 'Two Much – Are Too Much!' one of the posters declared, with both rather beautiful young men lifting their Roaring '20s-style skirts provocatively and pouting heavily lipsticked mouths at the camera.

"Oh yes!" Roger cried, as I studied each picture wandering along behind him. "We were very much in demand, Gladys and I! Glad was a crimper by day, hoofer by night!" He let out an ear-piercing shriek and pointed at one of the posters. "She looked gorgeous in slap, don't you think? And vada those lallies, dear!! Pins to die for! God rest her soul. The gin got her in the end."

Not sure whether to laugh or offer solace, I followed him as he skipped through to a large sitting room, full of a kind of decayed grandeur. Heavy velvet-swathed curtains, plush dark green carpets covered by exotic, threadbare rugs, on which several rather worn chaise-longues were dotted around. It resembled a period Victoriana film set, complete with a huge Steinway Grand which stood centre stage. Roger stood aside, sweeping his arm dramatically around as I wandered in, making little gasps of delight as my eye was caught by different little touches.

"You obviously love old things, dear. So I'm in with a chance!"

He shrieked again, clasped his invisible pearls and sailed by me in a gust of Paco Rabane:

"Enough nostalgia for one evening, dear," he declared and ran to a door leading off the sitting-room. "And the boudoir!" He threw open the door. "This would be yours, if you decided to take it, of course. Mustn't be presumptuous, must we?"

He giggled and watched me take the room in:

"It needs a lick of paint but it's very comfortable! Are you handy, dear?"

It was a dark, once again heavily decorated room, with massive beaded lamps on the bedside tables which stood each side of a King-size mahogany bed. An ornately brocaded bedspread was set off with fussily crocheted pillowcases and a rather creepy Victorian doll staring at me.

"Oh don't mind Belinda. She's my mother's pride and joy, been here for decades. A bit like mother!!". He saw my face, and banged my arm with more of a punch than I would have expected. "Oh! Now, don't worry your pretty little eek! Mama doesn't live here any longer, she's in a living-assisted flat in Sheen. Darling woman but has no idea I'm gay! She'd be horrified!"

'Then she must be blind' I thought but continued to follow Roger round the house, making suitably approving noises as he showed me every room like a tour guide, providing me with a potted history of how their decoration and furnishing came about. When we got to the bathroom which had not been altered since the 1930s, he clasped his face and exhaled loudly:

"Did you read about that poor boy who broke his neck trying to give himself a blow-job under the sink?!"

Apparently, as Roger told it, he'd wedged himself down there and was in the process of self-fallating when his neck snapped. Roger shrieked with mirth as he recounted the story, which he'd read in the News Of The World a few days earlier.

"At least he died happy!" he cried, and swished out to the kitchen, asking me if I wanted a cup of tea. "I only have Typhoo, dear, nanti all that foreign muck!"

For the next twenty minutes, as we sipped our tea and nibbled on rather delicious biscuits his mother had made, Roger nattered away about himself. Finally, he grabbed my arm and cried:

"Oh, hark at this old queen. All me, me, me! Tell me about yourself, darling. Just why does a Northern young man like you come to a soiled old city like London?"

When I told him I was a pianist-singer he cut me off in mid-sentence and clapped his hands:

"My dear. You must play for me."

He took my hand and led me, like a maître d would a new starlet, through the door and to the piano.

"Bona!" he cried. "Un peu de musica!"

As I tinkled out a few warm-up chords he got out two wine glasses from his mother-of-pearl inlaid drinks cabinet and filled them from his cut-glass decanter. Placing one on the piano for me, he clinked his against it.

"The last time someone played on this old thing," he trilled, "he had a heart attack and was rushed to hospital!" With an ear-splitting hoot he settled himself on one of the chaise-longues behind me. "The poor queen survived, but she wouldn't tinkle my ivories ever again!"

I smiled at him, he fluttered his eyelashes and adopted a 'listening intently' pose. I wasn't sure what to play for him but decided on something dramatic, it seemed to suit the room. I belted out 'Kid In A Big World', and as I whispered the final 'Take care...' Roger yelled out, "Fantabulosa! Oh, my dear! I am in *bits*!! That was totally marvelloso! Did you write that yourself?"

"Yes," I replied.

"Wonderful. Play me another. This is utterly fortuni. Mother would adore you!"

And so, as I played, he poured me several glasses of wine and finally moved to the piano, where he stood watching my hands and smiling at me indulgently during each number. I decided to end my recital with 'Werewolves'.

"Bravo!" he cried as I finished. "That one is SO sensuous, my dear! All that flesh!" Then, he looked at his watch. "Well. Can you believe it? Doesn't time fly when you're having a ball. It's more than likely you've missed your train home, my boy."

I looked at the Grandfather clock in the corner. It was eleven o'clock. I couldn't believe I'd been playing for two hours. Roger purred at me and said, "So why not stay here for the night? You can try out the bed!"

As it turned out, it was his bed I tried out, and, to my surprise, he was extremely impressive between the sheets.

The next morning, he brought me a cup of tea and tickled my nose.

"You thought it would be tootsie trade, didn't you, love? Bread and bread!"

Not sure quite what he meant, I sat up and sipped my tea.

"People think I'm such a camp old queen," he continued, "but I am a tiger in bed."

He growled loudly, and ran off to take a shower

"Brekkie in half an hour," he called out from the corridor.

Later that morning, we munched on granary toast and honey and lots of pots of tea, as Roger regaled me with more outrageous stories he'd either read about or heard 'on the queer-vine'. Without warning he changed the subject.

"You do know that if we do begin to date, you can't live here."

I looked puzzled. I hadn't considered sleeping with him again. But he took my expression as disappointment.

"Oh, there'll always be room at the inn for you, darling, you'll always be welcome to stay... but only for one night." He started rummaging through his diary, and continued to twitter away. "I'm a butterfly when it comes to sex, you see, dear, pollinating whoever I can whenever I can, cartes and dish at least three times a week. But if you lived here, and watched me dragging back dolly omis, one after the other, you may get jealous and bash my head in. I wouldn't want to end up like that poor Joe Orton." He stabbed his pen at a date in his diary. "How's next Monday?"

At the door, we agreed – or rather he told me – that I would ring him over the weekend to confirm our next rendezvous. He stepped out of the house ahead of me, looked around the street, ushered me out as quickly as he could and very formally and firmly shook my hand. I went to peck him on the cheek but he held me in my place with a definite straightened arm. In a voice lowered by at least an octave, he bellowed, "Well, thank you for coming round, Jon. You've been most helpful."

As he waved me off and dashed back inside, he poked his head through an almost closed door.

"Call me," he mouthed, miming a phone dial.

I never did.

The small amount of money I'd saved was fast running out, so I decided to look for a temp job. I walked into Alfred Marks Bureau in Oxford Street and half an hour later had secured one, at Telephone Rentals in Knightsbridge. In those days there were temp jobs galore, which suited me down to the ground. There was no commitment, no expectations of working out a career path with the company, I would just go in each day, do the job in hand, clerical stuff, filing, filling in forms, and then, at the end of each week, go home with a welcome £16 in my pocket. Around the same time I also found a flat, though it took a couple of weeks to finally be offered a room there.

I'd gone straight from work to a '60s block of flats in Shoot-Up-Hill in Kilburn, and queued as usual with a crowd of other hopefuls up the stairs to the 6th floor. It was like an audition, as two bright young things stood in the doorway and interviewed each person for a few minutes, quickly showed them round and, thanking them for coming, moved onto the next person in the queue. I finally made it to the front, was introduced to Phillipa – "call me Phil" which she'd said to everyone in front of me - and her room-mate Diane – "Di will do" - who both seemed very excited when I told them I was a singer-songwriter.

"Bry!" Phil called out into the flat and told the large chap in his forties who emerged, "Jon here is a singer! Just like you!"

"Oh hi!" Bry said, "What kind of singer?"

"Singer-songwriter," I replied.

I could hear the woman behind me in the queue starting to get fidgety and mumbling, "Oh get on with it."

"Really!" Bry said, ignoring her. "I'm Brian Keith, from Plastic Penny."

I remembered the group's hit single from 1968, 'Everything I Am', a cover of an old Box Tops song, and although much broader round the beam since those Top of The Pops appearances five years earlier, he was still recognisable. I mentioned that the band had featured Nigel Olsson on drums and Paul Raymond, who had later replaced Christine Perfect-McVie in Chicken Shack. Brian's face lit up.

"And weren't you the lead vocalist on The Congregation's hit as well?" I asked, recalling a Radio 1 DJ saying he had once been with Plastic Penny.

"Yes! I was! 'Softly Whispering I Love You'. Big hit! Wow! You're a knowledgeable guy!"

He led me into the flat and showed me three large-sized rooms, a compact kitchen, no-frills bathroom and a minute bedroom right at the end of the corridor. There was just enough room for a single bed and a very thin wardrobe.

"This would be your room," Brian said, "it's not much but we spend most of the time in Phil and Di's room of an evening. It's a friendly place, Jon. Nice people."

The rent was £8 a week, which left me with the same amount for food and the tube. It was do-able, especially as I had begun earning the occasional £10 playing the odd gig at folk clubs Peter had told me about.

I gave Brian my number, shook his hand and smiled at Phil and Di, who were chatting to the woman who had been in the queue behind me. Phil waved as I left and, above the woman's head, shouted,

"We'll def be in touch, Jon!"

The following evening, sure enough, Phil rang me. However, it was to say that, although they had decided to rent the room "to a fab clothes designer called Kerry", there would be another room coming available very soon and they would like me to take it.

A couple of weeks later, that room came available and after a fairly emotional farewell to Ann, and with Sophie, Jake, Carl and Matty squeezed into the back seat, Peter drove me to the station and dropped me off with a big hug.

"I am so sorry it didn't work out, you know, me getting you a deal and everything," he murmured into my shoulder.

At which point Matty burst into tears and hugged my legs.

"Don't leave, Jon!" he cried, which set off the other three kids. Peter gently extricated Matty off my legs, and told his children that I would come and see them soon. That seemed to calm them, more hugs followed and, finally, they waved me off, like a family saying goodbye to a son off on travels far away. I was very touched but knew that this was the right decision.

The Kilburn flat was perfect, even though I actually had the tiny room at the end of the apartment I had originally viewed. Kerry, the clothes designer, had simply moved out of that room and into one of the bigger rooms, after it too had been vacated by someone I hadn't met when I was there a couple of weeks earlier. My four flatmates were fun to be around. Phil, swanning round the flat in silk kimonos and satin slippers, usually painting her nails and telling us that she'd had an 'excel' day, was 'def' going places, and destined for a 'tremen' career. She was training to be a beautician and never looked less than perfect; Di favoured 'comfy jamas', as she called them, in the evening, and power-dress suits by day. She tended to listen more than talk, tipping her head to one side as you told her or the room something. She was studying law, and possessed that quiet confidence which made one immediately trust her; Kerry, an American-looking thickly-moustachioed handsome chap with eyes that twinkled as you spoke, liked to smoke 'weed' and often could be heard singing appallingly out of tune in his room to King Crimson records; and Brian, our pop star landlord, the daddy of the group. He collected the rents every Monday evening, and would regale anyone listening with his tales of appearing on Top Of The Pops and touring Europe in the late '60s.

We would all spend evenings in either Phil and Diane's large room, which had once been the flat's sitting-room, or in Brian's equally large room, listening to records and drinking wine. It was the closest I had come to that art college fraternity feeling I'd enjoyed in the early '70s, where I was part of a group of ambitious young people who spent wonderful endless hours talking about how we were going to change the world. Kerry would sometimes bring home his designs, one-off's which had been rejected by his tutors, but which I loved and would model, with much hooting and cat-calling, for my flatmates and then, without really asking, take them over as mine.

"When you become a pop star," Kerry would say, "I'll design your stage clothes."

We both knew that would never happen but it was a fun dream to have.

One evening, Brian came into my room and asked me if he could come and see me at my next gig. I'd done an open mic session at The Troubadour in Earl's Court a few evenings earlier and they had asked me back to perform a proper set the next weekend.

"We'll all come to see you," Brian said.

Sure enough, they were all there, smiling away at me as I sat at the battered old upright piano and did about six numbers. The place was full and my set went down well. Phil actually stood up and shouted "Bravo!", which got Kerry on his feet to do the same. The guy who ran the club came up to me as I was leaving and asked me if I would be interested in doing a Guest Night, when I would basically top the bill and get paid. Of course, I said yes.

"That was great, Jon!" Brian told me outside. "There's a guy I want you to meet. He's the Head of Chappell Music. I think he'll love your stuff."

As we went home by cab, going through St. John's Wood on the way to Kilburn, we passed Abbey Road Studios. I'd only travelled to Kilburn by Tube before so my eyes were on stalks:

"Wow!" I said, staring out of the window. "Abbey Road! And oh my God, the actual zebra crossing!"

"You could be recording there one day!" Brian said to me, enjoying the wonder on my face.

A few nights later, I went with Brian, Kerry and Phil to a club called Hatchett's in Oxford Street to see a band Brian was helping get a deal. Phil quickly got off with the drummer and disappeared after their first set and Kerry began chatting up one of the girls behind the bar.

"Alone at last!" Brian said laughing, just as a rather smart-looking older chap, and an equally nicely-dressed lady, wandered through the door and waved at us. As they came over to our table, Brian introduced them to me as Stuart Reid, from Chappell Music, and his wife, Patsy. I guessed Stuart was in his fifties, Patsy a little younger. They both smiled broadly at me and asked if they could join us. As Stuart began asking Brian about the band they'd come to see, Patsy chatted easily with me about London, how I found living there, and how my music was going. She had a very caring way about her, seeming genuinely interested in what I was telling her, as I rabbited on about myself for about ten minutes. As the band arrived on stage for their second set and were tuning up, Stuart said to me,

"Brian tells me you're a singer, Jon."

He had such an energy in his voice, an enthusiasm which I would have expected from a man half his age.

"He also writes his own songs," Brian interjected.

"Really? Are you playing anywhere soon, Jon?"

I told him I had a guest evening at the Troubadour the next weekend and asked him if he fancied coming along.

"We'd love to!" Patsy answered for him.

"Yes, we'll see you there. What time?"

"I'll be going on about nine o'clock."

Happily, the club was full as I sat between Stuart and Patsy watching the first couple of acts. As a particularly intense folk singer sitting crouched over his guitar finished his final, rather tortured song, Stuart leaned towards me and said,

"Well, I hope you're better than this guy, Jon."

"I am, Stuart," I replied, evincing a huge smile and a wink at Patsy.

The club's manager introduced me and I went to the piano and launched straight into 'Guess Who's Coming To Dinner'. I looked over at Stuart and he was positively beaming at me. Patsy smiled in a way I soon got used to, a protective love seemed to literally pour from her in my direction, it was almost tangible. I performed eight songs, finishing with 'Kid In A Big World'. The place burst into applause and as I did a little bow at the piano, the manager came forward, shook my hand delightedly and gave me a beer.

Stuart and Patsy were already making a move to leave but came over to me and told me how much they'd loved my set.

"Oh, Jon!" Patsy said, hugging herself, her eyes welling up.

"Bring Jon to my office on Monday at twelve, Brian," Stuart instructed my landlord. "We'll have lunch and talk things over."

It was hard to keep the excitement out of my voice and instead feign sickness, as I rang my boss at Telephone Rentals on Monday morning to tell him I was feeling rather ill and wouldn't be coming in today.

"What's wrong with you?" he asked, rather angrily.

"I'm feeling rather light-headed," I told him, completely truthfully.

Brian and I met Stuart and Patsy at a lovely Austrian restaurant in St Christopher Place, off Oxford Street. It was the poshest eaterie I had ever been to. As we walked in, Stuart dashed forward and shook my hand warmly, sitting me next to Patsy at the table and ordering me a drink:

"You were drinking vodka and tonic at Hatchett's the other night, Jon. Is that ok for you?"

Indeed it was, and helped along by several glasses of beautifully dry chilled white wine which followed, I listened in a dream as Stuart praised my performance at the Troubadour and how he saw me as "The Next Noel Coward!".

As he chatted away enthusiastically, a gorgeous moustachioed thick-set man came rushing over to our table and shook my hand.

"Friedrich," Stuart cried at him, "this is Jon Howard I was telling you about."

Friedrich gripped my hand firmly and beamed at me.

"Welcome to my restaurant, Jon," he said, patting me on the back. "Stuart has told me all about you!" His beam grew even broader as an extremely handsome young woman rushed out from the back of the restaurant to join him.

"Jon," he said, "please meet my wife, Sascha!"

Fantasy over, I shook Sascha's hand warmly, and sat down as they both suggested some 'exquisite dishes' from the menu.

"They're not joking, Jon," Patsy murmured into my ear, "the food here is fantastic."

I chose a chicken dish in a goulash sauce with sauté potatoes – after Patsy had told me what sauté potatoes were – and settled down to listen to Stuart's extremely exciting plans for my career.

"You are a star, Jon," he told the table, Patsy and Brian nodding in agreement. "You radiate something extremely special when you are performing, and I am going to make sure the whole world gets to hear the music of Jon Howard!"

I remember little else about the lunch. My head began to swim with the wine and the compliments, which flowed in equal measure.

After lunch, from which I'd sobered up with the help of several black coffees Patsy had ordered for me, we walked up Oxford Street and into Hanover Square, Stuart and Brian pointing out various landmarks to me, Patsy smiling benignly as I looked in wonder at yet another architectural or historical feature. We followed Stuart as he strode into Chappell Music's headquarters and up the wide sweeping staircase like a twenty-year old, and led us into his huge office, which opened out into an even larger room where sat the most beautiful white grand piano.

"You are welcome to come and play that anytime, Jon," Stuart declared.

"Anytime," Patsy murmured in agreement.

"Isn't this great, Jon?" Brian said, looking at me like a father might at a successful son after he'd won a part in a movie.

Stuart clapped his hands:

"Now, to business."

He sat down and motioned for us to do likewise, passing a document to me across his desk which I could see was a contract.

"It's a very simple management agreement, Jon," Stuart explained as I looked at it, "basically, if you're not happy with us, or vice versa, we just..." and he mimed tearing it up. "I want to be involved with you, Jon, I want to make you a star, I believe you will be, we all do." He looked around the room and, as if on cue, Brian and Patsy murmured their agreement.

I noticed that my name had been spelt 'John Howard' on the first page of the contract, and was just about to correct that when Stuart wrote the name down on a pad in front of him, admiring it like a work of art.

"Such a great name, so very British," he said, his eyes sparkling at us. "John Howard, Noel Coward, could be one and the same."

He stood, we stood, and he shook my hand firmly:

"John, welcome to our family. We're going to have a lot of fun, I can promise you that."

"Come to dinner at our house this evening," Patsy said, putting her hand on my arm. "I don't want this day to end."

As Brian and I left for the tube station and back to Kilburn, he slapped me on the back and said,

"Well, John, this is it. Stuart will do his best to make you a star. I hope you're ready."

"Oh yes I am,' I said to myself, 'I have been for years."

Chapter Fourteen

The Business Side Of Beauty

The first thing Stuart Reid did when he'd signed me to a management deal in September 1973 was put me in the studio to demo the songs he'd heard me play at The Troubadour a few evenings earlier.

The studios were situated between Bond Street and Hanover Square, down some steps outside Chappell Music Publishing's offices, to the basement. This meant that Stuart could leave his office and pop downstairs anytime to see what I was working on, but he usually gave me a couple of hours to put some demos down before he joined me and the engineer, Chris.

My first session went well, Chris was a really enthusiastic and sympathetic engineer, who genuinely seemed to like my stuff and worked hard at getting a vocal sound he thought suited my voice. What impressed me was how impressed *he* was by the speed at which I recorded the piano backing tracks, then the lead vocal, then double-tracked the vocal and added a harmony line where needed. We got the tracks, 'Guess Who's Coming To Dinner', 'Family Man', 'Cue Dream Sequence', 'Werewolves', 'Party Deux', 'Black Leather Lucy', 'The Business Side of Beauty' and 'Kid In A Big World' recorded and mixed in just under three hours, just in time for Stuart to come down and have a listen with Patsy.

"My God!" Chris enthused as his boss took his seat by him at the mixing desk, "This guy is SO fast, Stuart!"

"But is he any good?" Stuart replied, winking at me.

"Listen to these," Chris said and started the tape.

Stuart started to smile as 'Guess Who's Coming To Dinner' played, and I knew I'd clinched it. What neither he nor Chris knew, of course, was that, since the age of fourteen, I'd been recording demos on my multi-tracking Grundig tape recorder at home, double-tracking, harmonising with myself, and always, as I'd written any song, imagined the vocal arrangement I would record. The process was second-nature to me, and oddly, a bigger, more professional studio like Chappell didn't faze me at all. In fact I upped my game, knowing I had to not only please myself but impress a good engineer like Chris and my new manager. Patsy stood behind Stuart and at one point in the second song, Family Man, she put her hand on my shoulder and blinked at me. I learned this was her way of saying, 'Well done!'.

As the tape played, I could see Stuart getting increasingly excited, his eyes widening when I did a double-tracked falsetto in 'Werewolves', or a harmony line in 'Black Leather Lucy'. Patsy was well away too, throwing her arms around in a kind of on-the-spot bop, thoroughly loving what she was hearing. As the final track, 'Kid In A Big World' ended, Stuart jumped up, clapped me on the back and began a little jig of his own.

"Fucking brilliant!" he yelled. "Stardom here we fucking come!"

After that first studio session, Stuart asked me if I would go to his office every evening after work (I was still temping at Telephone Rentals during the day) and continue to write more songs. It wasn't a difficult request, he had a beautiful white grand piano for me to play and always left a bottle of whisky and a glass on a table beside it. I'd arrive about 6.30 in the evening, bid farewell to Stuart as he left for home and settle down until about 10 p.m., happily working on song ideas to my heart's content. I'd play them for him the next evening and if he liked any of them, he would book Chappell's for the first available night and I'd go down there to put some more demos down with Chris.

One evening I arrived at Stuart's office and was introduced to a chap called Eddie Pumer. He was a handsome man with dark brown eyes that burnt into you as he spoke, but he also possessed an endearingly respectful demeanour too.

"I love your songs!" he cried, shaking my hand, as I sat down. "That line in one of them, 'beetroot love bites', great line!"

'The Business Side of Beauty,' I told him.

"That's the one. Love it. I would really like to record some songs with you, with my band!"

Eddie told me he had been in Kaleidoscope and Fairfield Parlour in the late '60s and early '70s, and was now keen to follow his dream to become a full-time producer.

"I think working with a band would be good for you, John," Stuart said, as if telling me that Eddie would be perfect for me.

So a few nights later, I sat down with Eddie's four-piece, all Italian chaps who were a delight to work with. I would play the song on the piano as Eddie would sit beside me, studying what I played and write the chords down, then he'd pass around his chord sheets to the two guitar players and bass player, and, along with the drummer, we would spend about twenty minutes routining the song till we were ready to record. They very quickly 'got' what I wanted for the song, Eddie egging us on as we got a groove going and then worked it up to a proper arrangement. Eddie would run into the control room, Chris would roll the tape and by the end of the evening we'd done '3 Years (I'm Gonna Make It)', 'Maybe Someday In Miami', 'Pearl Parade', 'Small Town', 'Big Adventures' and 'Third Man'. When Stuart arrived at the end of the evening he literally jumped up and down during each track.

"We've already got nearly enough for an album, John!" he shouted as Eddie beamed at me and Chris.

Over the next few weeks I wrote several new songs on the white grand, including 'Spellbound', 'The Flame', and 'Deadly Nightshade'. They all excited Stuart enough to get me to demo them downstairs but it was when I played him 'Goodbye Suzie' that I thought he was going to cry.

"That's a hit, John! It's a fucking hit!" he shouted. Patsy's blink meant she agreed.

Stuart compiled a track-listing for what he saw as my 'album', his favourite demos, which Chris put together on a reel-to-reel for Stuart to play to record companies.

"They'll be queuing up to sign you," he assured me.

On one of my evening visits to Chappell's offices, I found Stuart looking a bit uneasy. He pointed to a chair by his desk, which was his silent 'Sit down, John', and, taking off his reading glasses, which always implied he had something serious to tell me, he said:

"A guy called Peter rang me today."

For a moment I wasn't sure who he meant, then as Stuart continued, I realised who it was:

"He said he'd recorded a tape of your songs earlier this year."

"Yes, he did," I replied without hesitation, and told Stuart the story of how I'd met Peter and Ann a few months earlier in a Manchester folk club and what had eventually transpired after I'd recorded that tape in the Civic Hall in Ramsbottom. "Is there a problem?" I asked, just checking my memory that I hadn't signed any pieces of paper for Peter. I hadn't, and said so.

"Well," Stuart said, starting to doodle on a pad in front of him, another sign I soon learnt which meant that he was concerned, "he is offering to let me have the tape, if I want it."

"Do you want it? I've demo'd all the songs which were on that tape for you downstairs, in a proper studio."

"No. I don't. Especially as this Peter chap has kind of intimated he wants something for the tape."

"Like what?"

"Not sure. Money, a stake in you, perhaps. I don't know. We didn't get that far. I told him I wasn't interested, that you were now signed to me, and that he should walk away and not call me again."

Although Stuart's story disturbed me, it didn't sound like Peter at all to make such a call, or to want anything from anyone. When I got home I rang him, but it was Ann who answered the phone. She was initially a little cool when she heard my voice:

"Peter's not here," she told me. "Shall I ask him to call you when he gets in?"

I heard a baby crying and realised,

"Oh! You've had the baby!"

"Yes! A little girl." Ann's voice warmed.

"I was thinking of coming to see you and Peter."

"That would be nice."

"When would be convenient for you?"

We arranged that I'd pop round that weekend.

Ann met me at the door as I walked up the path and welcomed me in with a smile, holding her new sleeping baby girl as she led me through to the sitting-room. I hadn't been back to the house since I'd moved out a few weeks earlier, but it was as cosy and homely as I remembered, with that recognisable smell of baking permeating through the house.

"Would you like some tea?" Ann asked me.

There was no Sophie this time to offer me Jasmine, in fact none of the kids were there. They'd gone out to the playground with their dad, Ann explained.

I followed Ann to the kitchen and stood leaning against one of the units as I asked her how she was coping with being a new mum again, watching her gently put the little girl into her 1950s style huge pram.

"Like riding a bike," she said, and went over to put on the kettle.

I decided to jump right in and risk drowning:

"I am so sorry about Peter's phone call with Stuart, Ann."

"Yes," she said, turning to face me. "He was, well, he was very hurt, John."

"I only found out about it when Stuart told me about it."

"Your manager seemed to think Peter wanted something for the tape." She glanced over at me with wide-eyes, tears forming in them. "He didn't, John. He just thought it might be useful, there may be something there your manager could use."

I didn't say anything of what Stuart had intimated to me, that he thought Peter did want something in return and just said,

"I know Peter wouldn't even think of such a thing. Obviously a misunderstanding. Stuart is a good guy, Ann. He really believes in me."

As she poured the tea into little bone china cups, added milk and handed mine to me she said,

"Yes, I'm sure he is. But, be careful, John. He did seem to Peter to feel like he now owned you."

"I guess, musically at least, he now does. I've signed a contract with him to manage me for the next five years. He's spending his money to put me in the studios, and next week his wife and I are going to look for clothes for me, which again Stuart is paying for."

"What's wrong with the ones you've got? You look fine to me as you are."

We sat down at the scrubbed pine kitchen table:

"Stuart feels I could be a star, so he wants to make me look like one."

Ann stared into the middle-distance:

"Hm. All I would say is...don't lose yourself, who you are is great, it was, apart from your music, what attracted Peter and I to you, you were so natural on stage. Not at all star-like, just lovely to watch."

I smiled at her, nodded my head, but inside felt she was wrong. If I was to be the Big Star I wanted to be, I had to follow what a professional manager planned for me. I knew nothing about how to make it, while Stuart had been involved with star names since the 1960s. At that point, the front door opened and in ran the kids, all excited to see me, hurling questions at me, telling me how much they'd missed me, Sophie asking if it was jasmine tea I was drinking.

When I told her, no, it was PG Tips, she turned to her mum and, looking very cross, said,

"Oh mum! John loves jasmine tea!"

"It's fine," I said, "you can make me a jasmine tea next time."

Then Peter walked in. He smiled a little distantly at me, came and shook my hand, but no hug, and leaned against a work-top, arms folded. He asked me how I was doing, what news I had, and listened intently as I told him about the demo sessions and Stuart's plans for me. Finally he nodded, almost to himself, and just said quietly, more to the floor than to me,

"Sounds like you've found the right guy."

When he looked up at me, he seemed very sad.

"I hope so, Peter," I replied, trying to throw him a smile, but it wasn't received and hovered above us. Ann caught it instead and smiled at Peter, going over to hold his hand:

"It's very exciting for you, John!" She nudged Peter who finally smiled at me.

"I wish you all the best," he said. "You deserve it."

We all sat round the table, with the kids running in and out all the while, and chatted amiably for another ten minutes or so, but it was obvious that Ann needed to get a meal going for her family, so I excused myself, kissed Ann on the cheek, said goodbye to the kids as Peter followed me to the door alone.

"Take care, John," he said as he shook my hand again. "A step at a time, eh?"

I wanted to apologise to him personally for the phone call but decided not to. It would have sounded rather empty and I hoped Ann would tell him what I had said about it. As I turned to go, Peter said,

"Be amazing. I know you will be."

I turned to reply but he was already closing the door with a final glance in my direction. I never saw him, Ann or the kids again. Our time together, and we all knew it, was over.

One little postscript to this. After my phone call to Ann before my final visit, I had called to chat to my mum, as I regularly did, and mentioned to her that Ann had had a new baby. Always thrilled about new arrivals, she had knitted a little baby outfit for her and posted it in a brown paper parcel to Ann. The next time I went to visit Mum, a few weeks later, she told me how she had never had a response to her gift, obviously hurt and disappointed. I said it had probably got lost in the post. It may have done. Who knows? I could have rung to find out if they'd got it but didn't. I should have, of course, if only to find out for my mum that it had never arrived. Anyhow, I thought at the time it was best to let Mum believe it had been mislaid in the post, and somehow, another uncomfortable conversation where misunderstandings could have been flying down the phone line, was not something I wanted to have with either Ann or Peter.

Have there been regrets I didn't call? Of course.

One crisp sunny morning in early October, feeling very excited, if a little apprehensive, I met Patsy at Chappell's from where we trotted off, first of all, to Biba in Kensington High Street. The huge art deco store had become the place all fashionable folk went to at that time, especially after Roxy Music had credited the store on their album sleeves, 'Clothes by Biba'. While it was great to visit and rather lovely to wander round its cavernous rooms and admire the satin shirts, billowing trousers, paisley scarves, sequinned shoes and various odd-looking cape things which were draped around naked mannequins, I wasn't in truth all that impressed. The store felt more like an art gallery or clothes museum, under-stocked, over-priced tat, as though someone with a lot of spare cash had bought the biggest shop they could find and then discovered they didn't have enough things to fill it. There were enormous areas of under-lit empty floor spaces filled more with the sound of David Bowie and Roxy Music blaring out from sound-surround speakers than actual merchandise, or indeed enough lighting to see what was on offer. Staff tended to stand around aimlessly in little groups looking gorgeously bored, more like models awaiting their call to strut their stuff than shop assistants. The latter part of their job description hadn't been explained to them, whereas 'staring vacuously' obviously had.

Still, we found a couple of nice blue satin tops and a pair of bell-bottom purple silk trousers, a sequinned top-hat, and a pair of six-inch heeled brown and gold platform shoes. And we enjoyed a snack lunch upstairs in The Rainbow Room restaurant, though the price of a fairly ordinary cheese and salad sandwich, which Patsy paid for without batting an eyelid, made my eyes water. Again the room was huge, all art deco back-lit splendour and Noel Coward trilling away in the background. I wanted to feel excited at being there, but didn't. I found the whole place pretentious, cheap-looking and ridiculously expensive.

Our next stop was far more productive. Herbie Frogg's in Jermyn Street oozed tailoring class and a sense of history. Smart shop assistants bubbled around busily, bidding you 'Good afternoon' as they walked past with a bolt of fabric in hand. It all felt purposeful and professional. A very pleasant Spanish chap walked towards us, greeted us charmingly, listened carefully to what Patsy told him we needed, and within a few minutes I was being measured for a new suit. We eventually plumped for a pinstripe double-breasted number, "accentuates your slim frame," Patsy advised. We also bought some white and red embossed cotton shirts and a few beautiful silk ties. I'd also seen in the window a couple of gorgeous wide-brimmed fedora hats, one white, one red, so I tried them on. Patsy and the enthusiastic salesman purred as I looked at myself in the mirror, so they were added in to our purchases. I'd also fallen in love with a pair of black and white brogues one of the mannequins was wearing, so tried those on too. Another box ticked. We got back to Chappell's laden down with 'HF' and Biba shopping bags, which we emptied on Stuart's desk and showed him everything we'd bought. He was impressed with the Frogg stuff, less so with the Biba frippery.

"The suit will be ready in a couple of days," Patsy told him.

"I'll come with you to have that fitted, John," Stuart said. "I know how a good suit should look and feel."

He took us for a quick meal to Kettner's in Soho, all high white stuccoed ceilings and huge sash windows overlooking the bustling West End streets. The dinner-jacketed pianist tinkled away on the Steinway Grand as we tucked into the most expensive egg and chips I had ever eaten. Every time someone walked in to take their table, Stuart would wave to them, then quietly tell me who they were. Artist managers, producers, publishers, people he'd known for decades. Patsy would reminisce about the Mediterranean holidays they'd taken with so-and-so in the corner, or about the DJ near the window who had played Stuart's first hit in the '60s. The Maître D', a dapper octogenarian gent with twinkling eyes, came over and shook Stuart's hand, kissed Patsy on the cheek and welcomed me warmly to "my beautiful restaurant!".

Then, meal over, out on the streets of Soho again, we bid Stuart goodbye and Patsy whisked me off to her hairdresser's in Knightsbridge. I was praying my bosses at Telephone Rentals weren't out and about there, as I'd rung that morning, once again, to tell them I was sick.

The brightly-lit establishment was a hive of chic and noisy activity as Susan, Patsy's personal hairdresser, took me to a chair and stroking and combing my long hair, excitedly declared that I had "great hair!" and all it needed was "a bit of styling."

"We don't want to lose too much length," she told Patsy, who nodded in agreement, "just give it a bit of body. Let's get a fringe thing going as well and go from there."

Half an hour later, after being preened, washed and cut, I looked in the mirror at this transformed kid, with shiny hair that no longer hung limply from a Lennon centre parting down my back, but now bobbed every time I moved my head with full-bodied life.

"You look gorgeous!" Susan exclaimed, as I swished my head from side to side like some Silvikrin model.

"He looked gorgeous before, Susan," Patsy said, doing her blink at me, "just even more so now."

As we walked back to Hanover Square to meet Stuart for dinner, Patsy told me she was even more convinced now that I would be a star.

"The way you handled everything today, John, it was like you were born to it. I can't believe that just a few months ago you'd come down from a tiny northern town with very little money and no experience of city life. Look at you now. You even carry yourself like a star!"

A cold autumn wind blew around us but I felt an inner glow no icy temperature outside could cool.

A couple of days later, I was fitted for my suit. Stuart watched me admiringly as I looked at myself in the mirror, the salesman picking at various parts of it and suggesting a nip here, a tuck there.

"I think you just grew another two inches, John," Stuart said.

"He has!" the salesman cried. "A man born to wear a good suit!"

That evening, Stuart and Patsy took me to the White Elephant restaurant. It was a hubbub of chatter, clinking glasses and crockery which chimed wonderfully with the sense of the confident enjoyment of success. I'd dressed in my new outfit of pinstripe suit, white fedora, white cotton shirt and striped black and white silk tie, finished off with my raised-heel brogues and felt like a million dollars. As we were shown to our table Stuart beamed around the room, waving at various smiling people, his glow reflecting on me like a stage spotlight. As we sat down a broad-shouldered handsome man came over to us, hand outstretched to Stuart.

"Mitch!" Stuart cried, grabbing his hand with both of his. "Let me introduce you to my artist, John Howard. John, meet Mitch Murray."

"Pleased to meet you, John!" Mitch said, oozing success and confidence. "You're with the right guy, that's for sure," and he patted Stuart on the back.

"Come for dinner!" Patsy said, "Soon!"

"That's a date, lovely lady," and he kissed Patsy's hand.

When he'd gone back to his table, I said:

"Mitch Murray! Wow! He's written so many hit songs!"

"So many," Patsy said, shaking her head.

"Yes, he and Peter Callander have a huge catalogue of smash hits to their name," Stuart agreed.

"Stuart and I have known Mitch for years, John. We celebrated his first Number One with him…"

"'How Do You Do It'," Stuart interjected.

"Gerry and The Pacemakers," I added. "Their first of three No.1s, and the first British act to achieve that with their first three singles."

Stuart's eyes widened, and he nudged Patsy:

"This boy is not only talented, he knows his pop music too!"

"Mitch wrote Gerry's second No.1, didn't he?" I asked, though I knew the answer before Stuart told me.

"Yep, 'I Like It'. Great song!"

The waiter came to take our drinks order just as another smiling chap strode over to our table:

"Stuart! Patsy!" he said.

"Les!" Patsy cried.

"Les Reed as I stand and breathe!" Stuart said laughing, and standing to greet him clapped him on the shoulder. "Let me introduce you to my artist, John Howard."

I stood and shook Les's hand.

"This is such a great guy, John!" Les said, pointing at Stuart. "The best! We have had so many hits together, Stuart and I!"

Stuart smiled at Les, then at me.

"What was our first hit, Les?"

"'It's Not Unusual'!" Les replied. He turned to me. "We offered it to Sandie Shaw, you know, John, and she turned it down, so we gave it to the guy who'd done the demo for me. A certain Tom Jones!"

"My favourite was 'The Last Waltz'," Patsy said. "Such a great song."

"How many million did it sell, Les?" Stuart asked. They were quite the double-act.

"Four million and counting, Stuart!"

Stuart patted me on the shoulder and winked at Les: "This guy, Les, is going to write songs that sell millions too. I guarantee it."

"With you, Stuart, anything is possible!"

As Les went back to his friends, the waiter, who had politely stood to one side until the jolly conversation came to an end, took our order.

"Champagne!" Stuart said. "I want to celebrate the birth of my new star!"

"Christ! You know everyone, Stuart!" I said, smiling over at Les Reed who smiled back.

"And everyone knows Stuart," Patsy said. "That, John, is your calling card."

Autumn 1973 London, my first London photo session, by Dezo Hoffman

The next stage in

Stuart's JH portfolio building was arranging a photo session.

"We have got you your Look, now, John, so we must now make sure everyone sees that, every record company A & R man will have your face looking at them as he falls in love with your songs!"

One rainy October evening, he took me to a tiny back street building in Soho, where we ascended a slightly seedy set of stairs and wandered through a scuff-marked off-white door marked 'Dezo Hoffman – Photographic Studio' into rather a large empty room. A sturdy middle-aged small man in horn-rimmed glasses came from behind a partition to greet us:

"Stuart! My old friend! How are you?" he cried in an Eastern European accent.

"Dezo!" Stuart cried back, slapping him on the back. "This is my artist John Howard."

I shook Dezo's warm large hand and he smiled at me, then at Stuart:

"Good looking boy!"

Stuart beamed at Dezo then at me.

We followed Dezo round the room, as he nattered away about what he could do regarding lighting, set-ups, and showed us various screens which were propped against the cream walls (they were actually white, but hadn't been painted for years). Lights of different sizes stood at ease as their master started picking out

Autumn 1973 London, my first London photo session, by Dezo Hoffman

some of them and positioning them, head tilted to one side as he made a lens square with his hands and pointed it at me.

"You have a good slim figure," he murmured, more to himself than to me, "a young face and good cheekbones, so I will not need to light you too kindly. You can stand some harsh lighting with your features."

What Stuart may have told me in part as we'd wandered through Soho to Dezo's studio that rainy evening, but which I probably hadn't taken in, was that Hoffman, a Slovakian photojournalist, had photographed some of the biggest names in pop music through the '60s and early '70s. The Beatles, The Rolling Stones, Dusty Springfield, The Kinks, Jimi Hendrix, Elton John and Pink Floyd had all been given the Dezo treatment. His black and white shots of pop stars had become iconic. He'd also photographed Charlie Chaplin, Marlon Brando, Frank Sinatra, Sophia Loren, Marilyn Monroe and Laurence Olivier in his long career. As a young man, he'd worked at Twentieth Century Fox in Paris and gone on various infamous assignments in the 1930s such as filming Mussolini's invasion of Abyssinia and surviving a period in Spain during the Civil War. He'd met Hemingway and became a great friend of his. In the mid-'50s he'd started work at Record Mirror and so began his long career photographing pop stars and celebrities.

In 1962, he had struck up a long-standing friendship with The Beatles, after travelling to Liverpool to take photos of the then largely unknown group, and immediately sealing a bond with them. His candid shots of The Fab Four through to about 1966, are now, of course, featured in numerous books and exhibitions. Paul McCartney reportedly once said that Dezo was "the world's best photographer."

That October evening, however, I just found him a pleasant little man who worked hard to relax me in front of his peering lens, as it closed in on me, the white lights slightly blinding me. Patsy turned up halfway through the session and Dezo was impressed by the change in my expression as I greeted her.

"Patsy!" he declared, "go and stand in front of John, out of camera range but close enough so he looks at you…" She settled herself on a stool a few feet from me… "Now, John, look at Patsy…There! You see, Stuart! His whole face changes, softens, relaxes when he's looking at your wife! You should be a worried man!"

Stuart chuckled, "Oh, I don't think I need worry about that, Dezo."

The two men exchanged glances and Dezo nodded knowingly.

"Still, he loves Patsy, that's for sure," he said, nodding at her and winking.

I found the session rather stilted and uncomfortable, not used to posing in various outfits as a photographer closed in on me, a bit like being in a dentist's chair, or having an eye test, the two-hour session was full of bright lights, peering eyes, and a sense that I was being judged every second, every twitch, look, smile, movement of the head was greeted by "Yes! That's good! Do that again! Lower your head! Look at Patsy! Stand up, over there, yes!"

The results, on sheaths of shiny paper with dozens of tiny black and white shots of me in various poses and settings, looked at through a magnifying glass with Stuart and Patsy the following afternoon at Chappell, were, for all that, rather splendid. Stuart circled about half a dozen of what he thought were the best shots and called in a young lad to take the envelope back to Dezo so he could make up Ten-By-Eights of them.

"Next week I begin the hard work, John. I'm going to put together several John Howard folders, photos, tapes, a biog, and take them to all the top A & R men in London, and wait for the phone to ring – it shouldn't be long before we're inundated with offers of a deal!"

After about two weeks, still arriving in the evening to compose new songs on the white grand with a bottle of whisky for company, I plucked up the courage to ask Stuart if he'd heard back from any of the record companies. He shuffled a little in his seat and looked down at his desk, fiddling with a pen, clicking it distractedly. Finally, he let out a long sigh:

"Well, John, I still believe in you, but sadly, I've had a pretty negative response so far. EMI and Warners have both said 'definitely no', Phonogram and Polydor can't make up their minds, and CBS seemed interested at first but have gone cool in the last couple of days, not returning my calls."

I tried to sound upbeat, but my heart was sinking. 'Here we go again,' I thought.

Stuart suddenly brightened:

"Jonathan King loves you though," he said. "He thinks 'Family Man' is a hit."

King was then a hit-maker in his own right, with eight Top Thirty hits of his own, and recently his label UK Records had enjoyed huge success with 10cc, who'd notched up three Top Ten singles and a growing reputation for perfectly crafted pop records.

"Why don't we sign with him, then?" I asked.

Stuart shook his head:

"I want you to have a deal with a big record company, John," he explained. "One-off singles are fine, but you should have a long-term career as an albums artist who sells millions of records, you are not just a one-hit wonder."

The truth was, at that moment, having even one hit single seemed like a great idea to me, and I wanted to push Stuart to accept King's offer of a singles deal, but I decided to trust my manager's judgement, and be patient.

The phone rang at my Kilburn flat one evening while I was sitting chatting to Phillipa and Kerry over a bottle of red wine. Philippa's eyes lit up:

"The call I was waiting for!" she cried and jumped up to answer it.

I heard her bright little voice deflate into disappointment as she said, "Yes, John's here, who's calling?"

She poked her head round the door-frame, trying a smile, "It's your manager, John."

Kerry held up the bottle of wine as Philippa sat down, "So Mr Right is Mr No-Show?"

"They're all Mr No-Shows these days, darling," she moaned and held out her glass for a refill.

Stuart sounded very perky on the phone:

"John! CBS's Head of A&R, Dan Loggins has called to say they love your tape and want to see you perform somewhere. I've booked a little eaterie-cum-night club in Knightsbridge, Small's. Do you know it?"

I didn't, and again hoped none of the Telephone Rentals crowd ate there after work as I'd had quite a few days 'off sick' in recent weeks. It was only a temp job and I just got paid for the days I worked. But still, I felt guilty at keep letting them down, even though it was a boring clerical job filling in cards and filing them which anyone with half a brain could do. However, it paid my rent and I couldn't afford to lose it.

"I've booked Small's for tomorrow night, John, meet Patsy and I at Chappell's at 6.30, you're on at 8, CBS are sending their A & R team to see you. Wear the full gear, glamour is the word!"

Small's was actually quite large, very chic with a lovely white baby grand in the centre of where people ate. As we arrived a handsome man with a thick bushy moustache and twinkling eyes marched towards us and shook my hand:

"John! Great to meet you! I'm Dan Loggins," he said with a languid American accent I immediately adored.

"Good to meet you too, Dan!" I said as brightly as I could muster, trying to match his American verve. "Loggins? No relation to...?"

"Kenny Loggins is my brother!" Dan said, with an expression

which said 'everyone asks me that.'

I'd loved Kenny's 'Danny's Song' which Anne Murray had had a hit with a couple of years earlier, and knew some of the Loggins & Messina records.

Standing behind Dan was a younger red-haired chap, who smiled at me rather shyly the whole time I was talking. Dan saw me looking at him and jumped backwards:

"Hey! Sorry Paul! I should introduce you. John, this is my A & R manager, Paul Phillips."

Paul stepped forward and in a soft Brummie accent shook my hand and said,

"I absolutely love your music, John."

Feeling very good about things again, I sang well that evening, and loved the piano I was playing. Other diners seemed to enjoy what I played as well. Whenever I looked across at Dan and Paul sitting with Stuart and Patsy, Dan was in deep conversation with Stuart while Patsy and Paul just watched me, smiling to themselves and nodding to each other at the end of each song.

After we made our goodbyes outside the restaurant, with lots of waving and 'I'll call you, Stuart!' cries from Dan down Knightsbridge High Street, Stuart and Patsy walked me to the tube. They seemed thrilled with how the evening had gone.

"I'm expecting a phone call from Dan tomorrow!" Stuart assured me as I went down the steps to take the train home.

I arrived as usual at Chappell's the next evening expecting some good news. So I was surprised to find Stuart looking rather glum, twitchy even. I asked him if he was alright.

"John, come and stand over here," Stuart replied, rather oddly.

I did as he asked and stood opposite him.

"Now, shake my hand."

I did.

"Yes, Dan's right," Stuart said rather despairingly. "Your handshake is terrible, John."

I was puzzled. He'd never said this to me before.

"Dan says you have to develop a much stronger handshake. He said it was like shaking hands with a waterfall last night."

"What has that got to do with my music?" I asked.

"Nothing, John, but it has everything to do with how you present yourself to CBS executives."

He could see how mystified I was.

"A lot of them are rough tough New York guys, John, they expect men to be manly. Soft is fine for women, but not for men."

I actually laughed out loud:

"What cave did they crawl out of? Hello? Ziggy Stardust was hardly Mr Butch! Marc Bolan was never going to win Mr Universe!"

"But you are not Ziggy Stardust, John. You are not Marc Bolan. You are John Howard, English gent. These Americans see you as an upright masculine British guy, dressed fabulously, chic, full of confidence. Then you shake their hand and they realise..."

"That I'm just a rather effeminate gay guy."

"Well..."

"And?"

Stuart looked slightly impatient:

"You can be what you are as often as you like when you're with friends, John, I don't give a damn what you do, who you sleep with. You can hang from a chandelier with carrots up your arse for all I care. But John Howard, CBS Recording Artist, he's a different guy. It's all about image, perception. I've sold you as an all-English boy next door, charming,, funny, erudite, and..."

"Straight?"

"I've never actually mentioned your sexuality, John. But we have to give them what they want. Or no deal. Now! Shake my hand again!"

Reluctantly, I did.

"Better. Now, shake my hand again, even more firmly, and stop dropping your wrist. It's like you're expecting me to kiss your hand."

"Maybe I am, Stuart!"

"If we get the deal with CBS, I will, John, believe me. But bear with me. Now, shake my hand again!"

Over the next ten minutes, we went through this bizarre process where I made each handshake firmer than the last, until finally, Stuart flinched:

"Perfect! Strong as a rod of iron! Now keep that up. I want Dan to be writhing in agony next time you shake his hand."

Disappointingly, after the Small's gig and the surreal phone call from Dan about my handshake, things went quiet again on the CBS front. I could tell Stuart was getting exasperated. They seemed really enthusiastic one minute then wouldn't return Stuart's calls for days. When someone did come to the phone it was to tell him they were still discussing me.

Towards the end of November, I was having dinner at Stuart and Patsy's house in Willesden Green, just a short walk from my flat in Kilburn, and enjoying the company of a young singer-songwriter called Biddu. 'Bid', as he was known, was a long-standing friend of the Reids, a very attractive beautifully dressed Indian man, great stature and a wonderful smile. As he sat playing us his new songs on the guitar he'd brought along, I could hear something special in there, and while he didn't have the greatest voice, there was a lovely melodic content to what he'd composed. As we went to the table to eat Patsy's as always glorious food, Bid turned to me and said,

"I really love your music, John. I'd love to produce you."

Stuart looked at Patsy then at me, and as we tucked into the starter, said to Bid,

"I think we really need a name producer for John, Bid. CBS have said they need a big name to get John noticed."

I could see how disappointed Bid was, but he took it in good cheer, and we continued to enjoy the meal, listening to Stuart's always entertaining stories of his time in the music business.

"How are things going at CBS, Stu?" Bid asked.

"Well, it's difficult to say. They seem really keen on John, love his music, then it goes quiet, then I get weird calls about his handshake..."

Bid look mystified.

"Don't ask, Bid. It's crazy. Then today I get a call from someone in marketing saying they want to change his name!"

This was news to me and obviously to Patsy too. She stared at Stuart:

"Change his name? To what?"

"They think Christopher Howard or Sean Howard is more interesting than John Howard."

"Utter nonsense!" Patsy huffed, helping herself rather stroppily to more salad.

"I can't see how either name is better," Bid added, taking the salad bowl and putting some on his plate.

"John?" Stuart said, "What do you think?"

Without hesitation I said, "No way. My name is John Howard. I don't suddenly want to become Christopher or Sean!"

Stuart banged the table, sending the salad bowl dancing across it:

"Great! My feelings entirely. I'll call CBS tomorrow and tell them it's John Howard or nothing!"

As we heard nothing more from the label through December, I assumed it was, sadly, nothing. Then about a week before Christmas, Stuart called me at home:

"John? Get your bags packed my boy, we're going to Madrid tomorrow!"

The first thing I thought was 'What am I going to tell my boss at TR this time?'.

"Madrid? Why?"

"Because, John Howard, you have been commissioned to write the theme song for the next Peter Fonda movie, that's why!"

It turned out Stuart was an old friend of the film director Peter Collinson, and in conversation he'd mentioned to Stuart he was looking for songs to start and end the movie he was filming with Fonda and William Holden in Spain. Stuart had sent Peter my demo tape and within a week received a call from Peter shouting down the phone, "I want John Howard to write my songs!"

"Right, what time shall I meet you?" I spluttered, down the phone.

"Taxi's picking you up at your flat at 7 a.m., John. Set your alarm for six. Don't be late!"

This was amazing news. Peter Collinson was an iconic director, *Up The Junction, The Italian Job,* to name just two classic films he'd directed. In fact he had featured his godfather Noel Coward in The Italian Job. And now, I was off to Madrid the following morning to meet him and watch the film rushes of his new movie.

As we were off so early in the morning, I begged Phillipa to call TR for me and tell them I had the 'flu. She was so excited for me she agreed without too much begging being needed.

Stuart chatted to me as we boarded the plane, telling me that Peter had said to him that, until he'd heard my demos, he had been considering Don McLean to write the film's songs. I was just digesting that information when the steward grabbed hold of my shoulder and said,

"This way, sir."

I was automatically making for Economy, but, with a thrilled smile, he gently redirected me through a curtain into the First Class seating area.

"If you'd like to take your seat, sir, and we'll be along shortly to take your breakfast order."

"This is how it's going to be from now on, John," Stuart said as we sat down and were offered a glass of champagne. He lifted his bubbling glass to mine and said, "To success, to stardom."

We were met at Madrid airport by a suited gentleman who shielded us from the pouring rain as he led us to a limousine, into which we sank, the smell of real leather, wood panelling and an expensive cologne permeating the car. Ten minutes later, we were escorted by the doorman into a beautiful hotel, probably with the largest foyer area I had ever seen, apart from in Fred Astaire movies. Whisked up to a suite of rooms by a respectful porter, I assumed they were for Stuart and I to share. But when he followed the porter along the corridor, I realised all this was mine.

"Settle yourself in, John," Stuart said over his shoulder. "I'll call you in a couple of hours and we'll have an early dinner, ready for tomorrow."

I closed the door and wandered around my huge suite which seemed to go on forever, comprising an enormous beautifully furnished sitting room, with a beautiful large vase of white lilies on the coffee table, two massive bedrooms, a bathroom which Cleopatra would have felt at home in, and my own fully-stocked mini-bar beneath a smoke-glass counter under dimmed spotlighting, packed with glasses and goblets.

I picked a bedroom, sat on the bed and fell back laughing my head off. Less than six months earlier, I'd been living in a tiny village in Lancashire, working as a postman, playing folk clubs at night for at most £5 a go, and dreaming that perhaps one day I would make it with my music and enjoy some success. And now, here I was, in the centre of Madrid, surrounded by rooms straight out of a Hollywood movie, treated like a star and about to begin work on writing songs for a Peter Fonda movie directed by one of the greatest living film directors. I picked up the phone and rang reception:

"Hello. Could you call a UK number for me and charge it to my room, it's..."

"Room 150, sir. Yes, immediately. What is the number you wish to call?"

A couple of minutes later I heard my mum answer the phone. She sounded tired, battling as she was with cancer.

"Mum?!" I shouted.

"Ee, hello, love! Are you alright?" Her voice brightened.

"You will never guess where I am right now…"

Stuart woke me at 6.30 the following morning:

"Good morning, John! Hope you slept well! Order breakfast from room service and meet me in reception at 8 o'clock. They're sending a car for us at 8.15."

The limo whisked us through the rain-drenched streets of Madrid as Stuart chatted about how this commission to write the songs for Peter's film may give CBS the "kick up the pants they need." Finally, we arrived at a large building on an industrial estate outside the city and, as the car pulled up, a bright-faced red-haired girl came running out of there to greet us:

"Hi! I'm Sue!" she cried, as we got out of the car, "Peter's inside waiting to see you! God! This weather! What a welcome!"

Trying and failing to shelter us under a tiny pink brolly, she ushered us in to a small ante-room where a tall, gangly bearded man sat smoking a Gauloise. As we entered the room he stood and strode forward:

"Stuart Reid! Do my eyes deceive me? You look even younger than you did last time I saw you!"

Stuart was indeed a very youthful fifty-eight. He laughed, shook Peter's hand and stood aside to introduce me, but Peter didn't wait:

"John! It is such a pleasure to meet you! I adore your music! I am extremely honoured that you will be writing songs for my movie."

I was about to say the honour was all mine when Sue dashed in with a clipboard:

"Peter! William needs to speak to you!"

Peter grinned at us and took a long drag on his cigarette:

"Excuse me, chaps, when the star of one's movie calls, one runs!"

Sue smiled at me as Peter rushed by her:

"William Holden," she said nodding excitedly. "You'll meet him later, John!"

'Christ!' I thought. 'The star of Sunset Boulevard! The fucking star of Sunset fucking Boulevard!'.

Sue offered Stuart and I a coffee and asked if we minded if she smoked. Once again, that exotic aroma filled the room as she blew impressive smoke rings, speaking animatedly about how the movie was going:

"Fonda's a darling but quite mad. Carries a gun everywhere. That's been a bit of a problemette in Spain, but we've managed to keep him out of jail. William is quite different, very quiet, very much a gentleman." More smoke rings rose to the ceiling, and she stared intensely at me. "This film will blow your mind, John. It will inspire you to write something truly great."

No pressure then.

Peter returned like a hurricane into the room, explaining to Sue that everything was fine with William, got a cigarette out of her pack, sat down next to me and, looking me straight in the eye, began a long, thoughtful monologue, punctuated with little wags of his finger to emphasise a point:

"John. This film is going to be very big. It's thought-provoking, yes it's brutal, but it's also touching, and it's heartbreaking. Your music, I know this, will be perfect for it. When I heard the tape Stuart sent me I literally jumped across the room and turned up the volume full... didn't I Sue?"

Sue nodded eagerly at us all and blew an even bigger smoke ring.

"Sue knows I am not an easy man to please." Raised eyebrows from Sue. "I demand perfection of my crew, my actors, my production people, and in your music I heard perfection. SO fucking amazing, man!! How old are you?"

"Twenty."

"Fucking incredible. You write like a man who has lived a lot longer than twenty years!"

Sue nodded even more eagerly at me.

"What I want you to be aware of, John, is that this film, your involvement in this film, will make the world talk about your music for years to come. This film will change your life."

Both Sue and Stuart were now nodding at me eagerly. I felt like joining in.

"Now, come with me gents and watch what I believe will be the best film of 1974."

In a fairly small viewing room, the large screen in front of us lighting up the smoke which rose from various seats - smoke rings rising regularly in the front row - I watched with Stuart as the uncut four hour movie unfolded. *Open Season* was indeed brutal, it told the story of three young guys, played by Peter Fonda, John Phillip Law and Richard Lynch, who had raped a young, under-age girl, in a car as students. As grown successful businessmen a few years later, and now damaged by their previous experiences in Vietnam, they go on their annual hunting weekends together, but, on this particular weekend, they decide to hunt a different kind of prey. They kidnap a young couple they see at a garage on the way, take them to their hunting lodge and proceed to rape, humiliate and torture them, until finally making them run for their lives as they hunt them down. Their wives back home have no idea what they are getting up to as they return home with a stag tied to the roof of their car, with jolly plans for a venison barbecue the following weekend.

The young girl they had raped years earlier had, unknown to them, given birth to a baby boy and shortly after had killed herself, the boy being raised by her grandfather, played by William Holden.

He turns the hunters into the hunted as he follows them to their lodge and, one-by-one, shoots them as they run from him in terror.

It made uncomfortable viewing and everyone was very quiet as the film ended with Holden's character sailing away from the lodge, job done. As I readied to leave my seat Peter walked over to us and introduced me to Peter Fonda. As I held out my hand to shake his, Fonda mimed shooting me with a gun, blew on his fingers and tipped his hat at me and winked.

"What did you think, guys?" Collinson asked Stuart and me as Fonda carried on up the aisle, slapping his co-actors on the back as they left the viewing room.

"Amazing film," Stuart replied.

"Incredible," I said, "really powerful. I've already got an idea for the songs I'm going to write."

"Yes, well...." Peter put his arm round my shoulder and led me up the aisle into daylight, "...I've been thinking. I want you to not only write two songs for the movie, how about also writing some music, or songs, for the scenes on the road and in the boat?"

Those scenes were very disturbing, the three men hailing the puzzled couple in their car, pretending to be traffic cops, kidnapping them at gunpoint, and then, later, taunting the man and woman on a boat as they sailed up a river to their lodge.

"Sure!" I said enthusiastically.

We had a great film crew dinner that evening in a large packed restaurant in the centre of Madrid, Peter regaling us with stories of his godfather Noel Coward, working with him and Michael Caine on *The Italian Job* and Dennis Waterman on *Up The Junction*. I felt completely at home with these wonderful creative people. Ramsbottom, Lancs seemed a million miles away.

On the flight home with Stuart the following morning, I wrote down the first couple of verses of what became 'Casting Shadows'. Stuart glanced over and said, "Inspired already, John?"

"Of course!" I said, writing down another line. "How could I not be?"

A few days later I was in Chappell Studios recording piano and voice demos of four songs I'd written for the film. 'Casting Shadows', which I saw as opening the movie over the scene where the raped girl lifts her hands to a rain-soaked car window after her ordeal; 'Missing Key', which I imagined as ending the film, over the scene with William Holden riding away on his power boat after killing the three rapists; and two others I saw for the road and boat scenes Peter had mentioned. Stuart sent the tape off to Peter and we waited for his reaction.

Just before Christmas, the response came, Peter calling Stuart as I was eating dinner with him and Patsy at their home. I could hear Stuart talking quietly on the phone in the hall as Patsy smiled at me across the dinner table. Finally, Stuart came back in, all smiles:

"Peter absolutely loves 'Casting Shadows'!"

Patsy grabbed my hand, "Fantastic news, John!"

"However…" Stuart sat down, "he now wants to use an instrumental of that song to end the film, rather than a different song, and has commissioned an Italian composer to write the incidental music for the rest of the movie."

"Why?" Patsy asked, incredulous.

"I would imagine pressure from the Italian sponsors. Still, we have the theme song for the new Peter Fonda movie! Congratulations, John! I'm very proud of you."

Patsy lifted her glass of wine and toasted me:

"To John!"

"To John!" Stuart repeated, clinking my raised glass.

Later in bed, I couldn't help feeling slightly disappointed that the other three songs I'd written hadn't impressed Peter as much as 'Casting Shadows'. Still, when I rang my parents a few days later and told them I would be recording my song for the film in Rome in the

New Year, they sounded suitably thrilled.

I went home for Christmas, knowing this was likely to be my last one spent with Mum. She was remaining apparently well after her operation a year earlier, but I knew the doctors had told my dad she would only last another eighteen months at most after the op. The cancer had spread to all her vital organs and there was no way they could halt it.

However, when I walked in and saw the Christmas Tree all lit up and her beaming face as I walked in, all that was forgotten.

"You got a real tree this time!" I shouted.

"Yes, son, I know how much you love real ones, so we decided to get one just for you this time."

I hugged her and realised how thin she was. Never a strong lady, always skinny, she felt very bony for all that, and somehow much smaller.

Stuart and Patsy held a party at their house on New Year's Eve and I returned to London for that. It was a wonderful evening full of some of the music business stellar people. John Burgess, who had started up AIR Studios with George Martin; David Platz who ran Essex Music and had once signed T.Rex, The Move and Joe Cocker to his record labels; songwriter Tony Macaulay gave us fantastic renditions on the piano of some of his hit compositions – 'Baby Now That I've Found You', 'Last Night I Didn't Get To Sleep At All', 'Love Grows', 'Build Me Up Buttercup', 'The Lights of Cincinnati', 'Home Lovin' Man', finishing off with his current smash hit, The New Seekers' 'You Won't Find Another Fool Like Me', which had entered the Top Three that week. Les Reed then took over and gave us 'The Last Waltz', 'It's Not Unusual', 'There's A Kind Of Hush', and 'Delilah', which had everyone singing along in the chorus.

After the sing-song, we'd all settled down to play a few games of charades, when the door bell went. Patsy went to get it and we heard her cry, "Jim!"

In walked Jim Dale, straight from his performance on that evening's Sunday Night At The London Palladium. He was covered in tinsel as he bounded into the room, shaking everyone's hands and settling down with a glass of wine cross-legged on the floor next to me. When I mentioned to him how much I loved Kenneth Williams, knowing he'd been in a couple of Carry On movies, he proceeded to give us perfect imitations of Kenneth, and telling us some lovely stories of working with him.

The evening was full of chatter and wine-pouring, everyone having a tale to tell of their careers in the music business, and during one of Stuart's stories of his time in the '50s as a record plugger for Robins Music Publishers, Jim turned to me and said,

"So, John, how do you fit into all..." he waved his hand around the room, "...this?"

"I'm a songwriter," I replied, feeling very inconsequential at that moment.

"So, is Stuart managing you?"

"Yes. He's talking to CBS at the moment about a record deal."

Stuart had finished his story, and had moved to a sofa above us, overhearing our conversation:

"Jim, John is being very modest. He is in fact a wonderful singer and pianist!"

Jim stood, made a sweeping gesture towards the piano and said, "Then, maestro, play for us!"

I hadn't intended to perform at all, not surrounded by a roomful of hit-makers, and Stuart had kindly not insisted I do.

"John?" he asked me, seeing how I felt about it.

Jim got hold of my hand, lifted me up and took me to the piano:

"If Stuart Reid says you're great, then you will be great! Now, please," he made a praying gesture, "please, John, play!"

So I sat rather nervously at the piano and played 'Family Man'. It was greeted at the end by a standing ovation. I felt my legs slightly shaking as I stood to bow.

"Another!" Jim Dale shouted, to cries of "More!" from everyone else.

I looked at Stuart:

"Do my favourite of yours, John," he said and I knew exactly what that was.

At the end of 'Guess Who's Coming To Dinner', Jim walked up to me, took my hand and kissed it.

"You are a bloody marvel, son!" he shouted and waved his arms at everyone to continue the applause.

Stuart proceeded to tell everyone about the commissioned song I had written for Peter Collinson's movie and, thankfully before anyone had the chance to ask me to play that, Patsy brought in hot snacks for us all. As we ate Jim leaned over to me and said,

"I would love to include 'Family Man' in a one-man show I'm planning, John."

Patsy, overhearing what Jim said, blinked at me and blew a kiss.

Later as we all linked arms and sang 'Auld Lang's Syne' to bring in the New Year, I couldn't help thinking that this year-end was leading to a truly exciting 1974. In just four months since I'd left home for London, here I was, surrounded by pop royalty, feted by them, feeling actually a part of them, and beginning to believe that I could soon be tasting the same success as them. But as always, the Roman Catholic voice of warning and rebuke, which one never escapes, even as a born-again atheist, nibbled at the back of my mind, drowning out the joy of the evening: 'Who DO you think you are?' it sneered. Mentally, I swiped it away.

For the first time in my life, I had an answer to that religious nutcase bastard in my head who had nagged away at me for years. While Stuart still hadn't heard from CBS since he'd informed them that we wouldn't agree to my name being changed, on that fabulous New Year's Eve of 1973 I felt it didn't matter. I had arrived and my self-belief was finally being borne out amongst people who did matter. Now it was just a matter of time.

Chapter Fifteen

Kid In A Big World

Early in January 1974, Stuart Reid and I flew to Rome. I was to record 'Casting Shadows', the song I'd written for the film *Open Season*. It was to be backed by a full orchestra playing an arrangement done by the movie's director of music, Ruggero Cini. It would be usual here to say it felt 'awesome' and I was 'shaking like a leaf', but neither was the case. In those days, I seemed to readily accept things, face them full on, and just get on with it. With age and experience, I have become far less immediately confident, needing time – and others' approval - to feel things I do are ok. I guess events which unfolded in my career had something to do with that. They rubbed away the edge of arrogance and utter self-belief which only youth truly possesses.

As we had when we went to Madrid a couple of weeks earlier to view the film's rushes, we flew First Class. The hotel was again rather splendid. I – less wide-eyed than I'd been in Madrid - sat in my enormous suite wrapped in the softest, hugest white towel dressing-gown I had ever seen, let alone worn. The two-hour bubble bath, quaffing a small bottle of champagne I'd got from the mini-bar, had completely relaxed me.

"This IS the life!" I told myself as I settled on my King-size bed, poured some more champers and munched the chocolates from my Welcome Hamper. It had been delivered by a stunningly good-looking porter who had placed it on my coffee table with a perfect smile and a handsome tip. The card attached to the hamper read, 'Welcome To Rome, John, SO looking forward to the recording session! – Love, Peter Collinson'.

That evening, Stuart took me to a busy restaurant just round the corner from the Spanish Steps, where I ordered spaghetti. 'When in Rome,' I told myself rather smugly. To my horror, when it arrived it looked nothing like the spaghetti rings my mum used to serve from the Heinz tin, dished up with chips. I stared at my plate, at the endless strands of spaghetti, woven around each other like some impenetrable bird's nest, then at Stuart tucking happily into his steak, and wished I'd ordered that.

I felt my face going redder as the unworldly little lad from Ramsbottom emerged from the outer covering of stylish London youth-about-town, which I'd begun to develop since meeting Stuart and Patsy four months earlier. It fell away from me like a poorly-applied new layer of paint. A minor panic began to enfold me.

"Are you ok?" Stuart asked.

"Erm -", I pointed at my spaghetti, on the verge of tears, "how do I eat this?"

Stuart chuckled and was just about to show me when…

"Can I help you with that spaghetti?" a rich, deep Italian voice said above me.

I looked up at a beautifully dressed, smiling handsome man, cocking his head to one side, waiting for me to say 'Yes'. Instead I just stared dumbly at him.

"I saw you looking a little, well, puzzled…would you like me to show you how to…get it in your mouth?"

I gulped and nodded as Adonis winked at me. His glorious cologne wafted over as he deftly, like a TV chef, demonstrated how to hold my fork against the spoon and spin it into a neat ring of spaghetti.

"Open wide," he said, and popped a perfect helping of the delicious pasta into my mouth.

"Mmm…! Thank you!…" I struggled to say, munching away and remembering my mum's constant mantra, 'Don't speak with your mouth full!'.

"There!" He clapped his hands. "Now you try!"

My face burning like a beacon, I carefully spun the spaghetti on the fork against the spoon and lifted it into my mouth.

"Bravo!" Adonis shouted and applauded, and with that his table of friends next to us joined in, beaming and cheering.

I thanked him again, thrilled and embarrassed all at the same time. He took my hand and shook it with a delightful little bow:

"My pleasure! Enjoy the rest of your meal!"

As he joined his friends, who were patting him on the back and joshing him, he winked at me once more.

"You should look helpless more often, John," Stuart said. "It's very effective."

The next morning, the limousine picked us up at nine-thirty and whisked us through Rome, past the Coliseum which had been clad in clear plastic. Covered in thousands of drops of the rain from the previous night, which twinkled like stars in the now sun-drenched day, it looked like a huge art installation.

"They're cleaning it," the driver told us flatly when I asked him about it.

'Oh well,' I thought, still wishing I'd brought a camera.

At the studio, the small sturdy figure of Ruggero Cini introduced me to the orchestra, and I saw the friendly face of Peter Collinson up in the control room. He waved and Stuart went to join him.

"Would you like to try the piano, John?" Ruggero asked me.

It was a Steinway grand, and as I sat down the musicians began studying the manuscripts in front of them.

"You begin solo, John," Ruggero told me, "and we come in on the second verse." He pointed at the manuscript he'd placed in front of me. It had been some years since I'd read a piece of music, but I pretended to know what he was talking about. When he'd walked off, I surreptitiously got my lyrics out of my pocket and put them over the manuscript.

"Shall we try a run through?" Ruggero said to his musicians, then smiled over at me. "Sing it too, John, but this will only be a guide vocal for the musicians at this stage, so don't worry about singing it very well."

I played it through, loving the sound of the orchestra as it came in, and aware of Ruggero conducting everything from his rostrum very gently and unobtrusively. At the end, he gave me the thumbs-up, and, after a few quiet instructions in Italian to one or two of the musicians, said into his mike, "We'll do a take."

I was aware of Stuart's face watching me from the control room, looking slightly anxious but smiling through it in case I saw him. Peter on the other hand looked to be in his own private heaven. My voice felt very tight, but it was only ten o'clock in the morning and the song was extremely rangy, as were most of my songs in those days. I used to write in ridiculously high keys back then, encouraged to do so by Stuart, who loved it when I 'soared' as he called it. I privately wished I'd written it a few semitones lower at that point.

I put on my headphones and heard the engineer say, 'rolling'. With a 'three-four' count-in from Ruggero, I began to play the arpeggios in the key of A. It seemed to go well, I played without a mistake, though my voice still sounded strained. Ruggero was, however, smiling broadly at me throughout, and as I finished the song the violinists and cellists tapped their bows on their music stands. I saw Peter striding downstairs from the control room to greet me:

"John!" he cried, grabbing my hand and hugging me. "Gorgeous! Simply gorgeous!"

His Gauloise wafted around the room as we chatted about my trip and I gushed about the hotel. Peter made a dismissive gesture, grabbed my shoulders with surprisingly strong hands and said,

"You are a star, my darling. Stars stay at the best hotels!"

"OK," I heard Ruggero say, and saw him walking towards us, looking at his watch. "Let's take a half-hour break then we'll record the vocal!"

My stomach churned. It was still only eleven o'clock! I'd hoped we'd break for lunch then do the vocal in the afternoon. I inwardly panicked that my voice would not be good enough for the take. Stuart appeared with a cup of tea and took me into a corner of the studio. He fidgeted and shuffled his feet as I sipped the welcome and warm Earl Grey.

"Are you going to be alright?" he said, his anxious face and the worried tone of his voice not helping at all. "Singing so early in the morning is never good, John."

I had no ready answer. Inwardly shaking, I just shrugged and held up crossed fingers. I must have looked much more sanguine than I felt as it seemed to relax him.

By midday, I'd recorded two takes of the vocal, both of which sounded, to me, in places ok, in others rather shaky. But, as we listened back in the control room, Ruggero seemed pleased, Peter Collinson looked thrilled, only Stuart paced up and down, looking like a man who had lost his winning Pools coupon.

"Is that really alright?" I asked Ruggero at the end of the playback.

Ruggero made a circled finger and thumb gesture:

"It's frail, John, it's young, it's rather heart-breaking in fact."

Peter nodded in agreement:

"Perfect for the scene it will accompany in the movie, John," he added.

"Truly." Ruggero agreed. "And we have two vocals to choose from, we can drop in the best parts of each take so we have the absolutely perfect one!"

Stuart looked unconvinced, but smiled at the fact they were happy.

In the taxi back to the hotel, I was still wishing I'd been able to redo the vocal once more when he nudged me out of my reverie:

"I rang CBS while you were recording," he said. "I told the Head of Legal Affairs that we were in a studio in Rome, where you were recording your new song for the next Peter Fonda movie."

"What did he say?"

"Well, his parting words were, 'Please call me as *soon* as you get back, Stuart!' Somehow, John, I think he'll be calling me."

Stuart had been absolutely right. That nugget of tantalising information had been 'the rocket up the arse', as he called it, that CBS needed. Their legal department called Stuart within minutes of him arriving back at his office, asking him to go over there for a meeting to discuss the contract. Later that afternoon, Patsy and I sat in the kitchen, sipping coffee, waiting for news. When the phone went in the hall, my stomach turned over and she went to answer it. I could hear her murmuring conversation with Stuart, with no sign of exuberance or disappointment in her voice.

Finally, she said, "Okay, I'll tell John."

She put down the phone and popped her head round the door. Very deliberately and slowly, trying not to reveal anything on her face, she said,

"Well. You are now a CBS Recording Artist!"

We met Stuart at his club that evening, where, looking a little flushed, he poured the champagne and toasted me:

"Congratulations, John! This is the beginning of what I believe will be a truly exciting adventure. I am very proud of you."

The deal, he told us, was a £10,000 advance, working with a producer of our choice on my first album. If the next option was taken up the following year, then an advance of £16,000 was promised for a second album. Not a huge amount of money, but to me it sounded like a fortune.

Stuart also told me that he would be leaving Chappell's very soon to join his old colleague and friend, Frank Coachworth, at their new management and publishing company, Mautoglade Music. This answered the question I'd never had the courage to ask – why Stuart had never signed me to Chappell Music. He duly gave me an agreement to read and sign, wherein I would be a Mautoglade songwriter, and as such they would pay me a weekly retainer of £30.

"All I ask," he said, emptying the bottle of champers into my glass, "is that you come to our house every day and work on new material there."

It wasn't a tough ask. I would make the fifteen minute stroll over to Willesden Green from Kilburn every morning at eleven, where Patsy would cook me Eggs Florentine for an early lunch, make great coffee and then leave me to write. She would go out at about 1 o'clock to join Stuart at his temporary tiny attic office in Bond Street, and I would work away to my heart's content on song-writing for the rest of the afternoon. They would both return at about six-thirty, and I would play Stuart what I'd written, while Patsy made dinner.

The day after the news of the CBS deal came through, I'd telephoned the Temp Bureau to tell them I would no longer be working at Telephone Rentals. When the girl on the phone asked me what sort of job I would prefer to do next, I just said,

"All sorted, thanks. I've finally found the perfect job, and it's hopefully for life."

So, deal done and signed, the next thing was to find the right producer for the album. Stuart went through the latest issue of Music Week, perusing the album chart. He made a ring with his pen around the names of the British producers of hit albums, and from that compiled a list of ten, with Tony Visconti at the top. He phoned Visconti's office, spoke briefly to the great man himself, and was asked to send a tape over for him to hear. Fully confident there would be no need to go further down his list, Stuart took the tape over there himself. A few days later, the tape was returned with a handwritten note saying, 'No thanks.' Over the next couple of weeks, the list became a page full of crossed-out names, all of them, with just one left untried, had turned us down. Finally, as we reached No.10, Stuart had good news:

"Chris White, used to be in The Zombies, John, he liked the tape and wants to meet you."

The Zombies were one of my favourite groups in the '60s, their *Odyssey & Oracle* album a classic. Chris had been one of the main songwriters in the group and had also co-written the recent Top Ten hit by Argent, 'Hold Your Head Up'. He'd also produced Colin Blunstone's lovely *One Year* solo album, which had included the astonishing version of Denny Laine's 'Say You Don't Mind'. So I was extremely excited when Patsy told me she had invited Chris and his wife Viv to dinner.

A few days later, the five of us were enjoying a beautiful meal cooked by Patsy, and it was obvious from what Chris and his wife said that they both loved my music. Chris's eyes lit up when Stuart said that I would play a few songs for them after dinner. I found him a very sympatico man, gently spoken and intelligent. I loved listening to his stories of recording with The Zombies, and especially working with Colin Blunstone, one of pop music's finest vocalists.

Somehow, we got onto talking about going to America, probably something to do with when The Zombies toured there, and Chris began telling us about his visit to Disneyland, laughing about when they went into Peter Pan World:

"It was fantastic!" Chris enthused. "Pirates were running around everywhere, setting fire to buildings and pillaging the village, it was mayhem!"

Stuart and I laughed with him, Viv nodding enthusiastically at me as Chris recounted his jolly tale. I was imagining the scene, and the atmosphere round the table was truly convivial. A real bond of friendship was developing between us. Then, out of nowhere, with Chris in full flow, an unexpected snort came from Patsy's end of the table:

"Pah!" she said, staring at Chris. "Pillaging the village? What *do* you mean?"

Chris stopped and looked unsurely at Patsy, who continued to stare back at him. With a nervous glance at his wife, he stammered,

"W-w-well...yes, that's what they were doing, Patsy."

"What? You mean they were *actually* pillaging?" Patsy snorted again and looked around the table for support. But, as one does when witnessing a car crash, we all just stared, fascinated and yet horrified.

Stuart stepped in to the rescue. He spoke to his wife as one would to a confused and stroppy child who'd wandered half asleep into an adults' party:

"Patsy, darling, come on now. Why don't we all have some more coffee?" He beamed round the table and back at his scowling wife, who prodded the table with her finger and sailed blindly on:

"No, Stuart! No! Chris said there were pirates pillaging!" She glared at the poor man, who resembled a scolded child. "That's what you said, isn't it, Chris?"

"We-e-ell, yes, but...that was the whole point of the show, Patsy... pirates in Peter Pan's world, pillaging."

Another snort from Patsy. Now Chris was looking annoyed:

"Of course I didn't mean real actual pirates! That would be silly. It's a show! It's fantasy! It's Disney! It's called using your imagination."

Patsy guffawed this time:

"More like exaggeration!" she crowed.

Stuart desperately stood up and pushed the coffee pot at Patsy:

"Darling! More coffee. Please!"

Chris stirred in his seat, looked at his wife, who nodded back at him:

"Er - No thanks, Stuart, I think we should make a move. It's getting rather late."

"Oh!" Patsy cried, looking crestfallen. "But we haven't talked about John's album! That's why you're here! He was going to play you some songs! Weren't you, John?" She looked at me with a motherly pity then beseechingly back at Chris. "You must stay for that!"

"No, I'm very sorry," Chris replied, standing up, "we really must go. Thank you for your hospitality, Stuart, Patsy," and shook my hand as I stood up. "John, it's been lovely to meet you. You write great songs. I'm sorry we couldn't stay longer. Good luck with your album."

Stuart bustled from the table, and went to shake Chris's hand, saying to Patsy en route:

"Darling, could you get Chris and Viv's coats?"

With a harrumph, Patsy left the room, empty coffee pot dangling from her hand like a rejected artefact. Stuart went into one of his charm offensives:

"Chris!" he said rather too loudly, grabbing both of his hands. "It's been really great to meet you! I do hope we can work together. John and I would love you to produce his album. Wouldn't we, John?"

I nodded at Chris but, while he offered a smile, I could see it in his eyes, for him the love had gone.

Coats delivered, a few more social niceties shared, the couple bid their goodbyes and left.

Shutting the door, Patsy said,

"Well, that was very strange!"

Stuart, sounding not a little annoyed said, "What?"

"Just leaving like that! Poor John!"

Stuart just sighed and went into the kitchen mumbling something about the washing-up. Patsy followed him and pushed the door to. All I could hear was the stern lowered voice of Stuart and the anxious protests of his wife. There was a slightly more raised cry from Stuart at one point of, "Why didn't you just let it go?", then the inaudible murmurings continued.

Finally, after about five minutes, the door opened and a surprisingly bright-faced Stuart emerged:

"Would you like a coffee, John, one for the road?"

My cue to leave had been signalled, and, duly prompted, I told him I was rather tired, kissed a subdued Patsy on the cheek, got my coat off the banister and thanked them for a lovely evening. As their front door closed and I wandered slowly back to Kilburn, I had an image of the final name on that list being crossed out.

At the end of January, I went to Cannes with Stuart and Patsy for the annual MIDEM music festival. We stayed at the Hotel Mediterraneo, with its lovely view from the patio of the harbour, full of hundreds of millionaires' yachts bobbing up and down on the sparkling water under blue winter skies. This was Stuart's opportunity to show me off to the world, the place being full of music business executives, producers, record company heads, songwriters, publishers, and he seemed to know them all. As we sauntered along La Croisette, or sat in The Grand Hotel's bustling outdoor café sipping Bloody Mary's, he would introduce me to everyone we bumped into:

"This is my artist, John Howard!", he'd tell them, and I would shake whoever's hand was proffered. Once they'd gone, Stu would explain to me who they were, which company they worked for and how useful they might be in the future for us on the international stage. I felt like a moving manikin in an enormous shop window, but enjoyed the feeling. If this was what it took to become famous, I happily took part in the display.

In the evening, we would eat in restaurants dotted around the old town, and again bump into music business colleagues of Stuart, the usual 'This is my artist,

Cannes, January 1974, by Dezo Hoffman

251

John Howard' introductions, shaking of hands, then settling down to a fun meal, where we were more often than not joined by Biddu and his beautiful wife Sue, a former model. She was probably the most vivacious woman I had ever met up to that point. She looked like a film star, thick blonde hair cascading round her tanned shoulders, large sunglasses perched on her head, always chatting, asking questions, fascinated and engaged by whoever was sitting next to her. She'd listen intently to what one was saying, nodding all the time as you replied to one of her questions, murmuring, "right,' as you waffled on and on, but never feeling you bored her in the slightest. It was a talent. She should have been an interviewer on a chat show. For the time she was with you, you felt like the only other person in the room.

I once told her she reminded me of Jacqueline Onassis, which she did, and she just threw her head back, chuckled, grabbed my arm and said, "Oh John!", with no sign of either acceptance or rejection of the compliment. I think she was the first person I'd met who seemed entirely comfortable in their own skin.

As she and Bid entered any room, heads would turn towards this gorgeous stylish couple walking into their midst. They sailed through a sea of faces, smiling charismatically at everyone, acknowledging the waves of admiration floating towards them, like pop royalty. I would watch how they carried themselves, aloof and yet connected, a perfect example of how to own a room without doing much at all. Such intangible star-like quality had always fascinated me, but I had never been at such close quarters to it before.

Bid had been talking enthusiastically all week about a new artist he was writing for and producing, Carl Douglas, and how sure he was that the guy would have a hit record soon. Although rejected by Stuart as 'not a big enough name' to produce me, Bid was obviously beginning to make inroads of his own into record production.

One afternoon, during one of my La Croisette strolls with Stuart, Dezo Hoffman came wandering towards us.

"Hey, Dezo!" Stuart said, shaking his hand warmly, and gesturing to the panoramic view of the sea and blue skies, "Why not take some photos of John while you're both here in the South of France?"

So, the next day, I was sitting, standing, pointing, and posing for Dezo in the hotel's roof garden; mock-steering someone's yacht whose owner Dezo knew and had persuaded him to let us take some pictures on it; and looking out enigmatically to the horizon from the Carlton Hotel's veranda. Dolled up in my suit, tie and white fedora, I loved the whole chic of Cannes, and felt enveloped by it like a comfy blanket. It radiated wealth and success, even the old ladies with enormous sunglasses, walking their tiny terriers up and down the street every morning, looked like retired Gloria Swansons.

Another chap we bumped into on one of our morning strolls was a very bright and breezy Tony King. He was an old friend of Stuart's and they chatted for a few minutes, with the usual "This is my artist..." introduction prompting handshakes and niceties. Tony joined us for a meal that evening and was a really funny and fascinating dinner companion. He had started his career as a promotion man for Decca Records, went on to work for Andrew Loog Oldham and the Rolling Stones, and then worked with George Martin at AIR London. He'd also been the UK Marketing manager for Apple Records and was currently their General Manager in the US. He regaled us with delightful stories throughout the evening, with me completely agog.

He'd recently worked closely with John Lennon on promoting the album *Mind Games*, which had been released a couple of months earlier. It was Tony who had come up with the idea of a TV commercial for the album, showing Lennon dancing with 'The Queen of England' - actually Tony in drag.

With his great tales about his times with The Rolling Stones, The Beatles, Lennon in LA (during his infamous 'Lost Weekend') and Elton John, I was glued to his every fascinating anecdote. He had actually 'been there' when The Fabs had filmed their Our World recording of

'All You Need Is Love' in 1967, which on its own would have been enough to raise him to legendary status in my eyes.

One anecdote, which particularly stuck in my mind, was of the time he'd been motoring down an LA freeway with Lennon. The Beatles' track 'Nowhere Man' had come on the car radio and, at the end of it, John had turned to Tony and said,

"That track is everything I hated about working with Paul, all those fucking harmonies were his idea, took a bloody age. I had none of that in mind when I wrote the damn song."

Nowhere Man, as all Beatles fans know, is a great track from the group's Christmas '65 gem, *Rubber Soul*, and a classic in our minds with glorious three–part harmonies which actually made it the brilliant recording it is. Lennon's barb about it to Tony, while surprising, was probably as inaccurate a reflection of how he really felt, as the time he'd unkindly told George Martin he'd never been happy with any of the Beatles recordings, and would love to redo them all. Martin had been shocked and rather hurt to hear that and had replied, "surely not 'Strawberry Fields', John?", which had brought the Lennon retort, "*Especially* 'Strawberry Fields', George!". In all the many books I've read about John, those who knew him well say that he was famous for saying things off-the-cuff, meant to shock or hurt, but which he would later regret, recant or apologise for.

The final evening of our week, we went to see Stevie Wonder perform at The Palais de Festival Theatre. While he was very good, no-one appreciated being kept waiting until one o'clock in the morning for him to appear. The show was a chaotic mess, with various presenters occasionally walking on stage, vainly trying to fill out the interminable wait by taking forever to introduce acts unknown to most of the audience. By the time Wonder finally appeared, and admittedly sang a strong set of his most recent material from *Talking Book* and the recent *Inner Visions* album, I actually just wanted to go to bed.

I'm not sure how much good it did my career going to Cannes that year, but it certainly made me feel like a star waiting in the wings. It also gave Stuart another chance to show me the kind of life he was certain I would soon be enjoying off my own back and future career, rather than as a preparation for the 'fame to come'.

For all that, back in London as a cold February 1974 arrived, the even harsher reality was that we had run out of potential producers to send a tape to. I'd been turned down by all but Chris White, and he was now obviously out of the running. As always, when down, Stuart came up with an idea...

...Although not on his list, he called Les Reed and asked him if he fancied recording three tracks with me. He promised Les that he would play them to CBS and, if they liked them, he could produce the whole album. It had been a few years since Les had produced those big hits for Tom Jones and Engelbert, but, he was still a name, albeit from the '60s rather than the present day, and, with no-one else in the running, it was worth a punt.

A week later, I watched from the control room as Les delightedly conducted his orchestra, while Tony Burrows, along with the pop duo Sue & Sunny, provided backing vocals to Les's choice of my songs: *Goodbye Suzie*, *Missing Key*, and *Guess Who's Coming To Dinner*.

Tony Burrows, as many reading this will know, was much more than just a session singer. I had watched him on Top Of The Pops in 1967 with his group The Flowerpot Men, whose Summer of Love single 'Let's Go To San Francisco' had climbed the charts to No.4. Then three years later, he'd been the lead singer on Edison Lighthouse's No.1 hit, 'Love Grows'. He actually became something of a chart phenomenon in 1970, singing lead on several hit records, the biggest of which were White Plains' 'My Baby Loves Lovin'' and 'Julie Do Ya Love Me', The Brotherhood of Man's 'United We Stand' and 'Where Are You Going To My Love', (which also featured Sue

& Sunny), and as one half of the duo The Pipkins' on their sole hit, 'Gimme Dat Ding'. His face became one of the most recognised on pop TV in 1970, and he was, in effect, the most successful pop singer that year, and probably in any year, certainly in chart terms.

So I was really surprised to see him singing backing vocals on my recordings. His was a face I had grown to know – and quite fancy - watching him each week on Top Of The Pops in the early '70s, in various guises and with different groups. It was actually only a few months later that he'd hit the Top 20 again, this time as lead singer with First Class on their summer '74 hit, 'Beach Baby'. Very much a gentleman during those Les Reed sessions, and interested enough in the tracks to come and listen to the playbacks with us in the control room, he was professional to a 'T'. With no side to him at all, he did the job he'd been asked to do, and it was obviously paying the bills. But it made me wonder just how much money he'd personally made from being the lead singer on eight British hit singles in one year. I would surmise it was probably not as much as his chart success would suggest.

Les's arrangements were big and lush, typically so when you remember the huge hits he had produced a few years earlier. After the sessions, he shook my hand warmly, praised my performance and told Stuart he'd have the mixes done within a few days.

True to his word, Les delivered the finished tracks to Stuart who took them round to CBS. They rejected them out of hand as "too MOR." Over lunch, Stu told me that he actually agreed with them, and thought the productions didn't get across the 'new exciting singer-songwriter' tag he was desperately trying to promote. I can't actually recall hearing the finished mixes and, sadly, they are now lost. When I asked Les years later what had happened to the tapes, he told me Stuart kept them and he didn't have copies. It seems they're gone to the great tape heaven in the sky. Although the tapes are gone, the memory of seeing a smiling Les Reed conducting the orchestra, and

Tony, Sue and the soon-to-be solo hit artist Sunny - her single 'Doctor's Orders' was just about to rise to No.7 in the charts - singing with such great gusto on three of my songs, will always be a dear one.

Undeterred, the slightly embattled Stuart continued to beaver away. He was determined to get some promotion and profile for me, regardless of the apparent cul-de-sac from which he was trying to escape, and, against the odds, secured me a BBC radio session. I was booked to record two songs to be aired on the David Hamilton Radio 1 show. We picked 'Goodbye Suzie' and 'Guess Who's Coming To Dinner' as the best representation of both my ballad style and the more quirky side of my song-writing. The station provided a drummer, guitarist and bass player for the session, and Stuart got 'top lines' - basically the melody and chords written out on sheets of manuscript - done by a friend of his in Denmark Street, which was the new larger location for his publishing company.

On the morning of the session I woke up with the most awful head cold, and was concerned it would affect my performance. But oddly, I sang mainly rather well during the recording, apart from a slight crack in my voice on the final chorus of 'Suzie'. I'd thought I should do it again but time was running out, so I let it go. The small combo read 'the dots' and played the songs solidly and professionally, while not particularly inventively. They were there to do a job as well as they could, with songs they had never heard before, not to give me an exciting new sound. The tracks sounded workmanlike to me but ok for a 'live' radio session.

A couple of weeks later, we all listened round the radio, in Mautoglade's spacious new 2nd floor office, to David Hamilton introducing me with his cheery Radio Wonderful voice:

"A new name on the music scene for you now, this is a very talented young songwriter called John Howard, and here's his first song of the week, which he's performing just for us today, *Goodbye Suzie*."

The performance sounded good, though that crack in my voice

on 'Suzie' niggled me. Stuart said that it sounded like emotion on a very sad song. He seemed convinced. I wasn't. I wished I'd insisted on doing the vocal on that chorus once more, and vowed never to let things like that pass again.

The next afternoon, Hamilton played the second song I'd recorded for his show:

"Many of you wrote in to say how much you liked John Howard's performance yesterday of his song 'Goodbye Suzie', so here's another one of his compositions, 'Guess Who's Coming To Dinner' – well, thanks for the invite, John!".

Again, it sounded fine, everyone in the room seemed pleased, Stuart's secretary making me a congratulatory cup of tea.

I'd rung my mum to tell her when the songs would be played on Radio 1 and she had recorded them off the radiogram onto a cassette (which I still have). When I called her the weekend after the broadcasts, she told me she had cried during 'Goodbye Suzie', but wasn't as keen on 'Guess Who's Coming To Dinner' – "it's a bit of a weird song, that one, love." Amazing how relations can always be certain to bring one's feet back onto the ground, just as you're beginning to slightly float above the pavement.

The Radio One plays gave me a bit of a fillip for a few days, but the fact was, on the recording front, things were not looking good. Despite Stuart's attempts, we still had no producer for my album. The CBS cheque for £10,000 was waiting to be spent, stuck stubbornly on Stuart's office wall where he had proudly pinned it when it had arrived in the post a few days earlier. It was now becoming something of a nagging reminder that we had no-one in place to spend it.

Then, early in March, Stuart rang me to say that he had met Tony Meehan at a music business function the previous evening, had mentioned me and, Tony having shown interest, had biked a tape round to Meehan's apartment in Maida Vale that morning.

"He's just called, John, he loves your songs and would like to meet you!" Stuart told me. "He's coming round to our house tomorrow afternoon at 3 o'clock. If you arrive about one for lunch?"

Tony Meehan had, as everyone knows, been the drummer in the first incarnation of The Shadows in the late 1950s. He was only fifteen when he began working with them, playing on such early 'Cliff & The Shads' hits as 'Move It', 'Living Doll', and The Young Ones as well as The Shadows' own No.1 smashes like 'Apache' and 'Kon Tiki'. He became something of an icon to burgeoning young drummers after his appearance in the movie The Young Ones in 1961, although by the time the film was released, he had left the group.

He had gone on to work as an arranger and drummer for producer Joe Meek, appearing on hit records like John Leyton's Top Twenty smashes 'Wild Wind' and 'Son This Is She' (I actually bought the latter single at the age of eight, loving its 'B' side, 'Six White Horses'). He then forged a fairly ground-breaking deal as an independent producer for Decca Records. It was Tony who had produced The Beatles' infamously unsuccessful Decca audition tapes in January 1962, recording for posterity Brian Epstein's first, albeit failed, attempt at getting his 'boys' a record deal.

Keen to get back into recording as an artist in his own right, Tony teamed up with another former Shadows member, Jet Harris, to enjoy three Top Five hit singles with him in 1963. The duo's biggest hit Diamonds ironically knocked The Shadows' Dance On! off the top spot. And, ironies abounding, as 'Diamonds' ironically knocked The Shadows' 'Dance On!' off the top spot. And, ironies abounding, as 'Diamonds' was dropping to No.3, The Beatles' 'Please Please Me' leapfrogged it to No.2! Cruel irony continuing, three months later, Harris & Meehan's second hit, 'Scarlett O'Hara' was kept off the No.1 spot by The Beatles' 'From Me To You'. In September, as The Beatles' 'She Loves You' was at No.1 and Cliff Richard's 'It's All In The Game' was stuck behind them at No.2, Harris & Meehan's final hit, 'Applejack' climbed to its chart peak of No.4. Tony's last hit was a solo Top 40 entry, 'Song Of Mexico' in January 1964, falling out of the charts just as The Beatles were conquering America.

I had been aware of Tony's name cropping up in the music press during the latter part of the 1960s and early '70s, when he'd produced the Apple Records group White Trash, and albums by P.P. Arnold and Roger Daltrey. So I was more intrigued than excited at the prospect of meeting him. He wasn't The Big Name I had thought CBS and Stuart were looking for to produce me, but Tony did have a pedigree as someone who had tasted chart success and worked with big artists.

On the day Tony was due, once Patsy had cleared away our lunch things, she made fresh coffee and sandwiches for our expected guest, while Stuart sat listening to me play a new song for him, 'Gone Away'.

"Great song!" Stuart declared, his eyes full of the fire he'd had when he'd first heard my Chappell's demos. "It's times like this that I actually love you, John." His eyes welled up with tears. "You've got to play that song for Tony!"

The doorbell duly rang at a few minutes past three. As Stuart brought Tony into the sitting-room, the first thing which struck me was how petite he was. I'd only seen photos of him sitting behind his drum kit back when my sister had pictures of Cliff & The Shadows all over her bedroom walls. Still youthful-looking but now with flecks of grey hair peeking through, he said a polite "Hello" when I shook his hand ('Firm handshake, John' I told myself) and settled down on the sofa while Patsy brought in the tray of coffee and sandwiches.

"Oh! I didn't know we were having lunch as well, Patsy!" Tony said, laughing, and I noticed how attractively languid his laugh was, with something of an American 'hip sexiness' about it.

"Just a little something for coming all this way," she joked back, knowing he had only travelled a short way on the tube.

Stuart began by saying how pleased he was that Tony liked my songs and suggested I play a few on the piano for him.

"Well, I have heard the demos, Stuart," Tony said, sounding a little surprised.

Stuart smiled around the room:

"But John is such a great performer, Tony, you have to see him in action to get the full picture of what he's about."

"Absolutely," Patsy agreed, sipping her coffee, as she settled into her armchair and studied Tony over her cup.

"OK," Tony said, munching on a sandwich and sitting back.

"Play Tony 'Gone Away', John," Stuart told me, then turning to Tony, "great new song, Tony, John only just wrote this one, so it's not on your tape!"

"Ah! An exclusive!" Tony said, brightening up and chuckling to himself. Draining his cup, he got out an old dicta-phone from his pocket. "I always carry one of these," he said, laughing again and holding it up. "You never know when you'll need to get something on tape!" He fiddled with the machine then looked over at me and said, "Whenever you're ready, John."

I trilled out the song, which was greeted at the end with a cheer from Stuart, smiles around the room from Patsy, and applause from Tony as he checked it had been recorded okay.

"Isn't that great, Tony?" Stuart enthused, as the tinny recording of my new song played out of Tony's cassette player.

"So good!" Patsy concurred, blinking across the room at me.

"Yes, it's a good song, Stuart," Tony agreed. "Anymore new ones, John?"

"Do 'Guess Who's Coming To Dinner'," Patsy said, without waiting for my reply.

"Oh yes! Another fabulous song!" Stuart cried.

"Yes, but that's on the tape you sent me, isn't it, Stuart?" Tony was now looking a little baffled.

Stuart ignored him and gave me an encouraging nod. I duly gave them a belting rendition of 'Guess Who's Coming To Dinner', with Patsy doing her on-the-spot bop and Stuart beaming across at Tony.

"Er -" Tony said as I finished, "very nice, John. I'm sorry, Stuart, but would you mind if I went and bought some cigarettes?"

It wasn't quite the reaction The Reids had anticipated, and they both looked at each other a little bewilderedly as Tony got up and walked into the hall:

"I won't be long," he said, and popping his head back through the doorway, "John, you do write great songs."

Turning to Patsy, he asked her where the nearest newsagent was. With a sigh, Patsy got up and walked into the hall with him:

"Left out of the door, walk up the road, turn first left and it's there, it's only about a five minute walk."

With a relieved "Great!" Tony was gone.

As we heard his footsteps disappearing down the path, Patsy exclaimed,

"Well! What do you say to that?"

She wasn't addressing anyone in particular, but Stuart replied with a shrug:

"Odd behaviour certainly. Maybe he's not feeling well."

"I think he's on something," Patsy declared to the room.

"He probably just needed some air," Stuart said, trying to calm an emanating sense of panic. I shut the piano lid and tried to steer the conversation back from its teetering brink:

"Maybe we should end the recital and just chat to him about the album when he gets back?"

A discontent pervaded from the other side of the room, which, forty-five minutes later, when he still hadn't returned, had become a black cloud of despondency.

"Where IS he?" Patsy cried, rushing out of the kitchen where she'd been banging dishes into cupboards for the last quarter of an hour. She stormed to the window and peered round her net curtains, as though that would somehow make him miraculously reappear. "This really is too bad!"

By now, she was even more convinced he was on some acid trip, and Stuart, no longer trying to be reassuring, was considering ringing his apartment. Then, like the sun breaking through after a storm, the doorbell rang.

"Hallelujah!" Patsy cried and went to answer it. I heard her saying less than sympathetically, "Are you alright?" and Tony's faint voice replying, "Yes, sorry about that, I got rather lost!"

His languid laugh was countered by a huffy, "Hm" as they both walked into the sitting-room.

"The wanderer returns!" Patsy announced.

"I'm very sorry about that," Tony said, smiling at us all. "I hadn't realised the time. Unfortunately, I really must go, I'm afraid."

"Oh!" Patsy and Stuart said in unison, looking equally aggrieved.

"But, you've only just got back!" Patsy protested. "We haven't discussed anything!"

Tony looked cutely abashed:

"No, well, we will, I'm sure." He looked over at a stricken Stuart. "I'll call you, soon. And thank you for your hospitality, Patsy. Very kind." He walked over to me and put his hand on my shoulder. "Thank you, John, for playing me your music, it's very good. Now I really must go. The sandwiches were lovely Patsy."

More mutterings in the hallway followed, and, with a close of the door, Patsy walked in and threw herself into an armchair, looking pleadingly at Stuart:

"What are we going to do?"

Stuart shrugged, poured himself a whisky, offered me one, and sat next to me.

"I'll call Tony tomorrow, John," he said, clinking my glass with his, "Don't worry. Everything will be fine."

Patsy, who hardly ever drank alcohol, stomped over to the drinks tray and poured herself a brandy.

"Well, we'll see about that, won't we?" she said, throwing it back in one.

"Oh dear!" Stuart said, mugging at me, "Black marks for Mr Meehan in Patsy's little book. Very few in there are ever redeemed."

To my surprise, I got a call from Stuart the following day with the news that Tony had, in fact, called him and said he'd love to produce my album, preferably at Abbey Road Studios. He wanted me to visit him at his apartment to discuss the songs he'd like us to record.

"On my own?" I asked, rather surprised I wasn't getting a chaperone.

"Yes, Tony specifically said he wanted to chat to you alone. Let me know how it goes, though. Here's his address."

Tony's apartment was just off Maida Vale and he welcomed me in with a hug and a glass of red wine. He was so much more relaxed than he had been at Stuart and Patsy's, and I said so. Tony laughed at that and said,

"First of all, John, I'd like to apologise for my rather odd behaviour there."

I laughed too, telling him that it hadn't worried me, but Patsy was rather put out. "Yes, I'm probably not flavour of the month with her right now."

"Possibly for longer than a month," I replied.

He clinked my glass, offered me a seat and said,

"Quite honestly, John, I'm afraid I found the whole situation at their house extremely claustrophobic. They were like two mother hens round you, and treated you, I felt, like a performing seal. Doesn't it get on your nerves?"

"They've been very good to me, Tony."

"Yes, I know, and I can see they're very fond of you, and rate your talent very highly. They're good people. But things are about to change for you, John." He became suddenly quite serious and sat forward as though he were about to tell me a secret. "You're about to make an album for a major record label, and it's likely to change your life. I'm afraid the music world won't want to know about all that – all that 'our clever little boy' stuff. They'll want to see and hear someone with an edge, someone who stands alone with something different and exciting to offer. I'm worried that they could blunt that edge."

"But Stuart got me the record deal."

"And well done Stuart for that. But he needs to stand aside now. Your songs are great, you have a wonderful voice. But you also have a certain style which could become…" he looked at me, unsure if I was ready for what he was about to say, "…well, too set, too pat, too easy, and I want to stretch you. I know what Stuart wants…he wants an album of production quality versions of the demos on his tape. But I'm not going to give him that." He sat back and poured himself more wine, studying my reaction.

I said, "I'm willing to try anything, Tony, but…Stuart and Patsy…"

"Are your managers! They are not your record producer, they are not your record label." He lit up a cigarette and took a long drag, blowing out the smoke as he continued. "You know, Brian Epstein never told George Martin what he wanted The Beatles to sound like. He trusted the group's record producer to find their sound and make it work." He looked at me and I nodded. "We are now the team, John," he continued. "We make the creative decisions. Not Stuart. Not Patsy."

With that off his chest, he handed me a list of the ten songs he wanted to record, 'Maybe Someday In Miami', 'Gone Away', 'Missing Key', 'Guess Who's Coming To Dinner', 'Kid In A Big World', 'Goodbye Suzie', 'Family Man', 'The Flame', 'Spellbound' and 'Deadly Nightshade'. He had marked the first five with a red-felt-penned tick and the words 'different arrangement' written against them. I looked up at Tony and raised my eyebrows. He refilled my glass and said:

"Stuart has employed me to record a great album with you. And I will. It just may not be the one Stuart's expecting."

The recording sessions were booked to start at Abbey Road studios in April, just after my 21st Birthday. After I left Tony's flat, instead of going to the nearest underground station, I walked over to Abbey Road and stood in front of those famous Beatles graffiti covered walls. As I strode across *that* zebra crossing on my way to St. John's Wood tube station, I felt that, finally, all the pieces were falling into place. I couldn't wait to get started.

Chapter Sixteen

Save The Days

A week before the recording sessions for my debut album were due to begin at Abbey Road, in early April 1974, I moved out of my Kilburn flat, which had now become an unbearable place to live. Three of my previous flatmates had, by the beginning of 1974, left and been replaced by four noisy male students. Their idea of fun was packing every chair in the place into the small kitchen, making it impossible to get in and out of there. They'd then nominate one of them to crawl over and under the stacked chairs so as to reach the fridge for the beers they filled it with every week. As the nominee crawled and manoeuvred his way back, beers in hand, his mates would stand outside in the doorway yelling their approval at the tops of their voices. This jape used to take place at about midnight, almost every night, when they'd got back legless from the pub. It would go on for about an hour, until they finally fell into a heap somewhere in the flat, passed out on too much booze, before retching up the takeaway they'd scoffed on their way home.

At the age of twenty, I felt extremely old as my protestations at being kept awake "yet again!", and having to remove several chairs from the kitchen to make my breakfast, were met with polite woozy stares and grimaces. The boys always very sweetly made promises to behave, then more of the same would occur the following night. Brian, our former-pop-star landlord, seemed oblivious to it all. Once our previous flatmates had gone, he had more or less cut himself off from the new occupants and taken to staying in his room singing himself to sleep with his headphones on. The nightly cat-on-heat noise of his out of tune whining to Led Zeppelin records, and the drunken laddie games going on outside my door, meant it was time to leave.

Patsy and I went to a flat-letting agent in Kilburn High Road, where the extremely camp, greasy-haired, long-dirty-nailed manager listened disinterestedly as Patsy explained I needed somewhere "in a better area than Kilburn."

He'd puckered his large lips at this, taken a long drag on his cigarette, and run his filthy fingernails down numerous thumb-marked pages of available dwellings. Finally, tapping the ash off his cigarette into a half-empty coffee cup, he said,

"Hm, this one might do," and showed us a photo of a 1930s block of flats in St John's Wood. "It's a studio flat on the top floor, what were the maid's quarters in days gone by, owned by the lady who lives in the apartment next to it. Mrs Skowalski is her name. Here's her address." He handed us a slip of paper. "I'll call her to let her know you'll be viewing it today. OK?"

It wasn't an enquiry, merely a raise of too-bushy eyebrows for confirmation that what he had suggested would happen.

Happily, the building, in Hall Road, welcomed us in with its sense of art deco history as we walked into the foyer, where a - now unused - concierge desk swept grandly around the marble walls to a large but long since deserted reception area. One of those old detective movie-type concertina-doored lifts had clattered to a stop, the gate had whooshed open and an elderly, but sprightly and well-dressed man, had stepped out, bidding us 'Good morning,' with a tip of his hat.

"Oh, this is perfect for you, John," Patsy had said as we'd stepped into the lift, closed the gate, pressed the brass button marked 2nd floor and clattered up there.

It was a lovely flat, comprising a large light-filled room with a huge window overlooking very pleasant gardens and a good view of the whole surrounding area. There was a Belling two-hob cooker in the bed-sitting room, which was enough for me as I rarely cooked for myself anymore, eating either at Stuart and Patsy's or out for dinner with them in the West End. Two ancient but recently re-covered armchairs faced the view, and a tiny wooden coffee table displayed a few old copies of Vogue. The room led to a small but well-lit spotlessly clean bathroom.

The rent was £14 a week, Mrs Skowalski told me, plus an extra 70p for the use of her cleaning lady, who would, she informed me, Hoover and polish my flat and clean my bathroom every Thursday.

"I'll take it!" I told her.

She clapped her hands and, holding them together as if in prayer, said, "So good to have a young gentlemen as a tenant! I never have young girls, they are so untidy!"

"Knickers and bras everywhere?" Patsy enquired conspiratorially.

Mrs Skowalski blushed at such words being said in front of a young gentleman, but nodded at Patsy and giggled with her girlishly.

Stuart had come along a couple of days later with Patsy and I to pay the one-month's upfront rent plus a month's deposit. He grandly signed the cheque as he told a breathlessly fascinated Mrs Skowalski that I had "Just recorded a song for the new Peter Fonda movie. And John is shortly to begin recording an album at Abbey Road Studios for CBS Records."

Mrs Skowalski purred as she took the cheque and, beaming at me, said,

"What a clever boy!"

"You have, as your tenant, a future star, my dear!" Stuart continued, winking at me. Patsy blinked, the landlady purred again, and I looked suitably shy and rather pleased with myself.

The day after I moved into the flat, my parents travelled down to London for my 21st birthday. I met them at St John's Wood tube station in the afternoon so I could show off my new home. I'd pointed out Abbey Road Studios to them, the three of us staring from the footpath at the famous white building, as I explained that it was where I would begin recording my album in a few days.

"This is the same zebra crossing The Beatles are walking across on the *Abbey Road* LP sleeve," I told them, as four giggling tourists posed a la Fabs for their friend with the camera. Mum and Dad did their best to look impressed but instead seemed rather puzzled.

"Oh, Bert!" Mum declared when she walked into the foyer of the apartment building, "It's like something from the movies!"

Dad smiled at her, and opened the lift door for us:

"Reminds me of the lifts in London department stores, when we had our honeymoon down here, Bren."

"Oh, yes, it does!" Mum said, laughing at the memories they shared of their first London visit in 1948.

Her face lit up even more when I let them into the flat,

"It's so London, Howard!" she cried. "And that view! Oh, it's lovely, son!"

I settled them into the two chairs and made them a cup of tea on the Belling hob. Sitting on the edge of my bed, I opened the present they'd brought me, a set of bottle green towels and matching flannel.

"John Lewis no less!" I said, rubbing the soft towel against my face.

"It's your 21st! We wanted to get you something special, something that will last. A bit of quality. And now with your new flat..." she looked admiringly round the room, "We thought you'd need those." I got up and kissed her on the cheek:

"They're perfect, Mum."

She looked well, considering she had been so poorly eighteen months earlier. She still was in fact, regardless of how she appeared. I was aware her time with us was limited. However, to look at her as she beamed over at me, you would never know she had less than six months to live.

I rather bizarrely then turned on Capital Radio on my transistor for them, I have no idea to this day why. I guess I wanted to show them what a London life meant, even having one's own Sound Of The City on the radio.

"Oh, it's very good," Mum said, unconvincingly, as Kenny Everett rabbited on about the new Chris Rainbow single and 'Solid State Brain' wafted around the room.

"Very interesting chords," Dad said approvingly. He always judged a record by its technical prowess, or lack of it. He hated Roy Orbison because he "breaks all the rules", which surprised me as Dad was a jazz musician, which I thought was all about breaking with tradition. Of course, as soon as he'd said that in 1964, when we'd watched Roy performing 'It's Over' on Top Of The Pops, I fell in love with The Big O immediately.

I told them that we would be going out for dinner that evening to La Dolce Vita, a restaurant Stuart and Patsy often took me to in Frith Street. The plan was that the three of us would have dinner there and then Stuart and Patsy would join us later for a drink. My parents had not yet met them and I could tell they were a little nervous.

"You'll really like them," I told Mum, but she still looked unsurely over to her husband, who just smiled encouragingly back at her.

After we'd had our tea and a chat about how things were going – "You've done very well for yourself, son"; "Oh, you have, Howard!" - they trotted off back to their hotel in Lancaster Gate to have a rest and get ready for our evening. I ran a bath and laid out my present over the original 1930s heated towel rail. Soaking in the fact I was now twenty-one and would soon be starting work on my first album, life felt okay. As the Liberty Bath Salts, which I'd treated myself to a few days earlier, permeated their perfumed sense of well-being around me, I sang Chris Rainbow's great new song to myself, *'Somebody gave me the sun in my hands and the clouds in the sky for my bed'*. I imagined myself, as I had so many times growing up with a teenager's burning ambition, standing at the microphone in Abbey Road Studios giving it my all. Now though, it was no longer an ambition, in just a few days I would be there, the dream had come true…as Chris sang, *'I close my eyes am I dreaming, but somebody's screaming it's me!'*.

Mum and Dad were waiting for me outside the restaurant when

I arrived. She was prettily made-up, enhancing her still porcelain complexion, which my dad had fallen in love with twenty-seven years earlier. Wearing a rather lovely dark red trouser suit I'd not seen before and a mauve silk scarf, she'd most likely bought them specially for the trip.

"How long have you been here?" I asked, knowing I was early.

"Not long, love," Mum said, kissing me on the cheek.

"About twenty minutes," Dad muttered.

I smiled at Mum who laughed back,

"Well, I didn't want to be late!"

"Why didn't you go inside?" My parents looked puzzled. "You should have gone inside and told them we had a table booked."

"Oh! I wouldn't want to…well, you know…"

"We're novices at this London way, lad," Dad said, coming to his wife's rescue.

I sighed and realised how my parents had become in some ways like children to me. I remembered Mum once telling me that, on their honeymoon, they'd taken a stroll down Piccadilly and discovered The Ritz. They'd looked uncertainly through the doorway and hovered for a few minutes as people strode in and out past them, before deciding "it was far too posh for us" and walked on. They instead found a café up a side street and had "a very nice cup of tea and a bun."

With my parents following close behind, I walked into La Dolce Vita and was greeted warmly by the Maître D', Francesco, who rushed up to us with a huge smile on his face:

"Signor Howard!" he cried, throwing his arms up in the air, "How very good to see you again." He looked round me expectantly, "No Mr and Mrs Reid this evening?"

"They're coming later," I said, and standing to one side, "this is my mother and father, Francesco. They're here to celebrate my birthday."

Francesco gave a delightful little bow, kissed my mum's hand and shook my dad's. Mum did a little coo and went red.

"Birthday boy!" Francesco cried, and winked at my mum. "And I can see now where Signor Howard gets his good looks!". His banter continued, both embarrassing and thrilling Mum. Her face was quickly beginning to team with her trouser suit very nicely.

Francesco showed us to our table, pulling Mum's chair back a little to allow her to sit down, which got a thrilled "Ooh, thank you!". She looked at Dad like a girl on her first date, as she settled herself. He was obviously loving every minute of his Bren being treated so royally.

"Now! What can I get you to drink?" Francesco boomed extravagantly. "On the house! For your son's birthday! A treat from Francesco!" He did his little bow again and my mum giggled.

"How nice," she said, nodding at my Dad, who tilted his head approvingly at the table.

"Mum? Dad?" I prompted them. "Would you like an aperitif?"

They both threw a look at each other:

"Ee, Bren!" Dad said, "Our little lad, asking us if we want an aperitif!"

"I know!" She looked proudly over at me, "You've come a long way, son!"

I had forgotten what life had been like before I came to London. I'd had dreams for years neither of my parents ever fully understood or probably believed would come true. While I had imagined one day living this metropolitan life, which I was now doing to the full, they had existed in another world, full of self-effacement and 'knowing your place'. I'd never 'known my place', always felt that the place I was in was not mine and I would have to leave it. I had finally taken the plunge and left all that behind eight months earlier, fitting into my new life straight away. But I suddenly realised now, as I watched them trying to feel at ease and failing, that it was totally out of my parents' orbit. The thought of simply walking into an eaterie in the West End of London and feeling immediately comfortable and at one with it, was completely foreign to them. I think it actually frightened them. Even more saddening, I could see them looking at me now as something slightly alien, changed, I was no longer their 'little lad'.

Just as we were finishing our desserts, the door opened and Stuart and Patsy walked in. Stuart smiled at us and I waved them over, but they were stopped in their tracks by a delighted Francesco. Stuart pointed over at us, whispering something in his ear.

"Let me introduce you to my mum and dad," I said, standing to kiss Patsy on both cheeks and shake Stuart's hand.

My dad did a little half-stand and shook their hands rather awkwardly. Stuart beamed at my mum who was looking up at everyone expectantly:

"I can see the resemblance to John, Mrs Jones," he said, grabbing her hand in both of his.

Mum laughed and looked pleased:

"Oh, I've never heard Howard being called John before!"

Patsy laughed and sat next to her on the chair Francesco brought over for her:

"Of course, Mrs Jones, he's Howard to you, isn't he? Do you mind?"

Mum looked confused.

"It must be strange for you, us calling your son, 'John'," Stuart stepped in. "Do you mind it?"

"Not at all!" Mum said, "It just sounds odd, to us anyway. Doesn't it, Bert?"

Dad nodded in agreement.

Very quickly, pulling up his chair, Stuart engaged my dad in amiable chat about their trip down, their hotel, if they'd been to London before, while Patsy did the same with Mum, both of them trying to put my parents at ease.

"You must be very proud of your son, Mrs Jones," Stuart said, grabbing my arm affectionately.

"Oh, please call me Brenda," Mum said.

"And yes, please call me Bert," Dad added, enjoying his wife knocking down a barrier.

"Thank you," Patsy said. "We are very fond of your son, Brenda."

"Yes, I can see that," Mum said, "and, yes, we are proud of How-er-John. Aren't we, Bert?"

Dad winked at me:

"I never thought I'd see this lad looking so fine, and happy, living this life so well. You've surprised us, son."

"He's fitted in like a glove, hasn't he, Patsy?" Stuart said.

"Like a man born to it," his wife added, and blinked at Mum.

At that point, Francesco appeared with a bottle of champagne, showed it to Stuart who studied it and nodded.

"I wanted to celebrate, John," he said, "not only your reaching twenty-one today, but also, with your parents, we'd like to congratulate you on the new album you will soon be recording. It's a cause for celebration that we are all here together, to toast your success and your continued success." Francesco poured the champagne into our glasses. "To John! Or, if you prefer, Brenda, to Howard!"

"To John!" Mum said happily and supped her drink daintily. "Ooh! That's rather nice," and she took another longer sip.

Glasses were clinked, and I watched Brenda Jones having the time of her life, even letting Stuart refill her glass. I felt grateful that at least she'd lived long enough to see for herself how good things were for me. She could now relax.

"I believe you're also a musician, Bert?" Stuart asked Dad, as always so good at bringing people out of themselves.

"Yes, I'm a pianist, like –er – John here."

"Do you play the same sort of music?" Patsy asked.

"Oh no, I'm in a little jazz combo, we play a couple of times a week. Nothing special but I enjoy it."

"He's very good," Mum put in.

"I'm sure he is, Brenda," Stuart said, giving my dad a huge smile. "It's in the genes, then, where John gets his talent."

"Well, I don't know about that," Dad said. "Brenda doesn't sing, and I've never written a song in my life, so I don't know where he gets that from."

A childhood memory popped into my mind:

"I used to listen to you play when I was a kid, Dad, and it made me want to play as well as you. But you're much better technically than me." Dad shuffled in his seat but looked pleased. Mum nudged me:

"You wrote a tune when you were about twelve, do you remember? Your dad transcribed it onto some manuscript for you, didn't you, Bert?"

"I'd forgotten that!" I said, laughing.

"You played it for all the ladies at my Tupperware party!" Mum said proudly.

"I'd forgotten that too!"

Patsy looked delighted:

"Do you remember what it was called, John?"

I couldn't, but Mum did:

"It was called, 'They Say', very pretty it was too. I've still got the manuscript somewhere."

Stuart and Patsy stayed a little while longer then left the three of us to finish our drinks before I walked my parents to the tube. I called Francesco over to settle the bill, only to be told that "Mr Reid has sorted it, Mr Howard!".

"How kind," Mum said. "Wasn't that kind, Bert?"

Dad nodded at the chair nearest to him.

Our coats brought to us by a smiling waiter, Francesco shook our hands warmly, and we were in the cool Spring Soho air, through which I walked my parents to Piccadilly Station.

"It's very lively, isn't it?" Mum said, eyeing the strip and girlie bars.

"It is that," Dad said, trying not to eye them.

"Did you enjoy yourself?" I asked them both once we'd reached the tube station.

"Oh, it was lovely, Howard!" Mum said, her face a little flushed from her two glasses of champagne. "And they are really nice people, aren't they, Bert?"

Dad smiled at me and said,

"We can go home tomorrow knowing you'll be alright, son."

After a hug and a kiss for Mum and a surprising hug from Dad, I watched them going down the steps to the underground, hand in hand. Waving at them, as they glanced back over their shoulders before they were surrounded by the mêlée of people rushing by them, I could see them still looking a bit nonplussed by it all. Mum pointed at what she thought was the right way, and they were gone. It was the last time I would see her looking so well.

Chapter Seventeen

Take Up Your Partners

One morning, in mid-April 1974, I woke up to the sound of the telephone ringing by the bed. I checked the clock, it was 10.30.

"Good morning, John!" Stuart's bright voice rang out like the sound of a bird at my window. "Today's a big day!"

It was the first day of my recording sessions with Tony Meehan at Abbey Road Studios.

"Thanks for the wake-up call, Stuart," I drowsily mumbled. I was still at an age where anything before midday was 'the crack of dawn'.

Tony Meehan, Peter Bown with me at Abbey Road, Studio 2 Control Room, recording Kid In A Big World, Spring 1974

"The session starts at two," Stuart breezed away as I yawned as quietly as I could. "I would suggest you arrive about one forty-five, Patsy and I will see you there around two-thirty, to give Tony time to set everything up."

"Ok, Stuart, see you then."

I turned on Kenny & Cash, the breakfast show on Capital Radio, where Everett and Dave would bring in the day with zany chat, brilliant Kenny-created jingles and great music. A fabulously bizarre new record was instantly chiming around my room, Sparks' 'This Town Ain't Big Enough For Both Of Us'. It would within a month be in the UK Top Ten, but as always London's favourite radio station was the first to play it. This was when it felt so good living in London, ahead of the game, the centre of everything cultural and new, at least to this twenty-one year old. I was about to record my debut album, and listening to amazing new singles like the one Kenny was now raving about, Queen's 'Seven Seas of Rhye'.

I had a long hot bath and mused about what life may hold over the coming months. Drying off and making myself a lapsang suchong tea, I chose my outfit for the day: a John Michael red woollen cardigan over a dark red silk shirt, grey Oxford bags, grey and red striped tie, maroon slip-ons over silver grey socks. A good look, I thought, for arriving at the studios for my first session, establishing a casual but stylish impression. I sprayed myself liberally with Pino Sylvestre, a cologne I had fallen in love with when I'd rolled around in its clean fresh essence, along with the one-night stand who was wearing it, a few weeks earlier. Dressed in my chosen attire, I checked myself in the full-length mirror and wandered out into the fresh Spring day. I turned the corner into Abbey Road, my heart thumping just a little as I anticipated what lay ahead.

Walking through the gates and up the steps to the studios, I stood for a moment, savouring it. I opened the door and stepped into the beginning of my recording career:

"Hello, my name's John Howard and I'm -"

"With Tony Meehan and Peter Bown, sir," the Abbey Road receptionist said efficiently. She ticked her pad and smiled up at me, directing me through the double doors and down the corridor to the door marked 'Studio 2'. I pushed it open and was met instantly by:

"John!" Tony shouted as I walked into the dimly lit inner sanctum. I glanced around the roomful of tape machines, piles of tape boxes and various lengths of cable hanging from hooks on the soundproofed walls. A dark-haired, Mop Top-fringed chap, in a bright floral shirt and red jeans, looked up from the mixing desk, where he was busily plugging in more cables.

"Very nice to meet you," he said over black-rimmed glasses perched on the end of his nose. "I'm looking forward to this!"

"This is Peter Bown, our engineer, John," Tony said.

"Very good songs, young man," Peter said approvingly, "a little Beatles with a touch of Bowie and a dash of Coward. Extremely tasty."

I shook his hand while Tony patted me on the back, looking delighted.

Peter's reputation preceded him. He was known to have 'two of the best ears in the business' and had long been recognised as one of the finest sound engineers in London. Tony had already briefed me on him, telling me Peter had begun working there in 1951, specialising initially in classical recordings, but moving seamlessly into engineering pop sessions in the 1960s. He was acknowledged as being technically responsible for the great sonic qualities of hits by The Hollies, Cilla Black and Gerry & The Pacemakers. George Martin had once referred to Bown as 'an electronics wizard', who astonished everyone with the results he achieved using EMI's then limited four-track equipment.

In 1967, Bown truly came into his own when he engineered Pink Floyd's ground-breaking album, *Piper At The Gates of Dawn*.

Produced by former Beatles engineer Norman 'Hurricane' Smith, who had actually been taught the art of great engineering by Bown through their years working at the studios together, the album set new electronic and sonic challenges. Smith and Bown, who proved a great team, faced them head on, giving Syd Barrett and the rest of Floyd an album to be proud of, and one considered amongst the best released that year. Especially important to the success of 'Piper' was Bown's enjoyment of experimentation, and his openness to the new sounds and effects the group was trying to create in the studio.

Peter worked on some of The Beatles' *White Album* in 1968, and a couple of years later he oversaw the infamous strings overdubs on *Let It Be*, with the enigmatic Phil Spector sitting beside him – and the ever-present bodyguard patiently waiting outside the studio during the sessions.

In 1971, Bown engineered one of the greatest albums of popular music, Roy Harper's *Stormcock*, which was produced by Peter Jenner. Together, the three men achieved some astonishing results, which regularly had blasted through my headphones that year as I'd sat mesmerised by its genius. The album has been named by Robert Plant as his No.1 favourite L.P. To this day, it's one of only a few albums I regularly play from start to finish, its four beautiful tracks a testament to inventiveness and experimentation working at its best.

As I stood chatting to Peter, I caught myself thinking how amazed I would have been, growing up in the '60s, to think that this legendary man, who had been a part of the some of the greatest creative production teams responsible for records I'd bought and adored in my little bedroom at home, would one day be working on my album.

I was dying to ask Peter all sorts of questions, but the ever-professional Mr Bown politely excused himself with a smile. "Okay, back to work," he said, and continued to plug in more cables, move a few faders up and down, mumble "Hmm" to himself, take the cables out and plug them in somewhere else. As he busied away, I became aware of the sound of a very jazz-tinged impromptu, not unlike the stuff Jack Bruce had done on his fabulous *Songs For A Tailor* album. I glanced through the control room window and saw a drummer and a bass player jamming away happily together. Tony nodded at me:

"Let me introduce you to the boys," he said, opening the thick control room door, with its quickly recognisable 'swish', and leading me down the staircase I had seen in so many Beatles recording session photos. As I followed Tony across the studio floor, I was struck by how truly huge the room was, something the *Beatles Monthly* shots hadn't really captured.

"Hi," said the drummer from behind his kit, doing a little stick-roll on a cymbal.

"Bob, meet John Howard," Tony said. "John, this is Bob Henrit."

"Argent's drummer?" I asked, wide-eyed.

"Amongst others," Bob said, and deftly twiddled his drumsticks.

I shook hands with the moustachioed, rather chunky bass player who Tony introduced as Dave Wintaur.

"Nice to meet you, man," he mumbled and carried on doodling.

"Okay!" Tony said, gently demanding attention, "The first number we're going to do today is 'Goodbye Suzie'."

"Good song," Bob murmured, Dave nodding in agreement.

"I sent the guys your demos, John," Tony explained. "Okay, if you sit down at the piano and give us a quick run-through of the song?"

The large Steinway Grand felt and sounded wonderful as I tried out a few chords, the bass notes huge and sonorous, and I imagined how many times McCartney must have stroked these keys. I immediately wanted to have a go at 'Maybe I'm Amazed' but instead I launched into 'Goodbye Suzie', while Bob and Dave began trying out various things as accompaniment. At the end, Tony went through the parts he'd liked and those which he didn't feel worked, lots of nodding from the boys as he took them through his thought processes, and then he turned to me:

"John, try making your piano less busy. The flourishes you did worked beautifully on the demo, but now we have Bob and Dave accompanying you, and there will be a guitarist adding stuff later, as well as other things we'll overdub, the simpler you keep your piano, the better it will sound. Try it."

He came and stood to one side of the piano and leaned into me, watching my hands as I went through it again, coaching the way I played it as we went along... "No, take that out, keep it just chords... don't slow down going into the chorus, keep the tempo going...that's better...do a looser Elton John-ish riff in the middle eight...great!"

He stood, rubbed his hands together, and said to the three of us, "Ok, guys, let's try another run-through."

Bob counted us in and I was amazed to hear how much more effective it sounded with me doing less on the piano.

"That's so much better," I said, looking at them all.

"Less is more," Bob murmured, and winked at me.

"It's what Paul McCartney does all the time, John," Tony said, "keeps his piano basic, simple and strong, and then adds the decoration with other instruments later. Welcome to proper recording!"

Just then, Peter Bown's voice boomed over the intercom:

"Just to let you know, John, Stuart and Patsy have arrived and say 'Hi'."

I looked up at the window at the top of the stairs and two smiling faces beamed down at us, hands waving happily. I waved back but Tony took no notice, instead rubbing his hands together again:

"OK! Let's go for one!"

Running up the stairs with a thumbs-up sign, he went back into the control room where I heard Stuart crying out, "Tony! Good afternoon!". The huge closing door silenced the reply.

Three takes of 'Goodbye Suzie', with me also singing a guide vocal for the boys, and we had it 'in the can'.

"That was great!" Tony said into our headphones. "Now, guys, we're going to try 'The Flame'…and then come up and hear them both."

I rifled through my lyrics while Bob and Dave put up chord sheets on their music stands, again doodling their way through it and developing it into a gentle jam. This is where I began to feel a little uncomfortable, as I have never been capable of - indeed get no pleasure at all from - just sitting at the piano and 'having a blast' through some impromptu bit of musical meandering. My father, on the other hand, loves nothing better. I've watched him at his gigs over the years, bouncing off his musical colleagues with pure joy as they all fit into their shared groove and play some unrecognisable bit of free-form jazz. I only feel in my comfort zone when I'm playing a song I've either written or routined several times alone beforehand, assured that I know exactly what I'm doing by the time I'm in the studios or at a gig.

Making changes on the spot to 'Goodbye Suzie', would, you may think, have freaked me out. But, if the structure of a song remains the same, I have a fixed template to work from. It's the tuneless, infinite jamming which I cannot do. For me, it goes nowhere, results in nothing, and is a waste of my time and effort. I am also probably just a little jealous that I can't join in the utter shared joy I see on musicians' faces as they contentedly jam and groove together.

Happily, on this occasion, Tony gently scolded Bob and Dave out of their jam with a "come on guys, time is money," and I gratefully counted us in and began the classically-influenced piano motif which opens 'The Flame'. It only took us two takes to get it down and then we all went upstairs to hear what we'd done so far.

Stuart and Patsy greeted me as I walked through the door, Patsy kissing me on both cheeks and Stuart warmly shaking hands as I introduced the guys to them.

"Would you like a cup of tea, John?" Patsy asked me.

"That would be great, Patsy, thanks!" I replied, and she disappeared in search of a drinks machine, with Bob calling out jokingly, "That'll be three sugars in mine, please!".

"How's the voice, John?" Stuart said.

"Fine, Stuart," but my reply was met with Tony adding,

"It doesn't matter, Stuart, he's only recording guide vocals today."

"Still…" Stuart said, almost to himself, as Peter began playing the two tracks we'd recorded up to then.

They sounded really solid. I was struck particularly by how sympatico Bob and Dave were, aware always of what the other was playing, and occasionally almost answering each other's deft touches with their own. They were also very sympathetic to what I was doing, supporting rather than outplaying me. Dave played a beautiful classically-influenced run during the piano motif breaks on 'The Flame', perfectly enhancing them, which delighted us all.

A little knock of the mike by Bob's drumstick during 'The Flame' – about 2 minutes 10 seconds in - caused initial concern, but then everyone agreed it was "texture", and was completely in time.

"Even when you screw up, it sounds great!" Tony chaffed Bob.

I turned to Stuart for his reaction and he nodded and gave me a thumbs-up, as Patsy returned with my tea.

"No, you're alright!" Bob joked again at Patsy as she handed it to me, but it sailed over her head.

"Ok, John," Tony said, "Next up is 'Missing Key,' and I want you to try a completely different approach to this song. I can hear a much slower, simpler ballad than the way it is on your demo."

"Really?" Stuart said, stepping forward a little.

"Yes, Stuart," Tony replied firmly, and turning to me said, "let's go down to the studio, John, and I'll show you what I mean."

I was aware, from the corner of my eye, of Stuart left standing alone, his concern almost tangible as I walked away. I purposely didn't look back, and followed Tony out, his chatter as we went downstairs dulling my sense of guilt.

On the demo of 'Missing Key' (and the version I'd recorded with Les Reed a few weeks earlier) I had used a florid syncopated piano motif throughout the song, almost like a guitar finger-picking riff. But as I began playing it, Tony stopped me and said he wanted me to just play very simple block chords, no decorative riff at all. And then, in the choruses, he asked me to play an accented beat anticipation thing, a la 'Golden Slumbers'. (He had in fact produced a version of that McCartney song by Apple Records group White Trash in 1969). Finally, he wanted me to start straight in with the vocal, very much like Macca did in 'Hey Jude'. As I fumbled my way through it, unlearning how I'd written it and slowly doing it the way Tony wanted, Bob and Dave began playing along. Once he was happy, Tony asked the three of us to have a run-through before doing a take. It did sound great, and I noticed how I now sang it, unconsciously phrasing the words quite differently from its original version. I smiled at my producer as he ran back up the stairs, thinking, 'This guy has great ideas.' I was also impressed by how prepared he obviously was for these sessions.

I was aware, however, of a very worried-looking Stuart standing up at the control-room window, peering down at me, and I saw him move quickly towards Tony when he'd got back in there, with a rather heated discussion obviously following on. Though we could hear nothing, from my vantage point I could see the two men waving their arms about at each other. Tony, however, looked the more insistent, as he made a 'back off' gesture to Stuart.

Bob, Dave and I just sat quietly for a few minutes, waiting for the go-ahead from Tony, until, finally, Peter's voice murmured into our headphones:

"Er – I think we're ready for a take? Ok, Tony?"

I could hear a mumbled conversation still going on in the background, then, at last, Tony's cheery voice cut through:

"Yes, sorry lads, minor disagreement in here but - " – languid laugh – "it's sorted now...OK, John, count-in please before your vocal. Let's lay this one down."

By about 4.30, we had three tracks, at least the piano, bass and drums, done. It seemed a good time to take a quick break. So I, along with Bob and Dave and Stuart and Patsy, trotted downstairs to the famous Abbey Road canteen, leaving Tony and Peter to stay back in the control room to run through what we'd recorded. Even this was, for me, hallowed ground, having seen photos of The Fabs tucking into egg and chips and cups of tea down there. I decided to follow suit, as did we all, and convivially chatted as we ate our British fry-up. Bob and Dave soon began their own discussion about a band they'd seen a few days earlier, and Stuart took the opportunity to lean into me and say quietly,

"Are you happy with how it's going, John?"

I nodded through my munching, took a sip of tea and said, as enthusiastically as I could muster,

"Yes, very. Are you?"

Stuart did a 'not sure' with his head, looked at Patsy, who shrugged but stayed silent, then he sailed in:

"'Goodbye Suzie' and 'The Flame' sound great, John, don't you think so, Patsy?"

Still remaining silent, she nodded. "But...what has Tony done to 'Missing Key'?"

I knew this was coming, but feigned surprise:

"I love 'Missing Key'! I think Tony's actually improved it. It's very Beatles now."

"It's not the same though, is it, John?" Patsy put in.

"And you're *not* The Beatles, you're John Howard," Stuart continued with moral support now confirmed from at least one of us.

"Your beautiful piano playing," Patsy added, "he's taken it away from 'Missing Key', John. Such a shame."

"Les loved that motif of yours," Stuart said, shaking his head.

At which point, whether he'd overheard the conversation, or was just calling time, Bob said,

"Ok, chaps, back to work I think!"

We all trooped up to Studio 2, and as we entered the control room and Stuart and Patsy moved towards the sofa, Tony looked at them and said, "Oh! You're staying, are you?"

"Well, yes, Tony," Patsy said defiantly. "Of course we are. Another tea, John?"

"Christ, John. Those two are driving me crazy."

Tony and I were back down in the studio about to start work on 'Gone Away'. I walked over to the piano and sat down.

"I know, Tony."

"We have to have a chat."

"I know."

Tony winked at me and then, clapping his hands, said:

"OK. Bob and Dave, you're with us until six o'clock – yes, guys?" They nodded. "So we'll get another track down now, and then..." he looked at his watch, "the studio's booked until eight o'clock... so I want to spend a couple of hours going through some keyboard overdubs with you on your own, John."

We all nodded.

"Now, 'Gone Away'...again, John – sorry about this! – I want to change the feel of the song from the way you played it to me a few weeks ago."

It had been the brand new song I'd just written when Tony had made his bizarre visit to The Reids at their home a few weeks earlier. He'd recorded my sitting-room performance on his cassette player, benignly smiling through Stuart's acclamations. I now sat there wondering just how much he wanted to change a song so dear to Stuart's heart.

It had been written as a kind of Burt Bacharach mid-tempo rhythmic pop ballad, with a similar feel to Carole King's 1971 hit 'It's

Too Late'. However, Tony had quite different ideas for it:

"Slow the song right down, John, use that intro motif you've got but also do it much slower, that's it, and then just play simple block chords as the guys accompany you. I have some overdub ideas I'll run by you later, but for now, just play the chords." I did a run-through, with Tony quietly telling me as I went along, "No, even slower, John… slower still, that's it."

My main concern was how rangy the song was, especially in the choruses, and I wondered if my voice could cut the mustard with this new slowed-down arrangement. But, after we'd tried a full run-through together, Tony seemed very happy and told us to get ready for a take.

As I played the intro, I could see out of the corner of my eye Stuart staring down at me, his puzzled expression saying everything that was going through his mind. Three takes later, we'd got it, and all climbed the stairs to the control room, where Stuart was in bits:

"John! What have you done to my song?" he cried as I walked in. "It's completely different!" He looked beside himself, pacing up and down behind Peter's chair. "And there's no way you can sing it like that, it sounds terrible!"

He threw out his arms, looking round the room for support. Instead, Tony shouted across the room:

"Stuart, please! Don't have a go at John, any problems, discuss them with me – later!"

Patsy shuffled in her seat and Stuart, crestfallen, sat down. I went over to them and said quietly,

"It'll be fine, don't worry. It'll be absolutely fine."

"Jesus, I hope you're right," Stuart mumbled.

Thankfully, the track suddenly blasted in as Peter hit play and the new re-structured 'Gone Away' filled the room. It did sound good, though, yes, my vocal, which was straining to hit some of the higher, now much more sustained, notes would need some work.

"Great take," Peter said as the track ended.

"Fabulous!" Tony agreed.

Bob and Dave simultaneously applauded, Bob winking at me and mouthing "Great!".

While, behind us, Stuart and Patsy were on the move:

"OK, gentlemen!" Stuart said as amiably as he could, "We'll be going. We have a dinner engagement this evening. Well played everyone! See you tomorrow!"

I followed them out, and, bidding farewell in the corridor, grabbed Stuart's arm:

"It's only a guide vocal, Stuart, don't worry."

"But, that beautiful song, John, it's…well, you seem relaxed about it, so we'll see."

I watched them walking away wondering what else I could say. They looked like parents who'd just lost a child. As I went back into the control room, the very walls seemed to be sighing with relief.

"Well, that was eventful," Peter said, still twiddling knobs and faders.

Tony was shaking his head, but, even so, everyone seemed in good spirits. We all listened again to the four songs we'd recorded that day, with lots of approving nods around the room.

"Great day's work, guys!" Tony shouted, and shook Bob and Dave's hands, as did I, thanking them both. As they left for the night, Tony turned to me:

"You happy to try some piano overdubs, John?"

For the next couple of hours, Tony took me through various overdub ideas he had, mainly on 'Missing Key' and 'Gone Away'. The first song needed just a doubling of my 'Golden Slumbers' piano in the choruses, which he would pan left and right, and a simple lilting right-hand overlay to the chords in the verses. I also doubled what I'd played on the grand piano, on an electric keyboard, which Peter set up for me. Happy with the results, we moved onto 'Gone Away'. For this, Tony had some very adventurous additions in mind. First of all, he wanted me to play an arpeggio rise and fall motif in the intro and verses and then double the piano chords in the choruses, so he could again pan both takes. Then, happy with that, he called Peter down again and asked him to roll the mellotron over to the middle of the room.

It was a huge wooden unwieldy thing, and Peter huffed and puffed it from the far corner of the studio. Once it was in place, Tony asked him,

"Do you know how we get a harpsichord on it?"

Peter looked mystified,

"Don't ask me, I'm just the engineer!"

Tony laughed:

"Don't be so modest, Mr Piper At The Gates!"

With a mock "shucks", Peter came over and very quickly showed me how to find various samples, finally picking a yellowing button marked 'H-chord'. As he pressed it, there began a deep rumble from inside the contraption, I could feel the wooden frame vibrating, followed by a loud whirring and then a heavy 'clunk!'. Peter explained it was locating the correct tapes sample, and – hey presto! – when he played a couple of keys a harpsichord rang out.

"Very 'Lucy In The Sky'!" I shouted, thrilled.

"Well, it is the same mellotron The Beatles used on *Pepper* and 'Strawberry Fields'," Peter said, smiling at my open-mouthed wonder. "The rest is up to you, my boy." He chuckled and went back upstairs.

"Peter?" Tony called out, "I need a pair of headphones so I can go through it with John while the track is playing."

"Behind you, over that mike stand in the corner," Peter called from the top of the staircase, and disappeared into the studio.

As the track played, Tony ran me through what he wanted me to do, literally doubling the arpeggios on the harpsichord which I'd just laid down on the piano. After two run-throughs, he ran back upstairs, and Peter asked me if I was ready. I looked up at the window and nodded and the track count-in started.

The harpsichord was ringing out in my ears, it sounded great. At the end, Tony shouted "Fantastic!" and then, "Now find 'strings' on it, John." I located the button, pressed it, and voilà, after more whirring, thumping and bumping, I was an orchestra.

"Now, give me a strings chordal wash in the middle eights and choruses, John."

When the middle eight arrived I played the mellotron and nearly wept at how beautiful it sounded.

"That's it, John! You're done! Well done!"

I took off my headphones and just sat for a couple of minutes, absorbing my first day in the studios. With a huge sigh, I climbed the stairs and was met by a big hug from Tony.

"That was really great, John!"

"Yes, congratulations, young man!" Peter said, lining up the track so I could hear what I'd just recorded.

As the track played through, Tony nodded at me and put his hand on my shoulder. I was finding it hard not to burst into tears.

Leaving the studios into a warm April evening, Tony asked me if we could meet up a little earlier the following day:

"There's a little wine bar just a few doors from here, can you meet me there at about 12.30 tomorrow?"

"No problem, see you then."

I walked round the corner to my flat, thrilled with how the recording had gone, but also aware that there was an interesting conversation on the cards before tomorrow's session began. I slept like a log that night.

I awoke much earlier the next day, had a long bath and took my time freshening up as I drank my tea. Seeing how casually everyone else was dressed the day before, save for Peter's floral shirt, I decided to dress down a little, and chose a white cotton shirt, jeans and a cream sweater slung over my shoulders a la Audrey Hepburn as my ensemble. I was just about to leave when the phone rang. It was Stuart.

"How did it go last night, John?"

"Great, Stuart. Really good."

"Look forward to hearing it all! See you about 2.30!"

I walked briskly along Abbey Road to the wine bar many of the studio engineers and staff used for their break-times. It was another lovely April Spring day, and the scene, as I strolled past the studio building where I would be recording in a couple of hours' time, reminded me of the Beatles album sleeve featuring this now-famous road, with its blue skies, a line of trees and a sense that all was well in the world. I'd just heard the Eurovision winner's record, Abba's 'Waterloo', on Capital Radio. They were a new name to me, and while I thought it was unlikely they would have another hit - most of the non-British contest winners were briefly successful one-hit wonders in the UK – their single had, for all that, just smashed into the Top 20 and looked set to top the charts. The record's bright clean joyful sound reflected how the air felt that day.

Tony was sitting at a table outside the café when I arrived and greeted me with a hug and his always welcome languid chuckle.

"Would you like something to eat, John?" he asked, but I demurred, never eating before a recording session or a gig. I did say yes to a drink, though, expecting it to be a coffee. He returned a few minutes later with a glass of port.

"For me?" I asked, surprised.

"The best thing for your voice, John. I know you're not doing your vocals for a day or two yet, but this will always help before any singing."

I sipped it and had to admit its warm richness felt very good. Tony smiled as I drank it down:

"The worst thing you can have before any singing is a cup of tea."

I knew it was a dig at Patsy, who had been constantly getting me fresh supplies of the stuff during the session the previous day:

"She means well, Tony."

"I know, but this brings me neatly to what I wanted to discuss with you…"

"Stuart and Patsy."

He chuckled again. "I know they're fond of you, and I respect the feeling is mutual from your point of view - "

"But?"

"But, they really must stop coming to the studios for hours on end, sitting there, judging, tutting, gasping and jumping up and down at things they don't like. Stuart is forever going into a mad panic every time you do anything he doesn't like."

"I've seen him staring through the window at me a couple of times - "

"Several times, John, happily you don't always see him, you're rightly too engrossed in what you're doing, but, quite frankly, it's driving me – and Peter – absolutely nuts."

"So…what can we do?"

"Well, I am quite happy to speak to Stuart about it, but I think it would be more kindly delivered if it came from you." I began to speak but he held up his hand. "However, if you're unhappy to do that, then I will speak to him, but I will be extremely firm with him. Patsy already doesn't like me, but after what I have to say to them, they'll both probably hate me! But that's fine. I'm not trying to win a popularity contest."

"Leave it with me, Tony, I'll have a word with them, quietly, on our own, tempt them down to the canteen at some point."

"They can come to the studio, of course they can, but only every couple of days, and just stay for an hour or so. They must stop this all-day attendance. I'm ready to snap, so is Peter. Doesn't it drive you crazy?"

Truth be told, I'd got used to it, the Reids' constant overseeing of my life, and it had been very welcome when I'd first arrived on my own in London, they'd become like second parents to me. But I could see how annoying such constant showing of affection and the chaperoning would be for others.

My glass of port finished, we made our way to the studios where we were recording four more tracks that day. Tony chatted about it as we went along, he wanted us to do 'Family Man', 'Guess Who's Coming To Dinner', 'Deadly Nightshade' and 'Spellbound'. That would leave two more tracks to do, and for those he told me he had an interesting concept which he would talk to me about soon.

We were just routining 'Family Man' when Stuart and Patsy arrived upstairs, smiles and waves through the window, and a sinking feeling in my stomach about the conversation I would have with them later.

It was a relatively straightforward track to do, Tony didn't have any changes to the way I'd done it on the demo, at least not at that stage. We then did 'Spellbound', its jazz-tinged feel a big favourite with Bob and Dave, who grooved along beautifully as I played the rather complex chordal run-downs. We went up to listen to what we'd done, everyone all smiles and handshakes, kisses from Patsy, Tony doing his best to move things along from a chatty social occasion, and glancing at me when I was offered the usual "cup of tea, John?".

"No thanks, Patsy, I've got a glass of water down there. I'm fine."

"Okay! 'Deadly Nightshade' next!" Tony said, clapping his hands, and off we trotted to do three takes of it.

Over the intercom, Tony said, "I'm coming down to chat with you about the next song, John."

That meant changes. And to 'Guess Whose Coming To Dinner', the song which, in its original form, had turned Stuart onto me all those months ago. I knew this would be major and likely to cause a terrible ruction.

At the piano, Tony explained that he wanted to give the song a much more ethereal dark vibe, rather than the camp Noel Coward-esque way I'd done it on the demo (and had always done it since I'd written it in 1973).

"Keep the camp, just make it more sinister," Tony said, smiling.

He didn't want me to play the grand piano on it at all, preferring the electric piano. And - I knew this would be an anathema to Stuart - he suggested:

"I know this is only a guide vocal, John, but try doing it with less of the Bowie-ish *Hunky Dory* effeteness, use more of a gutsy style, stretching the lyrics out, less clipped in their delivery. It's great fun, the way you did it on the demo, but I want more depth vocally."

So, instead of *"And Flash just flew past my window"* delivered in perfect Coward Englishness, he wanted me to lengthen 'Flash', with more of an American sound to it. As Bob hit the cymbal on the following beat, I doubled that accent on the piano, as did Dave on the bass, so it went *"And Fla-a-a-sh"* – accent – *" just flew past my windo-o-w"* – accent. As the three of us went through it in this radically new style, I saw Stuart, while not flying past, but certainly rushing to the window, almost banging on it, looking completely distraught.

"Oh God," Tony muttered.

"I will talk to him," I said quietly.

"Please, John, do."

As soon as Tony had gone upstairs and Peter told us the tape was running, Bob quickly counted us in and we were off, no time to worry about what was going on in the room above us. For now, that was Tony's problem.

I actually felt sorry for Stuart when we arrived in the control room to hear the takes back. As 'Guess Who's Coming To Dinner' played, he looked anguished and bereft. I went and stood with him and smiled at Patsy, mouthing "It'll be fine!". It was becoming my studio mantra to The Reids. Neither looked at all convinced.

"OK," Tony called out, "time for a break while Peter and I do some tidying up, so, people, relax for half an hour!"

This was my cue to invite Stuart and Patsy down to the canteen, while Bob and Dave, perhaps put in the picture earlier by Tony, stayed in the control room.

Stuart ordered us egg and chips and cups of tea, and we sat down together in a thankfully otherwise empty room. Before I'd even asked him what he thought, Stuart began:

"John, what is Tony doing to our songs?"

"You don't like what we're doing?" I asked innocently.

I knew the answer but wanted to tread carefully.

"Some of the tracks are great, I love 'Suzie' and The Flame', and 'Family Man' sounds good, 'Spellbound', 'Deadly Nightshade', fine, but 'Missing Key', 'Gone Away' and 'Guess', Tony is completely changing them...".

"And not for the better," Patsy added.

"They're not the songs I fell in love with, John," her husband continued.

I had to grasp this argument and pull it back:

"There's still a lot of work to do on them all, they're in their very early stages, nowhere near finished."

Glances between The Reids spoke volumes, but I had to continue:

"And this is what I need to speak to you both about...".

I looked at them as affectionately as I could, and took a deep breath:

"I know you both care deeply about this album, and the songs – as do I - but, well, is it possible that you could let Tony just get on with it...and by that I mean..." I mentally ducked from the oncoming flak... "not come in so often?..."

Stuart then took me completely by surprise:

"You've taken the words out of my mouth, John."

I sat up as Stuart smiled back at me:

"Patsy and I were only talking about this last night, weren't we, darling?" Patsy nodded. "I think we – Patsy and I – should back off and let you, Tony and Peter get on with it. Then, when it's all done and dusted, we can make our minds up if we're happy with the results. I know what I think about some of them already, but, let's give Tony the benefit of the doubt at this stage."

Feeling a mixture of utter relief and stunned shock, with that sense, after a frank discussion, that a tangible tension had evaporated, I could hear the relief in my voice as I said,

"Right! Great!"

The Reids continued to smile at me as I searched for words:

"I mean, by all means, come in every couple of days and have a listen - ".

"Oh we will, John," Stuart said.

I looked at Patsy who was blinking at me. Stuart patted my arm:

"I don't enjoy conflict any more than you do. But, after all, *we are* paying Tony. And by that, I mean me *and you*, John." He looked at me very seriously for a few seconds and then got up. "OK, enjoy the rest of the session. Call us in the morning to let us know how it went. We'll pop by in a couple of days."

The two of them looked back and, with a wave at the door, left me sitting alone, wondering if what had just happened was a dream.

When I returned to the studio minus Stuart and Patsy, Tony gave me a quizzical look, and I replied with a thumbs-up. He mouthed "OK?" and I nodded. But, in truth, I felt that I'd let them down, the two people who had supported me – in more ways than one – so steadfastly through the previous few months. But I knew it was the right thing for this situation. Tony, Peter and I could now get on with what we were there for, with a clear path ahead.

Chapter Eighteen

Cue Dream Sequence

After we'd recorded the first eight tracks of the album with Bob Henrit and Dave Wintaur in Abbey Road's Studio 2, I spent the next four days recording the vocals, some of them in the smaller, more intimate Studio 3. There were still two more tracks to be done to complete the album, but Tony had an idea for those which would not include the usual piano, drums and bass basic backing we'd had so far.

For the big ballads, 'Goodbye Suzie', 'Gone Away', 'The Flame' and 'Missing Key', he chose Studio 2 for me to do the vocals. He felt its spaciousness would add to the drama, the vastness, of the songs. For the more up-tempo pop numbers, 'Family Man', 'Deadly Nightshade', 'Spellbound' and 'Guess Who's Coming To Dinner', we used Studio 3. It had a boxy comfy feel about it and probably added to the dry sound he wanted on those numbers.

Most of the time, it was just Tony Meehan, engineer Peter Bown and me, along with the tape op, with Stuart and his wife Patsy only popping in every couple of days for one or two hours, and throughout sitting quietly listening. They had taken on board my request to keep their visits to a minimum, and it meant we could concentrate on getting each vocal right without Stuart panicking every time I sang a bum note.

I did walk into the control room one afternoon during a minor disagreement, after I'd done the first lead vocal for 'Gone Away'. Tony was patiently explaining to a worried-looking Stuart how we were going to approach these sessions:

"John isn't Tom Jones or Des O'Connor, Stuart, doing a song all the way through for us to applaud at the end at how great he is. He isn't a cabaret spot. This is modern recording in a state-of-the-art studio with a recording artist of today. We're using the latest technology we have to get the best results possible for a hopefully exciting new album."

"But he went wrong so many times, his pitching -"

"Will be fine. He's getting the verses done now, which sound pretty great to me, then, when those are perfected, we'll tackle the choruses and middle eight. They're particularly taxing vocally so we'll drop in and then work on them in isolation until they're perfect."

Peter turned round in his chair:

"If you'd heard the early stages of Beatles tracks on things like *Pepper* and the *White Album*, you'd have been amazed at how rough and unfinished they sounded."

"Exactly," Tony added, nodding at Stuart.

"And things have advanced much more since then," Peter continued. "We get each section done and dusted before we move onto the next, overdubbing and doing retakes where we need to. Like a jigsaw."

"It's part of the fun of recording now, Stuart. The whole performance doesn't have to be done in one take all the way through anymore."

"But John is first and foremost a performer," Stuart continued to protest, "that's what impressed me so much when I first saw him!" He looked over at me as if trying to get me to recall that evening, just a few months ago.

"On stage, yes, Stuart," Tony replied. "I'm sure John's great. But here, with me and Peter, he's a recording artist, and the two are entirely different animals." He looked at me, his expression one of exasperation masked in a benign smile. "John, do you want to hear what you've just done and we'll go through it together?"

He put his hand on my shoulder as the tape started, speaking quietly to me as a section he wanted me to redo came up:

"There, that line, you can do that much better…and there, just a couple of lines could be crisper, but apart from that, John, it's fantastic."

Then, smiling broadly at me, he said,

"OK, do you want to try those sections again?"

I nodded, smiled over at Stuart who still looked unconvinced, and went back down the stairs, put on my headphones, stood at the mike and waited for the right parts to be spun through to me. Two attempts later Tony's delighted voice rang into my ears:

"Perfect!" he shouted. "Now. We'll have a go at that pesky middle eight...."

The part I loved the most about recording was the double-tracking. I'd enjoyed the process ever since I'd recorded home demos as a teenager, overdubbing my voice onto a lead vocal, and trying to get the second voice as tight in time with the first as I could. Their brilliant double-tracked vocals was what had first impressed me about Lennon and McCartney, true masters of it. My attempts at being as good as them had obviously been great practice. As I went through the sections Tony wanted double-tracked, I heard him whistle into my headphones:

"I'm going to call you DT King in future, John. That was amazing. So synchronised!"

I then heard Stuart's overjoyed voice in the control room:

"John has always been fabulous at double-tracking!"

"We're all very happy, John," Tony said, adding that languid laugh of his.

He wanted me to triple-track the choruses on 'Gone Away' and 'Goodbye Suzie', which he thought should sound "huge", and so I got to work on that, loving the sound of three JH's singing in unison in my headphones! It's a sound I have never tired of creating.

When I went back into the control room, Stuart was now beaming:

"Brilliant, John! That sounded so great, didn't it Patsy?"

Patsy blinked across the room at me, stood, kissed me on both cheeks and said,

"We'll leave you to get on with it now, John. It sounds fabulous!"

As they left, Tony grinned over at me, shaking his head.

The vocals for the eight songs were completed as planned in the four days allocated, so, over the following week or so, Tony began bringing in the extra musicians he wanted on the tracks: a saxophone combo for 'Goodbye Suzie', 'Deadly Nightshade' and 'Spellbound' and a solo sax part on 'The Flame'; a guitarist for several of the tracks; an accordionist for 'Guess Who's Coming To Dinner' and a moog synthesiser on 'Guess Who's Coming To Dinner' and 'Family Man'. For that he booked Rod Argent – so I now had two members of his band Argent on my album!

I was fascinated watching Tony down in Studio 2, singing the parts he'd arranged in his head to the various musicians, 'blahhing' away the sax parts to the four players, air-guitar playing his parts to a terrific guitarist whose name I now have sadly forgotten, and humming the accordion parts – which came after the choruses on 'Guess Who's Coming To Dinner', unsurprisingly following the line *'And I'll play my accordion like all accordions should be played'* - to a sweet little man who looked extremely tiny and rather lost down in the vastness of Studio 2, as he played Tony the parts he'd been given beautifully.

Then it was time for Rod Argent, who arrived full of beans and energy. I was struck by his sparkling eyes, and the intelligent way he listened to whoever was speaking to him, almost soaking in what they were saying, enthusiastically nodding as he listened. Tony first of all played him 'Guess Who's Coming To Dinner' and told Rod he wanted "spooky". Rod looked at the floor and listened intently, before glancing up at me and giving me a 'perfect' finger-and-thumb circle:

"Great song," he said. "Well done, man! Did you write it?"

I nodded.

"Clever guy! It's a sort of comic-book song."

"Exactly, Rod!" Tony said. "So think cartoon sound affects, weird motifs, ghostly accompaniment."

"OK! Let's give it a go," and Rod was off down the stairs where Peter had just positioned his moog for him.

"Can I sit down there and watch Rod?" I asked Peter.

"Of course! There are plenty of headphones hung up around the room, pick any pair."

Listening to Tony's instructions through the 'phones, and watching Rod trying out various sounds and effects, as 'Guess' blasted through, was fascinating. It was a real blast watching him pull cheeky little faces as he tweaked various fun sounds out of his keyboard, winking and grinning at each new effect, like a little boy who'd found a new toy, occasionally glancing over at me to see if I approved. I must have resembled a nodding dog.

I still remember the delight on Rod's face when he first played the squealing 'flying' sound which goes through the choruses, and Tony's delighted "Yes," through our headphones as he played it.

Then it was onto 'Family Man', and Rod quickly came up with a great swooping accompaniment, recording that in just two or three takes. As the synth did its thing, a backing vocal motif came into my head in the choruses, a sort of counter-melody to the lead vocal. So when Rod had listened to his work and gone away satisfied, I sang the motif in my head to Tony:

"Go and do it," he said.

So off I trotted, pulled on a pair of headphones and quickly recorded a double-tracked 'Oh I am a Family Man' counter-melody to the chorus vocal, followed by a falsetto 'Aaah!' through the second half.

"Fantastic, John!" Tony shouted in my ears, "I'm coming down!"

As he arrived at the mike he said:

"Play me 'Deadly Nightshade', please, Peter, I've been hearing some backing vocals in the verses and choruses on that one."

He smiled at me and gave me a thumbs-up, mouthing "It's

sounding great!".

'Deadly Nightshade' suddenly blasted into our ears. Tony put his arm over my shoulder to pull me into the mike with him and sang a couple of "Ooh-ooh-ooh's" on the verses. I loved it, it was very Motown. So we recorded those together, and tried a few things out in the choruses too. Happy, Tony took off his headphones and beckoned me up the stairs to have a listen to what we'd done. And there we had it, eight tracks virtually completed.

We broke for a drink and a snack at the local wine bar in Abbey Road, where Peter, Tony and I discussed what was next as we tucked into our cheese and salad baguettes. Sipping his small beer, Tony said,

"I have a chap called Harry Gold coming round to my flat tomorrow, John, to talk about him doing some arrangements for 'Maybe Someday In Miami' and 'Kid In A Big World'. Do you know him?"

I didn't, but immediately Peter's face lit up:

"Harry Gold's Pieces of Eight!"

Tony laughed:

"That's right! One of the really successful Dixieland jazz combos in the '40s and '50s, always on the wireless. Harry's in his sixties now, of course, but I met him the other evening by chance and he's a really lovely guy, and so musical. I want him to do a kind of Dixieland Palm Court Orchestra-style arrangement, and have his band play on those two songs."

"I may have worked with him years ago," Peter said, mulling over his beer.

"So, it'll be like old times," Tony quipped.

Peter arched an eyebrow:

"Less of the 'old'!"

The following day, as we waited for him to arrive at the flat, Tony told me about Harry, who'd played saxophone in a band led by Oscar Rabin in the late 1930s. When Rabin told him he needed more variety to broaden its appeal, Harry offered him 'a band within a band' – and this became Harry Gold's Pieces Of Eight.

On the day war ended, Harry was in Paris with the Services' entertainment troupe, Ensa, one of a group of musicians asked to broadcast to a home audience from the grounds of the British Embassy. The Pieces Of Eight regularly appeared on the *Music While You Work* radio show, and the band had many big-name admirers, including Hoagy Carmichael, who invited them to accompany him on tour in 1948.

Harry also freelanced as an arranger for the BBC, sometimes collaborating with Norrie Paramor, the producer of early '60s hits for Cliff Richard, Billy Fury, Helen Shapiro and Frank Ifield.

With that foreknowledge, I viewed Harry quite differently as I shook his hand when he walked into Tony's sitting-room on that early summer's day, a bespectacled, unassuming elderly chap with a leather briefcase under his arm. Here was a man with a great musical pedigree. Even so, as I tried to imagine him blasting away on his saxophone in a Dixieland combo, I couldn't see it at all. There's youth for you. Appearances are everything at that age.

It soon became clear that Harry's musical knowledge was extremely wide. He completely surprised me when he said he really liked the new Cockney Rebel hit, 'Judy Teen'.

"Very clever song, great arrangement. A pinch from 'Catch A Falling Star,' of course. But that's music, nothing's original."

"Do you like David Bowie?" I ventured.

"'Life On Mars', loved that, not sure about his other stuff though. But he's a clever lad."

Tony laughed delightedly as Harry and I chatted amiably on about pop music, me waxing lyrical about The Beatles, Harry saying he preferred The Kinks:

"'Sunny Afternoon', what a great song, I could see my band playing that one."

Cups of tea finished, and time marching on, Tony switched on the tape recorder on the coffee table:

"I'm going to play you these piano/voice demos of John's, Harry. Try not to hear them as they sound now, but rather how you would arrange them."

As 'Kid In A Big World' and 'Maybe Someday In Miami' trilled around the room, Harry reached into his briefcase and took out a piece of manuscript and a pen, listening to each song carefully, making notes as they played:

"I can hear strings on them both," he said as the second song ended. "The ballad – lovely song, John - is very much a torch song isn't it?"

"Yes, but forget how they sound on the demos," Tony told him. "I'd like you to imagine them quite differently, as 1930s style songs, *Kid* with a lovely gentle Palm Court Orchestra-style backing, and *Miami* with a swinging Dixieland arrangement."

For a moment, Harry looked puzzled, furrowing his eyebrows at Tony. Then, as an idea came to him, his face lit up. He casually crossed out the notes he'd made, and wrote something else down:

"Al Bowlly," he said.

"Exactly!" Tony cried.

Harry smiled:

"Al Bowlly and Ray Noble – that's the sound you want."

I was mystified. I'd never heard of Al Bowlly or Ray Noble. Tony saw my face.

"Al Bowlly was the first British crooner, John, one of the most successful Dance Band singers before the war. Along with the Ray Noble Orchestra he sold a lot of records."

"He was killed in 1941 when a Luftwaffe parachute mine

detonated outside his flat in London," Harry continued. "He was only forty-three. Such a pity. A real waste."

Tony stood up and went to his record collection:

"Somewhere here..." he searched through his LPs, "Ah! Here it is!"

He held an Al Bowlly record in his hands like a little boy finding his favourite Christmas annual. "Listen to this, John."

As Bowlly's 'Midnight, The Stars and You' floated round the room, with his mellow, warm voice crooning above the orchestra backing him, I knew immediately then what Harry – and Tony - had in mind.

"Perfect for 'Kid In A Big World'," Tony said.

"Have you got 'All I Do Is Dream Of You' on that album?" Harry asked.

Tony scanned the back of the L.P. sleeve:

"Yes! That's on here too!"

He moved the stylus onto that track and we all listened as the lovely Swing orchestra gave Bowlly a wonderfully evocative, foot-tapping backing.

"How would that kind of thing be for 'Maybe Someday In Miami'?" Harry asked us both.

"Fantastic!" I said, getting excited now, imagining my song with this great period sound.

"It's going to be beautiful, John!" Tony said, smiling at Harry who beamed back. "I'd like you to book the band as well, Harry, your pick of musicians who you think can get us the sound and feel we need."

"No problem!" Harry said, delighted.

Packing the demos into his briefcase, he bid us a jaunty goodbye, promising us we'd have something to hear within the week. Tony shook his hand warmly and said,

"I'll book the sessions for a week today, Harry! See you at Abbey Road, Studio 2, at two o'clock, with your chaps!"

When he'd gone, I said to Tony that I thought it might be better to wait until Harry had done the arrangements and got the musicians sorted, before booking the studios. Tony smiled:

"I've actually already booked the sessions, John. I knew Harry would be the right man, and he will have it all done and ready in time. He's the old school kind of guy, efficient and trustworthy. Don't worry. He'll be ready!"

And sure enough, he was.

I stood at the mike in Abbey Road's Studio 2, as Harry, standing on a little raised platform, counted in 'the boys' – average age about sixty-five. As he conducted his small orchestra, I thrilled at the stunning arrangement he'd written for 'Kid In A Big World' as it wafted around us. The whole scenario seemed like a dream, me here in Abbey Road Studios, with one of the legends of 1940s dance band music conducting his orchestra on one of my songs.

It was the first time I'd heard the song played like this, so for a couple of takes I was getting to know the variations Harry had written. For a start, he'd put in an intro, which my original piano/ voice version didn't have, and the pauses I'd got so used to – 'So hey!' – pause –"Hey you there...' etc · performing the song as I had at the piano for the last twelve months since I wrote it in 1973, had been shortened or simply taken away. It was like a completely new song in many ways, and though I loved what Harry had done, I struggled to get it right to begin with. The only positive thing at that point – apart from Harry's beautiful arrangement – was that Stuart was not sitting in the control room listening to me make a hash of it, dashing to the window like a man imprisoned.

But after the first couple of takes, and Harry's extremely kind patience as he explained the changes he'd made, I started to get the hang of it. Rather brilliantly, at one point as I was going through a second take, Tony came over my headphones and said, "John? Try imagining yourself as Al Bowlly, as a 1930s crooner, not the John Howard we know, but as though you're playing a part in a movie... you're on a glossy Art Deco film set, singing out front in your black tie and tails, with Harry's orchestra behind you…".

When Harry counted us in for the third time, I was ready, and taking Tony's advice, adopted the persona of one of those dance band singers I'd seen in Fred Astaire movies, with a smoother, less dramatically pop-py approach to my vocal. With Harry's kindly face occasionally looking over at me, I let his orchestra guide me, rather than trying to force my style on the arrangement. I even had a go at 'poshing up' my pronunciation – though I came to regret doing that quite quickly. At the end, Harry put down his baton and smiled, even the drummer, who'd seemed lost in a world of his own, nodded at me and winked.

"This is only a guide vocal, John," Tony was saying, "but it's sounding great, we may even keep some of that. Harry…that was wonderful, come and have a listen, guys."

Most of the orchestra stayed down in the studio, chatting about what kind of weekend they'd had, but Harry and I and, surprisingly, the drummer, went upstairs to hear the take we'd just done.

As the track soared, like a World War Two radio broadcast, around the control room, I fell in love with Harry's sound. The little touches he'd put in with the strings and woodwind and the lovely cascading piano runs, were the stuff of spine-shivers. My only concern was how I was singing it, to my ears it just wasn't good enough, didn't sound natural, and I hated the 'forced-posh' thing I'd attempted. But, for all my concerns, both Tony and Harry seemed delighted, so we went back down to the studio to try a few takes of 'Miami'.

I found this one much easier to sing, and didn't attempt an upper-crust voice, just sang it naturally. I loved the way the orchestra belted along, carrying me on its great rhythms, the drummer especially having a wild time. If anything, Harry's arrangement had confirmed what I'd heard when I wrote it, a kind of Bryan Ferry camp '30s pastiche, *"with the stars lighting up the night, as we leave the car far behind, time is no problem, we've got our whole lives before us, and the wine made our heads a little light last night."* It was pure Glam-Camp fluff, and the Swing backing really swept it along on its fantasy-world journey. I got it in just two takes, and when we listened in the control room, I felt much happier. Again Tony said he'd probably keep some of the guide vocal.

With much shaking of hands, occasional manly bear hugs and delighted congratulations all round, Harry and his boys packed up and left. I then got to work at the mike again, on my own, recording three or four takes of each song once again. Tony wanted me to keep the poshed-up crooner style for 'Kid In A Big World', and although I wasn't happy about it, I did as he asked.

We were just listening to the tracks in the control room, Tony telling me that "we'll pick various parts of each vocal take, the best bits, and mix them together into one take", when Stuart and Patsy arrived.

"I was looking forward to meeting Harry," a disappointed Stuart said when we told him he'd just missed the great man. "I remember his band so well from my youth."

"Well, have a listen to this, Stuart," Tony said, looking over the moon at me.

'Maybe Someday In Miami' obviously entranced the Reids, but I could tell that, like me, Stuart wasn't entirely happy with my vocal on 'Kid'. It was 'Casting Shadows' in Rome all over again.

"Tony's going to mix the best bits of my vocal from several takes into one good one," I told him, trying to sound convinced.

He nodded, not wanting an argument, but I could see he wasn't entirely happy.

With sessions finished for three weeks until the mixing began, I walked out of the studios and blinked into a sun-drenched late afternoon in early June. As I wandered the five minutes back to my flat, I tried to imagine how the album was going to sound when pressed up. It felt like the whole world was offering me my future, a feeling I hadn't allowed myself before.

Arriving home, I turned on the radio and the beautiful strains of The Isley Brothers' 'Summer Breeze' cascaded round the room. I ran a bath trilling to myself, *'Makes me feel fine, blowing through the jasmine in my mind.'* Life felt great.

During the months of recording, I'd purposely kept away from frequenting the gay pubs around London, which had become my regular haunts over the past six months. I'd wanted to wake up each day well-slept and refreshed and ready for the long hours ahead, rather than groggily coming-to beside some one-night stand whose name I often couldn't recall, wondering where the hell I was, what the hell I'd been thinking, and how I was going to get home.

Now though, having completed the album on time, and with – nearly – everyone happy with it, I decided to treat myself to a well-deserved night on the town. It's odd how quickly one forgets the dire nights of boredom in some stranger's godforsaken bedsit miles out of central London, wishing you'd not bothered and dying for a toothbrush and a hot bath, when the possibility of finally meeting some gorgeous hunk you want to lie in bed with forever replaces those awful memories with once again excited anticipation.

Now as I languished in my long hot bubble bath, enjoying 10cc's brilliant new album, *Sheet Music* blasting out of my record player, I mulled over which establishment of the night I'd pick to go on my hunt this time.

An hour or so later, drying myself off, I poured a vodka and lime, cheered myself in the mirror – "To you, my darling," - and picked Stevie Wonder's *Inner Visions* from my collection of LPs. Bopping around the room to my favourite track on there, 'Misstra Know-It-All', I prettied myself up for what – and who - the night ahead might bring. I'd decided on the Duke's Head pub in Dean Street, Soho. It was a bit of a dive but I liked its tawdriness, it had an edge, a sense of decadence, and I found something rather Genet-esque about its clientele.

As I strolled into the pub, dolled up to dazzle these rough diamonds, I had no idea of the folly of my decision to go there that night. I stood at the bar and scanned the room, as I always did, for my possible Mr Right. Then someone caught my eye. He was a handsome, rough-looking little guy, mid-30s, jeans and white T-Shirt giving him a Marlon Brando look. Sitting by the window across the room, he half-smiled then winked and beckoned me over. I sauntered through the packed room, ignoring - but loving - the occasional 'Hello cutie' comments, and sat in the space he'd made for me beside him.

"Hello gorgeous," he said, in a broad East End accent. I was already hooked.

"Hi. I'm John," I said, checking out his broad shoulders and five o'clock shadow.

"I'm Ray," he replied. "Ray Robinson. But you can call me Sugar."

Throwing my head back and laughing, I thought, 'How *do* you do, Mr Right?'.

But how wrong I was…

Chapter Nineteen

Just Waiting Here For You

"I like people like you."

'Sugar' Ray smiled at me over his third pint of beer I'd bought him, looked me up and down and winked a slow, enticingly tipsy wink. His eyes were the lightest ice-blue I'd seen, and seemed to stare into your deepest self. It was an oddly disconcerting feeling, but also rather thrilling. He possessed a gently mocking persona and had seemed amused as I'd wittered away, completely foolishly, that I'd recently been paid £500 for writing a song for the new Peter Fonda movie, and was currently recording my first album at Abbey Road studios, for which I'd received an advance of £10,000. His widening eyes and slight tip of the head should have set alarm bells ringing, but, like the naïve fool I was back then, I inwardly preened.

"People like me?" I asked disingenuously. I sipped my vodka and lime and stared coquettishly back at him.

"Successful people," he said, nudging my knee. "Like you. I like success. The sweet smell and all that."

I breathed in the aroma of Pino Sylvestre which wafted round me, having virtually bathed in it before I'd left the flat that evening. I'm not sure if was the vodka or my cologne, but, without much forethought, I said,

"What are you doing later?". It elicited a broad smile from my East End trick.

"Don't waste time do you?"

"When I see what I want, I usually go for it." ('Who *is* this talking?' a voice inside me said. I ignored it and felt myself smiling provocatively).

"Coming home with you, I hope," he replied, finishing his beer with a huge thirsty swill.

My heart actually fluttered. I'd only read about fluttering hearts in Victorian romance novels, now I knew what it felt like. Legs a little shaky, and again ignoring the inner warning voice, I stood and said,

"Let's go then."

On the tube to St John's Wood, Ray continued to banter away with me, chuckling gorgeously whenever I said anything mildly amusing.

"You got a nice flat in St John's Wood then?" he asked, as the train flew through the tunnel from Baker Street.

"I like it, it's small but perfectly formed."

Another chuckle as we reached our stop. I felt his hand rubbing my back as the doors swished open. It was my turn to chuckle.

On the short walk to Hall Road, we were chatting away easily when Ray took something from his pocket and casually threw it in a garden. I heard it fall with a clatter onto the path and slide away.

"What was that?" I asked him, and he shrugged.

"A knife," he said matter of factly.

"Why did you throw it away?"

"'Cause I won't be using it on you."

I stopped in my tracks. He stood very still next to me as I shivered slightly, unsure whether to speak or run. I heard him take a deep breath before he walked in front of me, dipped his face into mine, forcing me to look at him, and said,

"Okay. Truth time. When I picked you up, it was part of a scam I have with one of the barmen. He scans the room for young, rich-looking, well-dressed guys, a bit, well, camp like you, gives me the nod, I approach them, give 'em the blah-blah sugar charm and get invited back to their flat."

"Such confidence!"

"Yeah well, it worked on you didn't it?"

Point made, he continued:

"Once in there, having a quick snog, I whip out the knife, threaten to cut their throat if they don't give me their cash, wallet, jewellery and what-not, and basically frighten the living daylights out of them. Having got all their valuables, which they can't unload quick enough, I scarper. I lie low for a week or so then go back to the pub, give the barman his half-share of the booty and sit and wait for the next pick-up."

As calmly as I could, but shaking inside, I said,

"Does it always work?"

He shrugged,

"We do alright. Never had any problems yet."

"You never get any return visits to the pub, with a policeman in tow?"

"Nah!"

"Do they never report it?"

"Young toffs steer clear of Lily Law. Too embarrassing, and mummy and daddy might stop their allowance. They're just relieved they're still in one piece, learnt their lesson and stay away from rough joints like The Duke's Head. I never actually hurt them, just make 'em think I will. And anyway, rich boys don't miss a few quid."

"So - why not me?"

"Honestly? I like you." I gave him a 'puh-lease!' look and he laughed. "I do! You're different. You're not stuck-up posh like the other guys I've picked up, all hoity-toity nose in the air, looking for a bit of rough." He moved closer to me, his expression the one we usually adopt when gently letting someone down. "I also realised early on you're not actually rich."

"Oh?" I felt slightly insulted.

He laughed,

"You went on a bit too much about the money you'd made from your music. It was obviously new to you to earn so much."

He waited a few seconds while I digested it all, then put his hand on my shoulder,

"I'd like to see you again. Or have I scared you off? What are you – twenty, twenty-one…?"

"Twenty-one."

"Yeah. Well, you probably wouldn't want to get involved with a thirty-five year old loser like me."

He leaned over and gave me a quick kiss on the lips. I could smell his leather jacket and the booze on his breath.

"So. Up to you," he said. "Do you want me to go or… shall we, you know…?"

In the early hours of the morning, I lay in his arms as he absent-mindedly curled my hair round his fingers. I kissed his arm and said,

"Me too."

"Hm?"

"I'd like to see you again too."

I woke up as the dawn chorus was singing its heart out by the window. I never drew my curtains, I loved daylight creeping in as the morning rose outside. It looked like it was going to be another lovely early summer's day. I could hear Ray humming to himself in the bathroom, and found him soaking in a steaming bath, covered in lather. He looked like a soaped-up teddy bear. He carried on singing and smiled like an angel at me:

"Good morning, gorgeous."

"Tea?" I asked, half hoping he'd ask me to join him. But:

"Great," he replied brightly. "Then I have to go. Work calls!"

I suddenly realised that I hadn't enquired what he did for a living. I'd assumed he earned enough money to live on from his pick-up scams – although as he'd promised me during the night that side of his life was now over…:

"Where is work?"

"The bookies. William Hill's."

"In the West End?"

"Nah. My stomping ground, Mile End Road. It pays the bills. Not far from my flat either. I can pop in and change before I go there."

I also hadn't asked him where he lived. The fact is, back then, in my world of one-night stands, you didn't give out too much personal information (unless you were a chatterbox preener like me). It was usually a casual no-questions-asked thing, certainly on the first date anyway, a mutual, unspoken understanding of 'That was nice, 'bye now, see you around sometime'. One learnt the rules of the single urban gay man very quickly – a hint of a desired attachment, voiced too soon, was a definite no-no. Exchanging phone numbers was sometimes delicately raised over a morning cuppa, if only – if you'd been so lucky - to arrange a repeat performance of the fantastic sex you'd just had. But it was the most upfront you could be without scaring off the pick-up for good. But to be brutally honest, you were usually glad to see the back of them.

Tea quickly knocked back, Ray gave me a peck on the cheek and went to the front door. I saw that he'd left his leather jacket perched on the back of one of the chairs and was about to get it for him when he said not to worry, it was going to be a hot day so he wouldn't need it. With another longer peck on my cheek and a delightful wink, he closed the door, saying "See you about seven tonight", just before it clicked shut.

I rang Stuart at ten o'clock to see if he wanted me in that day. Most afternoons, I went into his office to work on new songs on the old upright piano. Today though, I just fancied a long soak, a snack at one of the salad bars in St John's Wood High Street, and a good sleep – I hadn't had much of that the previous night. I was very relieved then when Stuart said,

"If you don't want to come in today, John, don't worry. I'm going to be having a few meetings here with overseas publishers most of the afternoon, so you won't be able to do much playing anyway. I'll need the larger piano room as it has the tape machine – and I'll be playing them some of your songs! Probably not good for you to be here while they listen, could make them a little uncomfortable... though I'm sure they'll love what you do."

Although we had the recording deal, Stuart was still 'working' my songs, trying to get some covers by other artists, or potentially interesting a publisher abroad, enough to want to do a sub-publishing deal for their territory and work the songs there. While I languished in my hot foam bath, I imagined one of Stuart's contacts raving about 'Goodbye Suzie' or 'Gone Away', saying how it would be perfect for a French chanteuse who he knew was looking for a hit. Such things my dreams were made of back then.

After a delightfully laid-back day, a light lunch and a wander round the shops in the High Street, I got back to my flat, lay on the bed and fell fast asleep. My last thought before dropping off was 'I'll get up at about five, have a quick bath and make a snack for Ray before he gets here.'

As I came to, I realised that night had fallen, the full moon casting spider-web shadows from the trees outside across the bed. I looked at the clock. It was nine o'clock! I jumped up in a daze, still not properly awake, turned on the light and wondered if I'd slept through Ray pressing the intercom buzzer at the main entrance. I imagined him standing downstairs, cursing me not answering. But that was unlikely, the buzzer was extremely loud. It had once shocked me out of a very heavy sleep when Patsy had popped round on the off-chance, to see if I fancied joining her for lunch at Fortnum & Mason. I'd been having a crafty post-late-breakfast rest and had had to feign hunger as she chatted away over our smoked salmon and scrambled eggs.

I paced the room for a few minutes, wondering what to do, and decided to make myself a cup of tea. By ten o'clock, I was sitting in the armchair, empty mug on my knee, staring out of the window at the dark blue sky tinted with the distant yellow miles of street lights. I glanced over at Ray's leather jacket slung over the dining chair, thought about it for a few minutes then went over and checked the pockets, there may have been a telephone number somewhere. But there was nothing, just a chewing gum wrapper and a screwed-up bus ticket. Wishing I'd insisted on giving him my phone number, I recalled him laughing when I'd offered it:

"Why do I need that? I'm coming back here later – aren't I?"

By midnight, I gave up waiting and went to bed. During the night, I had one of those dreams-while-awake – I was staring into the darkness of the room when Ray walked in and stood over the bed. He hovered over me for a few seconds, smiled, then turned and left the room again. When I actually woke up as the sun was coming through, my first thought was that he'd been killed and had 'come back' to me for one last time during the night. Telling myself to stop being so melodramatic, I got up and ran a bath.

Stuart rang at eleven, and told me he'd had a great reaction from one of the French publishers – maybe my daydream about the chanteuse covering one of my songs hadn't been so world-of-my-own after all. Visions of trips to Paris came into my head and brightened me a little, as he suggested we meet for lunch at Kettner's. "It's time we had a catch-up. Haven't talked properly for ages."

Before getting ready to go out, I put on the new Alan Price album I'd bought a few days earlier, *Between Today and Yesterday*. I'd got it on the strength of his brilliant new single, 'Jarrow Song', which was constantly on the radio and climbing the Top Ten. The album didn't disappoint either, with its mix of piano-led wistful songs, Nina Simone-like blues, and McCartney-ish pop, it was just what I needed that morning.

Sitting on the tube to Leicester Square, and mulling over the mixing sessions which were due to start in a couple of weeks, I had a surge of panic...would Ray have come back by then?...how would I concentrate on the mixing if he was still missing? Should I go to the police? No, not a good idea, given Ray's rather shady background... should I tell Stuart?

JOHN HOWARD

I felt completely dislocated. Unusually for me, my concentration was poor. I wasn't able to think things through. I tried to read the Time Out I'd bought at St John's Wood station, but realised I'd read the same paragraph several times of a review of the new Neil Sedaka album, *Laughter In The Rain*. With the side-thought that I'd read it properly later, and probably buy the album while I was near HMV later that afternoon, my mind went back to Ray. Maybe I should discuss his disappearance with Stuart. Talking things through often helped clear the mind. But then I decided that he would probably wave away my concerns as rather silly:

"You only met him last night, John," Stuart would say. "What's the fuss? So, he's gone. So what? Plenty more fish in the sea."

Yes, I told myself, I was just worrying about nothing.

"You always make mountains out of molehills," my mum used to tell me.

She was right. Simple answer was he'd decided one night was enough and gone back to his 'former life'. But then, why leave his jacket behind? Maybe I should take it back to the pub where we'd met. I had an image of me striding up to the bar, handing Ray's jacket to the barman and shouting grandly,

"Give this to Ray Robinson when you see him next. You know, the petty thief."

But what if he was there, in the middle of one of his pick-up scams? Then what? Another image came to me, flouncing over to him, throwing his jacket in his face and telling the queen he was chatting up that the hunk he was making goo-goo eyes at was a crook.

"Got yourself a new knife, Ray?" I'd say cattily. Then to the queen, "Watch yourself, love. He might use it."

I smiled at the silly daydreams of a dumped fool. I actually had no desire to darken that particular pub's doorstep ever again.

The train was coming into my station, and, as I stood amidst the tourist mêlée waiting for the doors to open, the thought floated by that

320

it was just a short walk from there to the pub where I'd met Ray. 'No,' I insisted to the niggling other voice in my head, 'don't be so stupid.'

As I stepped onto the platform, a very handsome Italian-looking chap waiting to get on gave me the eye. I returned his gaze but, carried along by the surge of disembarking passengers, was swept towards the exit. When I managed to glance round, I caught his resigned shrug through the carriage window as the train set off and sped away through the tunnel. Yes, I told myself, definitely more fish in the sea.

I wandered into Kettner's, past the white grand piano where a tuxedoed chap was playing Gershwin's 'Summertime'. Walking into the huge dining-room, I saw someone put his jacket over the back of a chair, and the unwelcome image of Ray's, lying forlornly on mine, made my stomach sink. Stuart's welcome smile was beaming at me from one of the window tables. I pasted on a smile and went to greet him.

"John!" he cried "How are you?" He grabbed my hand and squeezed it in both of his.

"Really good, Stuart," I lied.

"Honestly?" He studied me. "You look a bit tired actually, John. You sure you're ok?"

I sat down, picked up my napkin and smiled:

"I'm fine! Didn't sleep too well last night."

"You been out on the town again, you rascal?"

I laughed, it felt empty but I hoped it sounded throwaway.

"If only, Stuart!" I replied, nodding to the waiter who offered me some water from the iced jug on the table. "Great news about the publisher!" I said, changing the subject.

"He really loved 'Gone Away' and 'Missing Key'."

"That's fantastic! Do you think he'll get a cover?"

Stuart shrugged,

"Who knows? But at least he'll be trying to."

The waiter arrived to take our order. I glanced at the menu.

"And the mixing sessions are not far off now!" I chatted away as brightly as I could, feigning reading but knowing what I wanted.

"Nearly there, John! Nearly there. It's going to be so great, I know it is. Now, what do you fancy – egg and chips?"

He'd read my mind. It was exactly what I needed right then. Comfort food.

On the day the mixing sessions began, it was almost two weeks since Ray had gone out, saying he'd be back that evening. The pang of not knowing what became of him after that had started to fade, but, regardless of all the voices in my head telling me to just forget it, move on, he's gone, I was still concerned about him. It had gone beyond missing him to 'What the hell has happened to him?'. I had a couple of hours in the morning before the sessions started, so I decided to ring Directory Enquiries for the telephone number of William Hill Bookmakers in Mile End Road. Half-expecting there to be no such branch, I was oddly relieved when the operator gave me the number. They answered the phone very quickly,

"Hello? William Hill. How can I help you?" an efficient-sounding lady chirruped. Startled into action, I was already wishing I hadn't called.

"Hello," I said as confidently as I could. "I wonder if you can…".

"I'll do my best sir," the lady breezed away, laughing when she dropped her pen. "Ooh! Clumsy me! Now! What can I do for you?"

'Breathe,' I told myself. 'Calm.':

"I'm trying to contact a Ray Robinson, who I believe works at your branch. He's left something of his at my flat and I want to let him know."

"Oh! Well, hmm, I don't believe we have anyone of that name working at this branch, sir."

She must have heard the disappointment in my reaction:

"Tell you what," she said, lowering her voice a little, "he may have moved to another branch, people do, for various reasons. Let me put you through to our Head Office. They can check the list of employees at all our London premises."

Thanking her gratefully, I heard a light click, silence, then a ringing tone. After waiting for about a minute with no reply, I was just about to give up and put the phone down when a gruff-voiced chap came on the line:

"Yes?"

I explained who I was trying to contact, ignoring his rather bored cough as I twittered away. Finally, as he cleared his throat yet again, I shut up.

"Robinson you say?"

"That's right. Ray Robinson."

"Is he a member of your family or...?"

"A friend. Just a friend. But I'm actually a little worried about him, he seems to have, well, vanished."

That elicited a kind of puzzled grunt:

"If your friend has, as you say, vanished, sir, then you should really call the police, report a Missing Person."

"I know. I will, but first I wanted to check with you, just to make sure whether he's been into work since I last saw him..."

"And that was?"

"Oh, a week or so ago." It was only a tiny white lie.

"Well, sir, while we've been talking, I've been looking through the R's on our employees listing for London, and I'm afraid there aren't any Robinsons working for us. There's a Robertson, a Joyce Robertson, so, clearly, that's not your friend, but, no, definitely no Robinson here." He hummed to himself then, "No. No-one called Robinson on my list."

I thanked him for his time, and put the phone down. My mouth was dry as parchment.

"Lying little toe-rag!", I said to the kettle as I made myself a cup of tea. Settling with my Darjeeling into the armchair by the window, and glancing over at the deserted leather jacket, I felt utterly foolish. "Sod him!" I said out loud.

Band On The Run, McCartney's best album since The Beatles had split up, was my choice of getting-ready music. It was Paul's first truly great post-Fabs album. He'd had a patchy three years. While George and John had come up with the nearly-amazing *All Things Must Pass* and *Imagine*, Paul had been messing about with nursery rhymes and oddly ragged LPs. Now, with his former muckers' stars decidedly on the wane, McCartney had finally given himself a good talking-to and delivered the album we all knew he was capable of. It was like having all of Macca's best tracks from The *White Album* on one L.P. *Band On The Run* was that good.

I smiled at the title track's rather unfortunate lyric, *'Stuck inside these four walls, sent inside forever, never seeing no-one nice again like you.'* I sang along, but changed the words to *'Man On The Run'*, and decided once and for all to put the last couple of weeks down to experience. Ray had been good company, lovely to be with, and he'd made me laugh. But that would have to be that. Move on. Next. 'Hello. What's your name?'. Smile. Look alluring.

But, truth be told, the 'once-only-and-goodbye' thing was becoming a little tiresome. I was beginning to want more, and I'd hoped that he might be The One. He had the looks, personality, under-the-sheets talent, and that frisson of Bad Boy which suited me down to the ground. He was in many ways the character I had written about for years in some of my more colourful songs. My Genet-esque Great Dark Man. With a glance at the dust-gathering jacket over my chair, and a vow to take it to the charity shop in Maida Vale as soon as I could, I put McCartney's masterpiece back in its sleeve, checked myself in the mirror, locked the door and went for the lift.

It was still a thrill being just a short walk from Abbey Road, I never got bored of enjoying that, and, as I walked up the steps to the studio's front door, full of anticipation for what the next few days would bring, I hoped that the mixing sessions would be the distraction I needed. Sadly, however, what I hadn't expected was how boring I found the whole mixing process. Back then, long before I'd started producing my own recordings, the technical side was way over my head, and the endless what-seemed-hours of sitting around while the producer and engineer listened ad nauseum to a bass drum drove me crazy. With a sinking heart, I watched Peter fiddling with the knobs on his mixing desk, playing it through, unplugging leads and re-plugging them into various other inputs, and playing it through again. Tony would bend an ear to check it until it had enough oomph or whatever, thumbs-up, move onto the snare drum. It all left me losing the will to live, hour after hour, doing the same thing with every instrument, every piece of percussion and every vocal, over and over again until, after the umpteenth "more top…no a little less, that's it…more middle…down a bit, yep, good, ok, hi-hat now…yep…", I gave up. With a quick "ok" nod from Tony, and Peter smiling understandingly at me, I left them to it and popped down to Studio 2, sat at the grand piano and began working on some new song ideas I'd had. I sighed with pleasure as the keys moved smoothly beneath my hands. The chords rang out through this cathedral of pop history. This was where I wanted to be. This I understood.

The first one, which I already had most of the lyrics for, was 'Just Waiting Here For You', written just a few days earlier. The inspiration for the song is obvious:

> The clock ticks on
> That makes the day so long
> If only you had called
> If only you had phoned

Just waiting here for you
Just waiting here for you
You could've called
Couldn't you?
These four walls look the same
No matter how many times
I change the chairs around

Writing songs on that wonderful piano seemed to give my songs a much more panoramic feel. The gorgeously resounding bass notes vibrated through my hands and truly inspired me. What a difference from my parents' old upright on which I'd written many of the songs I'd recorded with Tony. It had most of its bass strings missing, destroyed by mice which lived inside it. This was, literally, chalk and cheese!

Another lyric I had sketched out a few days earlier was 'Hall of Mirrors', again reflecting my sense of detachment at that time, an odd feeling of empty abandonment I hadn't experienced before. It was my lullaby to loneliness:

Loneliness has never been
A very faithful lover
Darkness has never been
Very much of a mother
She leaves her kids crying every night
With a goodnight kiss
You cry for more
Like moths to light

I was dying to play the new songs to Tony, and was just about to go up and ask him to come and have a listen when the studio monitor boomed out:

"John? Want to come and have a listen? We have our first mix!"

As 'Goodbye Suzie' rang round the control room, I suddenly realised how all of Tony's and Peter's endeavours and efforts, getting everything on the track just right sonically, had paid off. It sounded huge, with its own space, and the vastness of the whole thing sent shivers down my spine.

"'Gone Away' is next, John," Tony explained. "I'll live with the mixes we do for a couple of days then Peter and I will tweak where we need to, to get the final mixes complete. Happy so far?"

"Over the moon," I replied. "It sounds amazing."

Tony smiled:

"I know it's tedious to watch and listen to if you're not involved in the process," he said, which elicited a crafty wink from Peter at me, "but it really is worth the time and effort."

"I can see that now. I just wish I understood more of what you're doing."

"Then stay and watch the next mix, I'll explain as we go along."

Over the next few days, standing behind Peter as he patiently worked at getting what Tony was asking for, I began to understand what he was doing. He stopped occasionally and told me which knob did what, and why such-and-such a channel needed less bass or more middle, or more presence. As the track built with each twiddle and listen, Peter fading channels up and down until he got the nod from Tony, I could see how it was like a collage developing, a collage of sound and atmosphere. Just a minor turn of a knob or lift of a fader a fraction of an inch, gave, say, the piano extra body, more depth, and sitting in the track just where it should be. What had initially bored me stiff became increasingly fascinating. I was actually seeing how all those weeks of recording with a great engineer like Peter at the helm had paid off. With neither fanfare nor ostentatiousness, he calmly got each track to sound exactly as Tony wanted it. They were a great team, and it was intriguing to watch their partnership turn my initial piano/voice songs into big-sounding productions. I'd never seen the process up so close and in such detail like that before. I stayed around for each mix from then on.

There was still time occasionally to wander down to Studio 2 and try out some new song ideas, usually at Tony's suggestion when mixing a track was getting tricky or required some time-consuming patchwork, so I did write three or four more, such as 'Lonely Woman', 'Blink In The Darkness', 'Oh Dad' and 'Take Up Your Partners' during those times. I also managed to complete a song I'd been working on for a while, 'Technicolour Biography', its rather dark and surreal lyric fitting my mood:

> It was midday
> By the flushed face
> Of the hunter with the slim waist
> Was a painter of Golden Age puns
> Runs on the shore
> Praising the sun for being a whore
> And the bar boy toyed with words
> He served them all as decoys
> To the poet Robespierre
> Who once climbed into his mind
> A mountaineer
> And from the shadows
> The songs were sung very low
> And the sky became yellow
> The ground like a pillow beneath them
> And the waves wound round their naked toes
> And the days seemed so endless
> But oh, how time flows!
> And the wine bottles strewn upon the shore were empty
> They were empty

And it was midnight
By the stark light
Of the actor with the dark eyes
Drank with all the stars
Slept in disused cars
And the bruises he got from the boozers
They left no scars
And the saga that he starred in
Was running in the back street cinemas
And his leading lady
Watched all her re-runs in the stalls
And from the shadows
The songs were sung very low
And the sky became yellow
The ground like a pillow beneath them
And the waves wound round their naked toes
And the days seemed so endless
But oh, how time flows!
And the wine bottles strewn upon the shore were empty
They were empty

And the bar boy toyed with no words
He'd served them all
Been destroyed
By the poet Robespierre
A mountaineer

With mixing completed by the middle of July, next came the sequencing of the tracks into a Side One and Side Two. I met up with Tony in one of the small ante-rooms at Abbey Road, where we listened to the ten tracks and he made notes where he thought they would fit into the tracklisting. He was keen that the album should open "with a bang", and wrote down 'Spellbound' as Track One. He played it again to me, saying,

"Imagine you've taken the LP out of its inner sleeve, put it onto the record player and dropped the stylus on the first track, then this - Bang! - comes in."

Bob Henrit's brilliant drum roll opening and the rather jazzy anticipated beat on 'You!' convinced me.

He followed this with a ballad, 'The Flame', then the Swing-style Harry Gold-arranged 'Maybe Someday In Miami'. 'Missing Key' followed that, and Side One ended with 'Family Man'.

"Now," Tony said, sipping his umpteenth coffee, "Side two has to come in with, again, something different, so I suggest 'Kid In A Big World'. All the time we're surprising people, just as they think they know where you're coming from, we switch gear and style. It's what The Beatles did on *Revolver, Pepper* and *The White Album*. Never allow your audience to completely know what's next."

He followed that with 'Deadly Nightshade', then 'Goodbye Suzie', penultimate track was 'Guess Who's Coming To Dinner' – at that point the album's title track – and finished Side Two, and the album, with 'Gone Away':

"Leave them wanting more – literally, John. Fantastic track to finish things. You've gone away – for now, until the next album."

"I've written some new songs for that."

"Already?"

"Yep. I wanted to play them to you at the studio during the mixing sessions but we didn't really have time."

"Sorry about that. We'll put some time aside soon, but for now…"

He chuckled as he looked at his tracklisting and handed it to me:

"What do you think?"

I suddenly felt excited. I hadn't really stopped to take in what was about to happen, until that moment. The previous few weeks had been a case of 'job to do, get on with it'. Each day of the sessions over the previous three months had meant getting the tracks recorded, with no real sense that these would all form part of an album. Just making sure they were all as good as we could get them was all that mattered. But now, with the album finished and the final tracklisting in my hand, all the hopes, all the possibilities, which I'd carried with me over the years since my teens, when I'd decided that I wanted to be a recording artist, they suddenly seemed tangible. Real. This was my album! We'd done it!

"Fabulous!" I said. "Really great, Tony."

"Excellent. I'll pop this down the corridor to Peter and he can make the album master and a copy for Stuart."

Sipping the dregs of his coffee he rushed out saying,

"Now let's see what they all make of it!"

I went over to the kettle and, as I stood waiting for it to boil, wondered which track CBS would pick as the first single. My bet was on *Deadly Nightshade*, but Tony thought they may go for a ballad to emphasise the singer-songwriter aspect. I was pouring the hot water onto an Earl Grey teabag, mulling it over, when the phone rang.

"Mr Reid for you, Mr Howard," the receptionist said.

"How's it going, John?" Stuart's bright voice chirruped in.

"Really well, Stuart. We've just finished the tracklisting. Peter's doing the copy master for you now."

"You pleased?"

"Very."

"Fabulous! Bring it in and we'll listen to it together. How about joining me and Patsy for lunch tomorrow, get here about 12.30?"

"Lovely, thanks, Stuart."

I was about to bid farewell when…

"Now! John. I've been having a few ideas about the album sleeve…"

"Ye-es?"

I hadn't expected that to be up to Stuart, more something CBS would arrange, but just then Tony walked back in and I mouthed to him who was on the phone. Meanwhile, Stuart breezed on:

"The album's going to be called *Guess Who's Coming To Dinner*. I think we're all agreed on that. So! Why not create a little mystery within that title?"

I could hear him getting really excited as he spoke more quickly. "This is my idea for the cover...I see an invitation card on a desk, with just the title of the album in beautiful handwriting. Your red fedora hat and a silver walking cane are lying beside it – very classy, John – and, here's the bit I love, we won't put your name on there!"

My silence must have spoken reams:

"Let me explain, John," Stuart continued. "Here's my thinking... when people see your album, they should be intrigued. 'Who *is* this?'. They get your album home, put it on and it's, 'He sounds wonderful, but what's his *name*?'. 'What does he *look* like?'. It'll create a real sense of mystery. Everyone will be asking about you. Then, when the media is begging to meet you, we reveal you to the world with a fantastic show and a press conference. Can you imagine it, John? You'll blow their minds! I have to say, it's a great concept."

I usually found his enthusiasm catching, but this time I wasn't convinced. I wasn't actually sure how to react. Obviously sensing that, he said,

"Look. Don't worry about it now, we'll discuss it over lunch tomorrow. But I've run it past Patsy and she thinks it's a great idea!"

"Have you run it by CBS?"

"Not yet, I'll do that when I take the tapes into them. Leave it to me, John, if I'm nothing else I'm a great salesman!"

As I put down the phone, Tony could see my concern:

"What?" he asked.

I started to explain Stuart's idea to him, but, even before I'd got to the bit about not featuring my name on the sleeve, he had buried his head in his hands:

"Christ Almighty!" he shouted through his fingers. "What is this guy *doing*? Does he want to fuck your career up before you've even got to first base?"

I didn't know what to say. I was still in shock at not having my name on the album. Tony stood up and began pacing the room:

"Paul McCartney, right?"

I nodded.

"He is probably the most famous guy on the planet, everybody knows what Paul McCartney looks like. Yeah?"

I nodded again.

"But what does he put on his album sleeves?"

I shook my head.

"He fucking plasters them with photos of himself, every fucking where! Front sleeve, back sleeve, inner sleeve, lyric sheet, Paul's face is on each and every fucking one of them!!" He laughed out loud, but in exasperation. "Stuart has spent the last six months – and God knows how much money – creating your look, buying you fantastic outfits, sending you to the best hairdresser's, make-up artists, getting photos of you done by Dezo Fucking Hoffman! And now...Now! He doesn't want anyone to fucking *see* you! Is he nuts?!"

"Well, in fairness, he doesn't want me to be seen on the sleeve, then, after the album's released, he -"

"It's a crazy idea, John! It simply won't work. Trust me. I gather from what you were saying that he hasn't told CBS about this?"

"Not yet."

"Well, if they've any sense, please God," he prayed to the ceiling - "they'll screw it up in a very tight ball and throw it through the fucking window. For Pete's sake, one of the reasons they're so excited about you is because of how you *look*! I don't understand, John. I really don't understand."

"He also -"

"Oh God, what else?"

I took a deep breath:

"He doesn't want my name on the sleeve either – he wants to create - "

"What?!" I thought Tony was going to explode.

"...a sense of mystery." I heard my voice wither away.

"A sense of *mystery*?!" He buried his face in his hands again and swayed from side to side. "Oh my God! What the fuck is he doing?"

I sat in silence as he continued to sway and moan into his hands. When he finally lifted his head, his face was red and I could see his eyes had watered up. He drew himself up, sat down very close to me, leaned forward and, grabbing me with his eyes, said,

"What do *you* think of Stuart's idea?"

I felt disloyal but couldn't lie:

"I don't think it'll work. I don't like it. It's – old-fashioned."

"Old fashioned isn't in it. Anyone seeing that cover will think it's a fucking Ray Conniff album. 'Singalong With John'. Sometimes I – well, frankly I despair."

He seemed to make a decision:

"Okay. I wasn't going to get involved in the sleeve, it's not my call, I'm not your manager and I'm not CBS, I'm just the producer, and my job is done. But! We've got to stop Stuart killing your album, because that's what his idea will do. And all our hard work will have been for nothing. Do you want that?"

"Definitely not."

"Okay. So, look. Forget what Stuart says. His idea ain't gonna happen. I'll make sure of that. We're going to have your face – and your name on this album, if it kills me. Fuck his bloody invitation card and silver cane crap. Who does he think you are, Maurice sodding Chevalier?! Right. Here's what I see. *This* should be the sleeve."

As he spoke, he painted a picture with his hands, bringing his vision to life:

"It should have you, beautifully, really tastefully made-up, with a white face, dark lips, dark nails, and wearing one of your fantastic suits, and that great white fedora of yours tipped over one eye. I see you standing in a really dark gothic interior, like you live in this off-the-wall, out-of-the-way place. A hermit genius living in some exotic mansion."

I smiled as his eyes widened, like a magician creating the sleeve for me out of thin air.

"Remember how great-looking Bowie was as Ziggy?"

I nodded.

"Bowie lived that image, he *became* Ziggy Stardust, his fans actually believed he was from outer space."

I laughed as I remembered almost believing that myself when I fell in love with Ziggy in '72. I knew he wasn't an alien, obviously, but I wanted him to be. I fully understood what Tony was saying - with a clever image, fully realised, you can excite pop music buyers. It certainly excited me. Then I thought of my little fourteen-pounds-a–week bedsit and my weekly allowance of thirty pounds from Stuart, hardly glamorous iconic genius. Tony must have seen the doubt crossing my face:

"I'm serious, John. You have to live this, *be* this. It's a big ask, I know, but it's the only way to really make it big. Twiggy was a fashion icon and always looked amazing, she lived what people imagined her to be. Bowie was a pop *and* fashion icon, and he lived it, he *became* Ziggy. To their fans they were untouchable, like Gods from another world. You can be that too. Really. Christ, why not?"

It was a lot to take in but I was really excited. Tony had this way of making you believe the impossible. He'd certainly stretched me during the recording sessions, shown me a different way of playing and interpreting my own songs, so why not now with my image?

Inside me, the little lad from Ramsbottom was shouting 'Don't be so daft!'; but the singer-songwriter with a CBS record deal was shouting back, 'You can do this!'.

"I love it, Tony!" I said.

"Good! So, this is how we play it…first of all, don't tell Stuart it's my idea, that'll put him off straight away!" He laughed. "Explain it to him like it's an image *you've* been thinking about and have come up with this great concept. Really sell it to Stuart as all your own idea. I'm not looking for any credit, I just want this album to be a fucking hit! I'm on a three per cent royalty on sales for God's sake!" He laughed loudly now, and so did I. "No. We have to go for broke. There's only one mystery we want to create, that's how all your talent comes in such an amazing-looking package. It's called marketing. Jeez. I wish I was your manager."

Happily, as I carefully explained 'my' idea over lunch, Stuart really loved it:

"You've been thinking long and hard about this, John."

"Absolutely," I lied through my teeth.

"Okay. I'll book the photo session, call the photographer and get a good make-up artist. Well done, John!"

Patsy hadn't said much, but seemed intrigued at least. I got an uncomfortable impression that she didn't believe it was my idea, but if that was true, she kept her counsel.

Once back from lunch, Stuart made a couple of calls and told me the session was booked for the middle of August:

"There's a young American guy who's been recommended to me, Mike Nicholson's his name. He loved your concept, John. He's going to call me later to discuss where we do the photos."

As Stuart was patting me on the back, Patsy looked at me rather oddly and said,

"Yes. Well done, John."

I thanked her, but still wasn't sure whether her congratulation was for 'my' concept, or the fact I'd successfully convinced Stuart it was my concept. I couldn't be sure. And I wasn't about to ask.

Whisky-on-the-rocks poured for me, red wine for Patsy and a Pernod and ice for Stuart, the three of us sat and listened to the album together. Neither of them said anything during the playback, and, when Side One was finished, Stuart just got up, put on Reel Two and sat down again next to me. I could hear the ice in his Pernod chinking in his glass, its strong aroma wafting over as the tracks played. With the ending motif of 'Gone Away', Stuart got up, took off the tape and looked over at Patsy:

"It's an excellent album, John," he said. "Very good indeed. I'm still not keen on a couple of the tracks...," another glance at his wife..."but overall I think CBS will love it." Patsy blinked in agreement at me across the room.

"Well done, John," she said, and this time it was definitely meant for me.

"OK!" Stuart said, putting the tape in its box. "I'll take the master tapes over to CBS now!"

I heard him crooning the opening lines of 'Kid In A Big World' as he went down the stairs.

A few days later, he still hadn't heard back from A & R Director, Dan Loggins, or indeed anyone from the label. The silence was killing me, but Stuart seemed quite sanguine.

"Give it time, John," he said. "They're a big company. This is a big album for them. They'll have to speak to the States before they come back to us. They'll call."

Finally, they did. About a week later, Stuart and I were in his office chatting about the upcoming photo session, when Paul Russell, then Head of Business Affairs at CBS, rang. The two men talked for about ten minutes, with me earwigging what bits I could make out. There were several 'Great's, a considered 'Understood', quite a few 'Mmmm's' and a final 'I'll speak to John'. When Stuart finally put down the phone I was gagging to hear what Paul had to say.

"OK," Stuart said, coming to sit next to me. "Paul thinks the album is really good."

'Really good' didn't sound as wholly enthusiastic as I'd hoped. I was partially right:

"He said there had been some very positive comments about it from the whole company. Different people like different tracks. Dick Asher, of course, loves 'Goodbye Suzie'."

The company's managing director had been very keen on 'Suzie' as soon as he'd heard my demo, apparently. Stuart had told me that, for him, it had sealed the deal. He went on:

"Paul especially likes 'The Flame' and 'Spellbound'. But - like me - he's not keen on 'Kid In A Big World', 'Family Man' or 'Guess Who's Coming To Dinner'. He loves the songs, just not Tony's production on those, he called them 'over-produced'. But, he stressed that these are his own personal opinions. Overall, he – and the label - think it's a very good album."

Seeing the relief on my face, he nudged me:

"*And* – this should prove to you how good he and the rest of the company thinks it is - he also wants to invite us - you, me and Patsy - to join CBS at their annual conference in Torquay at the end of August. Your album will be presented to the sales and marketing teams from across the world. And we will be there!"

"Wow!" I shouted, "Now *that's* great!"

He took a sip of his Pernod and nodded:

"Yes, John. It is. But – and I've told Paul I need to speak to you -". My heart began to sink. What now? "They want to change the title of the album."

I actually sighed with relief,

"Not my name this time?" I said wryly, referring to a few months previously when the label had said they wanted me to become Christopher Howard, which we'd rejected out of hand.

Stuart smiled,

"No. But they think *Kid In A Big World* is a more fitting title, to get across your youth to people when they see the album in the shops. He also feels it will be a better hook for the marketing people to plan a campaign."

I had no objection to the title change, but wondered if 'my' concept of the white-faced oddity in his gothic mansion, 'coming to dinner', was now right for such a youthful, ingénue-esque title. I voiced my concern and Stuart slapped me on the back,

"No! Don't worry about that. It's still a great idea. The photo session is on. Everything is coming together, John!"

I got back to my flat, put George McCrae's wonderful 'Rock Your Baby' on the record player and, screeching along to the high falsetto bits, ran a bath. I fixed myself a vodka and lime, cheered my reflection and wandered through to the lavender-scented steam-filled bathroom. Already imagining the heaven of languishing in the hot, scented water, I got undressed and was just about to lower myself in when there was a knock at the door.

Reluctantly, I threw on a dressing-gown and turned down the music, hoping my landlady wasn't in the mood for a chat:

"Hello Mrs Skowalski!" I said, opening the door. "I was -"

But it wasn't my landlady.

It was Ray.

Chapter Twenty

Hall Of Mirrors

I lay in the bath listening to the soft sound of Ray's gentle snoring from the next room. In a kind of dream, I reflected on my shock, half an hour earlier, at seeing him standing there outside my flat. His unexpectedly sudden return, after weeks of not having a clue where he was, rather than prompting spluttered shrieks, in fact turned me quite speechless. I'd simply waved him inside and then just stared at him. Several questions jostled in my head but my mouth wouldn't turn them into actual words. Finally, with a faint smile flickering across his face, he'd said,

"Aren't you going to say hello?".

He looked terrible, exhausted and pale. The swagger he'd possessed on the night I met him weeks earlier was now replaced by an air of a defeated prodigal son. The question I'd kept on the tip of my tongue, if he'd ever returned, now sounded rather lame:

"Where have you been?"

"Make me a cup of tea first?" he asked, his usually sparky wink now a rather tired attempt at cute.

As I boiled the kettle and poured the hot water onto his teabag, he collapsed into an armchair and watched me busying away for him. The look on his face was like a child's watching his mother baking in the kitchen.

"Okay," I said, handing him his tea, which he slurped down as though he hadn't drunk anything for days, "now tell me. What's going on, Ray?"

Draining his cup, he sighed heavily and, as I sat in the other armchair cradling my mug like a comfort blanket, he began his sorry tale:

"Right...". He glanced over at the chair by the table and smiled,

"Oh! You've still got my jacket!"

I responded with a look which said, 'Get on with it', and so he did:

"First off, I want you to know that none of the last few weeks were planned. I fully intended to come back that night, I wanted to come back! I did. Honestly. But I couldn't."

"Why not?"

"When I went back to my flat, my -", he looked across at me and winced, "my girlfriend, well, ex-girlfriend, was there."

He watched me as I took in that bombshell. All I could manage was a mouthed, 'Wha...?'

"Yeah, I know. I should have told you but... I'd been living with her for a couple of years, but it was over! Honest! She'd moved out. Anyway, I walked in and there she was, sitting there like nothing had happened. I'd kicked her out, for God's sake! She was waving a set of keys at me, said her brother had given them to her...he and I go back a while...and telling me her family want me to help them with another job. If I said no, it'd be curtains for me, that's what she said anyway, and I believed her. They're a nasty bunch."

"What kind of job?"

"A robbery. I used to be their driver, all sorts of stuff, usually big jobs, lots of cash, she and I did very well out of all that. Unfortunately, we drank most of it away."

I put down my half-drunk tea and decided I needed a proper drink! I poured myself a vodka with a dash of lime, offering him one, but he declined with an emphatic, "No thanks."

With a mixture of fascination and shock running through me, I took a large swig of my drink and sat down:

"So...did you do this job?"

"Yeah, that night, they robbed some jewellery shop in the East End, it went fine, I got them away ok...but, anyway...when I got back she was still there. She had some stuff with her...you know..." He mimed shooting up. "We used to do it together a lot but I've been off it for months. Thought I'd kicked the habit. But when it's offered... it's like..." He looked haunted. "Oh Christ, it's all such a mess, such a fucking mess!"

"So - are you back with her, this -?"

"Sarah. Nah! She and I got wrecked for a few days, too fucked up to fuck. I actually can't remember most of it, we were out of it for God knows how long. Anyway, her brothers have taken her home now, thank God. They say I'm a bad influence!" He laughed ruefully. "Me! It was always her, she's the bad 'un, but they think she's little old weak-willed Sarah under my spell. What a joke!"

He looked at me, his eyes resembling a lost kitten, but I resisted. Truthfully, I was wondering who the hell and what the hell I'd got myself involved with. I found myself wishing he hadn't come back at all. As his tale sunk in and I desperately tried to think of what to say and do, his plaintive voice cut through my thoughts:

"Can I just stay tonight? I need to get some sleep and get myself sorted. Please. I'll be gone tomorrow, I promise. This is too much for you, I can see that. I'm sorry."

"What about your flat?"

"Kicked out. The landlord turned up for his rent a couple of days ago and found the place looking like a drug den, it was a real shit-hole. That's what she does to me, I end up being nothing better than a strung-out tramp. But at least her brothers have ditched me, thank goodness. Out of my life at last. I slept on a friend's sofa last night, you know, the barman who -"

"Oh yeah, another one of your salubrious friends!"

I saw a flash of anger in his eyes, but only for a moment, then he laughed:

"Fair enough! I don't keep good company, it's true. Never did. You brought home a bad lad, John." He leaned over to grab my hand but I moved it away. "When I met you, I thought, at last, someone nice, someone good, someone who likes me, doesn't want anything from me, except - me. And I've fucked that up now, haven't I?"

The abandoned kitten look again attempted to melt me, almost did, but again I resisted:

"Okay!" I said, standing up. "My bath is going cold, and I definitely need one now. You go and lie down, get some sleep and we'll see what the morning brings."

As I walked towards the bathroom a terrible thought struck me:

"Er - your girlfriend and her brothers – they don't know where you are, do they?"

Ray was already settling himself on the bed:

"No! No, don't worry about that! They have no idea about you, about my 'other life'. I've never mentioned it to any of them. They wouldn't believe me anyway. Tough ol' Ray a pooftah? They'd just laugh! And anyway, they're gone now. That's all finished."

By the time I'd finally lowered myself in the thankfully still hot water, letting the rainbow-coloured suds climb deliciously up to my chin, he was snoring soundly.

"Why don't we get a flat together?"

Ray's whispered question in the dark woke me up. I realised I was snuggled in his arms and reluctantly turned on the bedside light:

"What?" I said, sitting up and wiping sleep out of my eyes.

"I think if we got a flat together, something a bit bigger, and set up a proper home, things would be better."

"For who?"

"Me for one. Wouldn't you like to?"

I had never even thought about it. For heaven's sake, we'd had just two nights together, with a very stressful and unsettling break of several weeks in between. I hardly knew him, and in fact I knew him probably less now than I had after our first night together. I didn't know whether to believe his tale of driving a robbery van, followed by drug-ridden days with his ex, and then magically turning up on my doorstep. It sounded genuine as he'd told it, but now –? Especially at the '3 a.m. Doubt Time'. But here he was, suggesting we become a couple! Talk about whirlwind romance watching your life get carried off. Without thinking, the words tumbled from my mouth:

"I rang William Hill. You know, Ray, the Bookies. Where you 'worked'."

Ray's head clicked towards me, his ice-blue eyes darting about as I spoke:

"They'd never heard of you, not the Mile End Road branch nor indeed their London Head Office."

He sat up and nuzzled me with his head:

"Yeah. That was a porkie."

"Another one."

"You calling me a liar?" It sounded angry, but he was smiling.

He leaned forward to hold me but I squirmed out of his grip and got up to put on the kettle. Making tea gave me something mundane to concentrate on. As I busied away, out of the blue I heard him say,

"I think I'm falling for you, John."

I actually laughed. Undaunted, he sat on the edge of the bed. I still couldn't help admiring his perfectly-formed stocky little body. But this had reached a point beyond lust:

"You're different from anyone I've ever met," he said, staring at me. "Man or woman – and I've had my share of both. You're the best." I gave him his tea. "Most people would have kicked me off the doorstep and down the corridor last night, but you -"

"Yeah, I'm a bloody fool," I said, sipping my tea and sitting by the window.

He started singing Elvis's, 'A Fool Such As I' and lurched off the bed, took my mug from me and put it on the table.

"Come 'ere," he said.

The gorgeous strains of The Stylistics' 'You Make Me Feel Brand New' floated out of the transistor as, over a breakfast of Muesli and toast, Ray and I chatted about where we could find a flat together. The fact was, while he'd declared he was falling for me, though I'd been loath to admit it to myself, I'd already fallen. On our first night. Our second night together had convinced me he was The One. Voices in my head were shouting 'No!'. I just re-directed them to my heart, which wasn't listening.

"You have such great bone structure," Jo the make-up lady told me as she applied the base for the work of art she was about to perform on my face.

I was sitting in one of the small anti-rooms in Les Ambassadeurs, the beautifully stylish restaurant inside The Inn-On-The-Park off Park Lane. It was a boiling hot early August morning, and I'd arrived that day feeling very positive about things. I'd drawn out £120 from my Midland Bank account the day before, to cover the deposit and four week's rent in advance on the flat in Harlesden that I'd found for Ray and me. Before I'd left, I'd given him the cash, the address of the flat and instructions on who to give the money to – a Mrs Rawindi, a very pleasant lady who'd shown me round the flat a few days earlier.

It was one of those typical London conversions, a once grand Edwardian house turned into several flats on three floors. A large, rather magnificently tiled hallway led to the flat's inner front door, which opened onto a spacious sitting-room, which led out down a narrow, windowless corridor, with a sizeable bedroom on the right, then opening out into a good-sized kitchen. The bathroom was just inside the back door which opened out onto a walled cemented-over courtyard. It wasn't a particularly pretty flat, but it was roomy, and I thought I could maybe make something of it, especially when Mrs Rawindi told me I could decorate the flat any way I liked.

Harlesden was a busy multi-cultural suburb of London, and the flat's lounge window looked out onto the main road, which was full of restaurants, deli's, a newsagent, several greengrocers and lots of different kinds of shops. It certainly wasn't St John's Wood, and I would miss its quiet subdued salubriousness. But the rent on the flat was basically the same as for my one-room bedsit. Even with the misgivings I still had about Ray, I was young and naïve enough to believe I could change him. I hoped that with a settled life he could leave behind whatever problems he'd had before.

Les Ambassadeurs Photo Session, August 1974, by Mike Nicholson

Even now I get cold chills when I think how trusting I was handing over £120 to Ray. It was a lot of money in 1974, a quarter of what I'd been paid to write and record the theme song for the forthcoming Peter Fonda movie, *Open Season*. I don't remember, though, having any sense of how foolhardy I was. I told him I'd see him at the flat later that evening, and happily imagined him sitting waiting for me with the keys to our new flat dangling from his fingers.

As Jo applied some dark blush rouge to my cheeks, Patsy sat watching the transformation. I decided to finally tell her about Ray (well, some details I kept to myself!). I prattled on about how marvellous he was, how in love I was, all the while knowing how much she'd disapprove. She and Stuart had given me a friendly career lecture just a few months earlier over lunch:

"Have fun by all means, John," Stuart had said, "but romantic attachments just get in the way of a career, certainly in these early stages anyway. My advice? Stay single. For now anyway."

As I chattered away like some besotted showgirl, casually dropping in the bit about the flat in Harlesden, I heard Patsy shift in her seat.

"Harlesden? That's miles away!"

"It doesn't take that long on the tube."

"But, John! The flat in St John's Wood was so perfect for you. Why would you want to leave it?"

Jo giggled and said,

"Love, eh? Makes us do silly things."

"Silly is absolutely right, Jo!" Patsy said angrily. "So silly, John!"

As the eye-liner was delicately applied, I looked up to the ornate ceiling above us. Being pampered must have emboldened me:

"I'm twenty-one, Patsy. I can make my own decisions."

"Yes, that's right. Of course you can. But Stuart and I are here to not only help you in your career, but also, I like to think, to protect you, advise you, John. And my advice would be that this is a very bad thing to do. You've given us no opportunity to talk about this. We haven't even seen the flat! Why didn't you tell us about this Ray person before?"

Jo carefully applied dark red lipstick saying,

"Lips together. Purse them. Perfect!"

Just then, I saw Stuart walk in and beam at me:

"Wow! You look sensational, John!" he shouted. "Doesn't he, Patsy? Amazing!"

"You do look fantastic," Jo murmured, giving me a mirror.

As I viewed the gothic beauty before me, I secretly congratulated Tony Meehan. He had suggested the white face and black lips, and, as he said it would, this look truly transformed me.

From a corner of the room I could hear Patsy quietly telling Stuart

Mautoglade Music, Denmark Street, August 1974,
by Mike Nicholson

about Ray and the Harlesden flat. Stuart mumbled,

"Who's Ray?"

"Exactly!" Patsy hissed.

I gave the mirror back to Jo who stood back to take a good look at her masterful creation:

"Stunning," she said, thrilled. "We should have Vogue magazine here!"

She took off the white linen cover from around my shoulders, handed me my black velvet jacket off the hanger, and looked excitedly over at Stuart.

"You look incredible, John," he said as I did a little pirouette. "Like a star."

Gently taking my arm, he walked with me, head down, a gesture which always meant 'We have a problem, John.'

"You and I must have a chat, young man," he said quietly.

I turned to him, feeling oddly masterful within my new star-like image:

"There's nothing to talk about, Stuart. It's done. I move into the flat this evening. Ray's already taking my stuff over there. As we speak."

Patsy, who had stayed close behind as we'd walked towards the photography set-up, situated by a huge and fabulously ornate spiral staircase, joined us and said,

"At least give us the address and phone number, John!"

"There isn't a phone."

They both gasped at that.

"I'll use the phone box across the road!"

They looked dumbstruck.

I didn't want to sound impertinent but I think I did when I said,

"What's the problem?"

Patsy stared at me:

"How are we going to get in touch with you if we need you?"

"I'll call in every morning to see if you need me for anything."

Stuart joined in:

"But what if something urgent comes up? What if CBS calls us *after* you've rung us, to say they want you there that afternoon? Or they've set up an interview? How will we get that message to you?

We won't be able to, John!"

I suddenly felt extremely stupid. It had never occurred to me. And should have done. With no answer for them, and seeing the photographer approaching us with a huge grin, the three of us made independent decisions to cease the discussion for now.

"John!" the photographer cried, extending his hand. "I'm Mike Nicholson. Wow! You look fabulous!"

He beamed at Stuart, then at Patsy, who both put on a steely smile and shook his hand.

"Where do you want John?" Patsy asked Mike, her voice revealing none of the anger of just a few moments ago.

"Oh, I think on this amazing staircase, don't you?"

For the next few hours, Mike photographed me; walking up and down the spiral staircase, both with and without the white fedora; standing and lounging in various wood-panelled rooms; sitting at the enormous exotically decorated bar with a multi-coloured cocktail the barman had created for me. All the while Jo occasionally stepped forward to touch up my make-up, getting rid of any 'sheen', and Patsy followed me from each set-up with the red and white fedoras at the ready for whenever Mike wanted me to don one of them for a particular shot. Meanwhile, I languished in the feeling of looking like a star. At one point, I caught myself in a gilt-framed full-length mirror, and inwardly gasped at how truly amazing I looked. Jo had done an incredible job transforming me into someone I found unrecognisable, and yet a person who had always lived somewhere within me.

Patsy's reflection came into view and stood behind me smiling. She put her hand on my shoulder and whispered,

"That is the star I always knew you were, John."

"Now," said a bright-faced Mike, "why don't we go outside? I'd like to photograph John in Hyde Park." He turned to me, "I have a little surprise for you, John!"

As we all emerged into the too-bright sunlight which seemed to scorch Park Lane, we were met by a superbly-smart lady, her perfectly coiffured long blonde hair fell around her pink Chanel frock, her bright pink stilettos reflecting the sun.

"Hello! You must be John," she said. "I'm Vicky."

In her hand she held two bejewelled leads, one blue, one pink, which were attached to two equally beautiful Afghan Hounds. Their exquisitely maintained manes seemed to float in the breeze, and rather matched her own, which she constantly swept back with an efficient flick of the head. She introduced her charges as Sara and Carn, and I said hello to them both. They smiled confidently back.

Mike kissed Vicky on both cheeks and grinned at me:

"I thought you could walk Sara and Carn through the park, John!"

"How divine!" Patsy exclaimed.

We all quickly crossed the busy road in a group, Vicky hurrying her charges along, Stuart waving at the cars to thank them for slowing down. Then, while Mike snapped away happily, I began sauntering through the leafy walkways with the impeccably-behaved Sara and Carn accompanying me. At one point Mike caught sight of a Victorian-style stone bench surrounded by trees, like a tiny magic garden, and suggested I sit on the bench with the dogs at my side. With just a single point of Vicky's finger, the dogs stood perfectly still and beamed at her. Mike took several shots

Hyde Park, August 1974, by Mike Nicholson

and then we were off again.

By about two o'clock we were finished, and Stuart invited everyone to his Denmark Street office for a snack and drinks. As we walked along all chatting together, I was aware of people stopping and staring at me, then walking on, or surreptitiously glancing sideways as they wandered past. I had become used to this kind of thing in my teens in Lancashire, my then shoulder-length hair drawing the attention of scoffers and name-callers. However, this felt different. I mentioned it to Patsy:

"Of course they're staring, John," she replied. "They're trying to work out who you are!"

"They think you're a star, John, they're trying to place where they've seen you!" Stuart said.

"Welcome to fame!" Mike said happily, and, running backwards in front of us, took more photos.

The walk to Stuart's office took about half an hour, and as soon as we entered the second floor room, Jo the make-up lady saw the upright piano and her eyes lit up:

"Oh! John! Will you play something for us?"

As Stuart handed round glasses of wine and Patsy busied in the kitchen preparing a large salad for us all, I played 'Kid In A Big World', while Mike again took more photos.

The dogs sat obediently at Vicky's feet as she sipped her wine and listened to me playing. At the end of the song, Patsy brought in the lunch and a large bowl of water for Sara and Carn. We tucked gratefully into the cheese salad, with various cold meats on a wooden platter, and chatted away happily.

Finally, as we bade farewell to everyone, Stuart came back into the office and declared,

"What a fantastic day!"

Any lectures about the folly of moving in with Ray seemed forgotten, for the time being anyway.

As I put my key in the lock, I wondered what I'd find inside. I half-expected an empty room. As I opened the door, the first thing I saw was a bottle of champagne on the coffee table, and beside it a set of keys. I looked up, and there was Ray, grinning at me from inside the flat.

"Bloody hell!" he shouted. "You look fucking gorgeous!"

Although I'd been stared at all the way home on the tube, having decided to keep my make-up on for a while longer, partly to see what reactions I got, I'd actually forgotten all about it by the time I'd reached the flat. Other more worrying thoughts had invaded my mind. Needlessly.

Ray picked me up, carried me into the bedroom, lay me on the bed and went to get the champagne. I heard the cork pop and that delightful chuckle.

"Here's to us," he said, walking back in with two glasses. "Our new life, and here's to you, you beautiful creature!"

At his request, I didn't wash the make-up off until, in the early hours of the morning, seeing my reflection when I went to the loo, I decided that, with passion-smudged lips and runny mascara, I now resembled Bette Davis's Baby Jane, rather than the pristinely made-up gothic creature of the previous day.

The next morning, I duly popped across the road at about ten o'clock to the phone kiosk and called Stuart:

"Steve, your press and promotion chap at CBS, has just called us," Stuart informed me. "He would like us to go and see him today. The photos are ready!"

That afternoon, Stuart, Patsy and I sat in a darkened meeting room while Steve, a pleasant enough guy who had chatted cheerily as he'd walked us from the lift, turned on the projector and began pushing each slide through for us to see.

I was astonished. The pictures were utterly breath-taking. As Jo had declared, some of them could have been Vogue cover shots.

There must have been about thirty which Steve showed us, each one as it clicked through emitting a 'fabulous', 'stunning', 'beautiful' from both Stuart and Patsy. My two favourites were the one of me sitting on the stone bench with the Afghan Hounds, and the other of me sitting at the Les Ambassadeurs bar with my exotic cocktail.

"That's the sleeve!" I said, as it came up on the screen.

"It's certainly a contender, John," Stuart murmured.

All the pictures viewed, Steve switched off the projector and got up to turn on the light.

"So, what do you think?" he asked us as he sat back down.

"They're fantastic, Steve!" Patsy said.

"Wonderful!" Stuart said.

Steve turned to me,

"John?"

"I'm thrilled with them, Steve," I told him, feeling very excited. "Mike's a genius!"

"And the make-up, John," Patsy said, "it looks beautiful – *you* look beautiful!"

"Don't sound so surprised, Patsy!" I joked.

As we both giggled like thrilled schoolgirls, Stuart turned to Steve:

"But what do you think, Steve?"

"Honestly?" Steve asked.

"Yes."

" I think they're disgusting!"

The three of us gasped at once.

He directed his gaze at Stuart:

"I can't believe that you, Stuart," his face and neck turning a baby-shade of pink, "allowed John to pose for these."

He stared down at the slides with disdain.

Stuart leaned forward:

"And I can't believe you've just said that!"

The two men glared at each other.

"Why don't you like them?" I asked Steve, utterly devastated, but keen to dispel the hostile atmosphere.

Steve turned to me and looked incensed:

"Because they're depraved, John, they are distasteful," he spat the words out, "and this –" he waved a hand over the slides, "is not how we want, how CBS wants you to be seen by the public."

I shook my head at him. I didn't know what to say. It was as though someone had thumped me in the chest. Stuart was staring at Patsy, who looked over at me with a kind of pity.

"You actually *like* them?" Steve asked me in disbelief.

"I *love* them!" I said. "This is *exactly* how I want people to see me!"

Steve stood up, meeting obviously over:

"Then we have a problem." He carefully put the slides back in their box, tapped the box on the table then, without warning, threw it across the table, where it clattered into the projector, the slides crashing out and laying strewn around it. Steve looked at me, then at Stuart. He walked forward and held up his finger:

"There is no way CBS will be using any of *those* photos."

He wagged his finger at the slides, then made a kind of helpless wave of his hand as he turned away from us and went to the door. He looked about to leave the room when Stuart also stood and walked up to him, faced him and, challenging his body space, said,

"So what now, Steve? Where do you suggest we go from here?"

Steve stepped back a little and raised his chin, obviously keen to maintain his superiority in the room:

"We arrange another photo session for John, but this time I get our sleeve designer involved, to make sure nothing like *this*..." he pointed again at the splayed group of slides lying by the projector..."happens again!"

He flounced out and left the three of us staring at each other.

"Oh Stuart!" Patsy wailed.

"I don't believe it," he replied sadly. "I'm so sorry, John."

In fact, I felt it should have been me apologising. After all, the whole white face/black lips look had been suggested by me, after Tony Meehan had come up with the idea. Maybe if we'd done what Stuart first envisaged, the invitation card and white stick concept, we wouldn't have been sitting there feeling like we'd just been severely scolded by the headmaster.

"I need a drink!" Stuart said, "let's have lunch!"

Feeling just a little tiddly from two vodka and limes and sharing a bottle of expensive red wine over lunch, I got off the tube at Harlesden, going over in my mind everything that had happened earlier at CBS, still not really believing it. As I reached the flat, I was looking forward to ordering a takeaway from one of the Indian restaurants in the High Street and telling Ray all about it.

But, when I walked into the flat, I could tell it was empty. On the table was a half-drunk cup of tea, which I'd made for Ray just before I'd left, a plate of uneaten toast, but no sign of Ray. The Beatles' *Blue '67-'70* sleeve was lying on the floor and the record was on the deck, the player still switched on. It looked like Ray had left in a hurry. I looked for a note, but there was nothing.

'Oh well,' I thought, 'I'll have a bath. He'll be back soon.'

The following morning, however, after a feverish night once again full of strange dreams, it was back to square one, he hadn't shown. I looked at the bedside clock. It was ten o'clock. I quickly got dressed, made a cup of jasmine tea, sat and cursed the bastard, and then went across the road to ring Stuart. I decided not to mention Ray's no-show. I hadn't told him about the first one yet, nor the still-puzzling aftermath.

Stuart's bright and breezy voice cheered me a little. He told me he'd heard from Roslav Szaybo, CBS's chief sleeve designer, that morning.

"We had a long chat. He sounds very positive, John. He's arranged a new photo session for us. I liked his ideas."

"Did you mention Steve's bizarre outburst yesterday?"

"Yes, I did. I expressed my anger at how Steve had treated us, well, how he'd treated you to be more exact. It was inexcusably rude."

"Did Roslav say what he thought of the Les Ambassadeurs photos?"

"All he said was he felt they didn't promote the image CBS wanted for you. He thought they were a little too camp, too outrageous."

I sighed loudly.

"I know, John," Stuart said in reply, "but let's see first what Roslav's photo session produces. If we don't like the new pictures, we'll say so. He's booking the session for early September. He must have liked something about the photos, he wants to use Mike Nicholson again."

My next call was to my mum and dad. They'd just moved out of their cottage in Ramsbottom and into the corner sweet shop in Heywood. I was keen to find out how the move had gone. But, unusually, Dad answered the phone:

"Hello, son," he said. "I'm glad you've called."

"Hi Dad, how did the move go?"

"Er, that's why I'm glad you've called…not very well, I'm afraid. It's your mum. I think you should come and see her. Soon."

Chapter Twenty-One

'Til Then

Looking through the window of the bus from Manchester Piccadilly to Heywood, smiling at the August rain which always fell here, I thought about all the times Mum and I had travelled on this route when I was a kid. She'd often take me to Manchester for the day to shop, and we'd always have lunch in the Kardomah café, the most exotic place I'd seen in my young life.

I used to love following Mum into the packed room, full of chatter and the delicious smell of fresh coffee, as she was shown to our table by the smiling, smartly-dressed manager. I'd admire the starched white tablecloth and beautifully sculpted cotton napkins, and the waitresses who always looked gleamingly clean in their brown and white outfits as they served us creamed mushrooms on toast and a pot of tea. At each corner of the large room stood an enormous wooden elephant, and I'd imagine they were guarding over us all as we tucked into our meals. It was the first time I recognised style, and always felt at home there.

Getting off the bus in Heywood all those years later, it certainly didn't feel like home anymore. It was more like looking at an updated movie of my past. I walked by the beautifully-kept Victorian gardens where I used to sit with Mum on the one of green metal benches and admire the white stone War Memorial, a bowing angel, surrounded by freshly-planted geraniums. I'd run my fingers through its engraved lettering of the names of local men who'd died in both wars and wait for Mum to tell me about her uncles who'd died in the 1914-1918 conflict, before she'd even been born. Multi-coloured geraniums still bloomed there, and while 1950s summer dresses had been replaced by T-shirts and jeans, it still looked the same.

I looked down the busy High Street, and thought of the time Mum and I would wander into the bread shop, where she'd buy me a mini-Hovis loaf so I could make myself tiny sandwiches for supper. The florist's where we used to buy carnations twice a week was surprisingly still there, and I recalled its heady bouquets from multi-coloured flower arrangements, as I wandered through the magic-garden foliage which seemed tree-high to me.

Sadly, the celery-scented greengrocer's was now a Spa shop. I used to love holding our carrier-bag open so the shopkeeper could empty a pound of potatoes into it with a great thumping sound. He'd always give me an apple, telling me it would stop my teeth from falling out,

"Like mine," he'd laugh, showing me his mouthful of gums.

It used to scare me a little and make me giggle at the same time.

I walked across the road, through the still well-kept grounds of the Anglican church where my paternal Gran used to take me to "show you a different kind of religion" from the Roman Catholic tradition Mum and her aunts practised. And there was the sweet shop, looking just as it had when I used to run in to buy an ice lolly on our way to Queen's Park. Mum, my sister and I would walk down the hill to meet up with aunts and uncles and sit on the slightly prickly grass with our picnic of egg and cress sandwiches. While the brass band played their hearts out on the nearby bandstand, Aunty Peg would tell my mum what a bonnie lad I was and give me wink. I knew a sixpence for an ice cream at the Mock Tudor tea rooms was in the offing after our snack.

"Don't tell your Aunty Chris," Peg would whisper, kissing my cheek and pushing the little silver coin into my hand, "she'll get jealous!"

It seemed odd now, standing outside the sweet shop, knowing that Mum was lying in the room just above it. Neither of us would have dreamed of that outcome all those years ago.

"Hello, son," Dad said coming out to meet me. He hugged me clumsily, an odd mixture of shaking my hand and pulling me towards him, and I wondered whether he'd planned it or if it had been an impromptu show of affection. He seemed very small and much thinner than when I'd last seen him, just a couple of months earlier. "I'm glad you're here. Come through."

The shop looked just as I remembered it, there were the glass display cases with penny trays and other sugary delights, and a line of various jars of sweets on shelves behind the counter. I used to love watching the lady open each jar and use the metal scoop to pour a few of each into a white paper bag which she'd put on the scales, adding or removing one or two sweets to get it to the right weight for 'threepence worth'. There was also still that distinctive smell of boiled sweets which must have permeated the walls over the years.

Dad led me through to the sitting-room at the back of the shop, and told me to sit down on a settee I didn't recognise. He went into the dimly-lit galley kitchen to make me a cup of tea, asking about what kind of journey I'd had and how everything was going in London. I looked around and thought 'What a bland unloved room.' It felt more like a waiting room, which was what it was, of course. Bringing the tea through, he sat next to me and slowly gave me the heads-up:

"Your mum fell ill on the day of the move. She couldn't get out of bed. I had to carry her out of the house and leave the removal men to it. I drove us to the shop and carried her in, thank goodness this settee was here."

I imagined him laying Mum down on it.

"Once the removal guys arrived they were great, they moved everything in very quickly, until finally I could take her upstairs to the flat and put her to bed. She's been there ever since. She's very weak."

"What did the doctor say?"

Dad made a resigned expression:

"Well, you know…"

I knew this day was coming since mum's cancer diagnosis almost two years earlier, even though she'd seemed to rally amazingly after her operation. Indeed, over the next twelve months, she'd taken on a new lease of life. She'd looked absolutely great when my parents had visited me in April to celebrate my 21st birthday, and they'd even managed a two-week trip to Newquay in June.

Her prognosis by the doctor in the Autumn of 1972, after Dad had found her in a coma when he'd taken in her morning cup of tea, had been eighteen months at most, so the fact she'd lasted this long was itself a testament to her strength of will and inherent refusal to give in.

However, when I'd visited them in June, just a few days after their holiday, Mum had told me that she now covered herself up with a towel before getting into a bath:

"I can't look. I have a wound, around my colostomy bag, which isn't healing. It looks like a squeezed orange. I haven't told your dad. I make sure I've got my nightie on whenever he's in the bedroom."

Mum used to confide in me about things she would never dream of discussing with Dad. She also often had me as her sounding-board, before she told him something which was worrying her. On one of my hospital visits, she'd just been told she had to have a hysterectomy and a colostomy bag fitted:

"What am I going to tell your dad?" she asked me, tears welling up in her eyes. "It will change everything…you know. What's he going to think?"

I'd held her hand and said,

"Dad will love you whatever, Mum. He adores you. He'll understand."

She'd smiled, squeezed my hand and told me I always lifted her spirits,

"You make everything seem alright again," she'd said.

Dad's voice interrupted my thoughts:

"Do you want to go up and see her?" he was saying. "She was so pleased when I told her you were coming. But – be prepared, son."

I nodded.

"Our bedroom's on the left at the top of the stairs. You can put your bag in the other bedroom on the right. It's not much but -"

I put my hand on his shoulder and went up the steep flight of stairs, gently dropping my bag outside the door. When I walked into their bedroom, Mum was asleep. I was struck by what a featureless room it was. It seemed so sad that she should die surrounded by these drab cream walls, no pictures around her, no reflection of the personality of the woman now occupying it. If she'd been up to it, she would have given it her own special touches of TLC in no time. As it was, her last resting place had all the welcoming atmosphere of a run-down hospital room. As I sat on the edge of the bed, her eyes opened:

"Hello, son," she said weakly. "How are you?"

I held her hand:

"Fine, Mum. You feeling a bit tired?"

She tried to shift herself to sit up but even that seemed beyond her. I slowly helped her up and packed the pillows behind her so she could get comfortable. Mum was always thin but I was shocked at how skin-and-bone she felt:

"I'm just a bit below par," she said as brightly as she could. "But I'll be fine soon, then I can get down to the shop and get stuck in." She smiled at me. "I'm really looking forward to that."

"Don't worry, Mum, there's no rush. Dad's got leave from work and he's coping okay, and Sue's helping when she can."

"Oh, I'll be down there soon. Just got to shake off this –" she pointed at herself, waving her hand up and down her body dismissively, "- this."

For the next half an hour, she listened happily as I chatted to her about what was happening with my career, about the recording sessions, and I saw her visibly seem a little stronger, especially when she asked me,

"Has Dad told you about our battle with the council?"

"No, what's that about?"

It was great to see her sit up a bit more and prepare herself for some gossip:

"Oh! Well! Listen to this!"

She told me with great relish about how Dad had had to fight with the council to get an extra dustbin in their backyard:

"He went down there and told them this is a shop, not a house, and we have a lot of boxes and stuff we have to throw out. The bloke at the council sounds like a right git."

'Git' was the strongest 'swear word' Mum ever uttered, but she always said it with such venom it sounded for all the world like 'fucking bastard'.

"Did you get your extra dustbin?" I asked, allowing myself a smile.

"Of course," she said proudly, giving me a wink. "You don't mess with The Jones's!"

Finally, she began to fade. I settled her pillows back down and she snuggled into the bedclothes, smiling dreamily at me:

"Thank you, my honey."

"Sleep well, Mum," I replied, but she was already asleep.

I could only stay for a couple of days, and I spent them mainly sitting with Mum, while Dad and Sue dealt with customers downstairs. Sometimes she'd chat away, about Sue's three young daughters, about her next planned visit to see me in London, and, surprisingly, about her desire to go to America with Dad and see his musician friend, Johnny, who'd moved there with his young wife in the '50s.

"Your dad was always close to him," she told me. "They were like brothers. He still misses him."

Other times she just slept while I read, and she'd occasionally wake up, smile at me, tell me she loved me, then go straight back to sleep.

On the afternoon I was due to leave, just as I was preparing to go upstairs and say goodbye to her, Mum appeared at the bottom of the stairs, looking dishevelled and confused. She stared round the room crossly and demanded that she be given the accounts to look at:

"I've had enough of lying up there worrying," she said. "I need to check everything's okay." She ran her hand over her hair as though preparing for an important job. "Where are they?"

Dad, who seemed thrilled simply to see her out of bed, went to the sideboard and took out a red exercise book and a tin box rattling with cash. I helped Mum to the table and sat her down. She moaned a little as I put a cushion behind her, but she was determined she would do what she'd come down for. Pulling her dressing gown round her and taking the box from Dad, she opened it and emptied the money onto the table. Then she opened the exercise book and began looking down the columns of takings Dad had entered over the previous few days in his usual neat hand.

"Now let's see, shall we?" she muttered to herself, purposefully adjusting her glasses.

I turned to Dad:

"I've really got to go."

"Go where?" Mum asked, not looking up.

"Back to London, Mum. I told you this morning. I have to go today. I've got things I have to be back f -"

"I'm sure you do," she said, interrupting me. "'Bye then."

She continued running her finger down the takings columns. Dad nodded at me and made a 'Come on then, let's make a move' gesture.

"Okay Mum," I said, going to kiss her goodbye, but as I bent down to her, she stared up at me angrily and pushed me away:

"Are you not combing your hair?"

I laughed,

"I combed it this morning, Mum."

"Then you need to comb it again," she demanded.

"I'm fine, Mum, I don't have time now. I have to go and get my bus, or I'll miss my train."

She sat as upright as she could and glared at me:

"And you're going to travel on the bus looking like *that*?!"

"Oh, leave him alone, Bren," Dad said, "he looks fine."

"Well!" Mum said looking from her husband to me and back again to Dad. "Then he can't leave by the front door." She looked me up and down with disgust. "I'm not having the neighbours seeing what a tramp my son is." She pointed towards the back door. "Go out through the backyard where the dustbins are. That's all you're fit for!"

Dad looked over at me and shook his head:

"Come on, son, or you'll miss your bus."

"Oh, you've always been soft, Bert," Mum said angrily. "I know when my son looks a mess!" She looked at me disdainfully, tutted and sighed. "Well, if you want to walk about looking like a tramp, go on! See if I care!"

With that she looked back down at her accounts columns and began very carefully putting the coins in little piles.

"Okay," I said, moving towards the door, "I'll be off then."

She waved her hand dismissively at me, still not looking up, her task too important to be interrupted. Dad walked me out.

"Don't take it bad, son," he said, opening the shop door for me. "She doesn't mean it. It's the morphine and, well, everything. You know she loves you."

"I know, Dad. I'll ring you tomorrow morning."

It was the last time I saw or spoke to Mum. For the next three weeks, the last in her short life, she was always in bed asleep when I rang.

At eight o'clock that evening, I walked back into my flat, feeling exhausted after a long, hot train journey with several delays. It had been such a relief when I'd reached Euston. I suddenly felt at home. Heywood was, in fact, full of nothing more than memories, along with a present reality I found painful, to say the least. I was still thinking about the bizarre conversation with Mum a few hours earlier when I realised that there was still no sign of Ray.

'Good,' I thought, kicking off my shoes.

I'd got to the point where I'd had enough. Of him. Of his lies (I was now sure that all his excuses and stories were just that), and I'd finally decided I was better off without him. I made myself a drink and put on my recently-bought copy of Bryan Ferry's *Another Time, Another Place*. As I sat back and closed my eyes to the soothing strains of Ferry's sophisticated warble, I reflected on how I'd moved out of my lovely St John's Wood flat at Ray's request so we could "be together", with his promise that he would "never disappear like that again." I got increasingly angry as I realised what an idiot I'd been, and wished I'd involved Stuart and Patsy in my decision-making. In fact, I felt quite pathetic and, even more pathetically, began to weep. The mixture of frustration about Ray and my utter devastation at Mum's shockingly deteriorated condition, became too much. I cried buckets, all over the record sleeve. As my tears flowed onto Bryan's dapper white tuxedo, he crooned consolingly:

> Now laughing friends deride tears I cannot hide
> So I smile and say
> When a lovely flame dies
> Smoke gets in your eyes

At the end of August, Stuart, Patsy and I were due to travel down to Bournemouth for the annual CBS sales conference. A few days before we left, Biddu and his wife, Sue, asked me to join Stuart and Patsy for dinner at their apartment in West London. It was to celebrate Bid's first hit record. Carl Douglas's 'Kung Fu Fighting', which Biddu had produced, had just entered the UK Top Thirty and looked set to hit the Top Ten very soon (it did, the following week). I was most fascinated when Bid told us that 'Kung Fu Fighting' had been planned as the 'B' side of the single, which Carl had written as a quick throwaway novelty thing. It wasn't until the track was recorded that everyone, including Pye Records, realised it was the stronger side. Although Biddu had written the original 'A' side, 'Gamblin' Man', he seemed very happy that Carl's composition had hit paydirt. Bid had the publishing on both songs and with them the potential of his first real earnings from one of his productions. As we sat in their cosy basement apartment, I surmised that, before very long, Sue and her husband would be entertaining friends in a much more spacious pad.

After a lovely evening, Stuart dropped me back at my flat at about eleven o'clock. As I waved goodnight to him and Patsy, I noticed the light in my sitting-room was on and the curtains were drawn. My heart sank. When I opened the door, Ray was draped on the sofa, eyes swimming, bumptious expression on his face, obviously waiting to see my reaction to yet another of his unexpected returns from God knows where.

"Hello," I said as casually as I could, my heart thumping in my chest.

"Alright?" he asked, his mouth curling into a combative grin.

"Fine, thanks." I walked through to the bedroom and over my shoulder said, "How long do you intend to be back this time?"

I heard him stir. The smell of booze on his breath wafted behind me.

"What's that supposed to mean?" he yelled.

I turned round and yelled back:

"What I mean, Ray, is what the hell are you playing at?"

He swayed unsteadily towards me:

"I've come back!" he shouted. "Ain't that enough?"

With that, my lips unleashed a torrent of anger and frustration:

"No it fucking isn't! How *dare* you swan in and out of my life like this? Who the hell do you think you are? I can tell you now, this is

367

going to stop! You are not going to ruin my life. You are *not*!!"

That was it. Ray's eyes seared into me, he lunged forward and thumped my arm. I was surprised at how much it hurt.

"Ruin your life! Ruin your fucking life!" he shouted, grabbing hold of me by my collar.

With a strength which surprised me, he threw me out of the room into the corridor, then proceeded to kick me along it, as I tried desperately to stay on my feet. All the while he yelled at me, most of it I can't recall now, but it was the usual 'Woe is me, I'm the injured party, you're supposed to understand' baloney which he spat out as I tumbled into the kitchen and ran for the back door. I managed to get out into the courtyard but he was right behind me, and kicked me in the small of my back which sent me reeling to the concrete floor. My glasses flew off my nose and clattered somewhere to my left. As Ray pummelled and punched me I instinctively adopted the foetal position.

"I've loved you more than anybody else in my life," he sobbed down at me. "But I knew you despised me! Just like everybody else! You're the same stuck-up pile of swanky shit I've had looking down on me, all my life!"

He grabbed my thin cotton jacket and dragged me round the courtyard, ripping my sleeve and collar, and scraping my arm on the rough ground. All I remember thinking was 'Where are my glasses?'. Without them, I was virtually blind. I could see this blurred seething, swaying mass of man above me, shouting, thumping and crying. Lying there, curled into a ball, I hoped it would end soon.

Finally, a sash window slid open in the flat above us, and a man leaned out and shouted,

"Keep the fucking noise down! Fucking yobs!" and slammed the window down again.

Thankfully, it stopped Ray in his tracks. I felt his boozy breath on my face as he moaned pathetically – and rather ironically – like a wounded animal.

"I fucking did love you," he half whispered.

He panted above me for a few seconds, and I was waiting for more punches, but instead, I heard him walk away. I glanced up and saw him going back into the house. He shut the door and locked it. I lay on the concrete for a few seconds more, to make sure he wasn't coming back, then crawled to where I thought I could see my gold-rimmed spectacles glinting. I grabbed hold of them and put them back on. They were a bit bent but the lenses, thank goodness, weren't broken. I got to my feet, realised I was bleeding from my ear, and my arm was cut. The torn jacket sleeve hung limply like a broken limb, but I was surprisingly okay. I walked quickly to the wooden back gate and tried it. It was locked, as I knew it would be, and the key was inside the house. I stared up at its seven-foot height and, as unbelievable as I still find it, I climbed up it like a toddler in a play-park, balancing myself on the handle and using it as a springboard to the top. I sat there for a few seconds, a little shocked at my own agility, and then jumped down into the alleyway. From there I sprinted past dustbins and abandoned bicycles into the High Street and ran down to the tube station. Thank goodness I still had my wallet in my back pocket. I bought a ticket to Willesden Green and boarded the last train which was arriving as I reached the platform.

Sitting in the thankfully empty carriage, still in shock at what had just happened, I glanced up and saw my reflection in the opposite window. I looked an absolute state. I went closer to the window, and with my nose almost touching it, checked out where I was cut – face, forehead and left ear as far as I could see – and quickly washed them in my own spittle. Both my hands were badly grazed and my left arm was bleeding slightly. I wiped them as best I could with a tissue and then settled back in my seat, just relieved to still be in one piece. I rolled up the torn sleeve and did the same with the other one. Even in adversity, vanity prevailed.

Willesden Green was only a few stops along and once there I found a phone box just outside the station and called Stuart. As soon as he heard my voice he said,

"SOS, John?"

Trying to hold back tears, I replied,

"Yes, Stuart."

"Come on, come home. We'll be waiting for you."

They left me in bed that morning, and I didn't wake up until two in the afternoon. As I studied myself in the wardrobe mirror, my cuts didn't look too bad now. Patsy had washed and disinfected them for me as I'd sat in their kitchen, drinking the honeyed tea Stuart had made for me, and told them the whole sorry tale of the last few weeks.

For about half an hour I just lay there, going over what had happened. At that moment, it all seemed rather unreal. I felt slightly sick, but more with the gut-wrenching knowledge of what a bloody fool I'd been. I thanked God for Stuart and Patsy as I got up and had a long bath. They had been the first people I'd thought of when I needed help. I realised, extremely belatedly, what great friends they were.

All the disagreements and feelings of conflict between us over the previous few weeks, starting with their dislike of Tony Meehan's production of my album, my dislike of Stuart's quaint concept for my album cover, and more recently their horror at my moving in with Ray, all that evaporated into the pine-scented steam of their bathroom. For me, they were now Number One. Always would be. Staunch friends. And, as I dried myself off, I resolved that I would repay their loyalty and friendship with my own.

That evening, Stuart rang my landlady, Mrs Rawindi, and explained that I had vacated the flat and that he would go over there to collect the month's deposit of sixty pounds which I had paid. Unfortunately, she replied that it was Mr Robinson who had paid her the money, and to whom she had given the receipt (which I had never seen). Stuart tried to gently tell her that Mr Robinson was a scoundrel, had never contributed a penny in rent, and would more than likely be leaving her flat himself quite soon, once any money he had was spent. She was adamant, however, and refused to pay anything to anybody until she had spoken to Mr Robinson.

The following morning, as Stuart was getting ready to go to the office and I was helping Patsy prepare brunch, the phone rang.

"Hello, Mrs Rawindi," I heard him saying from the hall.

A few minutes later, he came into the kitchen and, with a wry smile, told us that Mrs Rawindi had gone round to the flat that morning to speak to Ray, and found not only him gone, but also some of the flat's contents – cutlery, crockery, even some bedding.

"I hope you don't mind, John, but I told her she should keep hold of the sixty pounds which should cover her losses. We don't need the hassle. She said we could come and get your belongings anytime, as long as she was there to oversee it. Of course, I agreed, the poor lady's distraught."

As Stuart was leaving the house, the phone rang again. Patsy answered it, but called Stuart back in. He took the phone from her:

"Yes? Mr Reid here..Oh, hello!..That's right, I am the guarantor for Mr Howard...". Long pause. "Oh! I see. Well, thank you very much for letting us know..Yes, I'll tell John, and he will be in later today to collect it. Goodbye, and thanks again."

Stuart was no longer smiling as he told us that it was the bank manager on the phone. As it had been Stuart who had set up an account for me at his branch a few months earlier, it was his number they had on file:

"Apparently, someone tried to cash one of your cheques yesterday afternoon, John. Luckily, the teller remembered you and realised it wasn't you at the counter. When she asked the chap for identification, he got verbally aggressive, so she called security. Ray - I assume it must have been Ray – then did a runner out the door and scarpered. They've cancelled your chequebook, and would like you to go and collect a new one."

"We'll go along later to do that, John," Patsy said, putting her arm on my shoulder.

"I left my chequebook in my bedside drawer!" I said, suddenly feeling sick.

"We'll go straight to the flat after we've been to the bank and collect your stuff, John," Patsy said.

"Can we?" I asked, feeling completely winded.

"John," Stuart said, sitting down next to me at the breakfast table, "this has been a lesson for you, I'm sure, but it's over now. He's gone for good. You won't see him again. You're no longer of any use to him. Now, get on with your life and enjoy the fantastic career which I know is ahead of you. In a couple of days' time we will be at the CBS conference, where you will be treated as you should be, like a star, and all this will feel like a bad dream. Let it go. Let him well and truly go from your mind, your heart, your life."

In fact, only my mind still held Ray, and I was never more keen to blank him out of there.

How different everything felt just a few days later, as I sat in the large dining room at The Imperial Hotel, listening to Leonard Cohen's astonishingly beautiful set come to an end with one of my favourite songs of his, 'Sisters of Mercy'. There'd been an extra frisson of thrill from the mainly male audience of CBS sales reps, departmental bosses and head honchos from both the UK and America, when Cohen had premièred a new song from his latest album *New Skin For The Old Ceremony*:

> *I remember you well in the Chelsea Hotel*
> *You were talking so brave and so sweet*
> *Giving me head on an unmade bed*

While the limousines wait in the street

I imagined several knowing glances going round the dinner tables from married men away from home, imagining their own unmade beds in their rooms down the hall.

There was another interesting episode during Cohen's thirty-minute set, which was both encouraging and disturbing at the same time. By the fourth number, the audience was becoming restive. Songs like 'The Partisan', 'Seems So Long Ago', 'Nancy', and 'Last Year's Man', not amongst what you could call his 'greatest hits', were reaching increasingly less highs with people who were more used to hollering at the latest smash by The Three Degrees or whooping along to 'All The Young Dudes'. The quiet sound of mumbling turned quickly into louder conversation, even from some tables into raucous laughter. Finally, as the company's legendary star ploughed on alone in the spotlight, the noise in the room got so loud that it became difficult to actually hear Cohen, who was seemingly undaunted by this appalling lack of respect. Unlike Dick Asher, CBS's Managing Director. He was sitting at the end of my table and, as the noise from his gathered executives rose to a din, Dick slowly rose from his chair, stood with his hands on his hips, Mussolini style, and did a one-hundred-and-eighty degree stare round the room. One by one, his employees became horribly aware of their prize-fighter-shaped boss glaring at them. Slowly but surely, the hubbub of fun-packed chat turned back into a mumble, until silence, except for the beautiful music Cohen was still making on stage, reigned once more. You could almost hear the executives' simultaneous thoughts in the darkness - "Oh shit, I'm in big trouble now" – as Dick sat back down with a final stare round the room. At the end of the number which Cohen had been singing, Asher stood and clapped loudly, again looking round at his now terrified minions, who all responded with ridiculously enthusiastic applause. There were even some cheers from those who were particularly afraid of losing their house.

I looked around the long top table where I was seated, to see how others were reacting to this show of power, and yes, Dick's patent support of and respect for his label's artists. I'd been placed next to David Essex, Michael Levy, Peter Shelley, Alvin Stardust and Ian Hunter. They were all smiling amiably, stars in their own firmament, at peace with their world of success.

Cohen ended his set, bowing to the room's applause as Dick once again stood and ensured it would last for some minutes. Cohen waved his trilby hat at us all and was gone. Just five years earlier, I had lain on my bed in Lancashire listening to his sultry dark voice floating from my record player. He was a hero to my generation. We adored his songs of exotic pain, love, lust and loss, in settings we could only imagine, glamorously bohemian, full of cigarette smoke and the sounds of a busy sidewalk café below. He told us of his life and we lived it with him. He was perfect for a teenager's dreams, creating worlds beyond what he or she would probably ever witness or experience. Cohen was the poet of our generation, but gilt-edged by the fact that he was also a folk music star who sold thousands of albums.

And here I was, watching this handsome brilliant man, alone on his tiny stage just a few feet away, having enthralled me with his quiet grace and a single guitar. I was still soaking in the magic of what I'd seen when Dick, with a wave of his huge arms, called for quiet:

"I now want to introduce you folks to some truly astonishing talent we have with us tonight, sitting at this very table." He looked paternally down at us all. "Firstly, let me introduce you to the magnificently talented and hugely successful David Essex."

David, dressed in a beautifully-tailored white suit, with a red rose in his lapel, and that goofy adorable smile which had melted millions of fans for the past twelve months, stood and waved to the applause from the people whose mortgages he had helped pay.

"David's new single," Dick went on, "will, I guarantee it, be No.1, very soon, and his latest movie, *Stardust*, which we will show you tomorrow, is, well, wow! It's just fantastic!"

More applause which David acknowledged with a wave and another gorgeous smile.

I was still clapping heartily when, through the dying applause, I heard my name:

"...John Howard, one of the most exciting singer-songwriters I have heard in a long time. John's new album is simply fantastic! We'll be playing you one of the tracks – a smash hit, folks – tomorrow. You'll be knocked out! Ladies and Gents, say hello to John Howard!"

I stood rather awkwardly as one does when sitting at a dining table ('how does David make it look so graceful?' I thought) and, the edge of the table digging into my knees, waved into the darkness. David caught my eye and grinned at me, a look on his face of 'I don't know this guy, must investigate'.

I lay in bed that night, feeling a myriad of emotions. I was thrilled at Dick's enthusiastic introduction, but still confused about the negative reaction to our beautiful photographs and a nagging feeling that the company was underwhelmed by my album, regardless of what Dick had said that evening. I dreamt that night that I was performing on stage to a huge audience. As I was singing, the words to my song, which sat in front of me on the piano, started to float away. I tried to catch them, knocked the mike stand over and found myself lying on the floor with a bunch of people standing over me, kicking me and shouting abuse.

The next morning, I showered and went down for breakfast where Stuart and Patsy were already halfway through theirs. A few people looked up as I went past them, one or two muttering, "That's John Howard." I grew a few more inches and, greeting the Reids, sat down.

"We've got the play-through of CBS's latest releases at eleven o'clock, John," Stuart said. "Your album is one of the 'star features', so I'm told."

Just then, a voice above me said,

"Do you mind if I join you?"

"Of course not, Paul," Patsy said. "Would you like some coffee?"

Paul Phillips, who I'd first met all those months ago at Small's Restaurant in Knightsbridge, where I'd done my intimate little show for him and his boss Dan Loggins, sat down opposite me:

"No thanks, Patsy. I'm fine. Good morning, John."

In the morning light, which streamed through several floor-length windows all round us, I noticed how fair-skinned Paul was. He was wearing glasses which had sellotape holding on one of the arms and must have seen me notice it:

"Forgive this," he said, laughing and playing with the tape, "I dropped them in the shower this morning. I don't always look like this!"

We all laughed, relaxing into the bonhomie of the moment, and I sipped my coffee as Paul said,

"I just want to tell you, John, how much I love your music. And I mean I really love it."

"Thank you, Paul," I said.

"Oh, how lovely!" Patsy added.

"He's fantastic, isn't he, Paul?" Stuart joined in.

"Really. And I also like your album, John." I heard the 'but' before he'd said it. "But, I would like to have a go at redoing a couple of the tracks."

He checked my reaction. I just nodded. He sat forward and went on,

"Basically, I'd like to record 'Family Man' and 'Kid In A Big World' again."

Without hesitation Patsy looked at me and said,

"Oh, that would be wonderful, wouldn't it, John?"

I wasn't so sure:

"What is it you don't like about Tony's versions?" I asked.

Paul held up his hands:

"What Tony has done isn't terrible, or even bad. But, for me, those songs should be done so that they're, well, closer to your original demos - which are what I fell in love with. Tony has effectively – for me anyway - turned them into different songs. They're such great songs already, I don't see why he's done that."

Paul smiled affectionately at me across the table. I could see how much my music meant to him, it was written all over his face:

"Okay, let's give it a go," I said.

"Sure?" Paul asked.

"Yeah."

"Great!" He started playing with the croquet set on the table. There was more. "I'd also -" he smiled at me nervously, "I'd also like to remix 'Goodbye Suzie'."

He again waited to see my reaction. I just raised my eyebrows slightly:

"Tony's production is good," Paul went on, "but I'd like to give it a slightly more commercial sound. It's a potential hit record, John, it just needs a tweak to get it there."

He sat even closer in:

"What I *would* like to continue is Tony's great idea of recording you at a studio associated with The Beatles. So we'll be doing the tracks at Apple Studios."

Now I *was* enthusiastic. He immediately saw that:

"And I'm going to book Phil McDonald to engineer the tracks."

Phil's name was known to me from the sleeve credits on John Lennon's *Imagine* album and he'd also had a 'Thank you' credit on *Abbey Road*. I mentioned that to Paul:

"He also did some of the engineering on *The White Album*," Paul said. "And Lennon's 'Instant Karma'. It all keeps that Beatles-related theme going on your album."

He was smiling almost coquettishly at me. I felt as though I was being wooed by a charming suitor. Of course, he could tell I was hooked.

"That is so exciting!" Patsy declared.

"Good! Excellent!" Paul said and stood up. "I'll let you know the dates in a couple of days. Really looking forward to finally working with you, John. I've been wanting to record you since the first time I heard your songs."

Stuart stood and shook Paul's hand.

"Lovely, Paul. Speak to you soon."

Paul smiled down at me and, looking like a man who had been told he could have my hand in marriage, wandered out of the dining room.

Although I had an inner glow of excitement, a tricky thought came into my mind:

"Shouldn't we tell Tony?" I asked Stuart, who looked puzzled:

"Why? He's done his job, he's been paid. This is – as I keep telling you, John – your album, not his."

It was almost a sonic reversal of what Tony had said to me months earlier, when he'd complained about Stuart's too-close involvement in the sessions at Abbey Road.

But, the excitement I felt – and admittedly, the attention Paul was giving me - persuaded me that Stuart was right. It was simply an opportunity I couldn't turn down.

At eleven, Paul joined us as we walked into a large function room with several other CBS people already seated, who greeted me with a wave as I arrived. We were led to our front row seats, and I noticed directly across the aisle David Essex and his team of people were chatting easily to each other. David turned round as we settled ourselves and smiled at me. Ian Hunter, sitting directly behind him, seemed coolly uninterested in anything going on in front of his large sunglasses.

Once everybody was seated, Dick Asher stood out front and welcomed us all, telling us we were in for "a real treat".

The lights dimmed and Dick gave someone behind us a signal. From the back of the hall, Radio One DJ Paul Burnett's instantly recognisable voice cheerfully rang round the room, as photos of the label's best-known artists faded in and out on the huge screen before us:

"David Essex, Mott The Hoople, The Three Degrees, Harold Melvin & The Bluenotes, Andy Williams, Charlie Rich, Barbra Streisand, The Isley Brothers, Bob Dylan, Paul Simon," Burnett intoned confidently. "Just some of the great artists on CBS Records. We are very proud to be unveiling to you today some of our fantastic new releases, which we believe will become globally some of the most important, and most successful records of our time."

Mott The Hoople's 'All The Way From Memphis' suddenly blasted around us.

"Remember this great hit from 1973? And this?"

'Roll Away The Stone', one of my favourite Mott records still sounded amazing.

"And this!"

'The Golden Age of Rock 'n' Roll' had Patsy bobbing her head around.

"This Autumn, Mott release their first ever live album…"

Burnett gave us release details of the album as the sleeve floated across the screen and a surprisingly polished version of 'All The Young Dudes', with the Bowie chorus vocals impressively replaced by female singers, blasted out. I looked across the aisle. Ian Hunter still sat unmoved by it all, his '66 Dylan-esque pose perfectly achieved.

The Three Degrees' 'Dirty Old Man' then turned up the heat as Burnett sounded excited:

"Three smash hits in 1974…!"

'Year Of Decision', followed by 'TSOP' sounded as sassy as ever:

"The girls' fabulous eponymous album has already sold millions in The States, and we believe it will be an equally big-selling release in the UK, including as it does this massive No.1 hit!".

'When Will I See You Again' melted all our hearts once more, I even heard a few sibilant sing-alongs on the line *"When will we share precious moments?"*.

Then without warning or introduction, some of my Hyde Park photos floated by us. Burnett allowed each startling image to appear in silence before he announced:

"John Howard! He's the man with a great look and a fantastic sound!"

'Goodbye Suzie' played as Paul nudged me from my left while Stuart did the same to my right. More images faded in. Enlarged for the screen before us, the Les Ambassadeurs shots looked truly gorgeous.

"This Autumn will see the release of John's first single, followed by his remarkable debut album in the Spring."

As the track faded out, I was aware of the sound of banging behind me. I turned round to see a burly, American-looking man with an enormous unlit cigar in his mouth thumping the arm of his chair and, with his other hand, giving me a meaty thumbs-up. Gradually, the room filled with applause and cheers. I almost stood and bowed but decided to stay put. As the noise faded, I heard Dick murmuring, "Great song," and my brief moment was over.

What should have been a magical moment was rather overshadowed by my puzzlement at CBS executives loudly applauding Tony's rejected mix of 'Goodbye Suzie', and the cheer that rang round the room at the photos which had been so disdainfully dismissed by my press officer.

I heard Patsy saying to Stuart,

"I thought they didn't like these pictures?"

Stuart just shrugged.

A huge photo of David Essex appeared on the screen. His first hit, the brilliant 'Rock On' played as Burnett said,

"David Essex, CBS's brightest and most successful British pop star today. Millions of records sold, a box office smash with the movie *That'll Be The Day*, and now, not only a new album due this Autumn, but also David's fantastic follow-up film, *Stardust*."

The film's title track burst out of the speakers, its stunningly odd stop-start arrangement and punchy production, which had been one of the striking features of David's first couple of singles, engaging us all immediately.

"And to trailer the album and film is this great track, David's new single, which I guarantee will be one of the biggest-selling records this Autumn."

As the strains of 'Gonna Make You A Star' blasted out, I looked across at David who was beaming at a room full of loud applause.

"Great record," Paul murmured into my ear, and I nodded back. It sure was.

What turned out to be CBS's biggest-selling British single that year faded out, Burnett thanked us all for being there, more light applause for a job well done, the lights went up, and Dick bounced back into view:

"OK, people, there's a buffet lunch just outside in the foyer area, and then we'll reconvene at two o'clock for a screening of David's new movie." He glanced down fondly at his most successful artist that year. David responded with a thumbs-up back. "I can tell you all now, *Stardust* is going to blow your minds!"

As I stood munching delicately on a small cold collation, people buzzing around me, queuing at the buffet spread or just looking for someone to chat to, a voice behind me said,

"Hello, John."

I turned round and a very pleasant-looking, rather slight chap was smiling at me. His overweight comb-over companion sweated profusely in the thick tweed suit he must have regretted putting on that morning.

"My name's Joe," the pleasant-looking man said in a velvety American accent, "I work in the classical department."

I shook his hand.

"And this is Terry. He's one of our sales reps. I thought he should have a chat with you."

I shook Terry's clammy hand and waited for Joe to explain why. He duly did, lowering his voice a little:

"Terry is thinking of coming out, and I suggested he talk to you."

I couldn't resist it:

"Coming out of where?"

Joe giggled girlishly, and grabbed his imaginary pearls:

"Oh! The closet, of course! He's married, well, separated now, and..." he prodded my arm campily, and smiled encouragingly at Terry, who continued to sweat buckets and look nervous, "...well, John, you're someone who I thought could, you know, give him a few pointers?"

"Haven't you done that already?" I asked, eliciting an oddly disturbing rapid flutter of Joe's eyelashes.

"Well, yes," he chuckled like a first date, "but, I'm not *Out*, am I?"

'Oh I think you are!' I thought, but instead, as kindly as I could, and trying not sound too Marge Proops, said, "you have to simply do what feels right for you, Terry. Take it step by step. We're all different, and want different things."

Joe was meanwhile standing on his toes and looking round the room, mouthing 'Hi' and waving celeb-like at various people:

"So," he said, preparing to dash off somewhere much more interesting, "could I leave you two to chat?"

'Oh no you don't, bitch!' I thought, but said,

"I'm sorry, Joe, but my manager's beckoning me over."

I pointed flamboyantly at Stuart, who was chatting with Dick Asher and Dan Loggins by the window. Thankfully - and I could have hugged him - he waved back at me to join him.

Shaking Terry's drenched hand, I took my leave, but not before muttering into Joe's ear,

"It's you he's after, darling, not me."

As I made my way towards Stuart, I glanced back at a crestfallen Joe, now stuck with his sweaty friend who'd obviously collared him earlier.

"John!" Dick declared, shaking his head in apparent disbelief. "'Goodbye Suzie'! A smash hit!"

Dan shook my hand – and I took great pleasure watching him flinch under my new vice-like grip.

"Great song," he concurred, grinning and nodding at us both.

I was about to discuss with them how we'd be remixing it in a few days, when a rather willowy, slightly unkempt man walked over and joined us:

"Hi John," he said, staring at me intensely and shaking my hand, "I'm Maurice. Maurice Oberstein. Deputy MD."

His sing-song Bronx voice, which went up and down in almost perfect octaves every couple of syllables, was truly fascinating. He wore a red baseball cap with 'Mott' emblazoned across it, a black T-shirt displaying 'The Hoople' in white letters, and a badge which read, "I'm A Dude." It was all teamed with an old pair of jeans and ancient–looking sneakers.

"Hi Maurice!" I smiled back.

"Call me Obie," he said confidentially, as though it were a secret moniker.

"And here's God!" Dick shouted, stretching out his arms in a prepared embrace. A large, elderly bespectacled man joined us. "Goddard Leibersohn in the flesh!" Dick muttered into Goddard's shoulder as they bear-hugged manfully.

As Leibersohn greeted Obie with a polite shake of the hand, I was struck by how out of place the company's Deputy Managing Director appeared, surrounded by these huge Armani-suited, big chested, big voiced guys. But his steely stare never wavered under their indomitable male bonhomie.

Extending an enormous fleshy hand, Goddard grabbed mine and gripped my bony shoulder with his other hand:

"John! Love your music!" he said.

"Thank you, er, God."

Dick chuckled, Dan laughed out loud, Obie just smiled.

"No, John, thank *you*," God said, "for coming to our label! It's an honour!"

"Praise indeed, John!" Stuart said. "Goddard *is* God at CBS!"

"Stuart!" God cried, as if he'd just seen him. "You look fantastic!"

It was all very American macho, and I tried not to be too gushy in its midst, but inside I was quite shaky and thrilled. You could smell the success, the wealth of these guys, they oozed the testosterone of being top of their game.

God then turned to Obie and asked him something about "Our market share". Obie moved closer in and replied something about "ship-outs", Dick was slowly nodding his head while Dan jumped in with something about "campaign spend".

Realising it was time to move on, Stuart took me by the arm, waved at the hunkered execs, and led me away from the mêlée:

"Let's leave them to it, shall we? Fancy a drink, John?"

We went over to the copiously stocked drinks table, where a handsome white-jacketed barman fixed me a very large vodka and lime with lots of greenery, and Stuart was given his usual Pernod with crushed ice.

"Enjoying yourself, John?" he asked, as we found a little corner away from the crowds.

"It's all a bit of a whirl, Stuart."

"Get used to it. These guys are convinced you are their next star."

With perfect timing, I turned round to see their current star radiating his divinely goofy grin at me.

"Hi John," he said.

I realised how small but rather beautiful David Essex was in the flesh.

"Love that song of yours, John. 'Goodbye Suzie'. What a hook!"

"Thank you! Love your new one too."

"So," David laughed easily, "glad that's settled. We love each other!" He made the peace sign. "All you need is love!"

"Looking forward to your movie," Stuart said, obviously thrilled that CBS's Number One star was chatting so amiably to me.

"Yeah," he said, suddenly shy and shrugging his shoulders. "It's ok. It's good."

As if on cue, lifting his head towards the throng, Dick shouted at everyone:

"Ladies and Gents, follow me, and we'll take our seats for your exclusive preview of David Essex's new hit movie, *Stardust*!"

Once we'd all taken our seats, a chubby, shiny-faced man in his forties appeared out front. He wore a T-shirt with the words 'CBS – The Family Of Music' on it, and seemed rather nervous, a little uneasy:

"People," he said very gently, as though not wanting to upset anyone, and clapping his hands with a reluctant gusto, "Family! Welcome!" His hands joined and cupped his chin. "Enjoy! Thank you."

He sat back down again, the lights dimmed and, just before the film began, Stuart whispered in my ear,

"That's Derek Witt, Artists Liaison Manager. Known as Woof."

David's movie was indeed excellent, though much less Mop Top-inspired than *That'll Be The Day*. Its time-line had moved on from 'Telstar'-playing fairgrounds and rock'n'roll, into a much darker, more recent period, as it followed Jim McClaine's ascent to global stardom followed by his steady spiral down into drugs, depression, isolation, and finally death. As the heartbeat-rhythm of the title track played over the credits, I wondered what David's millions of teenage fans would make of it. It was heralded by the CBS press release, which we were all given a copy of as we entered the screening room, as, "movie-wise, David's *Sgt Pepper*". I thought, however, it may be a little too soon for that. He was, for me, still at the 'I Want To Hold Your Hand' stage of his pop career. Certainly the catchy new hook-laden single seemed to reflect that.

As Stuart, Patsy and I wandered along the corridor back to our rooms, chatting about the movie, I saw Derek Witt walking the other way towards us.

"Stuart," he said, coming over and shaking his hand. "Woof!"

"Hi Derek! How are you?"

Derek looked a little distracted, keeping an eye on people wandering by, studying them briefly, then looking back at us:

"Oh, coping, you know. Busy busy. Has everything been okay?"

"Yes, great thanks. You know my wife, Patsy."

"Woof!" Derek said and shook her hand gingerly.

"Derek," Patsy said a little witheringly.

"And my artist, John Howard," Stuart continued.

"Woof *woof!*" Derek said much more enthusiastically, squeezing my hand and holding onto it. "Very good to meet you, John. Welcome to The Family Of Music!"

"Thank you, Derek."

"Please! Call me Woof! All my friends do. Oh, where are they going?"

A group of people wandered past us, and, hurrying towards them, he said over his shoulder,

"Must dash! Drop by the office anytime, John!"

As we carried on to our rooms, Patsy snarled,

"I do wish he wouldn't do all that Woof stuff!"

"He's harmless," Stuart said, "and very good at his job, darling. Artists love him."

"Does he actually expect us to Woof back?" Patsy continued unmoved.

"I think he'd be more than happy if John woofed back!" Stuart said, winking at me.

"Hm, I think John has had quite enough of odd men for the time being!" Patsy huffed on.

Just then, the smiling, burly man, who'd banged his chair during 'Goodbye Suzie' that morning, still with a huge unlit cigar hanging from his mouth, marched up to us and buried my hand in both of his. He beamed at me and took the cigar out of his mouth:

"John Howard," he declared. "Can I tell you something?"

He stepped back to give himself an eager audience of three:

"You're gonna make it, John! You're gonna make it big! And you know why?"

We waited:

"'Cause you got *class*!". He put his cigar back into his mouth, nodded his head at me and winked. "Real class! That's why!"

"Now, isn't that great, John?" Patsy said, looking much happier.

As I walked into my room and saw my reflection in the dressing-table mirror, the image of me being kicked and dragged around a courtyard in Harlesden jumped into my head. I wryly wondered if our friend would have been declaring that I had 'Real class' if he'd witnessed that just a few days earlier. The bare truth was that I currently had no home of my own, a disastrous love-life, and a career which, to date, I'd found occasionally exciting, but mostly confusing. I should have felt wonderful after the couple of days I'd just had. A year earlier I certainly would have done. Suddenly, however, at the age of twenty-one, I felt rather old.

Chapter Twenty-Two

Life Is Never The Way We Want It To Be

"Just lean out a little more, John," the photographer, Mike Nicholson called up to me from the cobbled street below.

The old window box in front of me, full of mainly dead flowers and dried-up spiders, impeded any particularly dramatic leaning, but I gamely stuck my head out a little more, which got a 'Great!' from Mike, who snapped away happily.

"Now, just slowly turn your head from left to right as I take the shots..Fantastic!"

Roslav Szaybo, CBS's Art Director, had found the location, an old empty 'two-up, two-down' in Shepherd's Bush. It was part of a lovely Edwardian red brick terrace, which would soon be pulled down to make way for one of the four huge tower blocks being built in the area.

Earlier that morning, I'd sat in the decaying front room while Jo the make-up lady once again got to work.

She told me that she'd been instructed by Roslav to "not make him so Gothic Nightmare this time" and to "go for a more natural skin colour. Nothing too outrageous."

After about half an hour, Jo had declared me "Done" and handed me a mirror. 'Yes,' I thought, studying my new face, 'it does look slightly more au naturelle.' But, while the white pan-stick and black lips, which she'd applied for the previous photo session, had been replaced by a fresh-looking pink complexion and subtly lipsticked mouth, I was also struck by the pale blue eye-shadow, the black eye-liner and the light mauve blush rouge on the cheeks. To me, I still looked as camp as a row of tents. Roslav, however, was thrilled when he walked in and saw the results of Jo's labours.

"More to your taste, Roslav?" Patsy asked him dryly.

"More to CBS's taste," he replied just as tartly.

"Gently effete rather than rip-your-heart-out vampire," I joked.

Roslav pointed at me as if to say,

"You got it!"

Suitably donned in my pinstripe suit, white shirt, striped silk tie, brogues and white fedora, I wandered around the abandoned house, striking poses in various rooms, and then moving on. I climbed up a rickety old staircase, precariously leaning on a very wobbly banister, and into one of the bedrooms. There I sat on a beautiful but dilapidated art deco sofa, and did my best to look chic and self-contained, all the while wondering if the roof was about to fall in on us.

Can You Hear Me OK album sleeve, August 1974, photo by Mike Nicholson

"These are going to be amazing!" Mike shouted.

Sure enough, as Stuart, Patsy and I looked at the transparencies in Roslav's office a couple of days later, I had to admit that Mike had indeed come up with some stunning pictures. I noticed someone had ringed one of them with orange marker pen. It was one of the window shots, my face in profile.

"Yes," Roslav said, "that's the sleeve! There can be no argument about it.

That -" he pointed at it with his Gitanes cigarette, "that is a beautiful picture. *That* is our Kid In A Big World."

A week later, I arrived at Apple Studios in Savile Row, to begin the recording sessions with Paul Phillips. Completely refurbished since Magic Alex had famously installed his useless 'multi-track system' five years earlier, it was now a state-of-the-art operation.

Paul greeted me at the door of the large control room:

"John! Come in," he said, and led me into where our engineer, Phil McDonald was setting up the tracks, and the musicians, Pete Zorn, Barry De Souza, Ken Nicol and Pete Marsh were standing in a little group having their coffees.

Stuart and Patsy were also there, settled on a sofa under the control room window, and waved over at me as I shook all the guys' hands.

"Okay," Paul said, looking through his piles of manuscripts, "I thought we'd start with 'Family Man'."

With that, we trooped

Kid In A Big World sleeve photo outtake September 1974, by Mike Nicholson

through to the studio, a nicely-sized room, with a beautiful grand piano awaiting me. Barry sat to the right of me on drums, Pete Zorn standing just in front of him on bass, Ken and Pete Marsh sitting to their right on guitars. We had one run-through, which sounded very smooth, and three takes later we had it.

We then recorded a song Paul wanted for a 'B' side, 'Third Man'. In 5/4, I'd modelled it on Dave Brubeck's 'Take Five', and the guys had a ball doing a full-on jazz interpretation.

"Okay," Paul said in our cans, "take a break, guys, but John? I'd like you to stay there and record 'Kid In A Big World' on your own. You sound in great voice, so let's get a take."

The boys took off their headphones and left the studio.

"I want to get the same kind of feel you got on your piano/voice demo," Paul continued, "so we're recording this like a live performance. No vocal overdubs. Just you at the piano, singing the song. This won't be a guide vocal, which you've been doing on the other tracks, this will be *the* vocal. Okay?"

Stuart's hand raised up above the desk, a thumbs-up sign of agreement.

I recorded two takes, Paul declaring the second one as the best.

After a short coffee break, Ken and Pete added acoustic guitar figures to 'Kid', onto which Pete Zorn then overdubbed some lovely flute and sax parts. He stayed at the mike for an overdub on 'Third Man', playing wailingly great free-form jazz throughout the song. It made it sound very 1960s New York, and I loved it.

Barry then played calypso style marimbas on 'Family Man', onto which Ken and Pete added their backing vocals.

Arranged by Paul, they reminded me of the backing vocals Paul McCartney and George Harrison sang on The Beatles' 'Help!', where they anticipated the next line John Lennon was about to sing:

(When)
When I was younger
So much younger than today
(I never need)
I never needed anybody's help in any way
(Now)
But now these days are gone I'm not so self-assured
(And now I find)
Now I find I've changed my mind
And opened up the doors

On *Family Man*, Ken and Pete did something similar behind my lead vocal:

I am a family man
(I do all I can)
I do all I can
(To bring it in)
To bring the money in regularly…

It was extremely effective.

After a brilliant morning's work, the boys took their leave and I re-did the lead vocals on 'Family Man' and 'Third Man'. I then double-tracked the choruses and put a doubled harmony line on 'Family Man'. Both songs were second nature to me, so it didn't take me long to get everything down.

"Fantastic!" Paul shouted as I came through into the control room. "You got those done so quickly!" I caught Stuart beaming over at me. "Just strings to do tomorrow, then the mixing!"

As Phil did some 'housework', as he called it, cleaning up the tracks for the strings overdubs, Paul and I chatted about the kind of music we liked. Unsurprisingly, our tastes were similar, both being big fans of Mott The Hoople.

"'Roll Away The Stone' is my favourite," I told him, "I love the 'rockabilly party on Saturday night' bit, really fantastic."

"Have you got 'The Hoople'?" he asked me. "It's a different 'rockabilly party' lady on there."

"No, I haven't got it yet."

"You should. It's a great album."

"It was one of the Thunderthighs on the single, wasn't it?"

"That's right. Lynsey De Paul does it on the album. BUT! My favourite track is 'Marionette', utterly stunning! Very Bowie-esque. You'd love it, John!"

"I must buy it!"

Paul laughed and looked puzzled:

"Buy it?"

"Yeah!"

"You don't *buy* CBS albums, John. I'll get it for you."

"Really?"

"Of course! In fact, give me a list of some other albums of ours you'd like, and I'll order them for you! You're a CBS artist now. You don't buy albums by other CBS artists! It's one of the perks!"

The next morning, I was woken by a knock on the door. I looked at my watch, it was eight o'clock. Mrs Mitchell, the landlady of the Earl's Court flat I'd recently moved into, opened it a crack and peeked in:

"I'm sorry, dear, but there's a call for you. It's your father."

As I quickly got dressed and walked to the phone in the hall, I already knew:

"Hello, son," I heard Dad say from an oddly distant place. "It's your mum. She passed away at three o'clock this morning."

For a moment I didn't know what to say. It felt rather surreal hearing the news I'd been expecting. Sounding surprised or shocked would have been dishonest, rather crass. So I asked the question which had immediately come into my mind:

"How are *you*, Dad?"

"She went peacefully," he sort of replied. "I was with her when she – when she went."

His voice sounded tiny.

"I'm really sorry, Dad."

"So am I. But she's at rest now."

I asked him when the funeral was and told him I'd travel up there the day before.

"It's next Tuesday."

"Okay. I'll see you on Monday afternoon then, Dad."

"It'll be good to see you, son. I just wish that -"

"I know."

When I arrived at the studio at ten o'clock, the orchestra was already doing a run-through, conducted by a small blonde chap who I vaguely recognised:

"Nicky Graham," Paul told me. "You probably saw him at the sales conference. He's one of our A & R guys. He can read dots so I asked him in to conduct."

What they were playing, along to 'Family Man', sounded lovely.

"I'm sorry about your mum, John," Paul said. "Stuart told me."

"Thanks, Paul."

"When's the funeral?"

"Tuesday. I'm going up there on Monday. I'll be back on Wednesday evening."

"Don't you want to stay a bit longer?" Paul asked. "Be with your family?"

I shook my head:

"No. No, I'd like to come back as soon as possible. This is home now."

"Okay then, so if I book the mixing sessions for Thursday and

Friday next week, is that alright for you?"

"Perfect," I said, knowing they would act as a lovely distraction.

"We're ready for a take, I think," Nicky's voice came over the intercom.

Paul dashed over to the console and switched on his studio mike: "Great! It's sounding lovely, Nicky." He turned to Phil, "Okay, Phil?"

Phil gave him a thumbs-up.

"Tapes are rolling," Paul said.

We stood listening to the orchestra, which melded beautifully into the track. As the chorus came in, Paul turned and smiled at me:

"Do you recognise the figure they're playing there?"

I didn't.

"It's the line you sang on Tony Meehan's 'Family Man', the one you did as a counter-melody in the choruses."

He sang it along with the orchestra for me and I could suddenly hear it.

"I didn't want to lose that, it's such a great melody. I just felt it intruded too much, the way you'd done it at Abbey Road. You were basically singing two choruses, and the original one is so great. Why take attention away from it? But as an orchestral line, it's really fantastic. You should be a strings arranger!"

I was touched that he had ensured my chorus counter-melody had not been lost, and hearing it his way now, it sounded just right.

Strings for both 'Family Man' and 'Kid In A Big World' were done and dusted by lunchtime and, as Nicky came through from the studio, he smiled and rushed over:

"John !" he shouted. "Lovely songs!"

He shook my hand enthusiastically and continued smiling at me. He was a handsome man, full of a wiry energy, which you could feel him wanting you to reciprocate, almost urging you to exude a mutual thrill. It was rather unsettling, and made me feel oddly tired.

"Good luck with them, John," he added, still beaming away.

"Thanks, Nicky!" I said, trying on a bright tone of voice, which I knew sounded forced. "The strings are great!"

"They are," Stuart's reassuringly sanguine voice came to the rescue, as he introduced himself.

Nicky pumped his hand quickly and beamed:

"Hi Stuart! Great musician you have here! Lovely piano work!"

Stuart smiled proudly at me,

"John is a huge talent. I hope CBS is proud to have him on the label."

"There's no doubt about that, Stuart!"

"Are you a musician, Nicky? I would imagine you are."

"Well, yes, now and again." He gave us a mock-modest look, like a flattered little boy. "I played piano for David Bowie a couple of years ago." He smiled at me, knowing I'd be impressed.

"Wow!" I duly gushed.

"On the Spiders From Mars tour."

"Wow!" I gushed again and was about to ask him what Bowie had been like, but one of the musicians came over to talk to him. He apologised to us, said goodbye and hurried outside for a private chat.

"Another young hopeful, looking for a record deal," Stuart joked.

As the musicians all began leaving, I took the opportunity, amidst the farewells, to go and sit next to Phil McDonald, as he worked on balancing the tracks:

"Hi," he said, "You happy?"

"Knocked out. Great studio!"

"Yeah, it is now."

"Paul told me you worked on 'Instant Karma'," I said, trying not to sound like a thrilled fan.

"Yeah! At Abbey Road. That session was a blast."

"It's my favourite Lennon track."

"Yeah, and it shouldn't have worked really. John insisted I push all the faders right up on everything, and mix it like that.* He wanted it recorded, mixed, mastered, cut and out within a week. He hated spending months on things. A bit different from doing *Sgt Pepper!*"

"Did you work on *that*?" I felt my eyes widening with wonder.

"I was just second engineer on some of it, but, wow, it was a trip!"

"You worked on *Imagine* too didn't you?"

"Yep!"

He nodded proudly at me and smiled. I could have talked to him all night, but I knew he had to get on.

"Do you think John will ever come back to the UK?" I finally asked him.

Phil shrugged:

"We can only hope."

*N.B. Phil Spector, the producer on 'Instant Karma', wanted to add strings to it, but Lennon turned that idea down. However, Spector did remix the track for the American release without John's knowledge.

I found it very difficult to cry at Mum's funeral. I was so relieved that she was now out of pain, I just felt rather numb, disconnected from the grief around me. It seemed unreal that she'd gone but in truth, she'd felt a rather distant figure the previous few weeks. Her light was slowly dying the last time I'd visited, and, because she'd become increasingly poorly, I hadn't been able to speak to her on the phone since then.

I'd accompanied Dad, my sister and Gran Wood to the chapel of rest the evening before she was cremated. When I walked into the room where she was laid out, I was struck first of all by a sense that no-one was there. Although I could see her lying in her open coffin, Mum's life force had completely gone. While that sounds an obvious thing to say, it was the oddest sensation. My eyes were telling me

'There she is, there's Mum', but, in fact, she wasn't there at all.

What disturbed me the most was her doll-like face. With over-rouged cheeks she would never have entertained, and a shade of lipstick which would have horrified her, her appearance drove it home that this was no longer my mum. It was akin to seeing a waxwork model in Madame Tussaud's.

I noted her expression though, frozen at the point of death, and one which I did recognise - total resolve not to give in. As though she were steeling herself for one more battle ahead. She aimed to go down fighting.

"Good for you, Mum," I thought as Dad held her hand and sobbed.

"It's so cold," he said. "She's so cold."

"But she's at rest, Herbert son," Gran said, patting his shoulder.

They'd never been close, Dad and his mother, at least he had never reciprocated her feelings for him. I knew her heart went out to him that day, and hoped he realised it.

"She always had such beautiful skin," Gran said, glancing down at the lady she had never wanted as her son's wife. I thought it was very touching that she was repeating what he'd told her, after his first date with 'Bren' in 1947:

"She has such lovely skin, Mum."

Ethel and Brenda's relationship had never been easy, consisting of a mutual toleration for "the sake of the kids." Now, as Gran finally saw just how much Mum meant to her son, all previous arguments and disagreements between the two women were forgotten.

That evening, I listened as Dad told me how he'd sat with Mum in her last hours.

"I thought she was a goner," he said. "She'd collapsed, unconscious, getting up to go to the loo while we were watching TV. So I lifted her onto the settee and just sat with her, holding her hand, waiting for her to - well, to fade away. I was there for about an hour, kept checking if she was still breathing, and wondering how long she'd last. I couldn't believe it when she opened her eyes and smiled at me. 'Hello, love,' she said, bright as you like. 'Have I had a little nap?'"

Telling him she felt better than she had for ages, she reminisced through the early hours of the morning about their life together; their summer wedding in 1948, complete with a chimney sweep for luck; their honeymoon in London, which had been Mum's first visit there; Sue and me growing up in their brand new council house in Heywood, where Dad grew peas, lettuce, gooseberries, strawberries and raspberries in his little allotment garden at the back; our trips to Butlin's Holiday Camps in the '50s, which we reached every year by way of various old jalopy cars, which often fell apart when – and sometimes before - we got back home; the first house they'd bought in 1960, a new-build in Bury which nearly bankrupted them, until they finally sold it in 1969 for four thousand pounds and bought a pretty little cottage in Ramsbottom, which cost them nine hundred. It put them 'in the black' for the first time in their twenty-six year marriage.

"And now," she'd said proudly, "we've got our own little business!"

Dad smiled at me ruefully,

"She was still talking about running the shop when she got better." He shook his head and looked away for a moment. "We should never have done it." He looked at me. "Coming here. Worst decision we - I - made."

"You did it for her, Dad. It wasn't a bad decision, it was the only one you could make."

He nudged me gently and smiled:

"She was bit worried about you, you know, being down in London on your own. But I put her mind at rest, I think so anyway. I reminded her what great people Stuart and Patsy are. That you had friends there. Good friends." He put his hand on my arm. "Your mum was very proud of you, son. She was talking about you when she -". I squeezed

Dad's arm as he fought back tears. "She suddenly gasped, sat bolt upright, looked kind of shocked, and fell back onto the cushion. That was it. She'd gone."

I felt such compassion for him at that moment, for a man who I'd always felt was one step removed. Our relationship had always been distant, since I was a kid really. The truth of it was that I was none of the things Dad would have expected when I'd been born. His first – and only - son, he must have thought what great times we were going to have together, going to football matches, playing cricket, weekends at the swimming pool or hanging out with other blokes and their sons. None of that ever happened. I was completely uninterested in energetic pursuits of any kind.

He tried to teach me to box once, when I was about six, and after a few minutes of his mock-punching me and trying to get me to punch back, I pulled off my gloves, declared myself bored and went up to my room to read. I think about that now, and wonder at how let down he must have felt, as I left him sitting there, holding my tiny little boxing gloves he'd bought for me specially.

As a child, I preferred watching Mum bake or sitting by her dressing table as she applied her make-up. I used to love listening to the gossipy chat amongst her friends at the Tupperware parties she hosted.

Dad did actually manage to get me to go with him, just once, to a soccer match – although it had really been at Mum's insistence.

"Go on," she'd said, when I moaned to her that I didn't want to go, "keep him company for a change."

As we walked into the football ground at Gigg Lane, he told me that Bury was "your team, they're the ones wearing blue and white", and that I should "cheer them on when they score." Inwardly I asked "Why?". Following a team of any sort has always been a mystery to me, and, freezing to death on a November afternoon, I gave up trying to work out what was going on and took to whining about my cold hands. Finally, he admitted defeat and took me home before the match was over. We hardly spoke on the bus home and he never asked me again.

He had no doubt looked forward, as I reached my teens, to meeting my girlfriends, and joshing me about them when I came home from 'a date'. Again, my score on that front was, obviously, zero.

Instead, I took to listening to records for hours in my bedroom and reading Virginia Woolf and Kafka novels in the garden. Usually after getting up to leave when Match Of The Day came on.

When I grew my hair down to my shoulders, he tried to scare me into getting it cut by pointing at his own bald pate:

"You'll end up like me," he said delightedly.

"No, I won't," I replied tartly. "Baldness comes down through the maternal line."

"You're such a know-it-all, aren't you?" he snarled, snapping his newspaper open and burying his reddening face behind it. "You look like a girl!"

"And that's a bad thing why?"

And so it ground on, our father and son war, while Mum listened from the ramparts of the kitchen, offering cups of tea while I stormed up to my room and put on *Highway 61 Revisited* or Zappa's *Hot Rats* as loudly as I could get away with.

At the age of eighteen, passing only two 'A' Levels, English and Art History - limiting my choice of Universities to none - I happily went off to do a 'Pre-Dip' art course. In Dad's book it was "wasting another year having a bloody good time while we feed you". I had finally become an alien living in his house. Nothing more than a "scruffy so-and-so" as well as a failure at everything else, I wholly disappointed him.

Even my song-writing bewildered him. It wasn't jazz, his first love, it wasn't catchy pop, it certainly wasn't going to make me rich. "Why is he bothering?" must have been his constant question to Mum.

He did come to my very first gig, at Accrington Art College in March 1970, and, after a really great evening where I was given a standing ovation from a packed theatre, I went to meet him and Mum in the foyer. All he said to me was,

"That's a great drummer you've got there."

I remember Mum staring at him, waiting for more.

"You were very good, love," she said, giving me a peck on the cheek, but Dad had already gone to get the car.

It wasn't until I moved to London three years later that, finally, it began to dawn on him. With a major record company signing me, a commission to write a song for a movie, and my first LP about to be released, he seemed to realise that his son wasn't the oddball loser he had thought I was after all.

Many years later, around 2005, when Dad was staying with me and my husband at our house in Pembrokeshire, we were sitting on the rear balcony, admiring the lawns I'd just mown, enjoying the smell of freshly-cut grass as we sipped our gin and tonics. Suddenly, out of the blue, he said,

"I wasn't much of a Dad was I?"

"You did alright," I replied.

"I wasn't very supportive of your music, not in the early days, when you needed it most."

I laughed and told him the story of what he'd said after that first gig in Accrington. He looked utterly shocked, like someone had slapped him:

"I didn't say that, did I?"

"You did."

He shook his head:

"I was so proud of you that night!"

"I wish you'd said so."

"So do I!" He sat staring out ahead of him, obviously going over it in his mind. He shook his head again and looked at me, his mouth quivering a little. "What a dickhead! Eh? What a prat!"

On my last night at the shop, before returning to London, I settled down in bed to read a copy of Melody Maker I'd brought with me. I must have been on the point of dropping off, when I became aware that the room seemed to be closing in around me, and I now inhabited a small cocoon, dimly lit. Outside of it was just darkness. I could sense a presence watching me from that darkness, but couldn't pinpoint exactly where. Then a strange whirring noise began, all round me. It was a rhythmic sound, like a low humming, getting increasingly louder. It seemed to envelop me as I lay there, forcing me to lie still. When I tried to sit up, I couldn't. It was as though a web had been wound around me, linked in some way to the sound pulsating in my little cocoon.

Oddly aware that the only thing I may be able to open were my eyes, I tried to force them open, really tried, but they wouldn't budge either. So I concentrated on one eye instead, and gradually, very slowly, it shifted, just a tiny bit, and with a strength which felt like it could normally move mountains, I prised my eyelid open and saw just a blurred greyness, with a slightly whiter light in its centre. No longer 'bound', I sat up and the whirring noise immediately stopped. I jumped out of bed and switched on the main light. Like someone who had heard a burglar breaking in, I stood there, staring round the room. The fact this was not my bedroom made me feel very detached from everything. Only my little suitcase on the floor, the only thing of mine in there, brought me back. I continued to listen and watch, and realised that there was no-one there. Nothing.

I left the light on and got back into bed. As I lay there, shivering slightly, thoughts scurried through my brain. Had I been asleep? Was it a dream? Maybe I'd been in that in-between-world just before falling, and unable to rise back to consciousness? Or was it something more? Could I have been experiencing Mum's imprisoning stillness, which she had fought as her life drained away? I had no idea, and, too exhausted to think about it anymore, fell asleep and dreamt of Mum…

…She was standing by a 1950s style, light brown tiled mantelpiece, in a dingily-lit sitting-room with flowery old-fashioned wallpaper and one overhead shadeless light. The walls looked nicotine-stained and it was all rather drab, even though the colours of the wallpaper had once been bright pinks, reds and yellows. I recognised the room, and yet I didn't know where it was.

Mum was crying and I couldn't tell why. I asked her and she just shook her head and looked at me.

Then, we were sitting in a bus stop, it was raining and she was crying again. I seemed unable to console her.

"What has happened to you?" she kept asking. "Why are you like this? What's happened to my little boy?"…

Waking up with a start the next morning, I quickly got dressed and went downstairs. I settled down with a bowl of cereal and a cup of tea as the clock struck six. Sitting alone in the back sitting-room, I remembered how, just a few weeks earlier, Mum had been there, counting the shop's takings at the small dining table, where only an Order of Service for her funeral now rested.

Dad moved out of the shop just a few weeks later. It had been Mum's dream to buy it, and now he no longer needed, or wanted, to be there. Too many memories and regrets inhabited those stark unloved rooms. He gave the shop to my sister, a little business she could run as an additional income for her young family, and found a very pleasant one-bedroomed flat in Bury. From there, he could rebuild his life as a single man in his late forties, and decide what his new future would be.

"This is a Christmas smash!"

Dan Loggins beamed up at me and laughed out loud as the just-mixed 'Family Man' played in the control room.

"It's an absolute smash, John," he said again, utterly delighted at what he was hearing. "It's the first single for sure!"

"Oh I'm so pleased you've said that, Dan," Patsy said.

Dan smiled at her, then at me:

"Fantastic, John!"

I looked over at Paul, who was watching proceedings with interest. I got the impression his Director/Manager relationship with Dan was not completely smooth-sailing. It always felt slightly prickly when they were in a room together.

"Great production, Paul," Stuart said, slapping Paul on the back, trying to bring a few congratulations his way.

"It's a great song, Stuart," Paul replied. "All I did was take John's demo and use that as the base for my production. It was all there already."

A few feet away stood Mike Batt, one of CBS's most successful artists of 1974, who'd popped in to have a listen. As the track finished, he nodded approvingly at me and said,

"What a fantastic track, John! I wish I'd written it!"

"I wish I'd written 'The Wombling Song'!" I replied, then hoped he hadn't taken that as a jokey dig.

The irony of Mike's situation was that, although he'd had three Top Ten hits and two Top Twenty albums so far that year, he was almost completely unknown to the young fans who bought the records he had written, produced and sung lead vocals on. At the beginning of the year, he'd turned the theme song he'd composed for the children's television series, The Wombles, into a novelty hit. By way of creating a 'pop group' out of the cute and furry Wimbledon creatures who kept the surrounding Common clean, he'd taken the single to Number Four in the charts. In what must have been exceedingly hot shaggy outfits under unyielding studio lights, the four Wombles pranced benignly around the Top of The Pops studio week and after week and stole the hearts of millions of kids. It was a catchy, extremely successful record, but everyone thought that would be that, just one of the many one-hit wonders which come and go in a heartbeat.

However, Mike – and I would guess CBS – must have been entirely unprepared for the phenomenon that followed. The follow-up, 'Remember You're A Womble', took just a few weeks to crash up to Number Three. By the end of the year, with five Top Twenty hits under their rather wide belts, The Wombles were officially the best-selling singles group of 1974, outselling Paul McCartney & Wings, The Bay City Rollers and The Stylistics. They also figured in the Top Ten best-selling albums listing for the year, alongside The Carpenters, Simon & Garfunkel, Pink Floyd and The Beatles.

"Love that 'reggae-reggae-regularly' bit, John," Mike laughed. "So good. Such a hook! Huge hit!"

"Fucking hell!" Paul shouted to the ceiling. "I've produced John Howard's first hit single! Mike Batt said so!"

The studio phone rang and Phil picked it up:

"It's for you, Stuart," he said.

As Stuart chatted amiably away, Paul and Phil began setting up a mix for 'Kid In A Big World'. Mike bid his farewells, telling us he was working on his next Wombles single, a Christmas song ('Wombling Merry Christmas', which reached Number Two, the group's biggest hit record).

"You might be in contention with John for the Christmas Number One!" Dan joked.

"Let battle commence!" Mike parried back.

Dan happily waved at us all and left with him:

"Really great, John," he said as the door closed.

With the opening strains of 'Hey, you're a 'Kid In A Big World' now' floating across the room, Stuart came and sat with Patsy and me:

"That was Roslav. He has the sleeve finished and wants us to go and take a look. We'll get a cab over there when the session's finished."

Half an hour later, we sat listening to Paul's mix of what would be the title track of my debut album. He'd added a lovely echoed tambourine towards the end, which perfectly captured the resigned quality of the track, like a sigh of understanding. The strings, the guitars, and the flute and sax overdubs fitted beautifully.

"That's exactly what I heard when Stuart played me your demo," Paul said, smiling over at me.

What particularly pleased me was how much better this vocal performance was than the one I'd done on Tony's version. It sounded much more assured, simply because this was how I'd written the song three years earlier, and how I'd been performing it ever since. Lovely though Tony's production and Harry Gold's 1930s arrangement had been, it never sounded quite there for me. I think if I'd written the song with a period feel in the first place, it might have been more natural done Tony's way. Now, it felt as though I'd got the song back.

"It sounds fabulous, Paul," I said. "I'm very happy."

I was even happier when I saw what Roslav and his design team had come up with for my album sleeve. It looked extremely classy and atmospheric.

"Terrific!" Stuart said, as we stood looking at it propped up against Roslav's wall, like viewers at an art gallery.

"The guys on the fifth floor love it too," he said, blowing out a Gitanes-scented smoke ring. "For the back, we are repeating the same picture but with you not there, as though you have left the little house for the Big World!"

That night, I had the best night's sleep I'd had for weeks. Finally, things seemed to be coming together.

The following day, Paul did the remix of 'Goodbye Suzie'. He lifted my vocal and piano, which had always sounded too low in the mix before, took out some of the guitar flourishes from Tony's production, and gave the track more 'top'.

"That sounds like a single to me," Stuart said, looking tentatively across at his wife, who had set her heart on 'Family Man' being the first one out of the stalls.

"It does, Stuart," Paul replied, "but we have to accept that it's too long for radio…four minutes twenty-five seconds, much too long. Radio One would never play it."

Patsy nodded and glanced at Stuart, while I silently argued 'Hey Jude', over seven minutes, 'MacArthur Park', over seven minutes,' but kept the thoughts to myself.

"So," Paul continued, with a wry smile, "we're going to look at doing an edit. Play it again, please, Phil."

As we listened to the mix again, I couldn't actually hear what Paul could cut out to bring it down to a more 'radio-friendly' length. Maybe a fade rather than a proper ending could work, but that would only take off a few seconds. As the middle eight came in - "And in the morning, all the shops will be open…" - Paul lifted his finger:

"There. That's where we do the edit. We cut the middle eight out, and cut in the final line of the first chorus, so it ends on the C chord, rather than F, then cut into the last verse and chorus."

"Okay," Phil said, rewinding the track, "let's give it a go."

Over the next ten minutes or so, the two men worked away and, voilà, without the middle eight, they had cut it to three minutes and forty five seconds. As an edit, it worked perfectly, but I wasn't happy about the missing F chord at the end of the penultimate chorus. It had led perfectly, with the following F7, into the B flat middle eight which I'd always been really proud of. I loved how it resolved back to the C chord - from E flat, into F with a D bass and then into C - ready for the last verse and chorus. I remembered going "Wow!" to myself when that section 'arrived' as I was writing the song. Paul must have seen the regret on my face:

"It'll only be on the single, John," he assured me. "The album version will stay untouched, it will be the original length." He looked at me. "Honest!"

"Okay," I said, a little reluctantly. "We need it to be a hit, I know."

"But which will be the *first* single?" Patsy said, looking from Paul to Stuart, and bringing us back down to Earth. "Dan clearly said he wanted 'Family Man' as the first one."

"He did, Patsy," Paul said, "but at the end of the day it's in the lap of the marketing gods – and probably a certain Dick Asher..."

"Hm," Patsy said, pulling a face, "that means it'll be 'Goodbye Suzie'. 'Bye 'bye Christmas smash!"

"Ballads *have* been Number One at Christmas," Phil interjected. "'Green Green Grass Of Home', also a story-song with a sad ending. Massive Christmas hit."

"'Two Little Boys'," I added.

Everyone pulled a face, including me.

"Well, let's just be happy if we have a *hit* this Christmas!" Paul said.

"I'll buy us all a case of champagne if we do!" Stuart said.

Patsy just sat quietly, not commenting any further.

Sure enough, 'Goodbye Suzie' was chosen as the first single. It was scheduled for release on October 25th, and, as I played my advance promo copy, I felt a pang of sadness that Mum had missed its release by just five weeks. She would have been so thrilled to have a copy in her hand.

The promotions team had about three weeks, prior to release, to get radio play in place, so that, by the time it came out, the public knew it and hopefully wanted to buy it. After the first week, Stuart told me that they'd secured a couple of plays on Radio Luxembourg, but Radio One were, for some reason, not biting. By the second week, it had entered Luxembourg's Power Play Top Thirty, but still no Radio One plays.

A few days before the release of the single, I sat with Stuart in

Fortnum & Mason, my heart sinking, as he explained the reason Radio One wouldn't be playing it:

"They say it's too depressing for their audience."

I nearly choked on my feathered eggs on toast:

"Depressing?"

"It's about death, they don't think it's right for their audience."

I dropped my fork noisily onto my plate, causing a few county ladies-who-lunch to glance over and look a little put out:

"What?" I hissed. "There have been *so* many hit songs about death! 'Tell Laura I Love Her', 'Leader Of The Pack', 'Terry', 'Ebony Eyes'." Stuart nodded sadly as I counted them off on my fingers. "'New York Mining Disaster', 'Ode To Billie Jo'. 'Seasons In The Sun' just this year, for God's sake! Number Bloody One!" (The second-best selling single of 1974, in fact).

"I know, John, but I think it's the suicide element they object to. A young girl drowning herself. They think it's too heavy for their primarily teenage audience."

He played with his food and seemed almost embarrassed.

"You don't agree with them, do you?".

"No, of course not! I absolutely love the song. You know I do. It's a great song. But what can I do? They're gods in their world, the Power People. But when I spoke to Paul this morning, he told me that the playlist committee at Radio One is adamant – they will not be playing 'Goodbye Suzie'. Period – their word, not mine. We're all devastated! I would imagine Dick Asher is beside himself."

"Maybe the Luxembourg plays will persuade them to think again?"

I was grasping at straws.

"The opposite probably, John. Radio One will be even less likely to start playing it, now that Luxembourg are supporting the record. They hate to think of themselves as followers of trends. It's not called Radio *One* for nothing. Damn and blast them."

On the tube back to Earl's Court, I felt a rage growing inside me.

'Here we go again,' I thought, 'another disaster, just when things looked to be getting better.'

That night, I went across the road to The Catacombs Bar in Finborough Road, a basement gay club which played the best disco music I'd ever heard. Entry was just fifty pence, and although it stank of burnt coffee and sweat, it was my idea of heaven. Through an orange-lit oasis of great music *and* attractive men, I made my way to the tiny, packed dance floor and joined in with the bumping and grinding mass of drenched, ecstatic bodies.

There was always a small group of guys who stood to the side and just watched. When one of them saw somebody they liked, they'd step forward and join in the dancing, moving closer to the object of their desire.

As I danced my depression away, a handsome Nigerian guy called Felix, who I'd spoken to briefly a few nights earlier with his American boyfriend Sy, caught my eye and smiled at me for a few minutes, nodding with approval. Finally, he walked onto the floor and began to dance around me. He could certainly move, but, tempting though he was, I wasn't about to steal someone else's guy.

"Where's Sy?" I shouted into his ear.

"Gone back to the States," he shouted into mine, his sweat dripping onto my face.

"For how long?" I yelled over the blasting music.

"For good. We're over."

I made an "I'm sorry" face but he laughed:

"No! I'm fine! It's fine!" he yelled.

He held my shoulders as I boogied in front of him, enjoying what he saw.

"You?" he said. "Are you good?"

I threw my arms in the air,

"I'm *great!*" I shouted.

With that, he grabbed hold of me, pushed me into him, tight

into him, and thrust us round the floor, ducking, diving, spinning, grooving. With no effort from me at all, we moved as one, so fast my heart was thumping. He was in total control and it was utterly divine. After months of feeling like my life and my career were unravelling, with nobody around to stop it, this was just what I needed.

For the next two hours, we bopped our butts off to amazingly funky tracks you never heard on Radio One, 'Do It 'Til You're Satisfied', 'Party Down', 'City In The Sky', 'You Got The Love', 'Skin Tight', 'Do It Baby', 'You're Welcome (Stop On By)', and the fabulous 'Higher Plane' where the whole room sang as one, "Gotta keep on liftin', liftin', liftin', liftin' you UP!".**

Chris Lucas, the 'Cats' DJ, played mainly American imports, months before they were released in the UK. It meant that we were amongst a very select few in Britain who heard them before anyone else. Every guy dancing felt that he belonged to an exclusive club. We were Underground, ahead of the game. Being gay truly meant being 'Where It's At!'.

"Those boring straights don't know what they're missing," one shirtless guy in tight white jeans shouted as he shimmied past me.

He winked at me, blew me a kiss and disappeared into the sweat-filled mêlée.

Chris's extra touch of 'Cats' magic came when he seamlessly mixed the 'A' sides into the instrumental versions on the 'B' side, then back into the 'A' side, so you literally had the equivalent of what later became 12" mixes, unknown in 1974. The records, and our joy, seemed to go on forever.

I whooped, I hollered, I was with probably the best dancer in the club that night, and I felt fabulous. And then, to top it all, The Pointer Sisters' live version of 'Yes We Can Can/Love In Them There Hills' gloriously shimmied in. It was a huge favourite at the club and the place went wild. Even those who hadn't been dancing joined us on the floor, everyone going crazy to one of the most uplifting tracks I've ever heard.

As the sweat poured off me, and the music took me to new ecstatic heights, I yelled for all I was worth:

"Go fuck, Radio One!!"

**For those who want to check out the great disco tracks mentioned above, to which I danced my tits off that late summer of 1974, here's a full run-down:

Do It 'Til You're Satisfied – B.T. Express (American No.1, not a UK hit)

Party Down – Little Beaver (Big R'n'B hit in The States, not a hit in the UK)

City In The Sky – The Staples Singers (American hit, not a UK hit)

You Got The Love – Rufus featuring Chaka Khan (American hit, not a UK hit)

Skin Tight – The Ohio Players (American hit, not a UK hit)

Do It Baby – The Miracles (American hit, not a UK hit)

You're Welcome (Stop On By) – Bobby Womack (Top Five R'n'B hit in America, not a UK hit)

Higher Plane – Kool & The Gang (the group's eighth American hit, five years before they'd have their first UK hit, *Ladies Night*)

Yes We Can Can/Love In Them There Hills – from 'The Pointers Sisters -Live at The Opera House'

Chapter Twenty-Three

Frightened Now

When I walked into Stuart's Denmark Street office late in October '74, I was still brooding about my first single being refused plays by Radio One. With no tours or live performances planned, and no TV in the offing, it meant, in effect, that 'Goodbye Suzie' was – ironically, given the lyric - dead in the water.

But seeing the smiling face of Paul Phillips, who was sitting chatting to Stuart as I entered the room, I inwardly felt better. He had the ability to make me feel good about myself whenever I saw him. He stood up to greet me:

"John, how do you fancy a cheer-up lunch?"

Stuart beamed over at us:

"Just what John needs right now, Paul!"

"Exactly. Let me take you to the Spaghetti House, you'll love it."

Fifteen minutes later, we were on the fourth floor of the enormously tall Italian eaterie in Goodge Street, having climbed up three staircases past packed rooms on the first three floors. With only one table remaining on the fourth, we grabbed it and sat down. I looked around the noisy, chatter-filled room.

"What a great place!" I said, watching numerous waiters flying from table to table, pads and menus under their arms, pouring more wine for diners happily tucking into gorgeous-smelling dishes. "Such a fantastic atmosphere!"

"CBS people use it a lot, it's really close to our recording studios for one thing. Which is -"

"Can I take your order, gentlemen?"

A smiling waitress stood with her pen and pad at the ready.

We placed our orders - Ravioli with spinach for me, Spaghetti Bolognese for Paul - and she whisked off to the table next to us.

Paul leaned in a little, pouring some iced water, which the waitress had brought, into our glasses:

"As I was saying before I was so rudely interrupted..." he grinned at me, "I thought this was a good place to meet up for a chat, apart from it being a fantastic restaurant, it's also very close to CBS's recording studios."

"Really?"

"Yes, the studios are in Whitfield Street, five minutes' walk away."

"I didn't know CBS had their own studios!"

"They're excellent, I think you'd enjoy recording there. Which brings me to my question...Have you been writing any new songs?"

I laughed:

"About three or four a day! I wrote quite a few during the Abbey Road mixing sessions."

"I don't enjoy mixing either!"

"I do now, but at first I found it really tedious. Once I understood it, though, I loved being there for the mixing."

"I will never love mixing, but it's a necessary evil!"

Our food arrived and we began to eat and chat:

"It's great that you've got some new material," Paul continued. "Have you demo'd any of the songs yet?"

"No, not yet."

"Would you like to demo them with me?"

"I'd love to!"

"With a view to recording your next album with me as producer?"

In truth, I hadn't begun to even consider what would be next for me recording-wise. I wrote so many songs as a matter of course back then, and I'd assumed they would at some point be recorded. But my attention had been so focused on the first album, which had yet to be released, the next one hadn't really entered my mind.

"Do CBS want a second album?" I asked.

It seemed a pertinent question, no-one had asked or answered it thus far, but Paul looked a bit taken aback.

"Er – yes! I certainly do! And I am your A & R manager!"

I had already taken it that Tony Meehan was now out of the picture. I hadn't spoken to him for months, not since we'd sat and done the album running order at Abbey Road in early August. There was no way that Stuart would have entertained him producing another album of mine. The twain would never meet between them, and while I'd really enjoyed working with Tony, the conflict which had arisen during the Abbey Road sessions between him and Stuart had made it difficult to truly enjoy the process.

Life was now running at a very fast pace, and, frankly, I was still young and thoughtless enough not to consider how Tony must have felt, having been basically abandoned after a job well done.

Paul sipped his water while keeping his eyes firmly on my face.

"Let's do it!" I said.

"Okay! Well, after lunch, I'll take you across to Whitfield Street and introduce you to the engineer I'd like us to work with. We'll do the demos there, and if you like the studio – which I think you will – we'll record the album there as well."

A couple of weeks later, I was walking to Paul's office in CBS's Theobalds Road building, when Roslav came running down the corridor and gave me a first-print of the *Kid In A Big World* sleeve.

"For your collection, John!" Roslav said happily.

It looked fabulous, even in its rough stage. Turning it over to see the lovely back sleeve, with, as Roslav had predicted, the 'kid' gone from the window, and then opening it up to find, housed inside it, a test pressing of the LP., made my heart leap. My first album!

"Wow! Thank you, Roslav!" I said, wanting to hug him, but instead just shaking his hand.

I noticed that the tracklisting had been altered from the one Tony Meehan and I had agreed on in August. The first single, 'Goodbye

Suzie', now opened the album, followed by the track that would no doubt be its follow-up, *Family Man*. Side Two now ended with 'Kid In A Big World', which made sense, as it had been elevated to 'title track' since Tony did his running order, when we thought that the album would be called *Guess Who's Coming To Dinner*.

"Looks good, eh?" Paul said as I sat on the settee by the door of his office, laying the LP like a favourite pet beside me. I couldn't take my eyes off it.

"Terrific," I said, stroking the sleeve. "It's finally real."

"Now we have to make sure plenty of people hear it and know about it." He gave me a coffee and sat down next to me, rather than behind his desk, immediately engaging me. "Has anyone told you our thoughts for a concert to promote the album's release?"

"No, not yet. I haven't spoken to Stuart today."

"How would you like to perform at The Purcell Room?"

I had no idea what or where it was.

"It sounds like a classical venue."

"It usually is. It's perfect for conveying the sense of class and intimacy we want people to experience when you perform. It's on the Embankment, a really beautiful venue, very stylish. It would suit you to a 'T'."

"Great! When?"

"Around the release date, end of February. The promotion guys are looking at dates when it's available."

I'd been a little concerned that the utter failure of my first single would have made the company less keen to release the album, let alone promote it. But with a promo copy now in my hands, a launch concert being discussed, and recording sessions being planned for the next one, my fears evaporated. For the time being.

That evening, after playing my LP three or four times and spending an age staring at the sleeve, I decided I needed to celebrate. I got myself schuchzed up and went across the road to The Cats club where, for an hour or so, I danced myself dizzy.

As I was getting myself a much-needed Coca Cola at the bar, a handsome, broad-shouldered man caught my eye. He reminded me of a taller version of Jack Lemmon and I wasn't surprised when, walking up to me, he said "Hi" in a gorgeous deep American accent. His greying flecks of hair at the temples added an air of sophisticated charm, which oozed from every pore as he studied me.

"You look like you're having a great time out there on your own," he joked, his lopsided smile and twinkly eyes inviting me in.

"Do you dance?" I asked, sipping my coke.

He threw up his hands in mock horror:

"O-o-o-h! N-o-o-o! My dancing days died with Elvis's 'Hound Dog'!"

I laughed, making a quick mental calculation about his age. He continued to look me up and down as I swayed to Barry White's 'Satin Soul'.

"Fancy a smooch then?" I said, feeling rather bold.

He raised his eyebrows, gave me another once-over and took my hand:

"You've convinced me," he said. "Let's go smooch!"

"So this is the same hotel your parents stayed for their honeymoon?" Roy Fitzroy Junior asked me across our croissants, honey and black coffees.

He had marched with great authority into the breakfast room of The Strand Palace Hotel, ignoring the suspicious glances from some of the waiters at his young companion.

"Yep," I replied. "Maybe even the same room!"

"Now that *would* be weird!" He chuckled, munching on his croissant. "I like being with you, Mr John Howard."

"And I with you, Mr Fitzroy Junior."

"You know," he dabbed his mouth with the starched cotton napkin,

"I'm old enough to be your pop! Maybe I should be calling *you* 'Junior'!" He sighed and swigged back the dregs of his coffee. "I wish I didn't have to go straight to the airport this morning. I'd love to have had a few hours with you in London. Why didn't you walk into that bar a few nights ago?"

"Do you have to leave today?"

"Yep. I have to get back to my ranch in Mexico," he said, filling me with images of Marlboro Man trotting on horseback through his acres of land, as the sun set on those greying flecks. "Will you at least accompany me to the airport?"

In the cab there, Roy told me he was born and raised in New Jersey, went to Hartford University in Connecticut, became a lawyer in New York, buying his ranch ten years earlier when his father died suddenly, leaving him a bursary:

"To be spent on starting up a business, was his dictum, but a business which would bring me 'Well-being'. That, of course, would not have been a law firm!" He slapped his leg and laughed, giving me Doris Day goosebumps. "So," he continued, "I decided that setting up with a small stock of cattle just outside Mexico City, where I'd spent a few summers as a teenager and loved it, as well as breeding Dalmatians, my favourite pooches ever since we had one when I was a kid, was good enough for any man in his mid-30s."

I had to ask:

"Do you have a partner over there?"

He scanned my face, the creases at his eyes deepening:

"I do. Alejandro. He's Mexican, we met about five years ago, he looks after the ranch when I'm away, and, well, he's a great person to have around, and be around."

"How old is he?"

Roy cocked his head and smiled:

"Well now, so many questions…what about you, Mr Howard? What about you?"

I'd told him I was a singer as we'd lain in the dark the previous night, but hadn't gone into any detail about the album or anything to do with my recording career. So, as the taxi sped along towards the airport, eating up our time together much too quickly, I gave him a brief résumé of what I'd been up to the last three or four years. He nodded as I chatted, listening without interrupting. Then, suddenly:

"Terminal Two," the driver shouted.

Roy paid the driver, bundled out, got his luggage and waved me to follow him.

"Okay, my musical friend," he said, slapping me on the back. "This way!"

I followed him to the First Class Departure lounge, where he signed me in as a Guest, ordered a rum and coke, a coffee for me, and we settled into the air of sophisticated quiet. He checked his boarding pass, sipped his drink and smiled at me. For a minute or so he just studied me, then said,

"How do you fancy coming over to stay with me in New Jersey? My mom would love you!"

"I'd really like that!"

"Okay! Let's keep in touch on it!"

An hour later, I watched him wander through into passport control. He glanced over his shoulder and gave me a friendly G.I. salute, I waved back, and he was gone. As I went to catch the bus back into London, I wondered if I'd ever see him again.

About a month later, a few days before Christmas, I was coming home from having one of my usual lunches-for-one at The Stock Pot restaurant, which was just round the corner in Earl's Court Road. It specialised in very cheap and tasty meals and, several evenings a week, on the way back from Stuart's office, I'd buy a music magazine from the kiosk outside Earl's Court station and eat there. I was always greeted by Juan, the maître d', order my Chicken A La King or Spanish

Rice, find a small table, prop up the mag against the napkin holder, and enjoy the Italian family ambience of the place and an excellent meal costing fifty pence.

Mrs Mitchell had, as usual, seen me walking by her front window, where she often sat watching the world go by. She waved at me frantically as I walked up the steps to the front door of the red-bricked Mansion building. As soon as I put my key in the door I heard her shouting "You've got a letter from Mexico, John!". As I walked in, she ran to me waving it in the air.

"Is this the American chap you told me about?" she said, grinning like an excited little girl as she handed me the letter. "Your Jack Lemmon?"

She'd often listen wide-eyed as, over a glass of wine, I sat in her room and recounted details of my various liaisons. She never tired of hearing the tale of Sugar Ray, which usually ended with her warning that I would "end up getting your throat cut by a madman one day, John!". I'd giggle as she dramatically threw her head in her hands, which would in turn make her laugh, with a final finger-wagging "You be careful, dear! All men are bastards, darling! I know!!"

With her invitation to "come and watch some TV with me later," which meant "to tell me what the letter says", I went into my room and opened the flimsy light blue airmail envelope. Folding it out, I read a short but really affectionate note from Roy.

"I wasn't kidding when I said my mom would love you," it said in his spindly handwriting, "and I will arrange a visit for you to stay with her and me in New Jersey. How would you fancy Christmas '75 in the ol' US of A??"

There was no mention of a trip to Mexico, but I'd already assumed that would never be possible, certainly not while Alejandro was around. I lay on the bed and, rather prematurely, began planning for my first trip to America. I fell asleep with vague thoughts of performing at The Carnegie Hall, which turned into a dream of duetting 'White

Christmas' with Bing Crosby, except Bing became Roy and I was swishing round him in a Rosemary Clooney tight-waisted swirly frock.

As for Christmas '74, I decided to stay in London, rather than go to see family. Mum had always been my draw to visit up North on a fairly regular basis, and the previous Christmas had been my last with her. Dad was now settled into his bachelor flat, and apparently already dating the occasional lady, and my sister had her own fairly sizeable family to see to. There was no reason to add to that number, and, frankly, London was now my home.

The day before Christmas Eve, I was invited, along with Stuart and Patsy, to Mike Batt's festive celebrations at his beautiful house on the outskirts of London. I met his wife, Wendy, who had the biggest beehive hairdo I'd ever seen. My sister had a back-combed and hair-sprayed one in the '60s, emulating Dusty and Ronnie Spector, but even they would have been jealous of Wendy's skyscraper-high bouffant.

She was thrilled when I mentioned the vintage jukebox underneath the sweeping *All About Eve* staircase. It was blasting out Wizzard's 'I Wish It Could Be Christmas Everyday' and I went to check out what else was on it:

"Choose one, John!" Wendy shouted.

"Any of Mike's hits on here?" I smiled at him and winked.

Mike threw his eyes to the ceiling:

"No, there isn't," he said, looking extremely uncomfortable.

"Christ! If I'd had your hits, they'd *all* be on here!"

"That's right, John, you tell him!" Wendy cried and squeezed her husband's arm. "You should have the new one on there at least, Mike."

The latest Wombles single, 'Wombling Merry Christmas', had just smashed into the Top Five, ready for its peak of Number Two at the beginning of the New Year. For a man who was the brains behind the biggest selling singles act of 1974, I was surprised, and actually rather impressed, by how shy and reticent he seemingly was about his success. I truly would have been shouting it to the extremely high ceiling if it had been me.

I did wonder how he would have reacted if the hits had been by 'Mike Batt' rather than 'The Wombles'. In fact, just a few months later, he did achieve a hit under his own name. 'Summertime City', the theme song he wrote for the BBC TV series *Summertime Special*, took just three weeks to hit the Top Ten in August '75, peaking at Number Four.

Early in the New Year, 6th January 1975, I was at CBS Studios, getting ready to record my vocal for 'Hall of Mirrors', one of the songs I'd written in Abbey Road's Studio 2 a few months earlier. Paul had asked me to overdub the lead vocal onto the backing track while sitting at the piano. It felt quite strange, putting my hands on my knees instead of the piano keys, but he explained his thinking to me through my cans:

"You sing in a much more intimate way when you're sitting down. I realised that when you did 'Kid In A Big World' at Apple. I think you approach a song differently when you're at the piano rather than standing at the mike doing an overdub. But if it feels too weird, just say so."

"No, it's fine," I said. "Let's give it a go."

When I'd done the first take, Paul literally shouted into my headphones:

"That was fantastic, John! Christ!"

I could hear Stuart also calling out to me from somewhere in the control room,

"John! Bloody marvellous!"

"Okay," I said, "let's double the choruses!"

"Just what I was about to say!" Paul said, laughing. "Do you want my job?"

"No, this one's just fine!"

That evening we demo'd - as well as 'Hall of Mirrors' - 'Technicolour Biography', 'Take Up Your Partners', 'The Other Side Of Town', 'Frightened Now' and, at Paul's request, 'Guess Who's Coming To Dinner'.

"I want to have a good quality demo of that song," Paul told me, "done as you originally wrote it, not Tony's take on it."

Stuart looked thrilled. Not only at Paul's comment on Tony's arrangement of 'Guess', which he'd always hated, but also by the fact that I was back to recording 'performances'. Songs done from start to finish with no drop-ins, then double-tracking choruses and adding occasional harmonies, was how we'd done the Chappell demos in 1973. It was one of the things he'd loved about the way I worked, very quickly and yet focused on getting everything done as well as I could in just a couple of takes.

He'd loathed the way Tony Meehan had concentrated, for take after take, on getting different sections of songs done as perfectly as possible, then moving onto the next section to work on the vocal for that, until he was happy with it. Stuart's beaming face, when I went into the control room to listen to the five demos I'd just done in three hours, took me back to those nights at Chappell's a year earlier.

We actually returned to Chappell's at the end of January, but not to the studios. This time we were in the Bond Street piano showroom, for a promotional photo session CBS had arranged. It was an enormous room, with various grand and upright pianos dotted around, all protected from the sun by thick red velvet floor-length curtains covering every window.

Jo did my make-up as the photographer, Tom, chose the piano he wanted me to sit at, and arranged the lighting around it.

Patsy helped me get changed into my black velvet suit, gave my hair a comb, and declared me ready.

One of the 6 foot high photos which stood in the foyer of the Purcell Room, February 1975, by Tom Sheehan

"Okay, John," Tom said, "sit here and play something, anything, and I'll just take some photos. Pretend I'm not here really."

"These are for the advertising campaign the label's doing for John's album," I heard Stuart telling Jo. "They're planning a big spread of ads in all the music papers."

My heart did a little flip of excitement as I began playing 'Hall Of Mirrors' for my small but attentive audience:

> One more exit to one more entrance
> One more bedsit to one more palace
> Oh, it's oh so easy

In early February, Stuart and I walked into CBS for a meeting with Paul when we saw him coming towards us with a single in his hand:

"Here's your promo copy of 'Family Man', John," he said. "I thought you'd like one."

As I was studying it, turning it over to find 'Missing Key' had been made its 'B' side, Paul said,

"Unfortunately, I've just heard that Radio One has refused to put it on the playlist."

"Not again!" Stuart wailed, looking utterly distraught. "Why this time?"

"They say the song is anti-female."

I snorted.

"Exactly!" Stuart said in response. "What do they mean 'anti-female'?"

"They told our promo guy that its lyric demeaned women."

"Christ!" Stuart put his arm on my shoulder, as though trying to protect me from the news. "Do you want me to speak to someone there? This is getting silly."

Dave, the Head of Press and Promotions, who I'd met at the CBS conference a few months earlier, overheard the conversation as he was coming out of his office:

"Hi, John, Hi, Stuart," he said, shaking our hands. "No point talking to them, Stuart. They're adamant over there. The single will not be put up for consideration again either."

"This is getting like a vendetta," Stuart said angrily.

"Something's going on," Paul said. He looked at Dave, "We've got to find out what the problem is."

"The problem is Radio One," Dave said, shrugging. "Okay, I have to go, but, yes, I want to talk to you, Stuart, at some point soon. There may be a chink of light!"

"Jesus, Dave, I hope so! Call me!"

As we sat in Paul's office, discussing an idea of his, that I give a show for CBS staff the week before the Purcell Room concert 'as a kind of preview of the launch show', I tried to stay engaged. Stuart declared it 'a great idea!' as Paul told us that the show – at The Langan

Hall in Earl's Court – would be 'really good for CBS people to hear John before the press do'. I nodded in all the right places, but was fast beginning to despair. Two flop singles to my name now. Just how long, I asked myself, inwardly shaking my head, would this company remain as enthusiastic as Paul obviously still was?

So, on that mid-February evening at The Langan Hall, Patsy and I were creeping, hand in hand, along the edge of the wall in almost total darkness. I

Purcell Room, concert to launch the release of Kid In A Big World, February 1975

could see what I thought was the grand piano quite a way ahead, lit with an orange glow, like a mirage in a desert of darkness. I could hear the buzz of the packed room, the hum of anticipation, but there was nothing to light our way at all.

I'd made one attempt to navigate my way alone, but, without my glasses – which I never wore 'in public' at that time - everything in front of me was a blurred mush. I almost went arse over tit at one point when my foot caught one of the floor cables, Patsy and Stuart running forward to stop me falling.

"Hold my hand, John," Patsy said, "I'll lead the way."

"You sure, Patsy?" Stuart said.

"Yes, we'll be fine, Stuart. I'll get him there," and onwards we crept.

As we nervously and very slowly rounded a corner, Patsy whispered,

"Not far now, John."

I stared out myopically, as, suddenly, the place burst into applause. I must have looked like a frightened rabbit in the white spotlight which hit me full on, blinding me totally. Patsy didn't flinch. She kept hold of my hand and walked me to the piano. We stood together like some bizarre double-act, grinning out at the cheering mass of people.

"We made it," she said to me. "It's all yours now!"

I turned and bowed and made my way to the stool like a man reaching a life raft.

"Good evening," I said, "and for my next trick…"

The place rang out with laughter, and from then on I was home and dry.

I opened with 'Kid In A Big World', and I'd forgotten what a powerful live number it was, having not performed it on stage for eighteen months. When the applause had died down, I asked them,

"Are we having fun yet?"

"Yes," someone, maybe Paul, shouted. I certainly was.

After the show, there was a small drinks party in the foyer of the theatre. Dick met me as I walked in:

"John!" he shouted. "That was really great! What a performer!"

"Wasn't he great?" Stuart said proudly, beaming from Dick to me and back again.

"I can't wait for the next show!" Dick laughed, surrounded by a group of his employees who all agreed, nodded, and made enthusiastic noises at me.

I spotted Obie in a corner talking to someone, and, leaving Dick and his coterie to chat to Stuart, wandered over. He watched me approach, expressionless, nodding in his usual sage fashion. "Hi, John, how are you?" he said in his sing-song, octave-altering voice.

"Really well, thanks, Obie! Did you enjoy the show?"

"It was okay," he said.

Whether I physically stepped back a little, I don't know, but in my head I did. The look he gave me was one I came to know well. His eyes never told you a thing, they only prompted questions of yourself, doubts in your head.

"Quite a beginning," his companion said jovially.

I laughed,

"Oh, yes! Patsy and I used to be a comedy duo!"

There was no reaction.

"Not really," I said, but whatever joke there may have been had given up the ghost and disappeared into their apathy.

Paul Phillips' enthusiastic cry behind me was like a welcoming brandy in the cold.

"John! Fucking amazing!"

I wanted to hug him as he said to Obie:

"Wasn't he fantastic?"

"When's the next one, John?" was Obie's reply.

"The twenty-eighth," I said, trying to maintain a positive note in my voice. "I hope you'll be there!"

He smiled thinly and politely took his leave.

"Thank goodness it's Dick who's the Managing Director," I said to Paul.

"Oh, Obie rarely enthuses," he replied. "When he does, you'll know you've made it. Now! Your show! Fabulous, John! The songs, obviously, were great, but it was your *chat!* It was amazing! I had no idea."

The fact was, I'd always nattered to an audience, ever since I'd begun playing live at the age of seventeen. People often used to tell me after a gig that it felt as though I was talking to them alone, chatting in a small room. It was all part of what I loved about performing, the intimacy, the feedback of laughter and appreciation, which, on a good night, was tangible.

As soon as I'd signed to Stuart in the Autumn of 1973, we'd concentrated on recording demos, getting a record deal and making an album. Gigging was put on the back burner but I realised, talking to Paul, just how much I'd missed it the last year-and-a-half.

"I just say what comes into my mind," I said, as Stuart approached us.

"Well, do exactly the same at your Purcell Room show," Paul enthused. "It works, it really works!"

"It's what I saw the very first time I watched John perform," Stuart added. "He's the whole package."

I looked across at Obie and Dick in deep conversation, wishing I could be a fly on their wall.

As I walked into the foyer of The Purcell Room, I was met by two huge double-lifesize photos of me, placed on either side of the double-glass-doors. They had been taken during the recent session at Chappell's. One of them, taken after I'd clasped my face reacting to something Stuart had said, and Tom had told me, 'Do that again', displayed embarrassingly large bitten fingernails, and I resolved to try to stop the nasty habit.

Having made my way to backstage, and been greeted with numerous telegrams from family and friends, I stood in the wings as Dick announced me:

"The artist you're about to see, John Howard, is one of the most talented young singer-songwriters I have come across for a long time. His songs are amazing for a man still so youthful, his voice blows me away, his piano-playing makes many of his now-established contemporaries sound like amateurs."

"Way to go, Dick!" Stuart said quietly.

"John Howard is not a come-and-go singles artist, we don't expect instant hit records from John. He is an albums artist who we will nurture over time. Because I believe he has the capacity to be as big as Laura Nyro, to knock the glitter-socks off Elton John, and to remain one of our biggest-selling artists for years to come. Ladies and gentlemen, please welcome – John Howard!!"

I walked out on stage and was surprised by the fact that I could see everyone. The lights had not been dimmed, so there in front of me was a roomful of expectant applauding people. I could see my dad in the front row, looking concerned, and as I turned to the wings and walked to the piano, Stuart and Patsy were there. Two sets of parents, worrying about their boy out there on his own.

They needn't have worried. The forty-five minute show went without a hitch. I began with 'Family Man', and ended with 'Kid In A Big World', sandwiching some songs from the album in between, along with one or two newer ones no-one would yet have heard, such as 'Hall Of Mirrors' and 'Technicolour Biography'.

I also performed a very recent song, in fact I was still working on it but thought I'd try it out on stage, something I did a lot when I first started out performing at folk clubs in the early '70s:

"I am a big fan of Kiki Dee," I began my introduction, "and I used to love a song she recorded a few years ago called 'Excuse Me, Did

You Say Something?' I always wondered what her partner would have said back, and it gave me an idea for a kind of answer song – it's called 'Can You Hear Me OK?'"

The place erupted in laughter.

As I walked off the stage to the sound of loud applause and heartening cries of 'More!', I was met by Dick, who shook my hand but looked upset:

"No 'Goodbye Suzie', John!" he cried at me. "Why would you not sing that?"

The honest answer was that I considered it a flop, not just for me, but for CBS, so I thought I should move on from it. His absolute despair at me not performing it felt as though I'd personally broken his heart. Stuart, as usual, saved the day:

"Thing is, Dick," he said, stepping forward, "John writes so many great songs, so many, it's difficult to choose which ones to include in a forty-five minute show, and which ones to leave out. We felt he should showcase some of his newer material now."

Dick continued to shake his head and look disappointed.

'Black mark, Jonesey,' I thought.

It took me a while to walk from the theatre, out of the doors past those huge photos again, and round to the main Festival Hall, where we were to enjoy a grand buffet lunch in the glass-fronted foyer. All the way there, I was stopped by various people who'd seen the show and wanted to congratulate me, and to ask me about various songs I'd done. One of them, a tanned American chap called Mark, told me he was from the gay magazine, After Dark, and wanted to do a piece on me.

"You remind me, musically at least, of a guy called Barry Manilow," he said." Have you heard of him?"

I hadn't. (In fact, his first British hit, 'Mandy', entered the UK Top Thirty the following week). Mark continued to talk as we walked:

"I think your music will appeal to his fans. He has a growing following in the U.S. and I believe they would love what you do too. Your style of performance is very New York supper club. Perfect for my readers."

"Here's my number, Mark," Stuart said, ushering me along, "do call and we'll have a chat. Sounds great. Excuse us but -"

One of Stuart and Patsy's close friends, Charles, who I'd always rather fancied, then walked up to me, got hold of my hand, kissed it and bowed grandly. I did a mock 'Oh sir' fainting gesture and, with Stuart's persuasive hand on my back, moved into the mêlée of people gathering for lunch inside.

"Look at this, John!" Stuart said, staring at them all. "They are all here for you! Isn't that wonderful?"

In front of one of the floor-length windows, one of my biggest pop heroes was smiling at me. He walked up to me and shook my hand:

"Colin Blunstone, John," he said, without any need for introduction. I had all his albums at home. "That was absolutely fantastic!"

"Well, thank you, Colin! That's extremely flattering coming from you."

"I believe we're sitting together," he said, "shall we be seated? No-one will sit down until you do."

"Finally!" I declared, "I am *truly* royal!"

As we sat down, I looked around the room for my dad, who I still hadn't talked to. I spotted him deep in conversation with a chap I didn't know, and, catching his eye, I waved at him:

"Catch you later!" I mouthed.

"Okay," he mouthed back.

"A triumph!" Paul said behind me.

"Paul!" Colin shouted and shook his hand.

"Two geniuses together," Paul said happily, "what a great sight!"

My main memory of that joyous afternoon is of talking endlessly to lots of people, all of whom were introduced to me as from this magazine, that paper, this radio station, that record chain. I recall smiling people all around me, not least Stuart and Patsy who looked on top of the world. My only concern was that Tony Meehan wasn't there, obviously not invited. I made a mental note to call him, and take him a copy of the LP, the least I could do.

I finally got to talk to my dad towards the end, as people began to leave, and things were quietening down.

"Fabulous, my son," he said. "Fabulous! Your mum would have loved today."

"She's here in spirit, Dad."

I didn't believe that for a minute but it made him smile, as he squeezed my hand.

"Bloody great," he said. "My boy, eh?"

I was just pleased that he'd finally witnessed his son amongst peers and fellow professionals, at the top of his game, and hearing the applause and cheers as I stood and took my final bow.

I missed my mum proper for the first time that day. She would, as Dad had said, have loved it and she should have been there.

There is a coda to this story, which I only became aware of thirty years later...

...In early 2005, Paul Phillips was staying for a few days at our Pembrokeshire home. One evening, we were listening to *The Dangerous Hours* album, which I'd just completed. It finishes with the song which has become my oft-requested, personal gay anthem, 'Dear Glitterheart'.

As the final piano trill echoed into the distance, Paul looked at me and said,

"Great song. I wonder if Radio One would play that?"

I laughed,

"Well, they certainly wouldn't play my records thirty years ago, so I doubt it!"

Paul shifted in his seat, studying his glass of wine:

"I'm not sure whether to tell you this…"

"Well, now you have to!"

"Okay. You know why Radio One refused to play your records, don't you?"

"Because they didn't like them."

"Oh, it was much more complicated than that, John. It was because of the homophobia which ran through the station."

I stared at him, shocked. No-one had ever mentioned this to me before.

"No! Really? How do you know?"

"Well, first of all, there was a sense of that coming back with the radio pluggers, every time they took one of your singles down there, they had a feeling that you were not welcome at Radio One. There was a kind of instant dismissal as soon as producers saw your name on the label. But - and this is something I never told you at the time, I was scared it might upset you - I personally experienced it first-hand after your Purcell Room concert."

As I listened gob-smacked, he went on to tell me that, after my final song that afternoon, as the audience were applauding, he'd turned to the chap sitting next to him, one of Radio One's senior producers on the playlist committee.

"Isn't he amazing?" Paul had said to – well, let's call him 'D'.

'D' turned to him and, standing up very resolutely, said,

"Hmph! Well we won't be playing *him* at Radio One!"

"Why not?" Paul asked, mystified, as shouts of 'Encore!' and 'More!' rang round them. "I think he's going to be huge!"

"We'll see about *that*!" 'D' hissed and marched off.

A couple of weeks after my revelatory conversation with Paul, I was visiting Patsy at her Bournemouth flat, and told her what Paul had said. Her response took me even more aback:

"Oh yes," she said, "I had virtually the same reaction from 'D'. I was raving about you to him after your show, and he just dismissed me with a snort, saying 'There is no way we'll be playing any John Howard records at Radio One!'"

The irony was that, years later, 'D' came out as gay after inhabiting the closet into his fifties. I remember chatting to him after the show, and he was the perfect gentleman. I got no homophobic vibes from him at all. But I now wonder if my obvious 'gayness' sounded alarm bells in his head – "Keep away! Can't be seen to support *you*!".

It's all history now, of course, and even back then, there was nothing I could have done to change their minds, even if I'd known the true reason for my being blocked by Radio One. Once I knew the truth though, all those years later, I wrote 'My Beautiful Days' as a direct reaction to my conversations with Paul and Patsy:

> Look this way, John
> Turn your head
> Not so gay, John
> Not so come-to-bed
> Lick your lips, John
> They're looking dry
> Don't flick your hips, John
> Like that – from side to side
> Be yourself, John…
> Oh well, we tried
> Those were my beautiful days

There's a final acknowledgement in the song's lyric, that times have changed, and younger gay artists no longer suffer such bigotry from others in the music industry:

> Just look at Rufus
> He does his thing
> Garlands of rainbows

Everytime he sings
He tells it like it is
He's not afraid
These are his beautiful days

It's an acknowledgement which is bitter-sweet for me. I was 'Born Too Early', to quote another of my more recent songs.

In the early part of March '75, I demo'd some more new songs with Paul, when we did 'Lonely Woman (Where Are You?)', 'Just Waiting Here For You', 'Oh Dad' and 'Blink In The Darkness'. After recording the vocal for the last song, I made a mental note to ask Paul to let me really work on it, section-by-section, when we came to record the album itself. The choruses shoot up into the stratosphere, which, although Stuart was in seventh heaven every time I did it, even at twenty-one it was a hike vocally. I didn't want to repeat the dissatisfaction I felt every time I heard my January '74 Rome recording of 'Casting Shadows', where I hadn't been given the opportunity to fine-tune my vocal over a longer period.

Ironically, during the session with Paul, he asked me to demo a new version of that song:

"I haven't seen the movie," he explained as I made my way through to the studio, "so I haven't heard the song, but I'd really like to. Can you do a version for us this evening?"

'Hm,' I thought as I went to the mike, 'maybe I'll get a chance to do a better vocal if we record it for the album.'

A few days later, I also went across the road from Stuart's office in Denmark Street, to Regent Sound Studios, to do quick demos of 'Don't It Just Hurt', and 'Coconut Bible', which Stuart wanted on tape as soon as possible after I played them to him that morning. The lyrics were actually written three years earlier, when I was staying with a college friend in Sheffield in 1972. I'd recently read that Dylan often wrote lyrics on his typewriter, and wanted to try the method out, so banged away on my friend's old Olivetti for an hour or so while he was out.

It certainly gave a lyric a different quality than writing them by hand on a pad, the rhythm of the typewriter keys suggested the staccato edge of the words and rhymes one typed:

> When you're lost and alone
> 'Cause you can't hear the phone
> Ringing in the empty hall
> No-one wants to call you
> And your eyes they are ready
> For weeping
> No sleeping tonight
> Hard floor hurts your back
> Hard times hurt your pride
> Don't it just hurt?

So that was eleven songs I'd demo'd for the next album, and I was very excited when Paul called me at the end of the week to ask me to meet him at CBS, so we could discuss recording it.

Dick Asher was in the A & R Department when I arrived for my meeting with Paul. He was chatting to Dan Loggins and Obie:

"You've been recording some new material!" Dan said.

"Yes, I've demo'd some new songs, and now Paul and I are going to talk about recording the next album."

Dan beamed at me, Obie nodded sagely, Dick slightly shuffled on the spot:

"We gotta have some hit songs, John," he said, his eyes darting towards Obie. "Write me some hits!"

Obie continued to nod in agreement, and yet with a mild disinterest.

"Have you *heard* the new songs, Dick?" I asked him.

"Yeah, but we need some *hit* songs, John."

This was a new side of Dick for me. He was no longer benignly praising my talent, as he always had before, this was like a direct order from above. I'd up to that point blithely assumed that the company wanted me for who I was, a singer-songwriter they rated highly. Now it felt like I was there to do a job, a specific job, and one on which I had obviously fallen short so far. I hadn't felt 'employed' before, but suddenly I did. The tectonic plates at CBS had obviously shifted and I was shaken by it.

When I sat down with Paul in his office, I was, not for the first time, feeling a little confused and off-balance. His obvious enthusiasm refocused my mind a little:

"Okay," he said, getting his foolscap pad off his desk, full of scribbled notes against song titles. He smiled at me and nodded.

"Onto the new album!"

I sipped my coffee and waited:

"Right. I think the title should be *Technicolour Biography*." He checked for my reaction, and must have seen my eyes light up. "It's – for me – your greatest song so far, it sets the scene beautifully, and allows us to be very expansive in our considerations for backings and arrangements."

Over the next half an hour, I became, in spite of my earlier conversation with Dick, increasingly excited as Paul explained his ambitions for the LP:

"Your first album was great," he told me, "but this second one I truly believe is going to blow people's minds. You're writing such amazing songs now, John. For me they are head over heels better than the 'Kid' songs – and I *loved* those!"

He talked about the orchestral arrangements he'd planned for each song in great detail, how he wanted this album to have its own atmosphere, its own texture "which was obviously missing on 'Kid' because two producers and different studios were involved. We'll record this one at CBS Studios - which I know you love."

I nodded, taking a deep breath, just thinking about how terrific this album sounded already, weeks before it was even recorded! As I left, shaking Paul's hand, soaking in the sheer joy on his face, I nearly told him about my earlier worrying chat with Dick, but, not wanting to ruin the moment, decided not to.

As I walked down the corridor to the lift, questions rattled round my brain - Had Dick told Paul he needed "some hit songs" from me? And, if he had, was Paul so certain our album was going to produce a hit single, he had simply dismissed Dick's concerns as an unnecessary distraction. I didn't know the answers, and as the lift arrived and I got in, I wished I'd discussed them with Paul when I had the chance.

A few days later, Stuart and I had just got back to his office, when the phone rang. I'd just recorded a demo of another new song, 'The Deal' in Chappell's Studios and was particularly looking forward to playing this one to Paul. I had an idea for a gospel choir backing for it, and I felt that this one *could* be the hit song Dick hankered after.

I left Stuart to chat on the phone while I went into the next room to try out some more new song ideas.

A few minutes later, Stuart popped his head round the door with a whisky for me:

"That was Dick. He'd like us to join him for lunch tomorrow."

"Great!" I said, sipping on my iced amber nectar. "Do you know why?"

"Nope. He said there was something he wanted to discuss with us. He sounded very excited. We're seeing him at Les Ambassadeurs at one o'clock tomorrow."

On my way home that evening, the heavens suddenly opened. It poured down, and, without a brolly, I made a quick detour towards a record shop which I knew had a rather handy awning over the front window. It meant I could also have a look at what new albums they had in. As I reached my shelter from the storm, I stopped dead in my tracks. There, taking up almost the whole window, was an enormous cut-out display of my album sleeve. Around its base were several fan-outs of the LP and, arched over the top of the picture like a visual fanfare, the title and my name with the announcement 'Available Here Now!' in embossed gold lettering.

My eight-foot tall be-suited figure stood out from the picture, giving a 3D effect of 'the kid' literally leaning out to 'the big world'. I just stood and stared, taking it all in as the rain belted down behind me.

I contemplated going into the shop and offering to sign a few copies of the album, but thought that would, first of all, be rather presumptuous, and secondly, potentially embarrassing. I tried to subtly mimic my album sleeve pose, as though I'd noticed something up the street, hoping that one of the shop assistants might see me and call the owner over:

"Look! It's him! That Kid bloke."

"Who?"

"Him! The one in the window!"

No such luck. So, finally, I leaned against the wall and posed nonchalantly beside the window display, like I was waiting for someone to arrive. As people rushed by on their way home in the rain, I glanced at them, thinking one of them might stop and say,

"Ooh! That's you isn't it?".

Again, nothing. The rain eased, I took one last look at the window display, and trudged home.

The following morning, on the tube from Earl's Court into the West End for my lunch with Dick Asher, someone across from me was reading the latest New Musical Express, which I'd planned to buy later that afternoon. The page facing me made my heart leap. It was the ad for my album. The photo, taken at Chappell's piano showroom a few weeks earlier, stared out at me like a surreal reflection.

'Christ!' I thought, 'I'm everywhere!'.

I squinted to read the small print, but as hard as I tried, even with my glasses on, I could only just make out the headline: 'A *debut album from the fresh emotive talent of John Howard'*.

I waited, as calmly as I could, for him to turn his paper round, see the ad, look across, clock me and smile. Maybe even ask me for an autograph! Sadly, by the time I'd reached my stop, he was still buried in whatever article he'd been reading when I got on. I got up and went to the doors, glancing quickly around the carriage to see if anyone else had noticed the ad, but of course no-one had. Nobody looks at anything on the tube, except people's shoes and, when that gets boring, the ads above the seats. As the train moved off, I had one last look through the window. The chap was still reading his annoyingly fascinating article.

Walking into Les Ambassadeurs, six months after the abortive photo session there, it felt rather strange. I could see the beautiful winding staircase through the glass doors to our left, which I'd wandered up and down as Mike Nicholson had snapped away. As we went through to the restaurant bar, I recalled sitting there holding the exotic cocktail the barman had made for me, and Mike shouting "Perfect, John! Hold that pose!". I'd been so certain the photos would make a splash when they were published. I wondered now, would they ever be?

Dick was already there at the table and waved at us to join him. The three of us settled into our seats, ordered aperitifs, and chatted inconsequentially for a few minutes. The waiter brought our menus and drinks and silence briefly fell as we decided what to eat. As I was toying with having either Dover Sole or Lamb cutlets with mint, Dick murmured:

"So, John, you written any hits for me yet?"

I glanced at Stuart. As we'd walked across town to the restaurant, I'd not only told him about the shop window display and the NME ad, I'd also mentioned my recent unsettling conversation with Dick at CBS.

As I considered my reply, Stuart just raised an eyebrow but didn't look up from his menu. I took a sip from my vodka and tonic:

"I hope I have, Dick," I replied. "I'm writing a lot of songs."

"We need hits, John," he repeated, then turned to Stuart. "*You* know that, surely Stuart? You're a music publisher, you always need hit songs."

Stuart put down his menu, took off his reading glasses and, after pausing for just a moment, said,

"Dick, I seem to recall you saying, quite recently, publicly in fact, telling a roomful of people just before John's concert, that he was *not* a singles artist." He did a mock search in the air for the phrase. "You said, and I quote: 'John Howard is not a come-and-go singles artist, we don't expect instant hit records from John. He is an *albums* artist who we will nurture over time.'" I looked at Dick who was smiling into his white wine and soda and shaking his head. "Those were your exact words, Dick," Stuart continued. "So, in what feels like a very short period of time, what's changed your mind?"

When Dick looked up from his drink, his face no longer seemed quite so benign:

"What's changed my mind, Stuart, is the fact that *Kid In A Big World* is not selling." His voice had taken on a more steely tone, his eyes glinted like a guarded warning. "We've spent an awful lot of money on promoting it, an *awful* lot. We have now had two singles from it, both of which have stiffed. Radio One won't touch John. We have to change their minds, and soon. The next single *must* get on the playlist."

"But you've only just started marketing the album!" Stuart protested. "Only this morning John has seen evidence of that."

I took my cue and gabbled on about the display and the ad. Dick nodded and looked disconcertingly sad:

"And there's a lot more – a *lot* more – of that sort of thing around the country, John."

"So how can you give up so soon?" Stuart demanded. "It seems crazy, Dick!"

"You should know yourself, Stuart, those kinds of marketing spends are done weeks, months, before a release date, to build on an album which we're sure is going to be a big seller. But it's not, and it's unlikely to be, without a hit single, without radio play, with just one fairly negative review."

"It's had a review?" I asked.

"Yes, John, Disc and Music Echo were, I'm afraid, not impressed. 'Could do better' was the gist of it."

I made a mental note to buy a copy that evening.

"We shipped out fifteen thousand copies of the album first week of release, and we've already had half of those back – eight and half thousand unsold returns. Have you heard the expression 'Shipped Gold, Returned Platinum', John?"

I shook my head but smiled inwardly at the expression.

"Well, it's beginning to feel like that with your album. Every day, more returns, no re-orders. We've not even had support from local radio. -"

"Luxembourg played 'Goodbye Suzie'. A lot!"

"And did it sell, John? Did it chart? And you know how much I love that song. I was sure it was a smash."

He shook his head at the table.

"Sadly," he continued, "there's no way of rescuing the album now. It's over. Unless a miracle happens, but - as our artist Colin Blunstone sang on *his* great hit record - 'I Don't Believe In Miracles'. There are no more singles on 'Kid', that's for certain -"

"'Deadly Nightshade'!" I piped up. "That sounds really commercial to me. A couple of people at CBS have also said that."

Dick looked unimpressed but was, as ever, charming in his dismissal:

"It's a good album track, John, but it's not a hit record."

Stuart began repositioning the salt and pepper pots, and, looking across at me, said,

"So – what do you suggest, Dick?"

Without pausing for breath, Dick replied,

"We get Biddu to produce John."

I found it enormously ironic that, eighteen months earlier, Biddu had told Stuart he wanted to produce me but had been turned down because he 'wasn't a name producer'. Now, with a multi-million selling single ('Kung Fu Fighting') to his name, and a new artist deal of his own with CBS, he was the hottest ticket in town. The female singer he'd brought with him as part of his deal, Tina Charles, was also starting to create waves at radio with her first Biddu-composed single, 'You Set My Heart On Fire'. Events had played their part in finally bringing me together with, as Dick now put it, 'the man who can give John a hit record'.

"I've spoken to Biddu," Dick continued, "and he would love to do a record with John."

This, I could see, surprised Stuart. He was one of Biddu's closest friends in the music business, and yet he obviously knew nothing about any conversation between Bid and Dick. The fact it had also been about me, his artist, clearly embarrassed him. He looked over at me, and, rather quietly, said,

"John? How do you feel about it?"

As when Paul asked if I'd like to record with him a few months earlier, I was torn – on one side by loyalty to the producer I was working with, and on the other by the excitement of trying out something new with someone I'd not worked with before. Loyalty and ambition, never great bedfellows.

Paul was now plainly no longer in the frame and, apart from taking away someone who I trusted and enjoyed working with, that effectively put the brakes on what I'd thought was going to be my next album, *Technicolour Biography*.

With a sense of dread at the reply, I asked,

"What about the songs I've demo'd with Paul?"

I stupidly hoped Dick would at least um-and-ah a little. But, of course, he didn't:

"No hits there, John. Good songs, lots of good songs, but no hits. Right now, we need hooky, catchy pop songs from you. The ones you've come up with so far are just a continuation of what you did on 'Kid'. And, great though that was, it didn't work. It flopped."

Dick looked at me like a concerned father, talking to his wayward son.

"You need a guaranteed hit-maker, John. And Biddu is that guy. I still believe in you, but I need the rest of the company to not lose faith. Anymore flops and, well, they will."

The waiter came over and took our orders. I watched Dick looking completely at ease. He was handling what could have been a sticky situation extremely well, and he knew it.

"Look," he said to us both, taking a drink of his iced water, "let's take things step by step. How does this sound? Biddu produces a track or two with you first, John, before we commit to a whole album. See how you feel after working on those with Biddu, and if you're happy, if Biddu's happy, and we're happy, then let's move ahead and do the album!"

"Makes sense, Dick," Stuart said, glancing over at me. "If John agrees."

"Okay, let's do it," I said.

Our food arrived, and Dick lifted his glass to us:

"Here's to a hit record, gentlemen!"

The following day, I sat at the piano in Stuart's office, intent on writing 'a hit song'. I had a week to come up with something. At the back of my mind was the fear that, if the tracks I did with Biddu were not to Dick's or CBS's taste, what would happen then? Do two more with someone else, followed by another "No thanks,", until, finally, everyone gave up and I went home, deal-less, career-less, back at square one?

I began doodling round an E flat chord, getting a rhythm going. That naturally moved to an A flat over the E flat root, then into B flat staying on the E flat root, and back to E flat. It was very much the same formula Elton John had used on his debut hit 'Your Song', and a similar rhythm naturally developed. Without thinking about it, fairly meaningless words and a melody flowed out of my mouth:

> *Feel good*
> *Feel fine*
> *Feel the breeze*
> *Feel the sunshine*
> *No cares are worrying me*
> *I got you baby*
> *And you got me*

Stuart came running through from his adjoining office:

"What the fuck is that?" he shouted.

"It's pretty lame isn't it?" I said, my shoulders sinking under his glare.

"No! It's bloody great!" he shouted even louder. "Patsy! Where are you?"

She came dashing in from the kitchen:

"Listen to this, Patsy!" Stuart said, sitting her down. "John, play the song again."

I did and, when I'd finished, looked over at Patsy. She was smiling at Stuart.

"It sounds very commercial," she said, twiddling her tea towel in her hands.

"And that's great, isn't it?" Stuart stared at her, almost demanding she loved it.

"It's what CBS want," she replied.

"Do *you* like it, Patsy?" I asked her.

"It's a good song, John. But the chorus," she frowned, as though searching her memory, "hasn't that been done before? – 'I got you baby'?"

"Sonny and Cher," I replied. "One of my favourite records, 'I Got You Babe'."

"I'd change that, too similar, but, yes, it's a good song. Dick will love it!"

"We'll go to Bid's place tomorrow," Stuart said excitedly, "I'll ring him now, and you can play it to him, John."

I hadn't seen Stuart so animated about one of my songs for months.

"Feel good, feel fine, feel the breeze, feel the sunshine, no cares are worrying me, I got my lady and she got me," I sang to Biddu in his garage-cum-writing-room.

Reworking 'baby' into 'lady' had created my first heterosexual love song. I had always tried to avoid the boy/girl thing in my lyrics, as it obviously didn't ring true with me. I'd purposely kept things impersonal, sexless, using 'you/me' instead, or writing in the voice of a third-person fictional character, such as with 'Family Man'. The only time I'd written to a girl was in platonic songs such as 'The Flame', based on a poem for Pauline, my best friend at school, which I'd found in a 1969 diary; 'Lonely Woman (Where Are You?)' was an onlooker's observation of lonely men looking for comfort in the night:

> *Nightbirds*
> *Those nightbirds*
> *They pass like spoken phrases*
> *They just come and go*

As I trilled 'I Got My Lady' to Biddu, a wave of absolute positivity filled the room. By the time I'd reached the last chorus, I could hear him behind me clicking his tongue in a kind of calypso rhythm.

"That's really great, John," he said. "I think you may have written your first hit song!"

"Love the new line in the chorus, John!" Stuart said, patting me on the back. He turned to Biddu, "It used to be '*I got you baby*', but Patsy suggested John change that - "

"Too close to the Sonny and Cher song, yeah, makes sense, Stu. Okay! If you can demo that, John, I'll ask Gerry Shury, my arranger, to get to work on it. Have you got one more song, I'd like to record two if possible, an 'A' and a 'B'?"

On the spur of the moment I picked 'Frightened Now', one of the songs I'd recently demo'd at CBS with Paul. It had a strong hook, no matter what Dick thought about it, and although the lyric was much more introspective than 'Lady', reflecting how I was beginning to feel about what was going on with my career, I knew it was a really good song and I wanted Biddu to hear it:

> *I didn't think I'd have to cry so much*
> *To be an independent man*
> *To cancel out so many dreams*
> *I never knew the masks that could be worn*
> *To get a whole new range of friends*
> *You throw aside the man you knew*
> *And lie alone and wonder why*
> *Do you have to die before you start to live?*
> *Do you have to lie to have something to give?*
> *And does the laughter die when you've nothing left to give*
> *Except the question why - the all-time loser's gift?*
> *And I can't remember when I last said I'm alive*
> *And I'm frightened*
> *Really frightened now*

"What a fantastic song!" Bid said when I'd finished. "It's much too good for a 'B' side, but, maybe we've got two 'A' sides! Perfect! Demo that as well, John. And then we'll make our first record together!"

"At last, eh, Bid?" I said.

Biddu glanced over at Stuart:

"Yeah," he said, "everything comes to he who waits."

Chapter Twenty-Four

I Tried

"It's a Summer smash!" Dan Loggins cried.

We were listening to the tape of 'I Got My Lady', which Biddu had just sent round to Stuart's office so we could hear the final mix while Dan was with us for a 'get-together-lunch'.

Patsy occasionally put these on for people who Stuart wanted to keep on our side, during what felt an uncertain time in my career. They provided an intimate, relaxed, while private atmosphere, where no-one felt intimidated by a restaurant full of people, which probably included several music business insiders.

"It's a hit record, Dan," Patsy said, serving the salad and cheese board while Stuart poured out a crisp chilled white wine.

"Absolutely, Patsy!" Dan said, grinning over at me.

I was tempted to murmur "'Family Man' is a Christmas smash" but demurred, not wanting to add a sour note to a joyful afternoon.

"So, when will it be released?" I asked.

"July, August," Dan replied, sipping his wine, "early August probably, right at the height of summer. Perfect timing!"

"Great!" Stuart said, then, winking at Dan, "and I suppose this means that John and Biddu can continue recording the rest of the album together?"

"I would say definitely yes! I'll speak to Dick when I get back to the office, but yeah, why not? When you're on fire, keeping stoking it up!"

Recording sessions for the album were duly booked to start on the 22nd April. Biddu always used Nova Sound in Marble Arch, then owned by Tommy Steele. It was the same studio where we'd done 'I Got My Lady' and 'Frightened Now'. The only difference would be that Gerry Shury, Bid's usual arranger, who was now busy working on the forthcoming Biddu Orchestra project, was replaced by Pip Williams, who would step in for the remaining eight tracks to be recorded.

The word coming back from CBS was that they were really thrilled with the two tracks we'd done so far, and had a campaign already being planned for the release of 'I Got My Lady'.

"Dan says he's asked Capital Radio DJ Greg Edwards to do the promotion for the single," Stuart told me, handing me a whisky. "So that should mean we at least get Capital behind it. Dan's going to arrange a lunch with Greg nearer release date to go through the campaign."

There was a new feeling of zest around us, a definite sense that we were back on track with CBS, after several stop-start moments. The even better news was that Stuart had secured me a spot on a new BBC TV show, The Musical Time Machine, where I would perform the new single to a live audience. The theme of the show was pop music through the years, so each week they would have an evergreen major star headlining, a current British pop star, and a new face being tipped for stardom. Guess which one I was!

"You'll be sharing the bill with Johnny Mathis and Lynsey De Paul," Stuart told me after confirming the booking with the producer Stewart Morris. "Filming is in early July, so that will be great timing for the release of the single."

In preparation for the upcoming recording sessions, Pip Williams would visit Stuart's office every day over the course of about a week and sit with me while I played him my latest compositions. From those he'd pick the ones he liked the best. He'd then record them on his cassette player and go off to work on string arrangements.

The one he liked the most was 'Two People In The Morning', which I'd written after watching a TV play about a married couple whose relationship was breaking down. The only time they actually communicated was at breakfast, but even then they found it difficult to think of things to say to each other:

Two people in the morning
Thinking about what they're going to say next
Wishing that they still knew how to connect
But not bothering to try
It'd have no effect

Most of the songs had a romantic or post-romance feel to them. I'd purposely stayed clear this time of comedy observation songs like 'Family Man', 'Oh Dad', Glam camp things like 'Maybe Someday In Miami' and 'Guess Who's Coming To Dinner', or tragic story-songs such as 'Goodbye Suzie' and grandiose surreal-scenario tales like 'Technicolour Biography'. Although I was manufacturing a new mindset for these songs, I also think the fact that I was in the midst of my own happy-sad romance at the time helped me find inspiration for the songs. I'd recently become - rather unexpectedly - involved with someone who was due to leave the UK for South Africa quite soon. It certainly helped me to write first-hand about the various stages of a love affair, albeit a fairly short one, from start to finish.

I'd met Bry in The Coleherne pub in March and he'd told me during our first night together that he had to go back to Johannesburg by mid-April. So I knew our time together was limited, which naturally intensified feelings between us. It was a tempestuously passionate six weeks, where the elements of love and loss, both anticipated and experienced, played a big part in each day.

In the early stages of our relationship I wrote 'You Keep Me Steady' and 'You're Mine Tonight'. By the time Bry had left, songs such as 'Missing You' inevitably arrived. I also completed 'Can You Hear Me OK?' after it had been received so well during my Purcell Room show, and again it had a romantic theme.

Another song Pip was very excited about was originally called

'Love', but I changed it to '19th September' as a tribute to my mum, who had died on that date the previous year. It wasn't about Mum per se, but the lyrics could have been both about Bry as well as my complicated feelings about losing Mum so early:

> I take time
> To really see what you see in me
> I'm just a man
> I had plans that died
> But now I can stand the tide
> With your love
> 'Cause oh your love
> Keeps me alive
> Now there's a seed
> You'll give it life
> Oh my love

"That one is going to have such a beautiful string arrangement! I promise!" Pip said when I played it to him. "Fucking lovely John!"

There was only one slightly barbed song in the selection, and while lyrically it didn't fit with the rest of the album, Pip was insistent we record it. 'Finally Adored' was written after I'd re-read a 1965 interview with John Lennon, from amongst my many clippings of articles on The Beatles. It was during what he later called his 'fat Elvis period', and he'd said, "Look at me, I'm rich, I'm famous, I've got everything I ever dreamed of, and nothing is happening!":

> Baby though you've probably made it
> You've still got to lose at least seventeen pounds
> Your photos deceive
> You look thin but you're round
> Your true-story scandals are not written down

Baby though you're finally adored
You can't believe it but you're bored
Just tell your doctor you're unsure
And so alone

True to his word, in early April, Mark from After Dark magazine arranged a photo shoot for me in preparation for the article he was planning to write. Patsy came with me, helping me carry various outfits up a narrow flight of stairs. The building, situated behind Oxford Street, was, as usual in that area, fairly seedy from the outside. But when we entered the studio, it was clean and brightly lit, and already set up with several large lamps concentrated on a Biba-esque leopard-skin cushion and different textured backgrounds against the walls. It looked very art deco. Sam, the photographer greeted us as we set the outfits down on a chaise longue by the door.

After Dark Magazine photo session, 1975

"This looks nice, Sam," Patsy said, looking round.

"Well, Mark said you were very Glam and chic," he replied, looking me up and down dismissively as I stood there in my old T-shirt and faded black jeans, "so I thought this kind of setting would fit that."

He stared at me again and went to the outfits we'd draped over the settee:

"Okay, what have we got here...? Hm, a couple of suits, yes, and some nice Oxford bag trousers...we can try those...but I'd like to see if I have anything a little more..."

He wandered out mumbling to himself and came back a few minutes later with a couple of white sweaters and various coloured tops, which, on my eight-stone frame, were all voluminous. He studied me, looked disappointed and rushed out again. Back he came with some safety pins and proceeded to pull one of the sweaters tight around me and pinned it in place:

"Christ! You're so skinny! Are you in there somewhere?" he joked, but still with that odd disappointed tone in his voice. "Okay, stand there...yes...hands on hips... look straight at the camera...great!"

He took a Polaroid, and, as it slid out, he looked at it, checked the lighting on me again, changed his camera to a much more impressive model, and he was off, snapping away for about ten minutes as I posed, pouted, looked over my shoulder, laughed, looked serious, looked moody, and did my best to 'be louche', 'be Glam', 'be like Bowie'.

He then asked me to change into my velvet suit, and to lie on the leopard-skin cushion. Another Polaroid, more lighting changes, another camera and then Snap! Snap! Snap!, as he called out 'look beguiling!', 'look glamorous!', 'imagine you're Marlene!', 'imagine you're Jerry Hall!' for the next ten minutes.

As we got ready to leave, I asked Sam if I could have the two Polaroids to keep. He gladly gave them to me, promising the photos would be sent to Mark who would choose the ones he wanted for his article.

I stepped out onto the street, telling Patsy I felt like I'd let Sam down.

"Don't be silly, John, you looked lovely," she replied. "Let's go for some lunch."

I never knew if the article was written or published as we didn't hear from Mark again. Certainly I didn't anyway. All I have from that unsettling photo session are the two Polaroids. If anyone remembers seeing anything on me in a 1975 issue of After Dark, do let me know!

CBS 'moved house' around Spring 1975, from Theobalds Road to the much swishier Soho Square. This was very handy for me as it was literally across the road from Stuart's office in Denmark Street. One evening, as I was working on some new songs, a girl called Sally in the press office called to ask if I'd like to visit the new building:

"Come and see our new home," she said brightly, "it's fantastic! You'll love it, John!"

I popped round the next afternoon, and, giving my name to the receptionist, took the lift to the fourth floor where I was met not by Sally but by her boss, Dave. We exchanged pleasantries as he walked me round the impressively spacious Press and Promotions floor, everyone waving and shouting "Hi, John!" from their work stations as I wandered by. Finally, we reached his huge glass-walled office and, pouring me a coffee, he sat on the corner of his desk:

"John," he began, "tell me something. Why has your manager turned down a middle-page spread I got you in Melody Maker?"

I was gob-smacked as I'd heard nothing about it.

"Stuart turned it down?" I asked, bewildered

"He did! A whole *middle page spread*, an in-depth article on you, including an interview." He shook his head and stared at me. "Why would he turn that down?"

I was searching my head for something to say.

"Hasn't he told you?" Dave asked, surprised.

"No! I am -" (the truth was I was devastated) "- puzzled to say the least."

"I've fought for weeks to get this, John, been working on them, bringing them round to the idea, telling them how amazing you were at The Purcell Room, bigging up your album, your image, your talent. Finally, I get a call *from the editor* saying he would very much like to do a piece on you. Middle page spread!! I call Stuart to give him the fantastic news and, cool as anything, he just says 'The timing's not right, maybe later.' I mean, fuck, John! What the *fuck*?! What *is* his agenda?"

"All I can promise, Dave, is that I'll speak to him about it. I want to know myself anyway!"

When I walked into Stuart's office the next morning, I was ready for a battle. He was as bright and breezy as always, offering me a coffee, but could see something was bothering me:

"What's wrong, mate?" he asked.

I told him what Dave had said the previous afternoon, ending with, "How could you turn such an opportunity down, Stuart? Why?"

He looked at me, smiled and motioned me to sit down. I realised then that I was virtually standing on my toes opposite his desk.

Stuart took a moment while I sat down, and then began:

"The timing isn't right, John. Dave's correct, that's exactly what I said." I got ready for another rant. But Stuart held up his hand. "But! *But!* What he obviously didn't tell you was that I explained to him, in much more detail, exactly *why* I turned it down." He took off his reading glasses, always a sign he'd thought something through before saying it. "Look. If Dave had brought us that article -"

"And interview!" I interrupted.

"And interview – when 'Goodbye Suzie' or *Kid In A Big World* was about to be released, I'd've jumped at it. Great promotion! The best! But what have we got to promote at the moment?"

He looked at me and waited for the light to come on.

"That's right. Nothing. Dick has already told us your album is gone, finished, no more promotion, no more singles, as if it never happened. CBS have no interest in it any longer. So why promote that?"

I nodded. It made sense.

"However," he went on, "you are now working with Biddu, one of the hottest names of the moment, and your next single is due out in about three months. So, let's wait till then! New single, new album just completed with Biddu producing – perfect! What a story! It's all about timing, John, and I'm afraid, while I admire Dave's tenacity, it's too late – or too early, depending on which way you look at it."

My weapons were quietly put away, the battle was cancelled.

"We'll get our moment, John," Stuart said, "but it has to be the right moment. I'm sure when Dave goes back to Melody Maker when 'I Got My Lady' is climbing the charts and CBS is raving about your forthcoming new album, they'll be even more keen to interview you – along with Sounds, NME and Disc. Now, how do you want your coffee?"

It wasn't only CBS moving home at this time. I left my Earl's Court flat for a much more spacious semi-detached house in Norbury, a short train ride out of central London. It was owned by Daniel, who Bry had introduced me to. He was one of a small circle of friends based in the South London area, who, after Bry had gone back to S.A., became staunch allies of mine, and in fact I am still in touch with a couple of the guys today.

When I'd first met them, they'd all viewed me rather suspiciously, mainly because Bry's long-term boyfriend, Cliff, a great friend of theirs, was waiting for him to return to South Africa. Bry had extended his time in the UK so he could be with me for a little longer, telling Cliff he had "something to attend to". I was that "something" and regarded as 'the little hussy' in their eyes, persona non grata.

However, once Bry had left, I became the 'abandoned one', and the group literally folded itself round me. For the first time since I'd moved to London, in fact for the first time in my life, I had a proper social circle of gay friends.

The oldest guy in the group, Terry, seemed to take me under his wing and began inviting me to his home near Wandsworth Bridge for weekend group get-togethers, where we'd all eat, drink, spend all afternoon chatting and scoffing hash cakes. In the evening, high as kites, we'd go clubbing until the early hours, giggling at anything and everything around us. We'd have a dawn breakfast at Up All Night, an eaterie in Fulham, and crawl back to Terry's where there was usually an empty bed for me in the basement.

One evening, I was enjoying a whisky and dry, which Terry had recently turned me onto, when Bob, who lived on the first floor of the house, came and sat with me. I was surprised as he'd been the coolest towards me up to then, hardly even acknowledging me.

"Terry played me your album yesterday," he said.

"Oh! What did you think?"

"Well, what I said to Terry, after he'd played just one track was, 'I fucking *hate* you!'"

I laughed, a little disconcerted. Did he mean me or Terry?

"I wanted to *loathe* it," Bob continued, "you were 'the other guy' messing about with my best friend's bloke, while Cliff was stuck in S.A. waiting for Bryan to come back. But, as soon as 'Goodbye Suzie' had finished, I knew – I fucking *loved* it! You fucking bitch!"

He made a 'cat hiss' gesture at me and giggled.

"You called him 'Bryan' just now," I said, a little puzzled.

"Yeah."

Terry overheard our conversation and hurried over, nudging Bob as he squeezed in next to him.

"Okay. Tell all," he said. "What did Bry tell *you* his name was?"

"Brylance," I replied. "Brylance Barrett Ford."

Bob and Terry stared at each other and burst out laughing.

"Brylance Barrett Ford??!! Fuck me! It's even better than the last one!"

Feeling myself going scarlet and wondering if I should go on...I went on:

"Brylance Barrett Ford, The Third."

The two of them stared at me, mouths open, and howled with laughter.

Through fits of giggles, Terry said,

"His name is Bryan, darling! Plain old Bryan Ford. Jesus, that guy and his stories!"

"So..." – Oh God, I thought, feeling my face burning – "the story about his grandfather – Brylance Barrett Ford, The First - coming from Boston, Massachusetts is - "

"Oh my dear!" Terry screeched, standing up and stamping his foot. "I can't stand it! His family is from *Streatham*, darling! The nearest his family have ever got to Massachusetts was listening to the fucking Bee Gees! I've met his grandfather. He is pure 'sarf Larndon', love! Wouldn't know Boston from Bolton."

Daniel heard the commotion and ran over to join us, wide-eyed and laughing.

"Is this Bry again? Telling porkies?"

I ploughed on, actually beginning to enjoy the attention and the shared laughter, albeit while realising what a gullible queen I'd been:

"He told me his grandfather's family is famous in America, art collecting millionaires, and that when his granddad died he left the money to his son, who moved his family to London just before Bry was born."

Bob just kept staring at me in disbelief:

"You actually believed all this tosh?!"

"Why wouldn't I? I never met any of them."

"His granddad worked at a printer's down the road from here, Bryan's dad's a railway porter!"

Terry squeezed my arm, "Don't worry, love, he told similar porkies to Cliff when they met -"

"But Cliff just laughed at him!" Daniel shouted.

"Unlike stupid little me," I said, staring into my glass.

Bob stroked my arm as one would a wounded animal.

"Amazing what a huge cock does for you!" Terry said. "Makes a queen believe anything!" He mimicked screwing a guy, "My dad's worth millions, my dad's worth millions, oh fuck I'm coming!!!"

"He's not a bad lad," Bob added, "just desperate to big himself up."

"Well," I said camply, "he actually had no problem doing that!"

We all shrieked as one, and a friendship was sealed.

Working with Biddu over the next couple of months, April to June, was a strange experience. The musicians were all session men who he used on everything he recorded, Tina Charles tracks, The Biddu Orchestra, and several other artists he was producing. So, although Biddu was, as always, the perfect gentleman, there was a kind of conveyor belt atmosphere during the sessions, as though I was just one of many artists in the line of sessions these guys had been block-booked for over the coming months. I hadn't noticed it so much when we'd done the first two tracks, but those were very concentrated, isolated sessions, done over a couple of days.

However, over the next eight weeks, recording the rest of the album with Biddu, something changed. Maybe simply working with a producer who was fast becoming CBS's Next Big Thing had created a new imbalance between us.

During the Abbey Road sessions with Tony and the Apple recordings with Paul, both producers consulted with me one-to-one, sitting with me, asking what I wanted from the songs, discussed ideas with me. I'd also had a small close-knit group of musicians, who seemed to truly want my tracks to sound amazing. One felt they were there to help achieve that, we worked as a team. It was extremely collegiate.

During the Biddu sessions, there was no interaction between the musicians and me, they were jobbing session men, who sat down, read the dots, played the notes, quick chat about the weekend, and onto the next one.

There was one point during the recording of the second or third track, I think it must have been 'You Keep Me Steady', when I became aware of the drummer and bass player, who were sitting to my left, chuckling at each other. The drummer began adopting a monotonous cabaret style, and the bassist followed suit, doing mock jazz runs. I glanced round and they were mugging at each other, doing a 'ain't we cool, man?' thing like silly kids. Thankfully, Pip Williams noticed it too. At the end of the take, which he attended from start to finish during all the sessions, not just the string overdubs, the door from the control room swished open and Pip stormed over to the musicians:

"You cut that out right now," he shouted at the drummer and bass player. "If I see you behaving like that, sending up this song once more, you're out, gone! I'll get two guys in who can play you both out of this fucking room. Real professionals! Now buck up, calm down, and treat John with the respect he deserves. Play the song properly or, I'm warning you, you'll never work for me – or Biddu – again!"

He put his hand on my shoulder and said quietly,

"You okay, John?"

I nodded and smiled at him.

"Good," he said, then to the band, "now, guys, another take, and play your fucking hearts out. This is a *great* song!"

I turned round as Pip returned to the control room, and saw him pointing at the two musicians he'd just barracked, and making his case loud and clear.

Pip's lambaste obviously had the desired effect, the next take sounded great, declared 'That's the one!' by Biddu over the intercom.

The next morning, I arrived at the studio a few minutes before ten o'clock. Biddu was there, Richard Dodd, the engineer was setting up the tape, and Pip was chatting to Stuart and Patsy.

"Hi guys!" I said, taking off my coat. "Let's make some music!"

"John," Biddu said sternly, "the session may start at ten but I expect *you* to be here by a quarter-to at the latest. We're all here for you, musicians ready to go, and I expect you to be here for us, in good time to start dead on ten o'clock. Time is money."

The room fell quiet, Stuart went a little red, but I didn't argue. This was Biddu's regime, his timetable, his method, he was the producer, and fast becoming an extremely successful one.

"Okay, Bid," I said. "Understood."

"'Two People In The Morning' next!" Pip said brightly, trying to lift the atmosphere. "Go knock 'em dead, John!"

"Would you like a glass of water, John?" Patsy said, looking concerned.

"After we do this song, Patsy, thanks very much!" I replied, blinking at her.

Pip's overdubs onto the tracks were a delight. For 'You're Mine Tonight' he asked Richard to slow the tape down to half-speed, recorded a finger-picking guitar figure which, when the tape was brought back to normal speed, sounded like a brilliantly played harpsichord. I loved the '60s style of that kind of thing, not unlike what George Martin had done on piano for the instrumental break in Lennon's 'In My Life' on *Rubber Soul*.

Onto 'Two People' and 'Missing You', he overdubbed beautiful sitar parts, reminding me of some of The Stylistics' records. In fact, Pip said he was trying to get a very Thom Bell sound on all the tracks.

On 'Play Me A Love Song' - which I'd actually written during a lunch break a few days earlier - he played some fabulous Spanish guitar, totally changing the texture of the track.

His string arrangements were truly gorgeous. Overdubbed in two days, the orchestrations blew me away. Apart from the sweeping filmic sound on 'You Keep Me Steady', Pip had put in lovely touches like piccolo trumpet – a la 'Penny Lane' – at the beginning and middle of 'Two People', a harp motif on 'Finally Adored' and 'Missing You', a lovely solo violin and flute on 'Can You Hear Me OK?' and oboe parts on 'You Keep Me Steady' and 'Finally Adored'.

But it was Pip's orchestral arrangement on '19th September' which gave me shivers down my spine. When I'd demo'd it with Pip, I'd started the song with no intro, playing one chord and going straight into the vocal. Pip had scored a sumptuous, almost classical short piece of music which he asked Richard to edit onto the start of the track. It announced the song and its lyric beautifully. As he'd promised, he hadn't let me down at all. When I heard it, I returned the compliment he'd given me when I'd first played the song to him in Stuart's office:

"Fucking lovely, Pip!"

Then it was time for me to do the final set of vocals for the eight songs. I'd expected this to take a couple of weeks but we sped through them at an alarming rate. There was a sense we were running out of time as I recorded three vocals a day, straight through, hardly any drop-ins, retakes or double-tracking, no harmonies or backing vocals. Again, this was so different to how Biddu had approached 'I Got My Lady'. Those sessions had felt much more intensive and in-depth, Biddu and I overdubbing double-tracked backing vocals together, my lead vocal doubled as well as me dropping in the lines I felt I could do better.

But now, going through vocal after vocal, I felt rather like some 'hired-for-the-day' session singer. There were a couple of vocals I did where, on long phrases, I ran out of breath. I would have loved to redo those lines, but it was very much "Next!" rather than "Okay with that, John?". I can still hear my lungs struggling to get enough air to finish a phrase properly on those tracks, and it drives me crazy every time I hear them. Just one or two drop-ins would have sorted it.

The final vocal I did, however, was probably my favourite. Pip's astonishing string arrangement on '19th September' was an utter delight to sing to, and even I had trouble not breaking up hearing those incredible cello and violin lines sweeping into my cans. When I'd finished, I went into the control room to find Patsy in floods of tears.

"Nothing like making someone cry to help you find out something's a hit!" Pip said.

"Oh John!" Patsy said, wiping her eyes, "that was so gorgeous!"

"Hit record!" Pip reiterated.

"*Lady*'s the first single," Bid said.

"This one should be the follow-up then," Pip replied. "There won't be a dry eye in a million houses!"

In early June, Stuart, Patsy and I were invited to a CBS function to bid a fond goodbye to Dick Asher, who was leaving the London office to become Chairman at the Columbia Head Office in New York. The rumour we'd heard was that his replacement would be Obie.

"If that's the case," I told Patsy, "then I predict I will be dropped from the label by the end of the year."

"Oh, I don't think so, John!" Patsy replied. "Not now you're recording with Biddu. He is such a big star at the label, they really love him. You're in his camp now. Things will be fine."

"And with Dick running the US office," Stuart added, "Obie would have to answer to him. I'm sure Dick will have our back regardless. He absolutely loves you, John."

It was a glittering occasion, everyone there to say farewell to their boss of many years. As I made my way through the crowds of people, I noticed David Essex and his wife and went over to say hello. We were chatting about who we thought would be taking over from Dick, when, from behind me:

"Woof!"

I turned round to see a beaming Derek Witt, extending his hand:

"Woof Woof!" he shouted, grabbing my hand with both of his. "You look ravishing, John! Doesn't he David?"

"Very smart indeed," David said, doing a theatrical little bow.

Derek continued to stare at me. I felt like a work of art in a gallery. I had a new swept-back hairstyle which my landlord Daniel had given me:

"You gotta look like a star tonight, girl," he'd said, as he crimped and combed, cut and blow-dried his creation in the kitchen, finishing off with enough hairspray to withstand a gale.

I knew I looked good, but I hadn't expected such a reaction. I'd only briefly chatted to Derek at the CBS conference the previous August but hadn't seen him since then. He'd been due to attend my Purcell Room Show, which he'd apparently personally organised, but he was too poorly on the day to get there.

"I never thanked you, Derek," I said, "for arranging my show. It was a great day!"

"I heard that. People told me you were wonderful."

"Well, thanks very much for all your hard work. It went like clockwork."

"You can thank me by joining me on my table this evening! I'm sure Stuart and Patsy won't mind." He smiled as we saw them walking towards us, and moved forward to shake Stuart's hand and give Patsy a full-on "Woof!". She visibly flinched but Derek was undeterred. "You wouldn't mind if John sat with me this evening, would you, Patsy? Stuart?"

Patsy looked slightly put out but smiled, as if at an annoying child:

"If John's happy," she looked at me, and I nodded, "then so am I!"

Sure enough, Obie was announced, by Dick himself, as the new Managing Director of CBS UK. After Dick's rather moving and voluble speech about his "wonderful years working with my London friends", Obie, very quietly, simply said thank you to Dick, who grabbed him in a huge bear hug, and waved at the applause which swelled round the room. The two men shook hands, posed for photos, and we carried on applauding. As I smiled along with everyone else, I knew that things would now be a-changing, not least, I presumed, for me.

Two or three weeks later, Dan, Biddu, Stuart, Patsy and I were sitting in a busy basement West End restaurant, waiting for Greg Edwards to arrive. The lunch had been arranged so that we could all discuss my forthcoming single, on which Greg was going to act as freelance product manager. Dan chatted to Biddu about the album he was recording, while Stuart, Patsy and I tried to keep our cool, as the room got warmer and Greg got later. Finally, after half an hour, Greg arrived down the stairs:

"Hey! I am sorry to keep you guys waiting!" he shouted as he came over and, beaming at each of us, shook our hands. "I've had one hell of a morning!" he yelled as he settled down in the vacant seat at the head of the table.

For the next hour we listened to Greg's litany of anecdotes. Amusing as they were - and *how* we all laughed - I wondered if we'd ever get round to talking about the single. He and Biddu seemed to hit it off immediately, but Greg was more interested in discussing Bid's own upcoming release, his orchestral take on the theme song from the movie *Summer of '42*.

"I call my sound Blue-Eyed Soul," Biddu was telling Greg.

"You're kinda the new Barry White!" Greg replied, obviously thrilling Bid. "That record is a hit, Biddu!"

Finally, Stuart took the reins:

"So, Greg, what kind of promotion do you intend to do for John's record? As you know, Biddu produced it."

It briefly rebalanced the conversation towards what we were there to discuss.

"Oh, we'll get it to all the radio stations! I'll give it my full backing, they will be *convinced* I love it!"

"And do you?" Patsy chipped in briskly.

"It's a great summer song!" Greg laughed, "There's always room for a summer song!"

"A summer *smash*!" Dan added meaningfully, beaming around the table.

When the lunch finally ended and Greg had bid his jovial farewells, disappearing back up the stairs, I had the definite feeling we would not hear from him again. And we didn't.

"John?" Stuart said to me, as I sat in my dressing room at BBC Television Centre, "Stewart Morris has had a word with me about your performance. He's asked if you can take some of the feyness out of it."

The day had begun so well. I'd arrived at the TV studios on that early July afternoon with Stuart and Patsy. We were there to film my sequence in the forthcoming Musical Time Machine show, where I'd perform my upcoming new single. Hosted by Vince Hill, who had greeted us as we arrived, it was a new series the BBC had high hopes for.

As we arrived, Derek Witt eagerly bid us good day with a loud "Woof!" and whisked me into Johnny Mathis's dressing-room.

"Johnny?" he said, standing aside and pushing me forward, "This is our new artist, John Howard. He'll be on the show as well."

"John-John!" Johnny said, "Is this your first TV?"

"Yes, it is."

"Then you'll be wanting some of this lovely champagne! CBS paid for it! Thank you, CBS!" He laughed at Derek. "We're both artists of theirs, so why not?" Derek poured the sparkling nectar into my fluted glass. "Cheers!" Johnny said, as we all supped and looked bubbly-eyed.

"I'd like a photograph with the two of you!" Derek said, "Where's Tom?"

A few minutes later, Johnny and I were standing at the stage door, as CBS photographer Tom Sheehan snapped away.

"My people!" Derek said proudly. "Two CBS artists across the generations, wonderful!"

"Is he calling you an old crock, John-John?" Johnny joked as Vince Hill arrived to join us.

"And now *three* CBS artistes!" Derek cried. "Even better!"

More photos, more grinning from ear to ear, and then we were back inside ready for a run-through of the show before the audience arrived that evening.

"Lynsey De Paul is in this room," Derek said, as he led us briskly along the corridor, knocking on the open door. "Knock! Knock! Lynsey?"

"Derek!" Lynsey shouted, running over to hug him.

She was extremely tiny and porcelain-doll-like pretty.

"Lynsey, this is John Howard, he's also performing on the show."

"John!" Lynsey said, shaking my hand. She studied me as I grinned at her. "Now! How would you like to choose my hairstyle for the show?"

"Love to!" I said, and followed her to the dressing-room mirror.

Lynsey stared at me in the glass, fiddling with her hairbrush and posing two different looks for me:

"I can't decide whether to have my hair curled in," she brushed her flowing, golden tresses inwards, "or out!" The brush did its work again. "In?" Brush-brush. "Or out?" Brush-brush. "What do you think, John?"

"I like it curled inwards," I said, "it's very coquettish."

"I agree, John," Derek said joyfully.

Lynsey camply winked into the mirror and clapped her hands:

"In it is, then! Fabulous! Thank you, John!"

Derek whisked me out again, along the corridor and into my own dressing–room. Stuart and Patsy were already there, enjoying hearing about all the attention I was getting from major pop stars.

"Quite right too!" Stuart laughed. "Thank you for looking after John, Derek."

"Always a pleasure, Stu!" Derek shouted.

"Okay, Derek," Patsy said, "John really needs to prepare now, so thank you very much for all you've done. We'll see you later."

He took his glaring cue and, with a wave at the door, left the room.

"That man exhausts me," Patsy said, laying out my outfit and various prettying-up accoutrements in front of the mirror.

A knock at the door, a man with headphones round his shoulder popped his head in:

"John? Can we have you on the floor in ten?"

"Certainly!"

The first thing I noticed, as I walked onto the bright yellow and orange set, was a Christmas tree to my left. Its multi-coloured lights and silver tinsel twinkled and looked very jolly, but it all felt rather odd when it was in the high 70s outside. However, my attention was quickly refocused on the job in hand when one of the cameramen asked me to sit at the piano:

"Is this your first TV?" he asked, walking round me.

"It is," I said, as I settled myself.

"Okay. Well, first of all, don't be nervous. The camera never lies. And one word of advice, don't follow me with your eyes as I walk round you. Just look out to the audience and pretend I'm not here."

I heard the orchestra leader shout,

"We're in on four, John!"

He counted four beats very loudly, the orchestra and I began right on cue together and we were off.

Feel good, feel fine
Feel the breeze
Feel the sunshine...

All the while those Christmas Tree lights sparkled merrily over my left shoulder.

When I finished the song, Lynsey came rushing over and hugged me:

"I was watching you from the wings," she cried. "You were lovely! I can't believe this is your first TV! Is that your own song?"

"Yes, my next single."

"Fantastic," she said.

"Lynsey?" The floor manager called over. "You're on next. Take your positions everybody!"

I stood in the wings this time watching her perform her hit from the previous Christmas, 'No Honestly'. It was a flawless performance. She looked completely at ease.

Then it was Johnny's turn. I was surprised to see him arrive dressed in a long red Father Christmas gown. As he stood for the camera-positioning, tinsel and false snow was thrown around the floor and at his feet.

"In four Johnny," shouted the floor manager, counting him in on his fingers.

'Winter Wonderland' blasted out around the studio, as Johnny smiled and crooned the seasonal favourite. He followed that with his evergreen hit, 'Misty'. My parents had it on a single when I was a toddler, and his voice was still as smooth as honey twenty years later.

We all applauded from the wings and then were ushered back to our dressing-rooms by a smiling lady with a clipboard. I heard Patsy asking her, "Is this a Christmas show?"

"Yes," she answered. "Isn't it lovely?"

My concern faded as I entered the dressing-room. Laid out on a large trestle table by the door was a beautiful buffet of sandwiches, various salads, crisps, desserts, and a large choice of different fruit juices. We all ploughed in, filling our plates.

"This is okay, eh, John?" Stuart said, munching away on a smoked salmon sandwich.

"It's great!" I said, "Everyone is so lovely."

"Showbiz people usually are, the nice ones anyway!"

"This is the Christmas edition!" Patsy said, joining us.

"Seems so, darling. Never mind. It's still great TV exposure for the single!"

"If a little late," Patsy said, chomping on a piece of celery.

Tucking into the fabulous grub, I saw a breezy chap pop his head in and asked Stuart to go and have a quick word with Stewart Morris.

"There's no problem is there?" Stuart asked him.

"No, no! Just a quick chat!".

Stuart disappeared as Patsy and I sat down to enjoy our tiramisus.

Ten minutes later, Stuart returned, looking mildly concerned:

"Stewart Morris has asked me, John, to have a quick word with you. When you do the actual filming this evening, he has asked if you can take some of the feyness out of your performance."

"Feyness?!" Patsy said, putting down her emptied plastic bowl. "John was perfect out there!"

"Yes, darling I thought so too, but Stewart has seen the rushes and says the camera has highlighted how John moves his head about rather a lot. He thinks it looks fey. Cameras have a propensity to exaggerate some idiosyncrasies..."

"John's too young to have idiosyncrasies!" Patsy said. "You and I have them, but not John, not yet!"

Stuart sighed heavily:

"Don't shoot the messenger, darling. I'm only passing on what the producer of this show has suggested John do, to be more televisual."

Patsy harrumphed:

"How very silly of him," she said, pressing the plunger down the cafetiére rather aggressively. "Coffee, John?" she said, ignoring Stuart.

When I performed the song for the live audience that evening, I made a conscious effort to keep my head still, looking straight ahead into my myopically blurred view of the studio. As the orchestra played Gerry Shury's arrangement perfectly, I felt an incredible surge of confidence. I was in my comfort zone once again, performing to a live audience. The applause at the end of the number was genuinely warm as I nodded a thank you at them.

Feeling very happy with how it had gone, I walked back to my dressing-room where I was greeted at the door by a beaming Lynsey De Paul:

"Brilliant," she said, "I watched you on my monitor! Such a pro!"

"Lovely, John," Patsy said, squeezing my arm, "and not a head move anywhere!"

"Aren't you allowed to move your head?" Lynsey asked conspiratorially.

"Not if you're a male performer on a BBC show, apparently," I replied.

"Have you *seen* the dancers on this show?" she laughed. "Try telling *them* that!"

The Young Generation were, as we spoke, strutting their stuff for the cameras, their spinning heads bopping all over the place.

I'd settled down to watch the rest of the show on my monitor, when the girl with the clipboard tapped on the open door.

"John?" she said, "My name's Cathy. Would you mind popping back to the studio with me?"

"He did *not* move his head about!" Patsy shouted at her.

Cathy looked mystified. "Er- no, of course he didn't! He looked lovely. We just have a minor technical issue, nothing to do with you,

John, but could you come with me?"

As we walked briskly along the corridor, Cathy explained that, as I was acknowledging the applause at the piano, the camera slipped, giving the effect of falling over. As I came back on set, the audience applauded.

"No, not yet," the floor manager shouted, "adorable though John is!"

He led me to the piano. "Could you sit down, please, John, and, on my cue, acknowledge the extremely enthusiastic applause " - he mugged at the audience – "as though you've just finished your song?"

I duly sat down, the floor manager waved his hands manically at the audience, they applauded very enthusiastically, and I smiled and acknowledged it.

Silence as the floor manager concentrated on what someone was saying to him in his headphones.

"Okay?" he said into his mike. He gave me a thumbs-ups. "Okay! Perfect! Thank you, John! Wasn't he wonderful, Ladies and Gentlemen?!"

I waved at the smiling faces and the loud applause, caught one or two cheers of 'More!' and went back to my dressing-room, where Stuart presented me with a bottle of champagne.

"Happy Christmas!" he shouted, getting three glasses and popping the cork.

By mid-July, with no news of a release date for *I Got My Lady,* Stuart rang CBS to find out what was going on. When he got off the phone after a fifteen minute chat in the next room, he came through:

"Your single has been dropped from the release schedule. Indefinitely."

"Why?" Patsy shrieked.

"The girl I spoke to told me their release schedule has become 'top heavy', and they needed to lose some planned releases to free it up."

"So when *will* they release John's 'Summer Smash'??"

"She said she had no news on when it would be re-scheduled."

"I'd like to get my hands on Dan Loggins right now!" Patsy shouted at the wall.

"Maybe when they hear John's album they'll find a new release date for the single," Stuart calmly proffered.

"Did she say that?" I asked, my heart banging in my chest.

"No. But I'm hoping when I take the tapes over there, once Biddu's mixed the tracks, they'll change their minds."

A few days after Stuart had dropped the album tapes into CBS, he invited Robin Blanchflower, who'd recently joined the A & R team there, to one of the lunchtime meet-ups at the office. He was hoping a relaxing chat over one of Patsy's delicious home-made shepherd's pies, and a good bottle of Chardonnay, would get Robin onside, and give us a chance to test the waters as to what the label people thought of the album, having heard nothing from them as yet.

After much banter about the two men's time in the music business, comparing notes and hits they'd been involved in over the years, Stuart managed to bring the conversation round to the album:

"I dropped the tapes into Dan's office over a fortnight ago, Robin," he began. "Have you had a listen yet?"

Robin took a sip of his white wine and dash of soda, and put his glass down:

"I did give it an ear, yes, Stuart. My question is to John really -". He turned to me. "Why haven't you recorded a Biddu album?"

I wasn't sure what he meant and just gave him a puzzled look. Patsy jumped in:

"It's a John Howard album, Robin, that's why."

"Okay, let me rephrase my question," Robin continued. "With all due respect to John, who's a very talented songwriter, why doesn't it *sound* like a Biddu album?"

"Why would it?" Stuart countered.

"Because that's why we asked John to work with Biddu, to give us an album full of Biddu-sounding, catchy, hooky tracks. Instead, we have a very pleasant, nicely orchestrated collection of John Howard ballads."

"Don't you like it?" Patsy said.

"I don't dislike it, Patsy, but it's not what we expected, and certainly not what John needs right now."

"I'm still not sure what you mean, Robin," I said, speaking for the first time.

Robin stared at me, and, without taking his eyes off me, began banging a fast, driving rhythm on his knee. He then proceeded to sing, with great gusto, a much-speeded up chorus of 'You Keep Me Steady' to his impromptu disco beat:

"You keep me ste-a -"
BANG BANG BANG
"a-dy"
BANG BANG BANG
"when things are swaying, I'm re-a -"
BANG BANG BANG
"a-dy"
BANG BANG BANG
"for no more playing ar-o-u-u-nd, I'm so glad I found -"
BANG BANG BANG
"you...".

He stopped and smiled round the table. We stared at him as he beamed at us. "You see?" he said cheerfully. "Great hook, John! And with that kind of driving disco pop beat, it could have been a hit record, *but*..." he folded his arms, "the way you've done it – it ain't!" He took a swig of his wine. "I don't understand."

Neither did I. Words at that point completely failed me.

"Well, it's too late to change things now," Stuart finally said.

"It certainly is, Stuart," Robin replied, finishing his wine. "Unfortunately."

August began with Biddu's 'Summer of '42' entering the charts at Number 45, and the not unexpected news that CBS had rejected my album.

"They said it's not strong enough," Stuart told me.

"What they mean is, 'it's not disco enough'," I said, desperation setting in.

"Well," Stuart replied, shaking his head, "one comment was 'what's happened to our 'Kid In A Big World John'?"

"He's on the tracks I recorded with Paul Phillips!" I shouted, completely exasperated. "For God's sake! I can't bloody win! One says he wants disco, another says he wants 'Kid In A Big World'. What does Biddu say?"

"He's rather taken up with promoting his own record right now, John."

"So! What now, Stuart? What do we do now?"

"I have no idea, John," Stuart replied. "I have absolutely no idea."

That night I went round to Terry's, joined him, Daniel and Bob in scoffing two very strong hash cakes and drinking several whiskies. We then went to a new club in Chelsea called Rod's, where, within minutes of arriving and the hash cakes kicking in with a bang, I picked up a guy who I was convinced was The Statue of Liberty. For what seemed like hours, I manically threw myself around him on the dance floor, soaking up the beats like they were the very essence of my being.

The next morning, I woke up with a thumping head in a room I didn't recognise, beside a guy who was neither statuesque nor about to free me from the massive depression which had begun to envelop me.

I put my key in the door and almost crawled into the hallway, grateful that Daniel had already gone to work at Redken Hair Care. There was a note from him on the telephone table which said, 'Hope your Statue of Liberty used his torch well! See you later, you filthy bag!'.

Under it was an airmail letter for me. I recognised the handwriting and the postmark. It was from Roy Fitzroy. I ripped it open:

"Well, hi there," it began. I sat down on the bottom stair and almost cried with relief. "So, only a few months to go before you come over to stay with Mom and me! Everyone's really looking forward to meeting you. How does arriving on the 23rd December sound? I can stay until the 28th."

Mulling over who 'everyone' was, I went into the kitchen and put on the kettle. I read the letter again, made a cup of fruit tea and carried it up the stairs to bed. I slept like the dead, dreaming of my very own Winter Wonderland.

Chapter Twenty-Five

The Dangerous Hours

"Fancy a trip to Malta, John?"

Stuart and I were sitting in Kettner's as he told me he'd booked me a week's break "somewhere sunny, to give you a rest after the dreadful time you've had lately."

I'd never been to Malta, and had not heard of the beach town of Sliema, but it looked lovely in the Thompson's Holidays brochure Patsy took out and showed me over our chocolate chip ice creams.

"You can lie in the sun, John, relax, read and recharge your batteries – I know the last few months have ground you down." She smiled sadly at me.

A few days later I was sitting in the lounge of a perfectly nice beach-front hotel, along with several other British holidaymakers, listening to the Thompson's rep, a jolly lady called Doreen, telling us, in perfect posh Northern, about "the fun days out" she had planned for us. We could join her "on trips to several themed restaurants with variously different themes" and on days out to "a lace maker, where they make lace," and to "a basket-ware shop where they sell all sorts of baskets."

"Come and tell me which outings you fancy after I've done my chat," she said, "and I'll pop your names down on my list." She waved a blank piece of paper at us and pointed at it with her pen.

As she sat dealing with the impressively large queue of people who all seemed very keen to "see the lace place", I slinked away hoping she hadn't spotted me. Unfortunately, the lift took a while to come down:

"Er – hello," she trilled. "Hello there! Sir!"

I turned round like a discovered schoolboy. She was beaming away across the lounge at me, holding up her now filled-up piece of paper.

"Do you want to come and put your name down for some of the outings?"

Just as the lift arrived with a loud 'Ding!', I contemplated just waving back at her and getting in, but she seemed perfectly nice, and I didn't want to be rude. So, I made my way through the crowd of people, hearing one couple discussing how they quite fancied buying a "locally made basket", and finally reached Doreen, all smiles and poised pen:

"Doreen," I began quietly.

She smiled up at me expectantly.

"I'm here for a complete break," I continued, "so I hope you don't mind but I'll say no to any outings. I just want to relax, read a few books, lie on the beach, you know, just -"

She looked disappointed, put her pen down, but pasted on a bright smile for me:

"Relax. Yes, I understand. Of course! But this is a great way to get to know everyone here," she said, pointing expansively around the room, as though announcing the next act in a variety show.

"I don't really want to get to know anyone here," I explained. "I'm very happy to stay solo."

She made a 'get you!' face and got up.

"Well, if you change your mind, you know where I'll be!"

I actually didn't but was quite happy not to tell her that, as she went to greet her party of eager 'outtingers'.

The next morning, after a late breakfast at a welcome set-for-one table, I walked out onto the promenade and wandered along, enjoying the blue skies and the heat on my back, when I spotted a little rocky bay just visible down from the road. I had to negotiate quite a few slightly treacherous steps, carved out from the rocky terrain, to get there, but finally, I reached the water's edge. It was worth it. The bay was completely empty, with just a still, blue ocean and me.

I put my towel down on some fairly smooth-looking rocks, applied my Ambré Solair sun-cream, and settled down with a wonderfully amusing biography of Noel Coward I'd bought at the Heathrow bookshop. Coward had died a couple of years earlier but the author, Charles Castle, brought the man back to life, with hilarious stories of The Master's wit and sharp tongue. I'd laughed out loud at some parts of the book on the plane over.

Although it was a great read, my eyes soon began to get heavy, so I tipped my straw hat over my face, put the book on my chest, and decided to have a snooze.

When I woke up, the sun had moved across the sky a little, now directly above me, so I guessed I'd been asleep about an hour. As I was looking up, the silhouetted figure of a man appeared, standing over me.

"Hello?" he said. "You English?"

I sat up, cupped my eyes so I could see him better, and a handsome smiling face stared down at me.

"Yes," I said, "I am."

"I am Marcellino. I live in the next village."

He sat down beside me and gave me a definite once-over.

"Hello, Marcellino -"

"My friends call me Marco." He grinned. He was quite lovely in fact.

"Hello Marco! My name's John."

"You speak nicely," he said. "I like your accent. It's very — theatrical." He looked me up and down again. "You look nice too."

'Don't look so bad yourself,' I thought.

"Thank you!" I said. "Are you visiting Sliema?"

"My grandmother lives here. I visit her every Monday."

"Good boy," I said.

He was about the same age as me, maybe a couple of years older, but possessed an innocent charm.

"Have you been to Valetta yet?" he asked me.

"No. I only arrived yesterday. It's on my list of places to see."

"I will take you there," he said, standing up. "Would you like that?"

"Yes, that would be very nice. When?"

"Tomorrow. I meet you here at eleven o'clock, the bus stop is just across the road."

With that, he smiled, let his eyes linger on me for much too long, and walked away along the bay, his open white cotton shirt billowing in the sea breeze as he waved at me over his shoulder. Finally, he stepped out of sight behind a rocky promontory. The sound of him singing floated away on the air.

"Well, Noel," I said, reopening my book. "Not a bad start to the week!"

I could almost hear The Master tutting delightedly.

"The architecture here in Valetta dates from the 16th Century," Marco told me as we wandered past cafés and bars, just beginning to fill up with people ordering beers and an early lunch. "There are palaces, churches and museums all over the city."

"You would make a great tour guide," I told him, and he giggled.

"Did you know," he said, studying me, "that one of your Prime Ministers, Disraeli, called Valetta 'a city of palaces built by gentlemen for gentlemen'?" I shook my head. "He said it compared to Venice for its noble architecture."

For the next two hours, we visited various sights. We stood in the stunning St John's Cathedral and stared for what seemed an age at a beautiful and huge Caravaggio depiction of 'The Beheading of John The Baptist'. We walked through the high Baroque interiors, past the carved stone walls and beneath the astonishing vaulted ceiling decorated with scenes from the life of John The Baptist. I was most intrigued by the figures painted on the ceiling, they looked three-dimensional, almost like statues looking down at you.

"A clever use of shadows, yes?" Marco said.

I had the feeling he'd done this tour for several of my predecessors.

We walked over the incredible marble floors with their beautifully designed coats of arms.

"These are the tombs of four hundred Knights," he told me, as I marvelled at them.

"What, under here, under our feet? These are tombs?"

"Yes! Right here!" He stamped his foot and mock shouted at them. "Are you awake?" He laughed. "They're all sleeping! So lazy these Knights!"

"I prefer lazy days," I replied.

He looked puzzled for a moment, then got the joke:

"Oh! You're witty! I like that!"

We wandered around the National Museum of Fine Arts – "once the home of the Commander-in-Chief of the Mediterranean Fleet, inaugurated as a museum just one year ago" Marcellino proudly told me.

I stood for a few moments to admire Turner's beautiful watercolour of The Grand Harbour.

"Your Mr Turner was a great artist!" Marco said, standing beside me, smiling.

When our feet began to ache, he took me to the port area, where we drank sweet black coffee, accompanied by delicious Baci chocolate cake which Marco had recommended I try.

On the bus there, I'd told him I was a musician and, obviously keeping that in mind, he took me to the Strait Street area, which was a big jazz music centre. There was quite an array of buskers playing some fabulous cool jazz on saxophones, clarinets and electric guitars.

"My father would love this!" I said, dropping some change onto the pavement where a particularly good group of musicians were playing Peggy Lee's 'Fever'.

"Is he a musician?"

"He's a jazz pianist."

"You don't play jazz?" Marco asked, surprised.

"No, I play the piano but I'm more of a pop singer."

"Ah! Like your Elton John!"

On the bus back to Sliema, Marco asked me if I wanted to go out with him that evening:

"There is a club, I think you'd like it. I can take you there. Shall I pick you up at nine o'clock?"

"Come to the hotel and meet me in the lobby."

He looked horrified:

"No! Hotel people don't like us inside the hotels, they're for tourists, not locals!"

"How silly!"

"I am a fisherman," he explained. "I go fishing with my eight brothers, every day. The hotel owners don't like us to upset their guests with the smell of fish!"

"You smell very nice," I said, nudging him in the ribs.

"So do you."

He was at the bus stop on the stroke of nine, though I'd arrived early in case I missed him. The club was a ten minute bus ride out of town, and as we walked in Marco was greeted by almost everyone packed in there. He led me through to the bar and gave me a seat. They were all smiling at him, giving him thumbs-up signs.

"They think you're very handsome," he told me, sitting next to me, ordering beers and letting his eyes linger up and down.

"Is this your local gay bar?" I asked him, returning the favour.

We hadn't up to that point mentioned the 'G' word, and he giggled:

"Yes, I guessed you were gay but I wasn't sure until -"

"Until?"

"When you told me I smelled nice, I knew then. Straight men don't tell other men they smell nice."

"No, but sometimes they think it!" I joked.

"You're naughty," he said, giving me my bottle of beer and taking a long slug of his.

The tiny dance floor was heaving, and as he led me onto it, Biddu's 'Summer Of '42' started to play. I laughed.

"What's funny? You think we look silly? Men dancing together?"

"No! No, not at all, I do it all the time in London, this is lovely."

Marco pulled me close and moved slowly round the floor, pushing his crutch into mine.

"This record," I said, my heart beginning to bang in my chest, "it's by the man who is my producer."

Marco's eyes widened like saucers:

"You know Biddu?"

"Very well."

He pulled me in even tighter, kissed my neck and I heard him giggle into my ear as Bid's hit single blasted out around us.

A couple of hours later, we walked out of the club into a warm night filled with the sound of cicadas calling for mates. Marco had linked his arm into mine and smiled at me coyly:

"I have nowhere to take you, I live with my brothers. I cannot come to your hotel, so…"

I pecked him on the cheek:

"Never mind, this has been very nice."

"I know a place, not far from here, everyone who wants to make love goes there."

Ten minutes later, we were standing in the middle of a large moonlit field, surrounded by the sounds of cicadas and couples screwing. The lights of Sliema blinked in the distance through the head-high grass, as he began to unbutton my shirt. He pulled me down onto the ground with him, just as the orgasmic shriek of a woman quite close by pierced the air.

"Straights come here too?" I asked him, as he nibbled my ear.

"As I said, everyone who wants to make love comes here."

Just then, the sound of two men reaching climax rang out from just a few feet away.

"Let's join the party then!" I said, as Marco pulled off his shirt.

I went to my little rocky bay again the next morning, but, by lunchtime, with no sign of Marco, I walked back to my hotel, had a snack in the restaurant and then up to my room for a snooze. I woke up with a start at about eight o'clock feeling absolutely famished.

The restaurant was just about to close but they agreed to serve me with a pasta bake and a green salad, washed down by a glass of their extremely dry house white. As I supped it and nodded at some of the earlier diners leaving for their evening walk along the promenade, cardies over shoulders and light macs over arms, I decided to get the bus to the club again that evening. I hoped Marco may be there.

A few of the guys from the previous evening smiled at me as I walked in. It was even more packed and I nodded at them, squeezed my way to the bar and ordered a beer. I looked around but Marco wasn't there. I was about to beckon over one of his friends to ask if he was coming along later, when:

"Hello," a deep voice said to my right.

I turned round and acknowledged the smiling, rugged face of a stocky, extremely tanned guy.

"Hello," I said, and cheered him with my bottle.

"You English?"

"Yes. You?"

"I am from Libya. I am here with my friends."

He pointed at a small group of four slightly older, swarthy men who literally leered across the room at me. One of them had a mouthful of gold teeth, the other three seemed to be missing most of theirs.

"We are fishermen," he said, clinking his bottle on mine, "we come here some nights. To meet nice men. You look nice. I like you."

Over the course of the next hour, he told me his name was Ibrahim, he was thirty two, married with two children in Libya but liked "handsome men like you."

His broad shoulders, deep voice, and the five beers – along with whisky chasers - he kept insisting on buying me persuaded me to go back with him to the house he told me he rented, a five minute walk from the club.

We entered a large bougainvillea-covered courtyard which led through to an open flag-stoned hallway. I followed him in, past a very basic, not particularly hygienic kitchen, and into a huge room which had five beds in it and a TV. Nothing else. Ibrahim took my hand, kissed it, and led me over to one of the beds, laying me down and immediately undressing me.

We were just getting to the interesting bit, when the door flew open and his four very drunk friends barged in and staggered over to us. The one with the gold teeth bared them at me like a mad dog, and said to Ibrahim,

"I watch, then I have him!"

The other three joined him and stood over me, glaring. One of them licked his lips and chuckled. As I lay there, almost naked, Ibrahim quickly climbed aboard.

"You have my friends when I've had you," he growled.

"Yes!" Gold-Tooth said, rubbing his hands, "Fuck him good, then I do him!"

Somewhere within me, as had happened before when I'd been in danger, I found a strength which always took me by surprise. I pushed a very heavy Ibrahim off me and he crashed onto the floor, where he rolled around shouting 'Bitch!' at the top of his voice. Like a gazelle in flight from lions, I jumped off the bed, gathered up my clothes and shoes, thrust my way through the leering mass like a rugby player, and, pulling on my jeans and shirt, backed away from them towards the door.

"I am not a prostitute!" I screamed, as the five men closed in.

I ran for the door which miraculously opened. An older man, who I'd not seen before, stood blocking my way. I was about to barge past him when, to my utter surprise, he moved aside, held the door open for me and shouted,

"Run!"

I certainly did. For my life. With shouts behind me of "We find you and fuck you to death!", I scurried into the courtyard, quickly slipped on my shoes and made for the street. There in the distance were the welcoming twinkling lights of Sliema and I ran towards them as fast as I could, until I felt far enough away to feel safe and able to slow down. As I caught my breath, I could smell jasmine floating on the lovely warm evening, I heard a church bell chiming somewhere, and a group of old ladies sitting outside their houses waved happily at me.

Every time a car passed me, I was sure it was going to stop and unload the Libyan hoard. But, thankfully, only a taxi slowed down. The driver looked at me and wound down his window.

"You need a taxi?" he said.

I made sure none of the hoard were in the back, and climbed in, giving him the name of my hotel. When we reached it, I thanked and paid him and ran up to my room, finally feeling safe. As I lay on the bed, staring at the ceiling, I tried to take in what had happened, going over it all in my mind. Then I realised I'd left my silver bracelet behind, which I'd taken off by the bed. It was a Christmas present from Stuart and Patsy, matching the ring they'd bought me from André Bourget in Knightsbridge for my twenty-first birthday. Right then, however, my regret at losing it was nothing compared to the relief that I was still in one piece.

"You stupid bitch!" I said to my empty wrist, turned over and fell fast asleep.

The next morning, I caught a bus and stayed on it until it reached its destination, a tiny coastal village with just a few goats scampering through the little market square. I asked the driver when he would return in the afternoon, and wandered off until I found a small quiet bay. I read, slept, swam a little, and ate a small tasty lunch at the taverna.

The bus returned at about two o'clock, taking me back to Sliema. I stayed in my room and read for a couple of hours, took a long, hot bath before dining in the restaurant and an early night. I did this every day for the rest of my vacation. It was completely uneventful, unremarkable, but entirely safe.

I never saw Marco again and wondered if his friends had told him what a wanton tart I was, going off with some Libyan fisherman who I'd just met. I imagine he might have giggled as I'd told him about my near-miss, or maybe not.

One evening in October, I was listening to Marvin Gaye's *What's Going On*, which I'd fallen in love with after finding it in Daniel's record collection, when the phone rang.

"John?"

It was a lady's voice which I vaguely recognised.

"It's Sue," she said, "Peter Collinson's assistant! We met in Madrid aeons ago!"

I hadn't seen or heard from her since I'd recorded 'Casting Shadows' in Rome in early 1974 for Peter's movie *Open Season*, which had opened to poor reviews and a low box office a few months earlier. I'd popped into the Empire Leicester Square to see it when it came out, and was sadly disappointed, not only with the empty seats around me, but by the extensive editing which had ruined the film for me.

I was particularly taken aback at the edit on my song. They'd taken out most of the final verse from 'Casting Shadows', and cut to just the last line of the song, so that the lyric no longer made sense. It had originally been, *'what's real now only yesterday was just a game,'*, but now, with the third line of the penultimate verse cutting straight to the last line of the final verse, it went *'the silly man who made you laugh – was just a game.'*

I couldn't believe Peter would have allowed that, so assumed he'd left the editors to hack his film about as they chose.

"Long time!" I said to Sue, going over to turn the music down. "What can I do for you, Sue?"

She proceeded to tell me that Peter was planning to start work very shortly on a new movie:

"It's called *The Shells*, and we've got Oliver Reed and Charlotte Rampling starring. It's a wonderful story, about a lonely teenage boy who collects shells on a beach near to where Charlotte and Oliver's characters have a holiday home. She watches him from her window every day, as her husband stays out day and night with his drinking and carousing mates in the village, before rolling in drunk at all hours, brutally screwing her as she lies there wishing him away.

One day, she plucks up the courage to go and talk to the boy on the beach, pretending to look for shells herself. Of course, she falls in love with him, they have a tender summer affair, and on her last day, before she and her husband go back to their city apartment, she shows him how the shells contain those wonderful sea sounds we've all listened to as children. She realises, watching the wonder on his face, how she must stay with him and leave behind her city life with a man she loathes."

"What happens?"

"Exactly! That's why it's so marvellous, everyone will leave the cinema wondering just that. Peter's very excited about it, and he has asked me to call you to see if you'd like to compose the music for it?"

"*All* the music, or just the opening song?"

"No! Peter wants you to compose all the music, the whole score! *And* he'd like you to write an opening theme song as well!

"Well, tell Peter I'd love to," I said, which garnered a delighted squeal from Sue.

"Wow! Fantastic! Peter will be so thrilled, John! We'll be in touch very soon! Give our love to Stuart!"

I put the phone down, thinking I'd better ask Stuart to get me edit approval on my music before signing anything. But that was for later. Already, ideas for a theme song had started to filter through. I lay back to the strains of Marvin's 'Save The Children', and imagined meeting Oliver Reed, one of my teenage lusts.

I never heard from Sue or Peter again. Peter left the UK a few months later and settled with his wife, Hazel, in Los Angeles, where he died in 1980 from lung cancer. I don't think anyone ever made the film Sue was so excited about.

On the evening of the 23rd December, I arrived at JFK airport, full of anticipation. Stuart had again paid for my trip, seeing it as a perfect opportunity for me to meet up again with Dick Asher, now President of Columbia Records. He'd called Dick to tell him I was due over there for Christmas, and had been promised that "We'll give John a great time while he's here!"

As I walked into the arrivals hall I saw Roy Fitzroy smiling at me:

"Hello Professor!" He greeted me with a hug. "I *love* the glasses!"

"Oh! I'd forgotten I had them on!" I said, still ridiculously vain about people seeing me wearing them.

"They look great on you!" Roy said, studying me with his head on one side. "Mmmm! They make you look extremely studious! Are you very short-sighted?"

He took my bag and marched out to the car park, as I tried to keep up.

"Blind as a bat actually!" I replied.

"So! You must be a bit shocked to see that I am, in fact, an ancient old crock!" He laughed and looked sideways at me. "I hope I'm not a huge disappointment!"

In truth, he looked even better in clear vision. Rugged, tall, wearing a red checked shirt, thick sheepskin jacket and blue jeans tucked into shin-high leather boots, his lop-sided grin sent my stomach churning.

"Now, it's about a forty-five minute drive over George Washington Bridge to Tenafly," he told me, starting up the engine of his four-by-four. "So settle back and take a snooze if you want to, you must be tired."

In fact, I was wide awake. It was my first trip to America and I wanted to take in every inch of it as we smoothly cruised along. I also wanted to stay awake and talk to this gorgeous man I'd dreamed of seeing again for over a year.

However, the spirit was willing but the body was weak, and I soon dropped off listening to Roy's deep rich tones telling me about "the Christmas me and mom have planned for you."

"We're here!"

I woke up in the drive of a lovely clapper-board house. It was surprisingly large and surrounded by trees and verdant greenery. Its post box by the road, and the wreath of green and red poinsettia welcoming us on the door could have been from every Doris Day movie I'd seen. The door opened and a tiny old lady came out, smiling and waving at me. She walked over to the car and tapped the windshield:

"Hey! John! Come and get warm," she shouted and ran back in, rubbing her shoulders and laughing at Roy, who hugged her and kissed her forehead.

I followed Roy into a homely and warm kitchen, smelling of great cooking and boasting an enormous fridge. It was like a walk-in wardrobe. Roy saw me staring at it:

"Mom always expects she'll have visitors at any point in the day, and she usually does, so she's well prepared to feed them all!"

Mrs Fitzroy laughed and joshed her son with a wave of the hand:

"They can't stay away," she said, shaking my hand with her tiny little doll-like fingers. "John! Welcome!" She stared up at me and studied me with her head on one side, exactly as her son had done. "Roy's told me all about you! You're a singer!"

She led me into a large bright sitting-room, with two white leather sofas against walls full of photos of Roy through the years, a huge Christmas Tree in the bay window and the largest log fire I'd ever seen.

"What a great fire!" I said.

"You can help me chop some more wood for it tomorrow if you like!" Roy said, winking at his mum.

"Oh, take no notice of this scamp," she beamed up at him. "I have enough logs for the next ten years of fires! My boys are very good to me."

I thought Roy was an only child and glanced at him:

"My cousins Art and Jerry," he explained. "They live in Hackensack, we'll be seeing them on Christmas Day."

"And all the kids!" Mrs Fitzroy beamed. "Can't wait to get a hundred hugs!"

"Thank you for inviting me, Mrs Fitzroy," I began but was interrupted.

"Thelma," she corrected me, "but all my friends call me Thel."

"Okay, Thel, thank you. Your home is lovely."

"My husband Alf built it just after the war. He and I, and Roy, we were very happy here, weren't we, son?"

"Was he a lawyer like Roy?"

"Yep! The best! I still miss him."

"We all do, mom."

She clapped her hands:

"Okay! Enough reminiscing! Are you hungry, John?"

I'd eaten on the plane and was really too tired for any more food.

"Or do you just wanna go and get some shut-eye?"

I smiled at her and nodded.

"Roy! Show this young man to his bed for the night. You'll be sharing a room with Roy, he used to sleep in there when his cousins were staying over."

"My room is now a crocheting centre!" Roy said.

"My ladies need space to crochet! It's for all the old folk down the road. Your room was the perfect size!"

"In your letter back to me," Roy asked, climbing the stairs ahead of me, "you said you'd appeared on TV in the UK, how did that go?"

"It's on tonight!" I replied. "I'd forgotten!"

We reached the landing:

"So you'll miss it?"

"Yeah, but I was there so…I'd rather be here."

Roy winked at me and opened the door into an L-shaped room with three beds, three chests of drawers and a World Globe by the window.

"Here's your pod for the next few nights." My bag was already on one of the beds. "Unpack, and get some rest." He leaned over and pecked me on the cheek. "I'm glad you came."

He looked thoughtful and sat down on the bed:

"Okay," he said, motioning me to join him. "There's something I need to explain. Mom has a habit of not knocking on doors before she walks in – well, she does knock but she does it while she's walking in, so…" He chuckled, crinkling the adorable lines round his eyes. "It used to drive me crazy when I was a teenager, lying in bed of a morning thinking of guys who looked, well, a bit like you – and she'd just breeze in with a cup of coffee."

He grinned at me and raised his eyebrows.

"So?"

"So, we won't be able to do what we both feel like doing while you're here." He raised his eyebrows again. "It will drive me nuts but we're going to have to be very careful. Mom is always in the house and liable to crash in at any time."

As if on cue, the door opened and Thel appeared with a mug of steaming something, tapping lightly on the door as she breezed in:

"Knock knock, boys," she said brightly, seeing us both sitting on my bed, definitely clocking it but pretending not to notice. "I've made us hot chocolates! Here's yours, John! That'll help you sleep! Roy, come and get it!"

As she bustled out, Roy growled lightly in my ear and, getting up with a little, shall we say, discomfort, said,

"Oh Mom!"

He went to the door and grinned at me:

"We rise early, but you come down when you're ready."

With a last wink, he shut the door. I put my bag on the floor, got undressed, tucked myself in, and fell asleep wondering how my TV spot would go down.

I awoke to the sound of shovelling and scraping outside. I looked at the clock on the wall, it was eleven a.m.! I jumped out of bed, went to the window and gasped at a sea of white covering everything. Snow had arrived during the night and was still falling, big heavy flakes. Below in the driveway, Roy, wrapped up from the cold which I could see on his breath, was removing it from around his car. He looked up and waved:

"Happy Christmas Eve," he shouted. "Fancy helping after breakfast?"

A white Christmas! I put on my dressing-gown, had an amazing power-shower, so strong I had to turn the pressure down, and was downstairs as quickly as I could get there. The delicious smells of a cooked breakfast, and Thel at the oven singing a hymn, greeted me like a Christmas card.

"Morning, John," she shouted over her shoulder. "Full-on breakfast coming up!"

I heard Roy clumping in, banging his boots against the wall, as Thel put the packed plate in front of me.

"Is that okay?" she asked, as I stared at it.

"It's – amazing!" I replied. "The biggest breakfast I've ever seen!"

"No wonder you're so skinny," she said, rubbing my hair. "I'm gonna fatten you up while you're here!"

I'd brought presents for Roy and Thel, copies of *Kid In A Big World*, but hadn't wrapped them yet. I was planning to do that later in the evening not being aware that in America gifts are exchanged at the end of the day on Christmas Eve. As we settled down to watch Andy Williams' Christmas Show, Thel began getting presents from under the tree.

"Oh! I didn't realise you did this now!" I said, jumping up. "I haven't wrapped yours yet!"

"You mean you've got us something?" Thel laughed, handing me a beautifully-wrapped gift.

"Yes, of course! But we give presents on Christmas morning at home. I'll just go and get yours now!"

I rushed upstairs, got the LPs, two prepared sheets of wrapping paper and sellotape out of my bag, and quickly wrapped them. As I walked downstairs, Andy Williams was singing 'Have Yourself A Merry Little Christmas' accompanied by an angelic-sounding Thel.

"You have a lovely voice," I said walking in.

"Mom was in the church choir," Roy said, smiling over at her.

"Oh, a long time ago. But yeah, I love to sing!"

"You can probably tell what it is," I said, giving them both their presents.

"Is it Frankie? I love ol' Blue Eyes," she said, dreamily.

"Not quite..."

"Wow!" Thel cried, opening it. "Is this you?"

"Looks like him, mom!" Roy said, opening his. "He looks like a star to me!"

"And to me! Put it on, Roy!"

"No, really..." I protested. "You don't have to."

"Are you kidding? Put it on, son!"

As the strains of 'Goodbye Suzie' filled the room, and I opened my presents – a calculator from Roy and a beautiful tie from Thel – she beamed at me and hugged herself.

When I'd recorded it over a year earlier, I never dreamed, in my wildest imaginings, that I would one day be sitting, as the snow fell outside the window on an American Christmas Eve, listening to my album playing.

On a snowy day in December...

Christmas Day, at Roy's cousin Art and his wife Carol's home in Hackensack, was fantastic. After a gargantuan gourmet meal which would have fed hundreds, during which we listened to and talked about *Kid In A Big World* - which Thel had proudly brought along – Carol brought in the largest apple pie I had ever seen.

"You're as good as Elton John," she exclaimed, cutting me a huge piece and handing it to me.

"I love Elton," her daughter Barbara shouted, passing me the cream jug. "But I love you too," she giggled at me.

Elton was absolutely huge at that time in The States, having enjoyed a three-year run of Number One hits there and a series of million-selling albums. In the UK, his star was actually beginning to fade a little, his most recent singles not even denting the Top Ten, his previous two albums failing to reach the top. But I was happy to talk about him while listening to their heartfelt praise of my album!

At about nine o'clock, we all bade farewell on the sweeping drive from Art's house, and Roy drove us back to Tenafly, where I'd decided to have an early night.

I was going into New York the next day to meet up with Dick Asher. He had apparently told Stuart that he had something very nice arranged for me, and not to make any after-dinner plans. As I was getting my clothes laid out for my day in the city, Roy walked in and brushed the back of my neck with his hand:

"You were great today," he said, "my family loved you!"

"I love your family!" I said, turning round to meet his smile. "I was also impressed by how openly they asked you how Alejandro was. They've obviously met him."

"Yeah, he came over with me a couple of years ago and spent Christmas here."

"So you're completely 'Out' with them?"

He looked thoughtful:

"I've never discussed it, they've never asked questions, but yeah, I'm sure they've worked it out. Forty-four years old, unmarried, living with a guy in his early thirties. Go figure!"

"And your mum? Does she know the situation?"

"She loves Alejandro, has never queried what he is to me, but she knows I'm fond of him. I don't know what she knows though, we've never talked about it."

I held Roy's hand,

"She knows."

The snow had largely turned to slush on the New Jersey roads by the time Roy drove me into Manhattan after lunch. He had a business meeting of his own in the city and dropped me off directly outside the Columbia building on Madison Avenue. I'd told him that I would be making my own way back later that evening.

"Last train back leaves George Washington Bridge station at

eleven o'clock," he shouted through the window as he drove away. "Don't miss it! Have a great day!"

Acknowledging his G.I. salute, I walked into the impressive skyscraper building with the Columbia logo proudly displayed over the large glass doors, and gave my name at the gleaming reception desk:

"I have Mr John Howard for Mr Asher," the receptionist said into her phone, looked up at me and gave me a name badge.

"Go to the Twelfth Floor, Mr Howard," she told me.

When the lift doors opened, Dick was there, beside a small, blonde lady who beamed at me.

"John! Great to see you in New York," he said, shaking my hand. "Let me introduce you to Bunny, she's going to take care of you."

"Bunny Friedus at your service, John," she said, giving me a surprisingly firm handshake. "Come with me. You want a coffee?"

As she led me through, I turned round to see Dick waving at me. He shouted "Have a great time," and walked in the other direction. I didn't see him again.

"Now, John!" Bunny said, pouring me a coffee and sitting down at her desk. "This evening I'm taking you to a fabulous Japanese restaurant for dinner after which we will be going to see a great new musical in town. Columbia has the cast album and it is completely tearing Broadway up!"

Bunny was then Director of Pop Product and had Dylan's latest album, *Desire*, on her desk. She saw me looking at it:

"Would you like one? It's a great album!"

"Thanks, Bunny. I'll get one in the UK." I didn't want to be carrying an LP around with me all night. "I love Bob!"

"I saw him on stage in the '60s, he was tremendous."

"Wow! During his folk period or when he went electric?"

"Both. I preferred his folk stuff personally, but those Hawks could certainly rock!" She smiled at me as she sipped her coffee. "So,

John! Tell me, what's happening with you? Do you have a new album ready?"

I wasn't sure how much she knew, so trod carefully:

"I've recently finished an album, with Biddu producing," I began. "I'm not sure when it's due out..."

"Biddu! He's making waves in the UK isn't he? Kind of a British Barry White? Wow! I must listen to it!" She made a note on her pad. "I'll order up a tape from London!"

It had been four months since the album had been rejected by CBS UK, so her ignorance of its very existence told me enough.

Bunny and I walked into a buzzing restaurant, a huge place, full of wonderfully noisy tables. As we were shown to ours, a smiling chef lifted up a folding section, walked into the hollow ring in the centre, replaced it and proceeded to cook various small dishes on hot plates in front of us, handing them to us as he began the next one.

"Isn't this great?" Bunny said. "I love it here!"

"Amazing!" I replied tucking into the delicious food.

I hadn't eaten Japanese cuisine before and, along with Bunny's great talent as a conversationalist, it was a fantastic fun evening.

She paid the bill and went outside to hail a cab. We were whisked off to The Shubert Theatre where one of New York's hottest shows, *A Chorus Line*, was playing.

As we made our way through the packed foyer to our seats, Bunny told me the show had opened in July there and was currently the most successful musical on Broadway:

"It looks like it's going to get several Tony Awards," she told me as we settled in our seats. "Amazing for a show which, when it first opened off-Broadway in April, the theatre showing it didn't have the cash to finance it, so it borrowed over a million dollars to put it on. That's called belief!"

Seats were quickly filling up around us, and the expectant hum around the auditorium was electric.

"Advance word alone ensured it sold out really quickly," Bunny continued, giving me a programme out of her handbag, "just three months later it transferred here to The Shubert."

"Amazing!"

"Just look around," she said delighted at the packed theatre, "it's doing okay!!"

I was totally gob-smacked by the musical, the songs were fantastic, the story drew one in immediately, the dancing was astonishing, recalling the very best of Bob Fosse. It was very affecting to be watching a hugely successful play in the heart of Broadway, which was set in an off-Broadway theatre, about a group of actors desperate for work.

"Enjoy that?" Bunny asked, as we walked out into the cold winter evening.

It had begun to snow heavily.

"Thank you so much, Bunny!" I said. "I really enjoyed it, well the whole evening has been great!"

"How long are you here?" she asked, lifting up her collar from the cold.

"I leave on the 29th."

"How do you fancy seeing *Equus*?"

I hadn't heard of it.

"Great play starring Anthony Perkins," she dangled her carrot at me.

Images of *Psycho* flashed into my mind,

"I'd love to!"

"Come by the office on the 28th! Be there at seven! You'll love it!"

I looked at my watch, it was a quarter-to-eleven, and I knew it was at least a ten minute walk to the station, so I picked up pace and reached there by five-to. Unfortunately, I didn't know my way around and wasted time looking for directions, walking onto the wrong platform, realising my mistake and rushing across to the right one – just as the train pulled away.

'Okay' I thought, trying to stay calm. 'I'm in New York, no train back to Tenafly, haven't a clue what to do now – I'd better call Roy.'

I wandered around looking for a phone and eventually spotted a bank of them against a wall near the exit. The first two were 'Out of Order', but I found one which worked, checked my pocket for change and took out a couple of dimes. When I picked up the receiver a bored-sounding voice said,

"Hello, who do you wish to be connected to?" I gave her the number. "One moment please…". The line clicked for a few seconds. "Please insert your money now, caller."

I got a dime and put it into the slot. It promptly fell through into the change drawer.

"Have you inserted your money yet, caller?"

"I'm trying to! It keeps…" The dime clattered into the change drawer again.

"I'm sorry, caller, unless you insert your money I cannot put you through."

Clatter! The line went dead.

I took a deep breath, tried not to panic, and decided to try something I'd seen in an old movie:

"Hello operator?" I said as a different voice greeted me. "Can you make a call collect to this number, please?"

Much to my shock and delight she replied,

"Of course. What is the number?"

I read it out to her, the line clicked, it rang a couple of times and I heard Roy answering.

"Good evening, sir," the operator said, "I have a call collect for you from George Washington Bridge station, will you take the call?"

"Yes, I will," Roy said.

"Go ahead, caller!"

"Roy?"

"John! Have you missed your train?"

"Yes! Are there any taxis from here?"

"I can come and get you."

"No, the weather's terrible. If there's a cab outside I can get that."

"Okay! Go outside and turn left, the taxi rank's there. The weather's gotten pretty bad here too, John, so make sure your driver takes it easy!"

I walked out into driving snow, saw the taxi stop with three cars standing idle. They were dark and there were no drivers in them, so I waited. About five minutes later a cab pulled up behind them with its For Hire light on.

"Where to?" the driver said, winding down his window.

"Tenafly please!" I replied, getting in out of the weather. I settled in the back. "The other drivers on a break?"

Without replying, he set off. I saw a man running along the side of the car and bang on the window, shouting at the driver. My door flew open, the man leaned in and grabbed hold of me, dragging me out onto the sidewalk as my cab took off at speed.

"You okay?" he shouted, helping me up off the pavement.

My knees were wet through and I was terrified, but otherwise fine. Two other men ran up and joined us:

"You alright, sir?" one of them asked.

"I don't know. What's going on?"

"We were sheltering in our hut," the first chap said, "I came out and saw you getting in the car."

"Jesus," the second guy said, "that was close!"

"What was close?"

"I'll explain on the way," the first guy said. "Where are you going?"

"Tenafly," I replied.

I followed him to his cab, he opened the door for me and I got in.

As he set off, he looked in the rear-view mirror and said to me,

"You had a lucky escape!"

"From *what*?" I realised my left side was drenched and brushed the snow off.

"That guy was not an official cab driver. He was here last night trying to pick up a passenger and we chased him off. I tried to get his number but he took off too fast. One of our guys managed to get a partial just now."

"Who was he?"

"Don't know. There have been two murders in the last couple of months, people seen by friends getting into what they thought were cabs, then found in a dumpster the next morning. We've been told to be on our guard for someone posing as a cabbie."

"He was a *murderer*?"

"Well, he certainly was not a cab driver, so…" his voice tailed off, as I imagined my possible fate if he hadn't dragged me out.

"Christ! Thank you!"

"I should warn you the weather is supposed to get worse tonight, especially in the suburbs, so this may take us a lot longer than usual."

I checked my wallet for cash, I had thirty dollars.

"How much do you think it'll be?"

"Not sure. Don't worry, I'll get you home."

For the next hour and a half, we crawled along through driving snow and heavy winds, which got more stormlike the further we went. Happily, he was a great chatter, asking me where I'd been, genuinely interested to hear about the musical, the restaurant, why I was in America, my recording career. I in turn wanted to hear about his family, where he lived – Yonkers – and where he originally came from – Chicago, about which his tales would have kept me enthralled for hours alone.

At just before one o'clock, he pulled up outside Thel's house. I saw her anxious face staring through the pane of glass in the door.

She waved frantically at me, and Roy came rushing out to the cab, opening my door:

"Gee, I'm pleased to see you! Mom's been going crazy with worry!"

"Roy, this is my knight in shining armour!" I said, smiling at the cabbie.

"You wanna come in for a hot drink and a snack, buddy?" Roy asked him.

"Nah! I need to get home. But thanks for the offer!"

"How much do we owe you?"

"Should be about forty, but, your friend here was great company, so... make it twenty!"

Roy got out a fifty dollar note and handed it to him:

"Take your wife out for a nice meal!"

I followed Roy into the house where Thel threw herself into my arms:

"Oh John! I thought you'd been murdered," she wailed into my chest.

"Almost!" I joked.

"What?"

"I'll tell you all about it in the morning!"

She led me through to the kitchen, sat me down at the table, made me a steaming hot chocolate, got some waffles out of the fridge and put them in the toaster. Jam, honey and a huge jar of maple syrup were on the table in seconds, and very soon, through mouthfuls of gorgeously sweet hot waffles, I was telling Roy and his mum all about my New York adventure.

"Jesus, Roy!" Thel said breathlessly, clasping her throat, "this boy knows how to frighten a woman!"

On the 28th, Roy drove me to the YMCA near Central Park where I was staying that night, gave me a big bear hug, and watched me walk up the steps:

"You take care," he shouted. "Stay safe!"

As I settled in my sparse but clean room, I got out the map he'd given me. I'd always fancied walking down 42nd Street, so found it on the map and set off. On the way I found a place called McDonald's. I'd never heard of it but it was extremely popular and served a tasty burger, fries and a large coke, all for under two dollars.

42nd Street itself was, frankly, a dump, a real disappointment, but I wandered into a cinema showing Diana Ross's latest movie, *Mahogany*. The film was okay, if over-long, but I was more entertained by the audience, who regularly stood up and shouted 'Right on, Diana,' and 'You go girl!' at various moments in the film. At the end, as the theme song played out over the credits, ladies all round me were standing up and joining in at the tops of their voices.

From there I walked across town to the Museum of Modern Art on West 53rd Street, where I enjoyed seeing Van Gogh's 'Starry Night' up close. I stood looking at it for an age, one of his most famous works and here it was, right in front of me. There was also a Dali, a Lichtenstein, a series of Warhol prints, works by Mondrian, Matisse, Cézanne, Magritte, Bacon, and the crème de la crème , Picasso's 'Les Desmoiselles D'Avignon'.

Next on my list was Times Square. Following the map Roy had given me, I thought I'd found it, but all I could see were a few theatres and cinemas, like a small Leicester Square. I eventually asked a passer-by where it was:

"You're standing in it," he yelled over the traffic noise.

The disappointment must have shown on my face.

"Yeah, it ain't as big as you think it is! But hey! It's Times Square!"

That evening I went to see *Equus* with Bunny. It was an odd, rather disturbing play, but just being a few feet away from the legendary Perkins was enough to blow my mind.

We went onto an Italian eaterie, where again we never stopped talking. Bunny was open-eyed at my tale of the murderous cabbie.

"Good God, John," she kept saying, as my story unfolded.

After we bid a final goodnight, I decided to walk back to the Y, to take in my last night in Manhattan. I made a detour to the Lincoln Center, where Roy had told me people skated on a specially constructed ice rink at Christmas, and it didn't disappoint. With Dean Martin crooning 'Jingle Bells' on the street speakers, and several Father Christmases skating merrily on the ice, it was the perfect festive end to my stay.

I got home late on the 29th, collapsed into bed and slept in until eleven the following morning. Daniel was away in Miami on a Redken training course, so I, thankfully, had the place to myself. I took a long hot bath and reflected on what an amazing time I'd had.

Making my way downstairs, I had a light snack and wrote a long letter to Roy. I gave my love to Thel and all his family, thanking them for their kindness and hospitality. Whether it was wondering if and when I'd see them again, or the jet-lag kicking in, I began to feel a little low, and my eyes started to get heavy.

What felt like a few minutes later, I was woken up by the phone ringing. I'd actually been asleep for over two hours. It was Stuart:

"So how was it?" he said.

"Incredible, Stuart!" I replied, trying to shake myself awake.

"You can tell us all about it tomorrow evening. Jim and Trish Dale have invited you to their New Year's Eve house party."

I'd met Trish a year or so earlier with Jim at one of Stuart and Patsy's dinners at home. They were a lovely couple, and of course I'd first met Jim at Stuart's Christmas '73.

"But what I rang to tell you, John, is that I thought you were fabulous on the TV show. Patsy and I watched it and felt really proud of you. Even better is the news that CBS have had such a great response to it, they've decided to rush-release 'I Got My Lady' as a single!"

"A Winter Smash!" I joked.

"Who knows, John? Wouldn't that be wonderful?"

Chapter Twenty-Six

Star Through My Window

In early January, CBS photographer Tom Sheehan called Stuart to ask if I would go along to the Soho Square offices for a photo session in preparation for the release of 'I Got My Lady'. This was good news, because it meant the company were finally serious about issuing it, after the disappointment of them cancelling its release the previous Summer.

I arrived in the morning, feeling just a little hung-over after a night on the town with Terry and the boys. I'd indulged in too many hash cakes and whiskies, as well as dancing the light fantabulous to a fabulous new record by Donna Summer, an album-length orgasmic fiesta called 'Love To Love You Baby'.

As Tom snapped away, he asked me to chat to him. It was probably to extract a bit of life out of his exhausted subject, but he graciously told me he wanted to try and give the photos a more impromptu feel, rather than staged poses. So I told him about the Donna Summer record, and how it was one of the best things I'd heard for a long time.

"It's unlikely Radio One will play it," I said. "Much too risqué for old Auntie Beeb."

"That should ensure it hits the top then!" Tom laughed.

"It didn't help my records! Maybe I should have done some heavy breathing on 'Family Man'."

Towards the end of the shoot, Tom told me he had been asked to go along to a Freddie Mercury recording session.

"They want me to take some promotional photos for a record Freddie's producing, would you like to join me? It could be fun. You'll love Freddie!"

On the way out, we bumped into Derek Witt:

"Oh excellent," he said. "I wanted to speak to you, John. How do you fancy being my first Pub Grub artiste?"

I looked puzzled.

"Pub Grub," he declared, as if it was all London was talking about.

I shook my head.

"Pub Grub," Derek explained, a little exasperated, "is my idea to get some of our newer artists better known by The CBS Family. It'll be a buffet lunch with lovely music at Ronnie Scott's, to an invited audience of our office and sales people. I'd love you to be the first to perform, John. Are you up for it?"

"When, Derek?"

"Next week. Great promo for your new single!"

"I'm okay to do it, but speak to Stuart as well."

"Wonderful! I'll call him now."

When Tom and I arrived at the studio, Freddie was sitting in the control room listening to the singer recording his lead vocal. The track, which I gathered from the chorus was called 'Man From Manhattan', sounded remarkably like 'Killer Queen', even down to the vocal which could easily have been mistaken for Mercury's. It struck me that this was perhaps the way pop music was moving, successful stars and producers being employed to clone their sound and layer it onto other budding artists' records, in an effort by the record label to replicate their success. That had obviously been what CBS had hoped when they'd teamed me with Biddu.

Tom introduced us, Freddie shaking his then long hair and proffering a black-nailed hand to brush fingers with. In his little bum-freezer fur jacket and tight jeans, he looked extremely frail and tiny. But his charisma was enormous, it filled the room.

"Eddie has a great voice, don't you think?" he said.

"Eddie Howell," Tom prompted me. "He wrote the song."

"Sounds great," I replied.

"John's signed to CBS," Tom told him.

"Hm. What do you do, dear?"

"I play piano and sing."

"Oh goodie," Freddie's eyes suddenly brightened and he clapped his multi-ringed fingers together. "Then you'll have a sense of rhythm! You can join me and Eddie to overdub some hand-claps!" He glanced at Tom. "Come on, you too, darling!"

He led us into a small cubicle, and arranged us in a semi-circle round the mike.

"Okay, dear, track please," he said to the engineer. Then to us, "just follow what I do."

As the track played, Freddie did a quick 'And-1' hand-clap, then another, very much a Queen trademark. We followed suit, he gave us a thumbs-ups:

"Let's do a take then!"

We clapped our hands, thankfully in time, and as the track ended he told us to double it.

"Thank you, Mercurettes," he said on our last hand-clap, snapped his fingers and moved into the mike on his own. "Now, off you go while I make magic! Do stay and watch, Tom. I love an audience!"

For the next half-an-hour, Freddie overdubbed a whole multi-tracked bank of perfectly sung, perfectly pitched harmony backing vocals. I was mesmerised, watching this tiny man creating a huge vocal sound all on his own, reminiscent of the amazing choir of voices on Queen's recent hit, 'Bohemian Rhapsody', which was currently in its sixth (of eight) weeks at Number One.

When he sang the final part, he took off his headphones and said,

"You see? Magic darlings," and came into the control room to listen to the slice of perfection with which he'd enchanted us all.

"It sounds like a Number One to me, Eddie," Tom said.

"Well, maybe Number Two," Freddie quipped, "but you'd be happy with that, wouldn't you, Eddie dear?"

In fact, the single didn't chart, even with Freddie's name associated with it. Perhaps people who loved Queen just wanted Queen to sound like Queen.

I'd never been to Ronnie Scott's in Soho, and as I began my forty-five minute spot there with my forthcoming single, I was aware of the legends who had performed here before me, and thought how thrilled my dad would have been to witness it.

There was no band, it was just me and an electric piano, and by the time I'd come to the end of the first song, even though it got a smattering of applause, there was already a sense of restlessness in the room. I didn't recognise many of the faces who stood and stared rather nonplussed at me as I introduced the second one, 'Family Man'. Even my usually appealing chat was failing, I might as well have been talking to a brick wall. Gradually, people began turning their backs on me, chatting amongst themselves, completely uninterested in what I was playing. I now knew how Leonard Cohen must have felt, when I witnessed CBS staff treating him with the same disdain when he'd performed at the company's sales conference eighteen months earlier. Sadly, unlike Cohen, I didn't have my champion Dick Asher to quell the noise, nor had I sold lots of albums, which must have helped the legendary performer cope with an apathetic crowd of philistines. He was the millionaire in the room.

By the third song, 'You Keep Me Steady', the wall of loud conversations and drunken laughter made it difficult to actually hear myself. Nobody applauded when I finished. I turned to Stuart, sitting with Patsy behind me, for support but he was frantically rubbing his forehead and saying something under his breath to Patsy. She looked at me like a distraught mother watching her child make a fool of himself in the school play. I was on my own. As I ploughed on, the only attentive face I saw was Derek's, who beamed obliviously at me from the back of the room, occasionally disappearing off to chat to somebody, then reappearing full of smiles.

I checked my watch and decided that, instead of doing my planned three-quarters of an hour, I'd just do twenty-five minutes. I wasn't being paid, and who cared anyway? The next ten minutes were excruciating, as my sound was entirely swallowed up by an avalanche of noise. I finished the last line of 'Goodbye Suzie', stood up and got absolutely no response. People were laughing amongst themselves, shouting jokes across the room at each other, and blissfully unaware of the turmoil going on within the artist who, so they'd been told only twelve months earlier, was their Next Big Thing.

My legs shaking and on the verge of tears, I went over to Stuart and Patsy, who looked shell-shocked:

"I hope to God I am dropped," I shouted down at them. "I don't want to record for people like this."

I walked through the crowd, avoiding making eye contact with anyone, and slipped out unnoticed by Derek, who was nattering to a group of people by the bar. As I escaped into a busy Frith Street, I felt extremely grateful for one thing, that my father had not been in the audience. That half-hour of ego destruction, dealt by disinterested idiots, was something I would not have wanted him to witness.

I got the tube to Waterloo and the train to Norbury. Once home, I poured myself a stiff whisky, ran a bath, disconnected the phone and went to bed.

The following morning, as I was making a cup of jasmine tea, the phone – which I'd only just remembered to reconnect - rang. It was Stuart:

"John? Are you alright?"

"Not really, Stuart. I feel like shit actually."

"I tried calling you last night, and a couple of times this morning, but there was no reply."

I sipped my tea and didn't respond.

"Look," he went on, "yesterday was not your fault, they were extremely rude to you. I couldn't find Derek after you'd gone, but when I do see him I'll give him a bollocking for not taking control of the situation. But these things happen occasionally, that's show-business, John. Some you win, -"

"And I certainly lost them!"

"Right. Yes. You did. So, here's a chance to prove to yourself that you can still keep an audience. The promoter Dudley Russell is a friend of ours and he would like to book you for a concert he's putting on at The New Victoria Theatre next week. He came by the office yesterday evening and we played him some of your music. He thinks you'd be great as support on the Max Boyce show."

I was aware of Max as his recent live album, *We All Had Doctor's Papers,* had stormed to the top of the charts a couple of months earlier. A Welsh entertainer, comedian, musician and singer, he specialised in singing about his beloved national rugby team, and was the darling of the South Wales mining communities, from whence he originated and where he'd worked as a young man. What Stuart hadn't told me - or hadn't been told - was that the concert was taking place on the day that the Wales rugby team was playing England for the Five Nations Championship at Twickenham.

When I arrived at the theatre and was introduced to Max, he shook my hand and laughed,

"Well, boyo, we trounced you lot today, eh?"

I looked puzzled and glanced over at Dudley Russell:

"Wales beat England at Twickenham today..." Dudley explained.

"Thrashed 'em more like!" Max said.

I was still confused and pulled a 'what the hell are you talking about?' face.

"You don't follow rugby then?" Max looked at me with a mixture of pity and amusement.

"No, I don't, Max, but I'm pleased for you."

"I should warn you, the crowd might be a little tricky tonight, John, but don't worry," he said, touching his nose, "I'll have a word with them."

He chuckled and patted my arm.

"Max," Dudley said, "you're frightening the lad!"

"No, it's okay," I replied. "I like a challenge!"

I was the first act on, with just a twenty minute solo spot. As soon as I sat at the grand piano and introduced myself, someone from the audience shouted,

"Get off, loser! Where's our boy?"

I went straight into 'Family Man', wondering if I'd survive in one piece, but actually got a mild scatter of applause at the end.

'At least they're not booing,' I thought.

I immediately followed it, without preamble, with Streisand's 'The Way We Were', the first time I'd performed a cover on stage. Dudley had suggested I do a couple of well-known songs to an audience who didn't know me, and it paid off. There was a definite increase in applause, and I even heard a cheer from somewhere.

I noticed that Max had walked into the wings and was watching me. When he heard the audience response he gave me a thumbs-up.

That relaxed me a little, and I chatted for a couple of minutes, telling the audience that my next number was "a Johnny Burnette song from the early '60s, which gave Ringo Starr a Number One hit in America in 1973."

As soon as I began 'You're Sixteen', a couple of people cheered, and at the end many of the audience were shouting "More!".

Max looked over at me and did a 'Champions' thing with his arms, and laughed.

I thanked the audience for being so patient with an English guy from Ramsbottom, which got a good laugh, and went straight into my final song, which I told them was available to buy "from next Monday, it's my latest single". When I finished 'I Got My Lady' and stood up, the place roared, people were standing and clapping me with raised arms.

I walked into the wings with applause still ringing round the theatre, and Max, looking utterly delighted, grabbed hold of me, shook both my hands and stared at me:

"Well, there's nothing of you, boy, but you were a lion out there! Well done, my son. That took guts. I am very impressed!"

At the end of the show, featuring a masterly performance by Max which I watched from the wings, he bowed to a roof-raising cheer and looked over at me.

"Ladies and gentleman," he said, "tonight you watched an extremely talented lad from Lancashire win your hearts, give it up once more for Mr John Howard!"

He beckoned me out onto the stage and the whole place went crazy, with cries of 'Bravo!' and the sound of stamping feet. Max stood to one side and joined in the applause, nodding with admiration. I looked stage left and Patsy was in bits in Stuart's arms.

As we were leaving the theatre, a girl ran over and told me how much she'd loved my music. Stuart produced a copy of the new single from his overcoat pocket and gave me a pen.

"I was going to give you this over dinner, John, but why not sign it for this young lady, with our compliments?"

She beamed at it and kissed me on the cheek:

"You were amazing," she said and rushed off, red-faced and delighted.

We reached the street and I saw Derek waiting for a taxi. I didn't know he'd been in the audience. He smiled and came over to us:

"Very good, John, but a little bit of advice – don't drink so much water on stage, you were taking a drink after every number. Makes you look nervous."

Stuart stepped forward:

"Did you hear that applause in there for John, Derek? Did you hear them cheering? Did you see him turn that whole fucking theatre around, he single-handedly brought them onto his side?"

"Well, yes, of course, he did well, but -"

"He did more than well, he was fucking amazing in there. It's a shame your Pub Grub pile of yobs didn't show John the same kind of respect last week. You need to have a little talk to your 'Family', Derek. They don't know talent when they see it."

"We all know John is talented, Stuart."

"Then they should bloody well show it – for a change."

As Stuart walked away and hailed a cab, Patsy turned to a shell-shocked Derek:

"Woof!" she said, and got into the cab, waving at me to follow. "Come on, John, we're having a celebration dinner."

"Do you want a lift, Derek?" I said.

"No thank you, I'll get my own. Good night, John."

The actor Gerald Harper – famous for playing Adam Adamant and Hadleigh on TV – had recently become a DJ on Capital Radio, with a weekly show on Saturday mornings. He liked 'I Got My Lady', and played it every week for about a month, telling his listeners that they "really should go out and buy this lovely record."

Biddu was currently big news again, he'd produced Tina Charles' latest single 'I Love To Love' which was already play-listed on Radio One and looked certain to be a hit. I was hoping this might help attract some attention to my single. Although Bid and I had made it ten months earlier, the public didn't know that.

Sadly, Biddu's name made no difference. No other disc jockey or radio station played it, Radio One as usual giving me their freezing cold shoulder. By early February, my "Summer Smash", released during one of the UK's coldest winters on record, was another damp squid. So, when Stuart went along to CBS to discuss whether the company would take up a third option on me, I knew what the answer would be.

"I'm sorry, John," he told me, as we drowned our sorrows in the office, "they just wouldn't spend anymore money on you. If the single had at least charted, anywhere, we may have stood a chance, but…"

"Don't worry, Stuart. Onwards and upwards, eh?"

He looked at me with a new expression – defeat. He was doing his best to look hopeful, but could no longer muster his old belief that we were going anywhere upwards, anytime soon. In just two and half years we'd gone from 'the world is our oyster' to 'the world doesn't give a shit'.

Patsy was listening to Radio One in the kitchen while she prepared a snack, and I heard Dave Lee Travis introducing the next record:

"Here's one which is destined for the top spot! In at No.23 this week, it's our own Little Miss Dynamite, Tina Charles, and 'I Love To Love'."

Three weeks later, Biddu enjoyed his second Number One, beginning a two-year run of Top Thirty hits for Tina. I'd bump into him and his wife Sue occasionally at Stuart and Patsy's house parties, but we never once mentioned the album we'd had such high hopes for, and seen buried with such ease by CBS.

I spent the next few weeks moseying round the house, playing records, visiting Terry and Bob in Wandsworth, not in the least bit interested in writing any songs. I had no direction, no incentive, and, I thought, no career. Stuart rang me every few days to ask when I'd be coming in, but I always put him off, saying I was feeling off-colour or visiting friends, promising, untruthfully, that I'd go in as soon as I felt better.

It was true that I felt under-par, but it wasn't just because I saw my career plummeting away from me. I'd got into the habit of imbibing a little too much whisky at Terry's, and then spending most evenings, stoned and pissed, dancing my ass off to the latest club sounds at

Rod's disco in Chelsea.

One afternoon, as I was preparing to go over to Terry's, Patsy called. She rarely if ever rang me, that always seemed to be Stuart's domain. But she was obviously on a mission:

"John," she said, "Stuart and I went to a restaurant the other evening in Knightsbridge, April Ashley's place, AD8, have you heard of it? It's very gay."

I hadn't.

"Well, the food was frankly ordinary, but we loved the ambience of the place. It feels very Bohemian chic, and it has a lovely white grand piano. There was a lady called Hebe on the night we were there, she had a pianist backing her, and she was adorable, very camp 1930s, she went down a storm. I think you'd go down very well there. What do you think?"

I didn't want to sound negative, but I really didn't see the point. I had no record to promote and I'd actually imagined that, after the triumph of my appearance in the Max Boyce show, I'd be offered more theatre gigs.

"Has Dudley not managed to get me anything else?" I asked her.

"Sadly, no, he did try but no-one was interested."

"Quelle surprise!"

"Now come on, John, you really have to snap out of this! I know how low you must feel but, well, we have to do something!"

I checked myself in the mirror. I was off to a Black and Gold party at Terry's, an excuse to quaff Guinness and champagne and scoff several hash cakes before going out on the town again.

"What would I play?" I asked her, deciding the sequin-covered Biba top hat Stuart had bought me two years earlier would be too much.

"Your music," she replied. "It's lovely!"

"They wouldn't want my songs in a restaurant, Patsy. They'd want things like 'The Way We Were', songs they recognise, and I only know two covers."

"Then come into the office, learn a few more, and I'll arrange an audition for you. I spoke to the manager, a lovely little Portuguese man called Georges, and he is definitely interested in hearing you."

"Let me think about it, Patsy. But thank you for thinking of me."

"Why wouldn't I? You're our artist!"

"I do have to go now, Patsy, but I will think about it."

"This could be the fillip you need, getting back to playing some music again. And anyway, we'd like to see you, it's been weeks."

The next day, as I arrived back at Daniel's, feeling like someone had been kicking my head all night, I went and had a long bath and decided to call Patsy. 'Why not?', I thought, 'what else do I have to do?'

AD8 was situated behind Knightsbridge at No. 8 Egerton Garden Mews, down a fairly steep staircase, into the smell of cooking and a rather damp aroma, being under the streets and drains of London. The restaurant itself, however, was very stylish. There was a sparkling mirrored bar directly opposite the pre-dinner seating area, with comfortable deep sofas covered in Biba cushions and throws. The tables were on both sides of a narrow long room which swept away from you, leading to the grand piano at the far end. It felt very cosy and yet extremely chic. Various paintings and candle-holders hung precariously on uneven walls, and behind the piano were four small-alcoved rooms, for the more romantic evenings by candlelight and soothing live music.

Georges stepped out from behind the bar and introduced himself:

"You must be John," he said in a heavy Portuguese accent. He was a tiny man in his late 30s and moved like a dancer, straight-backed and full of poise. Still quite attractive, with high cheekbones and a floppy mop of shoulder-length hair, which he swept off his face like a movie star as he spoke, one could see he had been an absolutely frail beauty in his youth.

"Would you like to play something for me?"

I tinkled on the piano for a few minutes, just some doodle which sounded pretty, then went into 'The Way We Were'. By the time I'd finished, Georges had moved to sit at the nearest table.

"Lovely," he shouted, clapping his hands. "You will be so perfect for us! Can you play this Sunday lunch? It's always full on Sundays."

By the following Sunday, I had two forty-five minute sets sorted, having gone into Stuart's office every day that week and learnt 'Send In The Clowns', What Are You Doing The Rest of Your Life', some Beatles tunes, a couple of Dusty songs, several Elton John numbers, and a few Coward favourites. I sprinkled in a small selection of my own songs like 'Family Man', 'Guess Who's Coming To Dinner', 'Maybe Someday In Miami' and 'Oh Dad'. They fit in beautifully with the well-known up-tempo pop standards like 'You're Sixteen' and 'Honey Pie'.

"Simply marvellous!" Georges cried after my first set, his customers applauding as I walked back to the bar. "And you look so stylish, my dear! Now, let me get you a drink, and what would you like for lunch?"

After my second set, a couple near the stage beckoned me over:

"Beautiful," the man said, "will you join us for a drink?"

As we chatted, he told me he knew the manager of Morton's Restaurant in Berkeley Square:

"You'd be perfect there. Would you like me to speak to my friend?"

Morton's was a large two-floored eaterie a few doors down from the Rolls Royce showroom, the manager, a surprisingly young chap called Chris, showed me to the piano and asked me to "just play a few things". The place was packed with people sitting and chatting at the long bar which covered one whole wall, and several groups of businessmen at the many tables having lunch. This was obviously the brasserie. From the grand piano I could see other more formally-dressed customers climbing the sweeping staircase to the a la carte restaurant above us.

I had now developed a technique of linking each song with an instrumental doodle of my own impromptu creation. I found it was a great way of giving customers a constant gentle flow of music, without them having to stop what they were doing, eating or chatting, and applaud every three or four minutes. These weren't theatre gigs, I was there to give people some music while they ate, which they could listen to if they wished, or treat it as they would a CD playing in the background.

By the second number, the noise of conversation in the room had quietened, people had stopped chatting and were turning round to see who was singing. Several businessmen even began tapping their feet to 'You're Sixteen'. Chris sat directly opposite me throughout, obviously clocking the reaction of his clientele. When I stood up, the place erupted into applause. Chris came over and shook my hand:

"You're hired," he said. "When can you start?"

This word-of-mouth growth of my reputation seemed to spread, as customers put in their own good words for me at other restaurants they frequented. By the end of April, I'd added Blitz in Covent Garden, The Last Resort in Fulham and Porters of Piccadilly to my venue list. My repertoire also grew substantially, new numbers added a couple of times each week, often things people had requested which, if I hadn't known them, I'd learn and surprise them with at my next appearance.

AD8 was often host to British celebrities like Diana Dors and Danny La Rue, who would send me a drink and ask me to play one of their favourite songs. April also visited a couple of times, which always caused mumblings of "That's her, isn't she gorgeous?" amongst customers. She was truly lovely, skin like porcelain and with an attractive reserved dignity. She'd make her way along the room towards her friends near the piano, stopping occasionally and bending her head to chat to thrilled diners.

The actual owner of the place, Mark, was a racehorse breeder from Ireland, and he would join me at my table while I ate, gently chat me up, and I'd josh him that his husband Georges would not approve.

Blitz, in Covent Garden, was then styled as a 1930s canteen, serving East End grub and with lots of pre-war posters for Ovaltine, Horlick's and Coca-Cola on the walls. There was no sign at that time of it becoming the infamous night-time haunt of future New Romantics like Boy George and Steve Strange. Biddy and Eve, a Coward-esque duo, were the main performers while I'd do lunchtimes and occasional evenings.

Porters of Piccadilly was a gay venue, more a club than a restaurant, although they served snacks. It had been decorated like an art deco cruise ship, lots of wood, chrome and mirrors, and palm trees dotted about. I would serve up my hors d'ouevres of slightly camp cabaret at the Steinway grand, before the DJ would kick in with his main course of banging dance music. It seemed to work, people happily listening at the bar or smooching on the dance floor as I played, before getting out the poppers and bopping their butts off to the early hours.

The Last Resort, in Fulham, was a slightly rougher joint, it felt very young mid-management London, serving burgers and chips, steaks, and the like, but the clientele was always very friendly towards me. While playing there one evening, I noticed a familiar face at one of the tables. It was John Kongos, who had enjoyed two or three big hits in the early '70s. He listened intently to what I was doing but his interest was definitely piqued when I played a new song I'd recently written, 'Star Through My Window'. It was one of very few songs I wrote around that time, the lyrics appearing out of the ether one afternoon when I was learning some new material at Stuart's:

Did I see a star through my window?
Or was it just a memory?
It was guiding gold and silver to my door
Then it went out
And daylight came shining through
So who in the world would have guessed
I'd be back where I started
Making plans once again
There's always a rainbow
When the rain's at an end
But no pot of gold for the taking
I'm shaking, I'm nervous
'Cause I know I'm right back in the middle
The road lies ahead me
The hurdles behind me
It's a new race I'm running
It's a new face I'm showing
I've been growing up slowly
Taking my time
And good friends of mine see my heart is beating again

Stuart loved the song, took me into Regent Sound Studios to demo it, tried to interest a few record companies but got turned down by everyone he approached. I didn't really mind. I'd found a new career, a new life, and a new audience who actually wanted to listen to what I had to offer. There was no pressure, no agenda, no longer any ambition except to play music I loved to people who wanted to hear it.

When I'd finished my set, John waved me over.

"Please, join me," he said, "would you like a drink?"

He told me he loved 'Star Through My Window':

"Did you write it?"

"Yes, quite recently."

"I'd love to make a record of it with you."

We chatted for about half an hour, until I was due on for my next set. He took his leave, saying he'd come back the next time I was playing there and we'd have a further chat, but I never saw him again. "Events, dear boy," as MacMillan once said, may have got in the way. I never knew.

One evening at Morton's, I was surprised to see Dan Loggins walk in, accompanied by a couple of friends. He saw me playing and waved, ordered drinks at the bar, and sent me a vodka and tonic over. I was just starting 'Send In The Clowns' and he gave me a thumbs-up and went and settled in his seat, cheering me with his glass of wine.

I was about halfway through the song when a small party arrived, at the centre of which was a petite, dark-haired lady in her 30s carrying a red rose, which matched her flowing chiffon red dress perfectly. She put the rose to her nose, looked over at me and beamed. Whispering something to her friends, who went to their table and sat down, she walked over to me.

"I love this song," she said, with a strong Italian accent. "Would you mind if I sang it with you?"

"Not at all!" I replied.

She sat on a stool by me, listening intently and smiling across at her friends. I nodded at her to take the next verse and, oh my word, she sang like an angel. The place stopped in its tracks, everyone gob-smacked by this vocal perfection soaring around the room. She gestured at me to join in, and made eye contact with me throughout our duet. I had a microphone, she didn't need one.

We finished the song together, where we harmonised as if we'd rehearsed it, and the place went wild. She stood up, did a little bow, handed me her rose and, blowing me a kiss, went to join her friends. They stayed until the end of my set, applauding each song, and then standing to applaud as I walked from the piano. She called me over and I kissed her hand.

"Thank you," I gushed. "You were wonderful. I loved that!"

"You, young sir, are a delight," she said. "Thank you!"

Her party stood, nodded at me, and walked her to the door, where, with one last blown kiss, she was gone. I never knew her name, but she never left my memory.

"Wow, John!" Dan said, as I went to join him at his table. "That was amazing!"

He ordered another drink for me from the waiter and asked me to sit down.

"So, are you still writing, John?"

"Not much, no. I haven't really felt like it since, well, since CBS dropped me."

Dan stopped drinking:

"Dropped you? We didn't drop you!"

"Really? So – how come I'm no longer signed to the label?"

"Stuart turned our offer down!"

The waiter gave me my drink and I knocked it back:

"What offer?"

"You don't know? Okay. We told Stuart we couldn't take up another album option, it was for twenty-five grand, we couldn't agree to that. But! We didn't want to lose you, so we offered Stuart a deal where you'd stay signed to CBS and continue to record stuff, bring it to us, and if we liked it, we'd release it, which could have led in time to another album."

"I had no idea!" I said. "Stuart just told me you didn't want to spend anymore money on me."

"That's true, and any recordings you made would be at Stuart's expense, but if we'd signed something you brought to us, we'd've reimbursed the costs and spent our money promoting it. It seemed a fair deal to me, but Stuart wanted another advance for an album and..." He looked at me and shrugged his shoulders. "It's not called the music business for nothing, John. We'd spent a lot of money on you, with no return. That couldn't go on, as much as we loved you. And we did! We miss you!"

At that point, one of Dan's friends, a well-dressed guy in his 30s, leaned over and thrust his hand down my bare chest into my crutch. I was wearing a one-piece denim outfit I'd bought in King's Road a few days earlier, which, he told me as he groped his way around, "matches your eyes!".

"Thought so," he said. "You're not wearing any underwear! You little tart!"

"Jack!" Dan admonished him.

"What? If you don't want customers, don't advertise the goods! That outfit is sensational on you, darling! I'd love to investigate further!"

He did, a few evenings later, arriving on his own and sending me several drinks, after which I spent the night at his rooftop Bayswater apartment.

The next morning, after enjoying a breakfast of champagne and scrambled eggs, with the added bonus of a bird's eye view of sleeping London, I went over to Stuart's office:

"Yes, he's right," Stuart replied, when I asked him about what Dan had told me. "But let me ask you this, John: would you really have wanted a situation where you recorded something, I took it to CBS, they turned it down, you recorded something else, they turned it down, going through that again and again, until – and maybe not even then – they liked something enough to put it out as a single? There was no album being offered, John, no money either. And frankly, I can't afford to pay for recordings which may not be released. CBS didn't want demos, they wanted full productions, with the money only being reimbursed if they took something on. I couldn't accept that, for me or for you. You're way better than that."

Stuart was right, of course. Dan had made it sound oh so easy, but the truth would have been a potential energy and confidence drain unlike anything I'd yet experienced.

This was a whole new period in my life, where I not only had a new audience, I was also earning more money than I ever had.

Stuart had been paying me a weekly retainer of thirty pounds since we'd had the CBS deal, but it only just allowed me to pay the rent and buy food for the week. Going out, buying clothes, having fun with friends – who all had good jobs and were getting paid a great salary - were things I could only do sparingly, always feeing like the poor relation.

Now I had the money to buy great clothes and feel financially equal to my friends. I could also finally ditch the pin-striped suited 'Kid' image, which Stuart had chosen for me in 1973 and was looking very tired. The suits, along with my recording career, were put in a box and replaced with the business of having fun.

My new look seemed to appeal not only to customers who enjoyed my music, but also to several new wealthy beaus who would visit the restaurant, send me a drink, invite me to join them, ask me out to dinner, followed by an invitation to stay with them for the evening. By the summer of 1976, I had several boyfriends, none of whom were looking for a full-time relationship, just good company and 'buddy sex'. It suited me down to the ground. I was twenty-three years old, feeling fabulous, playing music I got an instant response to, and finally living the London lifestyle which my CBS promotional photos had - misleadingly - pictured me enjoying.

One evening at Morton's, a beautifully-dressed chap in his 40s arrived with a lady I assumed was his wife. They sat at the bar and, while she chatted to the barman, he watched me and listened to me playing. They sent several drinks over, and, after an hour or so, left. A couple of evenings later, he was back, this time with a male friend, and, sitting at a table near the piano, invited me to join them. He introduced himself as Clint and, over several glasses of very good red wine, began complimenting me on much more than my music:

"But you're married," I told him, as he fondled my thigh under the table.

"So what?" he purred, discovering my knickerless state.

A couple of hours later, we were rolling around the bedroom at his friend's flat in Mayfair.

The next day, over a late cooked breakfast, which his friend's manservant delivered to us in bed, he told me he wanted to see me again.

"I'm playing at The Last Resort this evening," I told him.

"I'll pick you up there at about, what, eleven-thirty?"

Sure enough he was there, sending over a vodka as I dedicated 'The Way You Look Tonight' to him. Looking forward to another night of unbridled passion, I was coming to the end of my set when Chas, the restaurant manager, walked up to me and murmured,

"Before you go over and join your friend, do come and speak to me."

As I stood with him in the staff nook under the stairs, Chas took a long drag on his cigarette, blew out the smoke a la Bette Davis and said,

"You know Clint well?"

"Intimately," I replied.

He pursed his lips:

"You know who he is, don't you?"

"Clint."

"Hm, thought so. Darling, he is part of one of the nastiest drug gangs in London. Very shady lot. Not to be messed with. Have you met his wife?"

"I saw her at Morton's with him the other evening, but we've never spoken."

"I hope you never do, darling. Cheryl wears the trousers, she calls the shots, her darling Clint is the occasionally disobedient lap dog. A friend of mine had a ding-dong with him a couple of years ago, Cheryl found out, and, well, if I tell you he could only now sing castrato in the choir, you'll get the idea."

My stomach flipped.

"That's right, dear. You'll be doing Tiny Tim numbers if she gets wind that you're screwing her darling Clint, Mr Fucks Anything That Moves, as he's known on the scene."

"What can I do?" I asked him, terrified.

"Leave it with me, dear. I'll have a little whisper in his ear."

A few minutes later, as I hovered in the nook, Chas returned:

"He's gone, dear. I don't think you'll see him again."

"What did you say to him?"

He buffed his nails:

"That's for me to know and you to feel fucking grateful for, dear. Now get back on and do your thing, darling."

A few evenings later, Cheryl arrived at Morton's with a female friend. She smiled over at me as I was singing, and sent me a drink with a note which read,

"Come and have a chat when you're finished."

With my heart beating like a drum, I went and joined her at the bar. She introduced me to her friend, Joy, and ordered me another drink.

"Love your music, darling," she said. "Isn't he fabulous, Joy?"

"He is, Cheryl," Joy replied, blowing smoke out of the side of her mouth. "I bet he breaks a few hearts with a voice like that."

"You've met my Clint, haven't you, darling?" Cheryl asked.

I attempted to swallow my vodka and replied, as nonchalantly as I could,

"You were here with him the other evening weren't you?"

"That's right, love. I absolutely adore that man, but he does have, shall we say, a wandering eye, doesn't he Joy?"

"Can't keep it in his pants, that boy," Joy cackled, stubbing out her cigarette.

"He can't," Cheryl went on. "He has, if you get my meaning, strayed over the fence a few times, but, when he does, I make sure it only happens once. You have to, don't you, love? Don't you, Joy?"

"You do, Cheryl," Joy replied, looking at me with half-closed eyes.

Trying to breathe as well as calmly sipping my drink, I could feel a small sweat breaking out on my forehead.

"Warm in here, isn't it, love? But," she looked me up and down, "you haven't got much on, darling, so you should feel pretty cool. Are you hot, Joy?"

"Getting a bit sticky, Cheryl."

"Okay doll, let's get some air." She gazed at me and smiled. "Listen darling, you keep singing those beautiful songs, someone will I'm sure whisk you away one day, as they should, you are quite lovely. But do make sure they're unattached. It'll make life much easier – for everyone. Know what I mean?" She stood up. "Joy? Shall we?"

She pecked me on the cheek and giggled about what smooth skin I had:

"Hm," she said, "I can see you're quite the little heart-breaker," and sauntered out, arm in arm with her friend, who gave me a 'Toodle-oo!' wave at the door.

Clint and Cheryl still came to Morton's occasionally, always together, sat at the bar, sent a drink over, and left again after an hour or so. We never spoke to each other, but Clint had obviously been beaten back into line, following her in and out like, well, like an obedient lap dog.

One summer afternoon at AD8, after a particularly well-received set, I was asked to join a couple at their table. Matthew, as he introduced himself, was, I imagined, in his late 30s, and about thirty years younger than his wife Beatrice. She obviously adored him. Every time he said something even vaguely amusing she laughed her head off, looked at me with widened eyes and cooed "Oh Matthew," like a love-struck little girl.

He was an attractive man with just the hint of a French accent, while she could have easily belonged to the colonial set fifty years earlier, with that brittle, slightly tortured Received Pronunciation one used to hear on old BBC newsreels.

"Bea and I adore your music," Matthew declared, as though addressing the whole room, "and Bea, my darling Bea, has something to ask you."

She welcomed his look of devotion with a nervous clasp of her expensive pearl necklace, beamed at me and said,

"John, would you play Elton John's 'Your Song' for me? The orchestra was playing that when Matthew proposed to me in Bermuda."

He grasped her hand across the table and she fluttered her eyes at him.

'This is true love indeed,' I thought.

I slipped Elton's debut hit song into my next set, rewarded with a sparkling smile from Beatrice and a blown kiss from Matthew, which he sent from behind his wife's head.

'Hm,' I thought.

I rejoined them after my set:

"John, that was simply wonderful!" Beatrice said, rubbing my cheek with her hand. "Now! Matthew wants to ask you something."

"Another song?" I joked.

"No," Matthew replied, "though that would, of course, be marvellous! What I – what we - would like to say is, we'd be honoured if you would be our guest for the night this evening, at our home in Kensington."

I had no gigs that night, so a few hours later I was sitting in their palatial apartment's dining-room, enjoying the delicious supper Beatrice had cooked. I looked around as we chatted at the beautiful antique furniture, and the enormous chandeliers which twinkled above our heads. We nattered into the early hours about their exotic travels around the world, which were obviously new experiences for Matthew, but not his wife.

"I am such a lucky woman," she said at one point, as Matthew fondled her hand on the table. "He makes me very happy."

Lit by the candelabras on the table, she seemed quite frail and vulnerable, while he was bounding with masculine energy, declaiming how in love he was with her.

As we bid goodnight, I kissed Bea on the cheek and was about to shake Matthew's hand when he pulled me forward and hugged me, very tightly, making it immediately clear how very pleased he was that I was there.

After finally extricating myself from hugs, kisses and my gushing hosts, I settled down in my exquisite four-poster bed for the night, dropping off very quickly.

I was woken by my door creaking open, glanced at the bedside clock, it was four a.m. The silhouetted figure of a naked man walked in and crept towards me. He slipped into bed and began passionately caressing, kissing and fondling me:

"I'm crazy about you!" Matthew whispered into my nibbled ear.

"But, what about Beatrice...?"

"Don't worry about her, it's you I want right now!"

His passion grew and developed alarmingly rapidly, and, throwing me onto my back, he lifted my legs into the air and rapidly moved in.

As he went at it hell for leather, I saw movement through the slightly ajar door. Beatrice was spying on us through the gap. When he climaxed extremely noisily, I looked over at the door again and saw her hurrying away.

Matthew rolled over, lit a cigarette and smiled at me:

"That was wonderful!"

"I think Beatrice enjoyed it as well."

Matthew glanced over at the door and chuckled:

"Ah! You saw her! She knows I have a penchant for attractive young men. She also knows it arouses me, and she will enjoy that later."

"But she seemed to rush away. I thought she was upset?"

"No! She was dashing off to pretty herself up for when I return to our boudoir!"

He took a long drag of his cigarette, put it out in the ashtray by the bed, heaved a huge satisfied sigh, rolled over and fell asleep in my arms. An hour or so later, I was woken by him creeping out of my room, no doubt going back to an expectant Beatrice.

The next morning, after a healthy breakfast of croissants, honey, coffee and orange juice, over which we talked about everything except what had occurred the night before, I bid them farewell at the door. Bea kissed me on the cheek and whispered:

"Thank you, John."

"Please do come and see us again!" Matthew shouted from the hallway, letting his silk bathrobe fall open just enough to show me what would be on offer if I did.

I didn't go back, and a few weeks later two friends of theirs, who were occasional diners at AD8, told me that Matthew had left Beatrice for the owner of the hotel where they'd been holidaying in The Bahamas:

"What about poor Beatrice?" I asked.

"Oh, she always finds a sugar baby, Matthew's one of many.

With her money, finding a man isn't the problem…"

"It's keeping him in her bed which is," said the other friend.

In May, Daniel was promoted to Director of Redken International Hair Care, which meant he was moving back to Johannesburg by the end of the month. It also meant I would have to find a new home.

I decided I wanted to be nearer the West End. Getting home after an evening gig had become something of a drag. Having to rush away from the restaurant by eleven o'clock, when customers were often calling for me to play some more, was often causing consternation from them and management. Being regularly courted, wined, dined and bedded by various customers had its uses beyond mere satiation of youthful lust, but if I didn't trick out, then getting home was sometimes very tight. A few times I'd had to make my way to Terry's, arriving after midnight, and knocking on his door until, bleary-eyed, he opened it and let me in so I could kip at his place.

I went to look at a flat in Finborough Road, which I found through an Earl's Court letting agency Terry knew about. The landlord of the first floor apartment, Vaughn, was Chairman of a successful wallpaper company. He was – as my mother would have said – a big-boned man, who told me, rather openly for someone I'd just met, that he used the flat as his weekend London getaway, where "I can catch up with my love life". He added conspiratorially, "I personally prefer Filipino and Thai men, always have." He explained that he financed their British education, in return for which they became his occasional companions for the night.

"Some people call it prostitution, I call it common sense."

The flat was a fairly basic but clean two-bedroomed apartment behind Redcliffe Square, and I told Vaughn I was definitely interested.

"What do you do for a living?" he asked me.

"I'm a singer and pianist, I play in various restaurants in London."

He suddenly became quite cagey:

"Isn't that rather insecure? How can I be certain you'll always be employed and have the earnings to pay the rent?"

Without pausing for breath I said,

"Come and see me performing at AD8 tomorrow evening, as my guest. I think you'll realise that my future as a performer is pretty secure."

I moved in a week later.

One afternoon, I was relaxing on the sofa in the sitting-room, listening to Barbra Streisand's *Stoney End* album. One of her most successful releases, it featured several rather splendid covers of Laura Nyro songs. The front door opened, and I turned expecting to see Vaughn striding in. Instead, a tiny Filipino chap appeared, looked down at me and chuckled.

"Hello," he said, "you're John, I presume?"

I thought he must be one of Vaughn's boyfriends:

"Vaughn's not here, I'm afraid, I'm not expecting him until -"

"Oh, I haven't come to see Vaughn," he replied dismissively. "God forbid!"

He marched over to a piggy-bank on the windowsill, where Vaughn had asked me to put my 10p coins whenever I made a telephone call. With a small penknife, which he produced from his trouser pocket, he proceeded to ease the change out onto the coffee table. He counted it, about a pounds worth, nodded and put the piggy-bank back:

"My spending money for the day," he cried. "So nice of the coin fairies to provide it for me!" He marched forward and shook my hand. "I'm Jun Terra, Son of The Perfect Earth to my father, June to my friends."

I was just about to explain that the money in his hand was in fact my contribution for the phone calls I'd made, when he marched towards the front door, turned round, grinned at me and said,

"We are going to have such fun, my dear!"

With a wink and a camp shoulder wiggle, he was gone.

And so began an episode in my life which, while certainly fun, ended rather disastrously just a few months later…

Chapter Twenty-Seven

'They'

"I think my head is falling off!"

I was lying in the middle of Terry's sitting-room, stoned out of my mind on hash cakes we'd all eaten an hour earlier. Usually I giggled for hours, finding everything anyone said or did hilarious. This time, however, I was terrified.

At first, there had been the usual sensation of things slowing down, and the realisation that I was staring at someone as they spoke to me for just a tad too long. Whenever I felt that happening, Bob always noticed and told the room,

"John's stoned!"

There were about ten people around me on chairs and sofas, enjoying floating away, one or two occasionally saying "Wow," to the ceiling or each other. But I was gripping my head as tightly as I could, certain that, if I let go, it would leave my shoulders and roll away on the floor.

As I frantically told everyone my fate, one Scottish guy called Bruce, who could cut you in pieces with just a couple of well-aimed tongue lashings, looked down at me and said,

"If your head doesn't fall off, I'll rip the fucking thing off myself! Now shut the fuck up!!"

I got up and wandered out of the room, leaving everybody having a marvellous time. I must have climbed the stairs and gone into Bob's room as I found myself standing in front of his floor-length mirror by the door. I stared at the bewildered-looking figure staring back at me, completely mystified as to who it was.

"Are you okay?" I heard someone say behind me. His reflection came into view and I recognised him, it was Bob. "You're not dealing with this are you?"

He took my hand and led me onto his bed, lay me down and sat with me, stroking my hair. His cool hand on my forehead was rather soothing and I closed my eyes, enjoying the comfort it gave me. I floated off and was walking on a beach on my own. It was completely empty under a sky which seemed to change colour every few seconds. A cloud appeared, opened like a trapdoor and released a shaft of light, which beamed biblically down in front of me. A voice from somewhere inside the light told me to relax, not fight it, join the slipstream and let it take me over.

I opened my eyes and I was back in the sitting-room, unaware of how I'd got there. Bruce was in a chair opposite, and staring at the ceiling as if he'd seen God. Very gradually, a sensation of slowly floating down, like a feather towards the ground, took over. I let it carry me downwards, enjoying the journey, until finally, I landed very gently.

As if a switch had been turned on in my head, things were suddenly balanced again. The picture made sense and the world felt like a solid place once more. It was as though all the bits of my brain, which had been scattered, had melded themselves back together. Bruce took his eyes off the ceiling, saw me and smiled, surprisingly benignly:

"Still got your head, then?"

"Yes. All here," I said, mock-checking it was there. "Thanks for the sympathy, by the way."

"So, I take it you've never had cakes laced with hash and opium before?"

"Opium?"

"Yes. It gives it that much more of a blast!"

It had certainly blasted me apart. Still feeling a little odd, I stood up and went outside into Terry's back courtyard. The smell of the damp ground after the rainfall we'd had that morning was like the best cologne I'd ever splashed on. I breathed it in and was probably there for a good half an hour – or it could have been a few minutes, time was still a little fractured - before Bob came and sat with me:

"You feeling better?"

"More or less, still a bit, well, jagged, but, yes, I feel better."

"I won't give you the opium cakes again, hash is obviously all you can deal with. You fought it, didn't you? The feeling."

I nodded.

"Fatal. You have to just go with whatever's happening, however weird or disturbing. Fight it, and it fucks up your head."

"The one I thought was falling off?"

"That one, yeah. Come in and we'll make a cup of tea, the more normality now the better."

After my next Morton's gig, Chris called me over to join him, and a lady he introduced as his girlfriend, Samantha.

"Sam wants to ask you something."

"How do you fancy a week in Corfu?" she said, smiling broadly at me. "All expenses paid, to play a gig at a hotel there?"

She told me that she was a tour operator who arranged musicians to play at various hotels on the Greek islands.

"Bring a friend with you, it's all paid for. All you have to do is one gig at the end of the week. I think what you do would be perfect for our hotel on Corfu."

Bob, who was fast becoming a good friend, was immediately up for it when I asked him if he fancied coming with me. I had to quickly arrange 'deps' at the other venues I played, ringing round several musicians who'd alternated evenings with me, and asking them to do my spots for a week. A couple of weeks later, with everything sorted, Bob and I were checking into a large hotel outside of the main Corfu town, way up in the hills, which the bus had struggled to climb. I'd looked out at the narrow dust road falling away from us into rocky valleys below and, although I had long ago lost my faith in God, I did pray to someone, anyone who might be listening, to help us reach the hotel in one piece.

"The name, sir?" the receptionist asked me at the desk.

"John Howard, this is my friend Bob Mantell."

She looked down the columns in her book, turned the page, looked down more columns, looked up at me and shook her head:

"No, nothing here."

"We have to be. I'm one of the entertainers. Samantha from Easytimes Travel booked me to perform here."

Her face lit up:

"Ah! Right!"

She put her red book away, got out a blue one from her drawer, found the right page, looked down the columns and pointed her finger at me.

"Yes! Mr Howard and Mr Mantell! Okay, here's your room key, just down the corridor, turn left at the end. You have a pool apartment."

"Very nice too!" Bob said, delighted.

As we were lifting up our bags, I thought I'd just check out the room I'd be playing in:

"Er - could I have a look at where I'll be performing?"

"Certainly, sir, down the corridor, turn right at the end."

It was a large room, obviously doubling as a dining room as well as where they staged their nightly entertainments for guests.

There was a small stage, with a set of drums, a couple of speakers, and long red and gold strands of tinsel along the back wall.

"Glitz and Glamour, eh?" Bob murmured.

I walked right round the room, but couldn't see a piano anywhere.

"They probably put it away when it's not being used," Bob said as we walked back to reception, where 'Shelley', according to her name tag, was just finishing chatting to a guest.

"Er- hello?" I said when the guest had gone.

She lifted her head and smiled extremely brightly at me.

"Everything okay?"

"Erm, not sure, where's the piano?"

She stopped what she was doing and stared at me as if I'd just spoken in Klingon:

"I'm sorry?"

"The piano, I can't find one in there."

"Piano?"

"Yes. Where is it?"

"Piano," she said again, as if trying to make sense of a word she'd never heard before.

"I'm the pianist. I need a piano."

The puzzlement on her face turned to horror:

"We don't have a piano here! Anywhere! We thought you were a singer."

"I am, but I play piano and sing. Didn't Samantha mention that?"

She took a deep breath and checked her register again. Shaking her head, she turned the book round and showed me. Sure enough, there was my name, and against it: 'Singer'.

"I'll get the rep to come and see you this afternoon," she said, obviously deciding this wasn't her problem. "About two o'clock? After lunch, in the dining-room?"

"The one with no piano?"

"That's it, yes."

The joy of finding our apartment, literally a few steps from the invitingly large pool, was quelled by the questions swirling round my head. The one which shouted the loudest was,

"So what the fuck are you going to do now?"

"Come on," Bob said, "let's get some sun, they'll sort it out."

About half an hour later, we were soaking up the rays, with vodka and tonics by our sunbeds, when a tiny lady's voice said,

"John Howard?"

I looked up and saw a skinny woman in a blue and white uniform, clipboard in hand, smiling nervously down at me.

"Yes," I replied, sitting up.

"I'm Sheila, your rep for the week. I understand from Shelley that we have a little problem?"

"I thought we were meeting up after lunch?"

"I decided we should talk now. Get it sorted."

Bob looked up at me with an expression which said, "told you they would."

"Well, there's quite a big problem," I told her. "There's no piano."

"That's right. There's no piano."

"Can one be hired?"

"I'm afraid not. No budget for that. Sam didn't tell me you were a pianist, we've never booked a pianist, because, well, there's no piano."

"So, what do I do?"

"Can't you sing without a piano? I've talked to the band, they're lovely guys. They're happy to back you, they back all our singers."

"But I don't have any sheet music. All my songs are in my head, and I wouldn't imagine the band are mind-readers."

She thought for a moment, glancing down at her clipboard as though an answer might be on there:

"Okay. Why don't you come and meet them? Have a chat. I'm sure we can sort something out."

The band, three guys in their late 30s, were sunbathing outside their apartment on the other side of the pool. They greeted us amiably as Sheila introduced us and I explained the situation to 'Paul, the guitarist', who seemed completely unfazed by my dilemma:

"Can you write music?" he asked.

"I haven't for a long time."

"But you can?"

"I was classically trained so...I can probably still do it."

"Joe?" Paul said to the drummer. "Can you get some sheets of manuscript from the room for John?" He turned to me, "I'm the dots guy."

For the next four days, I sat by the pool, not only getting a great tan, but also writing out the sheet music for eleven songs. I surprised myself that I could still do it, and by the Thursday they were all done. I found Paul having a cigarette on his veranda, and handed him the pile of manuscripts:

"Bloody great," he said, looking through them. "Nice selection too! We'll be fine, John. Let's break legs!"

On the Friday evening, I was suited and booted up, waiting to be introduced by the evening's MD, 'Laughable Larry – Your Holiday Happy Chappie', as he was billed on the felt-penned poster by the door. I'd had no rehearsal with the band, Paul had assured me we'd be fine. So, feeling very nervous, I looked over at Bob sitting at the front, who smiled and gave me a thumbs-up:

"Ladies and Gentlemen!" Larry shouted in full Butlin's mode, "Our next entertainer is a talented young man from London. He has made several big-selling albums for EMI, working with Cliff Richard and The Shadows and Tina Charles. He's now making a name for himself on some of the UK's top TV shows, so give a big hand for Mr John Howard!"

I walked into a roomful of warm applause, wondering where the hell Larry got his information – and the audience probably wondering why they didn't recognise me. Larry passed me his mike and the band struck up 'All My Loving'. Then something very bizarre happened. I became Mr Entertainment. As I made my confidently breezy way around the room, trilling McCartney's hit to the band's beaty rhythm, I smiled at the ladies smiling back at me, and belted the song out like

Sinatra at The Sands. I think I even did a Frank-esque 'Ooooh!' at one point. It went down a storm, applause and whistles everywhere.

I was expecting to feel naked without the prop of a piano, which I'd always had glued to me on stage before, but I rather enjoyed the freedom of being able to wander around at my leisure, with just the mike and its lead snaking through my hand for comfort.

'You're Sixteen' was next up, and that also raced along nicely. I even got the audience to sing along with me in the choruses, mugging at the more elderly ladies clapping their hands in time to the music on the lines, 'You're sixteen, You're beautiful!, And you're mine!'

I was on a roll. This cabaret lark was a piece of cake! I'd decided to slow things down a little for the third number, and introduced 'Killing Me Softly With His Song':

"Thank you ladies and gentlemen! I'd now like to sing you a beautiful song, written by Lori Lieberman after she'd watched Don McLean performing in concert in 1971," I told them slightly inaccurately. I later discovered that it was actually written by Charles Fox and Norman Gimbel in collaboration with Lieberman, after she'd told them how seeing McLean on stage had affected her.

Paul counted us in with a sprightly '1-2-3-4', and the band kicked in with exactly the same jaunty tempo and rhythm as 'All My Loving' and 'You're Sixteen'. There was nothing I could do, so I cheerily bopped on with the band who were racing along like a high-speed locomotive. I actually began snapping my fingers in time to the driving beat, like some Cruise Ship star turn.

I grinned at the audience, doing my best to look perfectly comfortable, performing what should have been a touching ballad in the guise of a banging disco number. As I belted out the chorus, half-wondering why the boys were steaming ahead at such a rate, I suddenly realised that I hadn't put any tempos on their sheet music. It meant they were playing everything at the same speed, regardless of what song it was.

Thankfully, no-one seemed to mind, in fact the place went mad, cheering, clapping and generally having a great time. They bobbed from side to side as I sang *'I felt all flushed with fever, embarrassed by the crowd, I felt he'd found my letters and read each one out loud, I prayed that he would finish, but he just kept right on strumming my pain with his fingers'* with the joyous bounce of a Jackson Five number.

For the next half an hour, I performed a storming, high speed set of finger-snapping favourites-which-should-have-been-ballads like 'And I Love You So', 'What Are You Doing The Rest of Your Life?', 'The Way We Were' and Nilsson's 'Without You'. They all bounded along at breakneck speed like a Holiday Bop-a-thon, interspersed with what should have been the light relief foot-tappers 'When I'm 64', 'Honey Pie' and 'Young At Heart'. Even 'Hey Jude' spun off at the rate of knots, with the *'Na Na Na'* ending sounding more like 'Land Of A Thousand Dances' than a reflective Beatles classic.

Emboldened by the love radiating back at me, during The Way We Were I sat on a rather handsome chap's knee, persuading him to join me in a duet. His wife was delighted, clapping and laughing throughout as we jollied away to each other, *'Memories, light the corners of my mind, misty watercolour memories of the way we were'* to each other.

"That was fucking amazing!" Bob shouted, as the audience yelled for more and I ran off waving to my newly-converted fans. "You have to go on and do another song!"

I encored with 'Send In The Clowns', which, again, resembled a rock 'n' roll evergreen in the hands of my band for the night. I bowed, the MD shouted 'Give it up for the fantastic John Howard,' and left the room like a champion athlete.

In the welcomingly cooler night air, filled with crickets and the muffled sound of the band doing a breakneck speed Elvis medley, we took off our shoes and walked along the beach, enjoying the sensation of the sand running through our toes and the thrilled glow of my having achieved a triumph against all the odds.

Early hours one September morning, I'd just got back from playing at AD8 and was making myself at cup of lapsang suchong, when Jun and several of his friends came running into the kitchen. They all dashed to the sink and washed their hands, giggling like schoolgirls at each other. Behind them came a stocky guy in his 40s, who nodded at me as they dried their hands and sat down at the table:

"Oh John!", Jun said, chuckling, "These are my friends Cid, Ricky, Lee and his partner, Jim."

Cid stood and shook my hand,

"So handsome! Be still my beating heart," he fluttered.

"Would you like some tea?" I asked them all.

"And domesticated too!" Ricky laughed, nudging Cid as he sat and beamed at me.

As I busied at the kettle, I asked Jun, "Why were you washing your hands just now?"

"Men's cocks, dear, lovely to hold but one needs to be hygienic!"

"Have you been to the Heath, John?" Cid asked salaciously.

I'd heard of Hampstead Heath of course, it was an infamous gay cruising area.

"No," I replied, "I've never had the transport to get there."

"You do now," he cried. "Come with us next weekend!"

Jim nodded at me:

"I can fit another skinny one in the back."

"You can squeeze in next to me!" Cid said, winking at me.

"We never have sex on The Heath, dear," Jun said, "we just put people together."

"We are the Sisters of Mercy!" Cid cried, and they all giggled uncontrollably.

"We facilitate the sex," Jun continued, as if giving an Oxford Union address, "then move on to the next hard cocks and guide them to where they wish to go."

"Do you get involved, Jim?" I asked him.

Lee shrieked and held his face with both hands:

"Jim? Oh no! He's our chauffeur. He sits and waits while we have fun, then, when we get back home, I tell him about all the men having sex and that turns him on."

Jim looked a little shyly at me and smiled,

"Works for me," he said, going red.

"So adorable!" Cid said, stroking Jim's hand.

"Come with us, John!" Ricky cried. "What night are you free?"

The following Friday night, I stood in the midst of a Heathful of screwing men, groups of five, six, seven and more, daisy-chains of sex, stretching round trees, growing increasingly longer as more guys joined in. The summer of 1976 had been one of the hottest on record, and the still, warm air was full of the sound of groaning guys reaching orgasm.

Jun and his friends merrily went on their way, pushing men together into an embrace, whispering to them, stroking and fondling them, until the union was made, then moving onto their next mission of baptising men in the joys of orgasmic group sex.

I wandered off on my own and found a small group of guys having fun and sidled in. Very quickly I was singled out by one of the guys, who took me off to enjoy a more private time together against a sturdy tree. As we took off our clothes and dropped them at our feet, I heard a crowd applauding in the distance.

"Someone's being appreciated for doing a good job!" I said.

"That's not applause," my partner for the moment chuckled, "it's the spanking section. There's an S & M section much further into the undergrowth. Fancy having a look?"

"No," I said happily, "this will do just fine."

This sojourn into the world of anonymous night-time sex became a regular event over the coming weeks. We'd all have our fun and journey home, packed into Jim's car, giggling like horny schoolgirls, comparing notes. Arriving back at the flat, we'd rush into the kitchen and wash our hands - and anything else which needed a quick rinse - then sit around a pot of lapsang suchong, rhapsodising over the size of the cocks on display that night. It was like being a kid again, sharing tales of naughtiness with one's chums.

"Did you see that one in uniform?"

"Enormous my dear! He was certainly standing to attention!"

"And so good at taking orders!"

The kitchen would be filled with our queenly hysterical mirth, as Jim stood in the doorway, looking at his charges like a benign nursery teacher.

"Have you ever been to The Gigolo, John?" Jun asked me one night, as I poured his tea.

I hadn't.

"My dear," he crowed, "we shall have to take you! It's wall-to-wall fucking! And in fashionable Chelsea too!"

"Fashionable fucking!" Lee cried. "You will love it, John!"

On my next night off, at about midnight, Cid, Jun and I walked the fairly short distance from Earl's Court into the King's Road, past the fire station where a few of the firemen were standing in the doorway having a cigarette,

"They're available you know!" Cid said, beaming at one particularly handsome chap. "A friend of mine had a six-some in there!"

"Note to self!" I joked, and on we went.

The Gigolo was a basement bar below a gay restaurant called La

Gourmet, and as we descended the stairs, the smell of the cooking above melded into the wave of body heat rising up. We walked straight into a boiling hot bar area, round which several groups of men were getting to know each other, and pushed our way through the snogging mass to order some cokes. Sipping them, we played voyeur for a few minutes.

"Look, John," Cid said into my ear over the loud music, and pointed at the dance floor, jammed with naked guys.

"Where did they put their clothes?" I asked him.

He nodded his head at a little alcove at the side of the bar:

"In there. If you want to join the fray, tuck your keys and money in your socks, and leave your jeans and shirt with the attendant, who'll give you a ticket for them."

We finished our drinks, stripped off, handed our clothes to a completely naked guy covered in tattoos, who duly handed us a pink raffle ticket, which, along with my keys, I pushed into my sock.

Jun and Cid quickly disappeared into the mêlée, as I was slowly carried along by the surge of activity around me. Several hands were all over me, as I moved with the undercurrent in an anti-clockwise-circle of groping, writhing men, until I was back where I started. I was about to leave the scrum and have a breather when a group of five good-looking guys, who I'd seen at the bar when we'd arrived, smiled at me and pushed their way through the crowd towards me. For the next half an hour, I was their main dish of the evening.

It was frantic, sweaty, and extremely exciting. I'd never been shy, and had enjoyed a good amount of sex over the years since I'd arrived in London, but this was completely new to me, sex-on-demand, wherever you wanted it, free and available at the point of entry. I'd always wondered what an orgy would be like. Now I knew.

The Gigolo became my almost nightly haunt after that. I'd finish at whatever restaurant I was playing, usually around one in the morning, and walk across a sleeping London to the King's Road, descending the steps into what I was certain would be a couple of hours of fantastic, orgiastic, anonymous sex with as many men as I could handle at one time. The only break from The Gigolo was our Heath night. My life had become a matter of performing: singing on stage to a roomful of appreciative music-lovers, and then the naked centre of attention in a circle of randy men. Who needed fame when this kind of popularity was such fun?

Amidst all this carefree debauchery, there were of course the necessary regular check-ups at 'The Clap Clinic', situated in Goodge Street. Rather than it being a roomful of pre-diagnosis misery, it was actually rather convivial. Queens sat chatting to each other about their spate of "crabs, dear" or "another dose, love", as if they were discussing their favourite cologne. Many of them used the monthly health visit as yet another opportunity to chat up guys they fancied and swap phone numbers.

"When you're clear, give us a call," came the cheery cry across the room as one by one, they each disappeared into various rooms for blood tests or the curative jab in the bum.

None of us escaped 'The Wrath of Vera Duckworth' as one queen called it, but, in 1976, we were all secure in the knowledge that whatever we'd caught could be cured very easily, almost painlessly, and, just a few weeks later, we'd be back on the pick-up scene, disease and crabs-free.

Life seemed to be going along completely at my whim and choosing, it was now solely my agenda which drove things. I was in control of my own adult life, with no-one else making decisions for me, for probably the first time. But, as the Summer turned to Autumn, I began to experience an occasional and disturbing sense of paranoia. I was initially worried, but brushed it off as a passing thing. Gradually, though, I felt increasingly detached from people and places around me, sometimes thinking that even Jun and Cid were plotting behind my back. I'd tell myself to stop being so silly, but the inner me wasn't listening.

Whether it was the build up in my system of the large quantities of hash I'd consumed for most of the year, or the after effects of the recent opium trip – which Bob had told me could create flashbacks and a sense of unease – I wasn't sure. Maybe, I told myself, the much-too-regular intake of copious amounts of booze, which I was sent every night by those I entertained at the restaurants, was the cause. Perhaps, I wondered as I lay in the bath one afternoon, feeling this sense of unease and slight panic starting to grow, I'd had an overdose of penicillin during my many trips to the 'Clinic'? Whatever was creating this inner unbalance, it was becoming a threat to my newly-found sense of well-being. As the Autumn evenings drew in, the nip in the air matched the chilling paranoia descending on me like a winter mist.

One evening, while sitting in a newly-opened bar in Notting Hill with Bob, two burly security guards in mobster-style suits walked in and wandered menacingly around the place, staring at the clientele to dissuade them from any kind of intimacy. Even hand-holding was discouraged by a pointed heavily-ringed finger stabbing the air.

One of them walked towards us and, as he got nearer, he opened his jacket, revealing what looked to me like a large gun in his inside pocket.

"He has a gun!" I hissed at Bob. "Look!"

"It's not a gun it's -"

Before Bob could say another word, I stood, a little unsurely, and pointed at the guard:

"He has a gun!" I yelled.

"John!" Bob said, grabbing my arm, "Sit down!"

"But he has a gun!" I yelled again.

In what felt like seconds, the two security guys had me by both arms and were quickly marching me out of the club and into the street, where they flung me onto the wet cobbles.

"And don't come back," said one, as I lay there trying to clear my blurred vision.

"Or else!" the other growled.

Bob ran to me and helped me up,

"What's wrong with you?" he said, checking me for any cuts or abrasions on my arms and legs.

"He had a gun!" I said to Bob.

"It was a walkie-talkie, you daft queen!"

"It was a gun," I mumbled, and stumbled off down the road.

Bob caught up and put his arm round me and, as I mumbled my certainties that we could have been shot, he got me back to my flat, put me to bed, and left me moaning into my pillow about men with guns.

On waking up the next morning, through an enormous hangover and half-closed heavy eyes, I saw a piece of paper on my bedside table. I put on my glasses and read it. It was an eight-line poem, the first verse of a lyric. I had no recollection of writing it down, but it was my handwriting. I vaguely remembered getting up to go to the loo during the night, so I must have done it then. It reflected my present state of mind, and a tune quickly started forming in my head:

> Jimmy was alright last night
> He didn't feel like getting high
> So we went out to paint the town
> Left him with some guy
> I took Suzie for a stroll
> Watched the sea come in at five
> When we got back Jimmy had gone
> Still don't know if he's alive
> Did they take him away?

No-one saw him after that day
Did they?

More lyrics followed, which I scribbled down, and pretty soon I had about half a song written. I got up, had a reviving cup of Earl Grey, dashed into the shower, got dressed and made my way to the tube. By the time I'd arrived at Stuart's office, the rest of the lyric and the song, which I turned over in my mind all the way there, were virtually complete:

Suzie was a sweet young thing
She had everything to gain
Signed-on on Friday
Went out Sat'day
Sunday out of her brain
Last time I saw her
Her dad's lawyer had made her a ward of court
So she barricaded doors
And boarded up the windows
Her bedsit was like a fort
Did they take her away
No-one saw her after that day
Did they?

I see 'em watching my home
I hear 'em tapping my phone
When Ma and Pa go out in the car
They know that I'm alone
Will they take me away?

So I ring up Lenny and Bri
Say 'Come on round here for a talk'

And we sit till dawn with the radio on
Listening for sounds in the hall
It's weird being told that the weather is cold
And feeling so hot inside
And how come my bedroom looks different each day?
Soon I'll have nowhere to hide

Will they take me away?
I know some people who pay
But still they take them away
And no-one sees them after that day
And if they take you away
No-one sees you after that day
Yes they

Stuart wasn't in, but Lyn, the office P.A., was there. I asked her if I could try something out on the piano and she seemed pleasantly surprised. I hadn't been in for weeks, certainly not to write a new song anyway. I went into the next room and played what had been in my head all morning. It had a similar rising F chord riff, and the same double-waltz tempo, as another earlier song of mine, 'Don't It Just Hurt', and, for the first time in ages, I felt extremely excited about a new composition.

I played it again, refining it as I went along and, just as I was putting the finishing touches to the final verse, I heard the main door open and Stuart's familiar voice:

"John's here!"

He walked in and beamed at me:

"John! It's so great to see you!"

Behind him came Eddie Pumer, who I hadn't seen since the Autumn of 1973, when he'd produced the set of Chappell's demos which had got me the CBS deal.

"John," he shouted. "That sounded great as I was coming up the stairs! Is it a new song?"

I nodded.

"What's it called?"

I didn't have a title, but plumped for 'They'.

"Fantastic! Will you play it again for me?"

He and Stuart sat down and listened as I did the song once more. At the end Stuart said,

"Fucking fantastic, John! Best song you've written for ages!"

"It's really great, John!" Eddie agreed. "I'd love to produce that!"

Stuart jumped up and went to the phone:

"I'm going to book a session at Regent Sound now," he told us. "Hello? Pete? Yes, it's Stuart. Can we book a session? As soon as possible."

He looked at me, covered the phone and said,

"When can you do it?"

I told him I wasn't performing on Sunday evening:

"Sunday, Pete? Okay, fine, yeah, that's great! See you then!" He came and sat down. "We're in Regent Sound across the road this Sunday evening. Take as long as you like, Eddie. It's an open-ended session, starting late though, ten o'clock."

There seemed to be a kind of serendipity to this, as Regent Sound was the studio where I'd demo'd 'Don't It Just Hurt' in 1975, and where I was about to record that song's musical 'soul mate'. Normally, I'd've avoided writing anything too close musically to a previous song, self-plagiarism wasn't something in which I'd indulged too much. But as 'Don't It Just Hurt' had never been released commercially, I decided it wasn't a problem.

"Have you got any other songs, John?" Eddie asked me. "It'd be great to do another one."

"Play Eddie 'Hall of Mirrors', John," Stuart said.

Like 'Don't It Just Hurt', it was one of the songs I'd written and demo'd for the abortive *Technicolour Biography* album two years earlier. Stuart had always loved it. When I finished it, Eddie clapped his hands,

"Fucking hell, John," he shouted.

He stared over at Stuart with a look which said, "What have you been doing with him?"

Stuart looked at me sadly:

"We've neglected John lately," he admitted.

In truth, Stuart had taken no interest in my restaurant gigs. As a publisher, my new career was of no use to him. Apart from 'Star Through My Window', which I'd written months earlier, getting zero interest from record companies, I'd given him no new material since the songs I'd written for the Biddu album. My maxim had unconsciously been 'Why create something no-one is likely to hear?'.

I explained to Eddie how I'd moved from writing and recording since being dropped by CBS in January, and had concentrated on performing covers on the restaurant and bar circuit instead.

"These songs will change all that," Eddie said. "You should be writing and recording, John. It's a fucking waste!"

He glanced over at Stuart, who looked rather shamefaced. I was about to say "It's not Stuart's fault" when there was a knock on the main office door. Lyn went to answer it and a man was there with a huge sack of mail. She led him into her office and told him to drop it by her desk.

"There are three more outside," he told her.

"Bring them in then!"

He carried each one in, dropped them on the floor, she signed for them and he left.

"More of Tina Charles' fan mail," Lyn told us. "We get about five sacks a day."

"I let her fan club use this as their official address," Stuart told us. "As a favour to Biddu."

"Those sacks should be full of John Howard fan mail," Eddie said.

"At one time I thought they would be," Stuart replied.

Eddie jumped up, got his briefcase and took out a cassette recorder:

"Let's do something about it then," he said. "I'll record your two songs on here, John. Whenever you're ready." He pressed record and nodded at me.

As he left promising to have "a great bunch of guys" to back me, Stuart glanced at me,

"Maybe our luck is finally changing, John," he said.

As luck would sometimes have it, another song came my way the following afternoon. I'd decided to go into Stuart's again and go through 'They' and 'Hall of Mirrors' on my own, to make sure I was fully happy with them before the recording session.

When I walked in, Stuart was sitting at his desk chatting to an old friend of his, who I'd met about three years earlier at one of Stuart and Patsy's house parties.

"John," he said, getting up to shake my hand.

"Norman, lovely to see you," I replied.

Norman Smith had been an engineer at Abbey Road in the 1960s, working on every Beatles album with George Martin up to *Rubber Soul* at the end of 1965, when he'd decided he wanted to go into production himself. He hit paydirt with his first album, Pink Floyd's debut release, *Piper At the Gates of Dawn*. Also recorded at Abbey Road, it brought together many of the psychedelic elements of what The Beatles, The Small Faces and Donovan were creating in the early Summer of 1967. *Piper* perfectly harnessed the band's 'mind-blowing' special effects they used on stage, as well as the song-writing talents of the group's leader, Syd Barrett.

He had written the group's hit singles 'Arnold Layne' and 'See Emily Play', and along with *Piper*, they cemented Smith's and Floyd's reputation as wielders of great, and big selling, pop Psychedelia. The album hit the British Top Ten at the beginning of September 1967.

Norman went on to produce another two Floyd albums, *Saucerful Of Secrets*, Barrett's final album with the band before his mental health began its steady deterioration, and *Ummagumma*, the band's biggest selling album by the end of 1969. He also produced The Pretty Things' late '60s masterpiece, *S.F. Sorrow*.

In 1971, after writing a song he'd hoped John Lennon might record, Norman was persuaded by his friend and fellow producer Mickie Most to record it himself. Released under the alias Hurricane Smith, 'Don't Let It Die' went to No.2 in the UK charts. He followed it a year later with 'Oh Babe, What Would You Say', which not only reached the UK Top Five, it also hit the Top Three in America. It was during this period that Stuart became professionally involved with Norman, acting as his tour manager during the promotion of 'Oh Babe' in Britain and the USA, the two men cementing a lifelong friendship thereafter.

"How's things?" Norman asked me.

"John's recording some new material in a couple of days," Stuart replied for me.

"How do you fancy recording one of mine, John?"

"I'd love to, Norman!"

He went to the piano and played a beautiful ballad called 'Is This My Love?'.

"What do you think, John?" he said when he'd finished. "I completed it this week."

"It's beautiful!"

"It's yours."

I sat down and began playing what I'd learnt watching Norman doing it.

"This boy is very quick!" Norman said to Stuart, as I sang it with him.

"John is one of the brightest musicians I've worked with," Stuart said proudly.

When Norman had gone, I recorded a quick demo of 'Is This My Love'. Stuart took it round to a cassette duplication company a few doors down the road, and returned half an hour later with it in his hand.

"I'll get this posted to Eddie today," he said, getting a jiffy bag from the stationary cupboard.

That night, I went with Jun and Cid to see Marvin Gaye performing at The Royal Albert Hall. He was fabulous. Magnetic, sexy and with the voice of an angel. As I was the only one of our myopic threesome to possess a pair of glasses, we shared my specs throughout the show, handing them down the line from one to the other for a quick in-focus glimpse of our hero:

"John, aiyee! Look at him!" Cid would cry, quickly handing my glasses to me so I could watch Gaye thrust his crutch at the audience singing 'Let's Get It On', like his personal invitation to us all for a great night between the sheets.

"Look at him now!" I'd shout, handing the specs to Jun as Gaye swivelled his hips at a girl in the front row.

"Wow!" Jun lusted. "He's amazing," handing the specs to Cid who shrieked in ecstasy at one of the sexiest men on the planet.

As Marvin went into sexual overdrive during 'You Sure Love To Ball', the three of us sighed as one, platonic sisters sharing a pair of glasses and a love for one of the greatest performers the world ever witnessed.

The day of the recording session at Regent Sound, I received an invitation to a wedding in Rochdale, taking place in three weeks' time.

On the 31st October, my dad was getting married to a lady called Sybil. I'd not met her, so I imagined the relationship had blossomed over the previous few months, since I'd last spoken to Dad on the phone at Christmas.

Since Mum had died two years earlier, Dad hadn't coped well without a woman in his life. Apart from missing the comfort of a life companion, he was your typical Northern man of an earlier generation, who couldn't boil an egg and was unsure how the vacuum cleaner worked.

I wrote a quick note in reply, that I'd love to be there, and that I'd call him soon. I wanted to know the full story before I met his wife-to-be.

Eddie had pulled together an excellent combo for my first recording session with a band for over a year. Two of the guys I'd worked with before, when Eddie had produced the demos of 'Small Town, Big Adventures' and 'Pearl Parade'. The guitarist, Sammy, was new to me. He was a boy wonder, about eighteen but played like a seasoned professional who'd been doing sessions for years. Whatever Eddie asked him to play, he did it, and usually in one take.

I gave the boys one run-through of the three songs, and they got them down in a couple of takes each, with Sammy overdubbing more guitar when the rest of the band had left.

I recorded my vocals for the three songs over the next couple of hours, and by about 2 a.m. we were finished, with the tracks recorded and mixed.

As we emerged into the cold Denmark Street air, Stuart carried the tapes like they were gold dust across the road to his office:

"I'll get copies made in the morning," he shouted from the door as he let himself in, "and shop them round to as many record companies as I can. These tracks will get you another deal, I'm certain of it."

The next evening, I played a good set at AD8, and got back to the flat at about two a.m., having resisted the urge to pop into The Gigolo en route for a bit of after-hours hanky panky. I'd even started having cokes, rather than vodka and limes, when customers had offered to buy me a drink. I'd made a conscious decision that this had to be when I got myself together. It was time to sharpen up and focus again. If nothing else, I owed it to Stuart.

When I walked in, the sitting-room light was on. Jun, Cid and Ricky were settled on the sofa together, a hefty stranger wedged between them with his dick out, which they were all fondling and admiring. Jun smiled coyly at me and said,

"Would you like to join in, John?"

"This is Dimitri," Ricky said, stroking his bearded face. "He's such a big boy!"

Indeed he was. He looked at me, got hold of his enormous appendage and waved it around, licking his lips.

"I'm exhausted," I told them, trying to avert my eyes from what was on offer. "I'll just leave you to it. Have fun!"

I went into the kitchen and put on the kettle. Taking a camomile tea to bed had helped me sleep during my recent unsettled nights. As I was getting a mug out of the cupboard, I turned round and there was Jun:

"Darling," he said in a excited low whisper. "Dimitri is a Russian sailor! We met him outside the Coleherne. He's divine, don't you think?"

The object of his admiration, now zipped up, appeared in the doorway:

"You are the owner of the flat?" he asked me.

"No, I rent it from a guy who uses it at weekends. Jun is my flatmate."

"Occasionally," Jun joked, sidling up to Dimitri and stroking his arm.

"Do you work with these boys?" he asked, moving Jun's hand to his crutch.

"No, I'm a singer," I replied, keeping my eyes firmly on his. "I do gigs at various restaurants around London."

"It pays you well." It wasn't a question.

"It pays okay. I'm not starving."

"So, when is the owner here again?"

I looked at Jun:

"In a few days I think," Jun said unsurely. "He comes and goes."

Dimitri left us and Jun hissed at me:

"Vaughn's here! In bed! With Michael!"

Michael was Vaughn's Chinese lover, who alternated at the flat with a Thai chap, each of them blissfully unaware they were not the only one in Vaughn's life.

"Does he know about…?" I nodded towards the sitting-room.

Jun widened his eyes and shook his head violently.

"I'd get your date out of here as soon as you can," I told him, unsure how Vaughn would react to an orgy going on while he slept.

Jun nodded, frowning sensibly, then smiled like an innocent child :

"We'll just have a bit more fun," he said, "and then I'll ask him to leave."

He winked at me and went out.

"We'll try not to wake you," Cid called out gently from the sofa, fondling Dimitri's cock as I walked past them towards my room.

Jun had joined them again and was stroking the Russian's hair.

"Are you sure?" he asked me coquettishly, while Ricky unbuttoned his shirt.

"So hairy!" he cried, giggling at me.

"Good night, gentlemen," I said. "Don't frighten the horses."

Jun gave me an understanding wink, I closed my door, got undressed and snuggled under my duvet.

As I drifted off, I could hear a lot of shuffling about next door, the occasional "Ooooh!", and lots of naughty giggling. But I was out for the count very quickly, completely unprepared for what would happen a couple of hours later...

...As I lay in my hospital bed, wondering what the hell was going to happen to me, a large bulky Captain Birds Eye figure of a man wandered down the ward, the male night nurse. He passed by the end of my bed and smiled at me, and for some reason I suddenly felt very safe, for the first time in a long time. I was taken back to when, as a small child, I'd watch my parents passing my bedroom door on the dimly-lit landing. My dad would pop his head in and whisper...

"Goodnight, son," Captain Birds Eye whispered.

And, as he wandered off along the ward, from my warm secure bed I whispered back, "Goodnight, daddy."